Praise for Marcel Gagné's
Moving to Linux: Kiss the Blue Screen of Death Goodbye!

"This is kind of a funny book for me to be recommending to readers of a Windows newsletter, but a lot of people ask me about this topic, so here goes. Author Marcel Gagné is a columnist for *Linux Journal*, and in *Moving to Linux* he's prepared a step-by-step guide to converting a Windows PC to Linux—or just trying it! The book includes a bootable CD with a version of Linux that you can poke around in without touching or changing anything about your Windows installation. If your boss is asking, 'What's with this Linux stuff?', *Moving to Linux* is a great way to show that you know what you're talking about."

— *Brian Livingston, Editor,* `WindowsSecrets.com`

"Pros: Too many to list in the available space. We liked the book from the very first page right through to the end. Gagné has done a solid job of exposing Linux and all its components in a way that is both inviting, useful, and easy to understand . . . We really liked this book—highly recommended."

—*Howard Carson, Kickstart News,* `www.kickstartnews.com`

"Marcel walks the user through each technique in a very chatty and comfortable style. In fact, when I put the book down, I had a momentary impression that I'd just finished watching a good cooking show with an entertaining chef. (Australian readers may understand if I say that it felt like having just watched Ian Parmenter do an episode of 'Consuming Passions'.)"

—*Jenn Vesperman,* `Linuxchix.org`

"Gagné's *Moving to Linux* is a straightforward exposition of just how a non-hacker PC user can get rid of 'The Blue Screen of Death.' If you have a friend, a co-worker, a significant other, or a relative who periodically screams, sighs, bursts into tears, or asks for help, here's the simple solution. It comes with a bootable CD of Knoppix, Klaus Knopper's variant of Debian."

—*Peter H. Salus, writing in ;login: The Usenix Magazine*

"This is a book aimed not at you, dear developer/techie/guru, but at your friends, acquaintances, and family who are lowly users of Windows. Yes, such people do exist even in the tightest of families. Fear not, however, because salvation is at hand should any of them decide that this Linux thing might be worth investigating. No longer will you be faced with the unenviable task of walking them through the process of switching OS. *Moving to Linux: Kiss the Blue Screen of Death Goodbye!* is a big, bold, and friendly guide to help them along. The emphasis is firmly on using Linux as a desktop system—this isn't a book about Linux as a file, print, or Web server."

—*Tech Book Reports*

D1476067

Moving to Linux

Second Edition

Kiss the Blue Screen of Death Goodbye!

Barnes & Noble Exclusive Edition

Moving to Linux®
Second Edition
Kiss the Blue Screen of Death Goodbye!

Marcel Gagné

♣ Addison-Wesley

Upper Saddle River, NJ • Boston • Indianapolis • San Francisco
New York • Toronto • Montreal • London • Munich • Paris • Madrid
Capetown • Sydney • Tokyo • Singapore • Mexico City

The publisher offers excellent discounts on this book when ordered in quantity for bulk purchases or special sales, which may include electronic versions and/or custom covers and content particular to your business, training goals, marketing focus, and branding interests. For more information, please contact:

> U. S. Corporate and Government Sales,
> (800) 382-3419
> corpsales@pearsontechgroup.com

For sales outside the U. S., please contact:

> International Sales
> international@pearsoned.com

Visit us on the Web: www.awprofessional.com

Library of Congress Cataloging-in-Publication Data
Gagné, Marcel.
  Moving to Linux : kiss the blue screen of death goodbye! / Marcel Gagné.-- 2nd ed.
    p. cm.
  Includes bibliographical references and index.
  ISBN 0-321-35640-3 (pbk. : alk. paper)
  1. Linux. 2. Operating systems (Computers) I. Title.

  QA76.76.O63G345 2005
  005.4'32—dc22

                                                                2005013056

ISBN 0-321-35667-5

Text printed in the United States on recycled paper at Courier in Stoughton, Massachusetts.
First printing, July 2005

This book is dedicated to Sally Tomasevic,
my wife,
my partner,
my best friend,
and the love of my life,
and
to my son, Sebastian,
who saved my life without knowing it.
I love you both.

Contents

Chapter 18
Linux Multimedia (If Music Be the Food of Love . . .)

Chapter 19
Fun and Games (Very Serious Fun)

Preface

Welcome to the second edition of *Moving to Linux: Kiss the Blue Screen of Death Goodbye!* This is my fourth book, and an exciting one at that. Back in 2002, when I first suggested the idea of this book, I had some serious selling to do. A Linux desktop book? In 2002, it seemed like a crazy idea. Not anymore. The first edition of *Moving to Linux* was something new on the scene, a book that promised the average user that moving to and running a Linux desktop was something anyone could do. Now, as I sit here writing this preface in May 2005, there are at least four other books dedicated to the Linux desktop experience for the average user. It's nice to see that you can't keep a good idea down, and also nice to see that I wasn't crazy.

Linux continues to grow by leaps and bounds. The face of Linux that most people see has changed quite a bit, with KDE 3.4 being the latest offering of the desktop environment itself. Below that desktop environment, the graphical engine that drives it all has changed as well. Linux distributions overwhelmingly switched from XFree86 to X.Org for the X window system software. Office productivity tools took another leap forward as OpenOffice 2.0 made its appearance, providing users with greater functionality, ease of use, and Microsoft document filters so accurate that they make the whole question of sharing documents between the two platforms a virtual nonissue. The Linux Internet experience has vastly improved, and Linux multimedia is now in a class all its own. A lot has changed, and the changes are fantastic. This is a great time to move to Linux and leave your old OS troubles behind, and I look forward to being part of that journey.

Writing a book is never a solitary experience. While writers certainly spend a lot of time locked away by themselves putting words to paper, this is not something you do entirely on your own. On that note, I'd like to take a moment to recognize a few people who have been with me through this process. First and foremost, I have to thank my beautiful wife, Sally Tomasevic. She is my love, my life, my inspiration, and my strength. My family and my friends, with their confidence, love, and support, have all played a part in the creation of this book. I love you all.

Many thanks to Mark Taub, my editor, and also to Heather Fox, Robin O'Brien, Don O'Hagan, Kathleen Addis, Beverley Carkner, Lara Wysong, and everyone at my publisher, Addison-Wesley. Many thanks also to my agent, Richard Curtis, a tough guy with a soft heart.

Sincere thanks to those people who reviewed my book along the way. They are (in alphabetical order by last name) Aeleen Frisch, Lew Pritcher, and Sally Tomasevic. The process of reviewing is hard work, and I truly appreciate their efforts, sharp eyes, and suggestions.

I would like to recognize and thank the Linux community: the developers and software designers, the members of Linux user groups (including my own WFTL-LUG), the many who share their experiences on Usenet, and all those unnamed folks who give free advice under pseudonyms in IRC groups.

Finally, my heartfelt thanks to everyone who made the first *Moving to Linux: Kiss the Blue Screen of Death Goodbye!* such a huge success. I thank you all.

—Marcel Gagné

Chapter

1

Introduction

Welcome to the Linux universe, one and all! Welcome also to this, the second edition of MOVING TO LINUX: KISS THE BLUE SCREEN OF DEATH GOODBYE!

Trying to pin down when something finally hits the mainstream is a crazy kind of game, fraught with danger. Linux has definitely hit the proverbial mainstream, and I'll explain shortly how I came to that conclusion. These days, the first question I get from people is no longer "What is Linux?" but, rather, "What do I have to do to get Linux on my system?" You can finally buy PCs with Linux preinstalled from Wal-Mart. The big names—HP, IBM, and Dell—all offer systems with Linux, and yet there is a better marker out there. Recently, my game-crazy 13-year-old nephew Paul asked me to switch his Windows XP system over to Linux. I, of course, happily did just that. While the infamous Blue Screen of the title is less of a problem in later Windows incarnations, viruses and spyware abound, thereby making Linux an intelligent choice, even for a 13-year-old gamer.

For those who may nevertheless want some clarification, Linux is a fully multitasking operating system based on UNIX, although, technically, Linux is the kernel, the master program that makes running a Linux system possible. That kernel, by the way, was written by a young Finnish student named Linus Torvalds. On August 25, 1991, Torvalds posted this now-famous (perhaps legendary) message to the Usenet group comp.os.minix:

```
From: torvalds@klaava.Helsinki.FI (Linus Benedict Torvalds)
     Newsgroups: comp.os.minix
     Subject: What would you like to see most in minix?
     Summary: small poll for my new operating system
Message-ID: <1991Aug25.205708.9541@klaava.Helsinki.FI>
     Date: 25 Aug 91 20:57:08 GMT
     Organization: University of Helsinki
     Hello everybody out there using minix -
     I'm doing a (free) operating system (just a hobby,
won't be big and professional like gnu) for 386(486) AT
clones. This has been brewing since april, and is starting to
get ready. I'd like any feedback on things people like/
dislike in minix, as my OS resembles it somewhat (same
physical layout of the file-system (due to practical
reasons) among other things).
     I've currently ported bash(1.08) and gcc(1.40), and
things seem to work. This implies that I'll get something
practical within a few months, and I'd like to know what
features most people would want. Any suggestions are
welcome, but I won't promise I'll implement them :-)
     Linus (torvalds@kruuna.helsinki.fi)
     PS. Yes - it's free of any minix code, and it has a
multi-threaded fs. It is NOT protable (uses 386 task
switching etc), and it probably never will support anything
other than AT-hard disks, as that's all I have :-(.
```

Much has happened since then. Linus somehow captured the imagination of scores of talented programmers around the world. Joined together through the magic of the Internet, they collaborated, coded, tweaked, and gave birth to the operating system that is now revolutionizing the world of computing.

These days, Linux is a powerful, reliable (rock-solid, in fact), expandable, flexible, configurable, multiuser, multitasking, and completely free operating system that runs on many different platforms. These include Intel PCs, DEC Alphas, Macintosh systems, PowerPCs, and a growing number of embedded processors. You can find Linux in PDA organizers, digital watches, golf carts, and cell phones. In fact, Linux has a greater support base (in terms of platforms) than any other operating system in the world.

What we call the Linux operating system is not the work of just one man alone. Linus Torvalds is the original architect of Linux—its father, if you will—but his is not the only effort behind it. Perhaps Linus Torvalds' greatest genius lay in knowing when to share the load. For no other pay but satisfaction, he employed people around the world, delegated to them, worked with them, and asked for and accepted feedback in a next generation of the model that began with the GNU project.

GNU, by the way, is a recursive acronym that stands for "GNUs not UNIX," a project of the Free Software Foundation. This project was started in 1984 with the intention of creating a free, UNIX-like operating system. Over the years, many GNU tools were written and widely used by many commercial UNIX vendors and, of course, system administrators trying to get a job done. The appearance of Linus Torvalds' Linux kernel has made the GNU dream of a completely free, UNIX-like operating system a reality at last.

Is Linux Really FREE?

When the discussion of what *free* means in relation to software, you'll often see the expression "free as in speech" or "free as in beer." Free, in this case, isn't a question of cost, although you can get a free copy (as in *free beer*) of Linux and install it on your system without breaking any laws. As Robert A. Heinlein would have said, "There ain't no such thing as a free lunch." A free download will still cost you connection time on the Internet, disk space, time to burn the CDs, and so on.

Walk into a computer software store and you'll see copies of Mandrake, SuSE, and Red Hat on the shelves, so this free software can also cost you money. On the other hand, those boxed sets come with documentation, support, and CDs that save you time and energy downloading and burning discs. Furthermore, there are boxed sets of varying prices, even within a distribution. For instance, you can buy a Red Hat personal or professional edition. The differences there may be additional software, documentation, or support.

Linux is distributed under the GNU General Public License (GPL), which, in essence, says that anyone may copy, distribute, and even sell the program, as long as changes to the source are reintroduced back to the community and the terms of the license remain unaltered. Free means that you are free to take Linux, modify it, and create your own version. Free means that you are not at the mercy of a single vendor who forces you into a kind of corporate servitude by making sure that it is extremely costly to convert to another environment. If you are unhappy with your Linux vendor or the support you are getting, you can move to the next vendor without forfeiting your investment in Linux.

In other words, "free as in speech"—or freedom.

The GPL

The GNU GPL permits a distributor to "charge a fee for the physical act of transferring a copy, and you may at your option offer warranty protection in exchange for a fee." This is further qualified by the statement that the distributor must release, "for a charge no more than your cost of physically performing source distribution, a complete machine-readable copy of the corresponding source code." In other words, the GPL ensures that programs like Linux will at best be free of charge. At worst, you may be asked to pay for the cost of a copy.

You should take some time to read the GNU GPL. For your convenience, I've reprinted it in Appendix A of this book.

So What Do I Gain?

No operating system is perfect, and nothing comes without some hassles, but as time goes on, Linux is getting closer and closer to perfection. These days, Linux is even easier to install than your old operating system, and you don't have to reboot time and again as you load driver disk after driver disk. I won't bore you with everything I consider an advantage, but I will give you a few of the more important points.

Security

Say goodbye to your virus checker and stop worrying. Although Linux is not 100% immune to viruses, it comes pretty close. In fact, to date, most so-called Linux viruses do not exist *in the wild* (only under tightly controlled environments in *proof-of-concept* labs). It isn't that no one has tried, but the design model behind Linux means that it is built with security in mind. Consequently, viruses are virtually nonexistent in the Linux world, and security issues are dealt with quickly and efficiently by the Linux community. Security flaws are well advertised. It isn't unusual for a security hole to be discovered and a fix created within a few short hours of the discovery. If something does present a risk, you won't have to wait for the next release of your operating system to come along.

Stability

The stability of Linux is almost legendary. Living in a world where people are used to rebooting their PCs one or more times a day, Linux users talk about running weeks and sometimes months without a reboot. *"Illegal operations"* and the *"Blue Screen of Death"* are not part of the Linux experience. Sure, programs occasionally crash here as well, but they don't generally take down your *whole* system with them.

Power

Linux is a multitasking, multiuser operating system. In this book, I concentrate on the desktop features of Linux. But under the hood, Linux is a system designed to provide all the power and flexibility of an enterprise-class server. Linux-powered Web site servers and electronic mail gateways move information along on the Internet and run small to large businesses. Under the friendly face of your graphical desktop, that power is still there.

Money

It is possible to do everything you need to do on a computer without spending any money on software—that means new software and upgrades alike. In fact, free software for Linux is almost an embarrassment of riches. In Chapter 7, I'll show you how to install (or remove) additional software on your Linux system.

Freedom from Legal Hassles

When you run Linux, you don't have to worry about whether you've kept a copy of your operating system license. The GNU GPL, which I mentioned earlier, means you are legally entitled to copy and can legally redistribute your Linux CDs if you wish.

Keep in mind, however, that although Linux itself can be freely distributed, *not all software* that runs on Linux is covered by the same license. If you buy or download software for your system, you should still pay attention to the license that covers that software.

Note I would be remiss if I didn't address a particular wrinkle in the free software world. In March 2003, SCO (formerly Caldera) with boss Darl McBride at the helm, launched an incredible $1 billion USD lawsuit against IBM. They later upped the suit to $3 billion and then later increased the suit again to $5 billion. This suit and SCO's allegations are largely seen as unfounded, an effort by a failed company to generate income through litigation. At the time of this writing, the case was ongoing and as yet unresolved.

As of February 22, 2005, things weren't going well for SCO. Their case was becoming increasingly shaky. On the stock trading floor, the NASDAQ had changed their symbol from SCOX to SCOXE. The "E" was added because SCO had failed to file its annual report with the SEC in a timely fashion.

What Do I Lose?

Nothing ever seems to be perfect. By moving to Linux you gain a great deal, but I would be doing a disservice if I did not mention the disadvantages.

Hardware and Peripheral Support

The hardware support for Linux is, quite honestly, among the best there is. In fact, when you consider all the platforms that run Linux, its hardware and peripheral support is better than that of the Windows system you are leaving behind. Unfortunately, there are some consumer devices designed with Windows specifically in mind. Consequently, certain printers or scanners may have limited support under Linux because the manufacturer is slow in providing drivers. That said, the vast majority of standard devices work very well under Linux, and you aren't likely to run into too many problems.

On the upside, you'll find that where you always had to load drivers to make something run in your old operating system (OS), Linux automatically recognizes and supports an amazing number of peripherals without your having to do anything extra or hunt down a driver disk. Furthermore, the Linux community is vibrant in a way that few businesses can ever hope to be. If you have your eye on a hot new piece of hardware, you can almost bet that some Linux developer somewhere has an eye on exactly the same thing.

We'll talk about devices and device drivers later in the book.

Software Packages

A huge amount of software is available for the Linux operating system. Amazingly, most of it is noncommercial and free for the download. There are *thousands* of games, tools, and Internet and office applications available to run on your system. You don't have to go far either. Most modern distributions come with several hundred packages on their distribution CDs, more than enough to get you going, working, and playing without having to look elsewhere. Once again, much of the software out there will cost you nothing more than the time it takes to download it.

On the other hand, commercial, shrink-wrapped software, including those hot new 3D games at your local computer store, are still hard to come by. As Linux grows in popularity, particularly on the desktop, this is starting to change.

There are ways around this issue however, and I'll talk more about that in Chapter 3. Since I mentioned running Windows games, I will tell you that you can pick up a package called Cedaga that lets you do just that.

A Step into the Unknown

Let's face it: For some, moving to Linux is a step into the unknown. Things won't be exactly as they were with your old operating system, and for the most part this is a good thing. You will have to do a little relearning and get used to a different way of doing things.

Even so, if you are used to working in your Windows graphical environment and you are comfortable with basic mousing skills, writing the occasional e-mail, surfing the Web, or composing a memo in your word processor, moving to Linux won't be a big deal. Your Linux desktop is a modern graphical environment, and much of what you have learned in your old operating system can be taken with you into this new world.

Some Tips on Using This Book

My intention in creating this book was to provide a simple move from your old OS to Linux. I'll cover things such as installation shortly, but the majority of the book has to do with working (and playing) in your new Linux environment. I want to show you how to do the things you have grown used to doing: surfing the Net, writing e-mails, listening to music, printing, burning CDs, and so on. Furthermore, I am going to tell you how to take those Word documents, Excel spreadsheets, and music files you have collected over time and start using them with Linux. In short, my plan is to have you move as effortlessly as possible from your old OS to Linux.

Working your way through the chapters, you'll notice that I am constantly inviting you to try things. That's because I believe the best way to learn anything is by doing. Yes, you're going to learn to work with a new operating system, but it doesn't mean you can't have fun. As everyone knows, all work and no play will make anyone pretty dull. Later on in this book (in an effort to avoid dullness), I'll take you into the world of Linux fun and games.

Quick Tips and Shelling Out

Throughout the book, I will occasionally provide you with boxed asides, "Quick Tips" that should serve as little reminders or simpler ways to do things.

You'll also notice boxes that start out with the phrase "Shell Out." Although I intend to concentrate on working with graphical tools and in a graphical way, much of the power of Linux comes from working with the command line, or the **shell**. The "Shell Out" boxes will guide you in working with the shell.

Learning to wield the command line is akin to getting a black belt in a martial art or earning a first aid certificate. It doesn't mean that you are going to run out and take on all comers or that you are going to be facing daily crisis situations. What working with the shell does is to give you the means and the confidence to step outside the confines of the graphical environment. The shell is power, and it is always there for you, so you should not fear it.

Meet Your Desktop

Modern Linux distributions come with powerful, easy-to-use graphical environments. There are many such environments, and in time you will learn about them. Part of that freedom I spoke about is the freedom to do things your way, and that extends to the type of graphical environment you may want to work in. The most popular desktop environments today are the K Desktop Environment (KDE) and GNOME, but WindowMaker, IceWM, and others have quite a following as well. *My* personal choice is KDE, but I often switch to other desktops when the mood takes me.

Although much of what you do with GNOME or KDE is pretty interchangeable, it makes sense in a book like this to pick one and run with it. Consequently, we will concentrate on the KDE desktop, primarily version 3.4 (although much of what I cover is very similar to what you would see in release 3.3).

KDE comes with most major distributions, including SUSE, Red Hat, Mandrake, Xandros, Linspire, and many others. I recommend KDE because it is more mature, beautiful, and better developed than the alternatives (yes, some of this is partly my opinion). It sports a clean, consistent, and integrated set of tools, widgets, and menus. Because of all these things, KDE is also much easier and friendlier to work with. In fact, many Linux companies install KDE as the default.

When you become comfortable with KDE and Linux, I invite you to experiment with other desktop environments. *Exercise your freedom to be yourself.*

Help Me!

Once you are done working with this book, I am confident that Linux will be your operating system of choice for the foreseeable future. That doesn't mean you won't have questions that aren't answered in this book. To that end, I give you a Web site address that will link you to the support pages for this book on my own Web site:

```
http://www.marcelgagne.com
```

My site has links to a number of other resources, including many articles I have written on using and administering Linux, links to other information sites, and much more. Click on this book's cover image, and you'll be transported to the support pages for this book.

I also run a few mailing lists for readers, which you'll find under the WFTL heading. WFTL is a short form I've used for years now. It stands for "Writer and Free Thinker at Large" (computer people love acronyms). It's also the hierarchy for the lists I'm talking about. One of those lists is the WFTL-LUG (a LUG is a Linux User Group), an online discussion group where readers can share information, ask questions, and help each other out with their various Linux adventures. I invite you to join any of the lists I offer there. There is *no cost*, and you can unsubscribe at any time.

If you check under the Linux Links menu of my Web site, you'll find a useful list of additional links to Linux information sources. One of these is the Linux Documentation Project (LDP).

 More Help In Chapter 4, I'll introduce you to your desktop's help system. It's a great tool with tons of additional information right at your fingertips.

The Linux Documentation Project

The LDP is a dynamic community resource. On your Linux distribution CD, you probably have a collection of documents known in the Linux world as *HOWTOs*. These are user- or developer-contributed documents that are maintained and updated by one or more individuals. You can find the latest version of these documents at the LDP site:

```
http://www.tldp.org/
```

The mandate of the LDP is essentially to provide a comprehensive base of documentation for all things Linux. If you've been looking high and low for information on installing that bleeding-edge FTL radio card on your PC and still haven't found what you are looking for, try the LDP. The LDP also makes a point of offering the latest versions of the man pages (also known as "manual pages," the default system documentation common to all Linux distributions) as well as user guides that tend to cover more ground than standard HOWTOs.

Linux User Groups

A few paragraphs back, I made passing reference to Linux User Groups, or LUGs. Let's put technology aside for a moment and explore something else you may have heard about: the Linux community. Yes, there really is a Linux community. All around the world, you will find groups of enthusiastic Linux users gathering for regular meetings, chatting over beer and pizza, and sharing information. This sharing of information is part of what makes Linux so friendly.

LUGs tend to run electronic mailing lists where informal exchanges of information take place (just as I do with my online LUG). New users are welcomed, and their questions are happily answered. These users range from newbies getting their feet wet to seasoned kernel developers. Should you find yourself stuck with nowhere to turn, seek out your local LUG and sign on to the mailing list. Today, someone helps you. As you grow more knowledgeable in administering your Linux system, maybe you will return the favor.

Locating a LUG in your community is as simple as surfing over to the Linux online Web site (`http://www.linux.org/`). Once there, click the User Groups button, and you are on your way. The list is organized by country, then by state or province, and so on.

About the CD

Included with this book is a full-featured Linux distribution called *Knoppix*. Knoppix is a Debian-based Linux distribution that runs entirely from your PC's CD-ROM drive (though slower than if you actually install Linux). That's right. You can run Linux on your system without having to change your system or uninstall Windows.

Note The version of Knoppix included with this book is *not* the official version but one that has been slightly modified by this humble author. I wish to express my admiration and thanks to Klaus Knopper, the creator of Knoppix, for his fine work. Any questions regarding the included disk, however, should be directed to me.

This CD is full of great software, some of which I will be covering in this book. You'll have access to e-mail applications, Web browsers, word processors, spreadsheets, games, and more. In fact, you should be able to follow along with this book and do many—*though not all*—of the things I talk about without having to install Linux at all. The bootable CD is a fantastic introduction, but there are limitations.

The first limitation is one I have already mentioned, but it bears mentioning again. The CD does run *much slower* than a hard-disk install, so keep in mind that the performance you experience from the CD is not indicative of the performance you can experience from a Linux hard-disk install. At their fastest, CD-ROM drives are no match for even the slowest hard disk drive. Furthermore, because this bootable Linux does not install itself on your hard drive, you are limited to the packages on the CD. In other words, you can't add or install any new software.

Ready to take Linux for a spin? The bootable CD is a *perfect* introduction. I'll tell you all you need to know in the next chapter.

When are truly ready to make the move to Linux, consider installing a full distribution. I'll tell you about how to find the distribution that's right for you and how to get a copy of Linux in Chapter 3. If you'd like to see some step-by-step installations, check out Appendix B in this book.

It's My Philosophy

I have a philosophy. All right, I have *many,* and this is just one of them.

Every once in a while, people tell me that desktop Linux is just crazy, that it is just too complicated for *the majority of people*. I don't know about you, but I am tired of being told that people can't learn to use something that is both good and powerful. With a certain amount of training and a little proper guidance, *anyone who is familiar with a computer can learn to use Linux*.

That isn't to say that working with Linux is difficult (it is not). But as you go along, you will be learning new things. This book is meant for users at every level of experience. It is meant to be read for fun as well as for reference. And because I'll ask you to try things throughout this book, it's also a training guide.

I'm delighted and thrilled that you've decided to join me in *Moving to Linux*. It's time to kiss the Blue Screen of Death goodbye!

Resources

Linux Documentation Project

>   http://www.tldp.org

Linux.org List of LUGs

>   http://www.linux.org/groups/index.html

Linux User Groups Worldwide

>   http://lugww.counter.li.org/groups.cms

Marcel (Writer and Free Thinker at Large) Gagné's Web site

>   http://www.marcelgagne.com

Chapter

2

An Introduction to the WFTL Edition Knoppix Disk

Included with this book is a full-featured Linux distribution that runs entirely from the CD-ROM. The WFTL Edition Knoppix CD is a Debian-based Linux distribution that runs entirely from your PC's CD-ROM drive. That's right. You can run Linux on your system without having to change your system or uninstall Windows.

Note Because it is running from the CD drive, WFTL Knoppix does run slower than if you actually install Linux and run it from the hard disk. Keep in mind that the performance you experience from the CD is not indicative of the performance you can experience from a Linux hard-disk install. At their fastest, CD-ROM drives are no match for even the slowest hard disk drive.

You should also know that the version of Knoppix included with this book is *not* the official version but one that has been slightly modified to provide you with a comprehensive companion to the software described in this book. I would like to express my admiration and thanks to Klaus Knopper, the creator of Knoppix, for his fine work. But any questions regarding the included disk should be directed to me via the WFTL-LUG or the forums on my Web site.

Running WFTL Knoppix is as easy as putting the CD in the drive and booting. A couple of minutes later, you are working with a great-looking, modern desktop (Figure 2-1). This CD is full of excellent software. There are hundreds of applications and literally thousands of programs on the disk. You'll have access to e-mail applications, Web browsers, word processors, spreadsheets, games, and more. In fact, you should be able to follow along and play with the software you'll explore in this book and do most of the things that are covered without having to install Linux at all.

The bootable CD is a fantastic introduction to Linux, providing you with a no-commitment way to take Linux out for a spin, but there are limitations. I've already covered one issue related to CDs, that of performance. The other limitation is also CD related. Because this bootable Linux does not install itself on your hard drive, you are limited to the packages on the CD. In other words, you can't add or install any new software. If you are truly ready to make the move to Linux, consider installing a full Linux distribution.

Note Actually, the WFTL Knoppix CD does have an experimental software installation mode for things like a Flash plugin for Web browsing, graphics drivers, some system utilities, and a few games. That option is under the main menu, KNOPPIX, Utilities, and "Install software while running from CD."

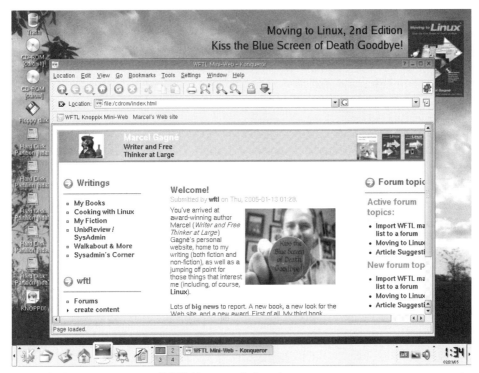

Figure 2–1   Meet your new WFTL Knoppix desktop!

Ready to Try Linux?

Loading Knoppix is easy because no installation is required.

Take your CD and insert it into your CD-ROM drive. Shut down Windows, and select Restart. Make sure your PC is set to boot from the CD. WFTL Knoppix boots up to a nice, graphical screen with a simple boot: prompt, from which you can simply press <Enter> and let Knoppix do the rest.

Note Most modern systems are set to boot directly from the CD-ROM drive (or DVD) if a bootable CD is found there. If your system does not, you may have to change the BIOS settings on your PC to allow this. This is generally done by pressing <Delete> or <F2> to enter Setup as the system is booting (you will usually see such a message before the operating system starts to load).

Because the menus vary, it is impossible for me to cover them all, but look for a menu option that specifies the boot order. You'll see something like A: first and then C: (i.e., your floppy drive and then the hard disk). Change the boot order so that it looks to the CD first, save your changes, and then restart your system.

The boot process is all text, but it is certainly colorful because Knoppix signifies devices, disks, sound cards, and so on in different colors. At some point, the screen will go dark as your video card is configured and X, the Linux graphical user interface, is started.

If the screen doesn't respond instantly, don't panic. Give it a few seconds. If nothing has happened even after you've waited a while, it is possible that your video card is one of the rare ones not included in the distribution. Never fear, most (if not all) modern cards support VESA. Reboot and type the following at the boot prompt:

```
knoppix xmodule=vesa
```

This prompt is an example of what is called a *cheat code* in the Knoppix world. If you have additional problems or you'd like to learn about cheat codes, head down to the HELP! section later in this chapter. For now, I'm going to assume that your WFTL Knoppix CD has booted normally and that you are sitting at the KDE graphical desktop (Figure 2-1).

Playing with WFTL Knoppix

Once the system has booted, you can start playing with Knoppix. If your system doesn't have a lot of memory, you can speed things up a bit right off the bat by letting Knoppix create a *swap file* in your Windows partition. This won't hurt anything on your system. All it does is allow Linux to use some of your disk space as though it were real memory. That is what we mean by *swap space*.

Doing this is easy. Click on KDE's program launcher (the big K in the lower left-hand corner), and move your cursor up to the KNOPPIX entry in the menu. There are five submenus here. One of them is Configure; under that menu, you'll see an entry labeled *SWAP file configuration* (Figure 2-2).

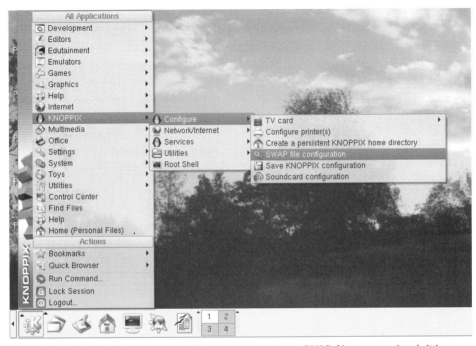

Figure 2–2 The Configure menu allows you to create a SWAP file on your hard disk.

Click this option, and you'll get a nice little warning that you are about to create a file named *knoppix.swp* on your existing DOS (Windows) partition. Click Yes, after which you'll be asked for the size of your swap file in megabytes. What qualifies as a good size depends on how much real memory you already have, but taking the default is probably a good bet.

Just Looking Around

The bar at the bottom of your screen is the panel, also called *Kicker* (Figure 2-3). Among other things, notice the large *K* icon in the bottom left-hand corner. This is the *Application Starter*, similar to the Start button on that other OS. Clicking the big K will bring up a menu of menus, a list of installed applications that you can run with a single click.

Figure 2–3 The KDE panel, aka Kicker.

You should take a moment to run through some of the included software in the menus. There you'll find the packages covered in the pages of this book. For instance, under the Graphics menu, you'll find the GIMP, a powerful graphic and image editing package that I cover in Chapter 17. Look under Multimedia and you'll see the Juk and amaroK audio jukebox players listed. I tell you all about those in Chapter 18. Under the Office menu, look for the components of the OpenOffice.org suite of office applications. This powerful suite is covered in three chapters in this book, Chapters 13–15. Altogether, there are hundreds of packages for you to run, ready for you to explore (Figure 2-4).

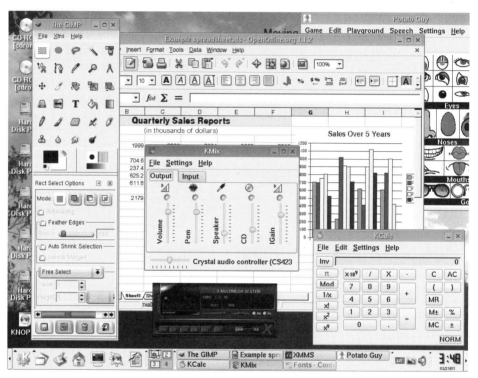

Figure 2–4   WFTL Knoppix comes with hundreds of programs and applications. In this image, you can see the GIMP, OpenOffice.org Calc, XMMS, Kcalc, Kmix, and the Potato Guy.

Speaking of running things, Kicker also has a taskbar embedded in it. When you start an application, you'll see it listed in the taskbar. This not only shows you what you have running on your desktop, but it also provides a quick way to switch from process to process. Just click on the program in the taskbar. Alternatively, you can press <Alt+Tab> to switch from one running program to another. The taskbar can be configured to list all processes from all desktops, group similar processes together, or simply show you what is on your current virtual desktop.

Virtual desktops are one feature you are going to absolutely *love*! On the default installation, you'll also notice four little squares labeled (strangely enough) 1, 2, 3, and 4. This is your desktop switcher, allowing you to switch between any of the four virtual desktops with a mouse click. If the concept of virtual desktops sounds a little odd, don't panic. I cover the panel, taskbar, and virtual desktops in detail in Chapter 4.

Configure Now, Remember Me Later

As you go through and try out the various things written about in this book, you will probably configure a number of things. Speaking of which, let's take another look at that Configure submenu under the KNOPPIX. Notice that you can configure a TV tuner, a sound card, or a printer as well (both local and network connected).

Look below that and you will discover two of the more interesting options, at least from the perspective of booting into Knoppix at a later time. There is an item on this KNOPPIX menu called *Save KNOPPIX configuration*. As you go along, you'll be making some changes, such as configuring printers or setting up your network. Using this menu option, you can save all of these configuration details to a diskette or to a disk partition.

The first dialog that appears (Figure 2-5) asks what settings to save. These include personal configuration files, network settings, graphics card configuration, and other settings, such as printers. Since the desktop icons are created by default when Knoppix boots, this is the only option that isn't checked. But if you have made custom changes to your desktop, you can override that now.

Then Knoppix reads your disk partitions and offers you a choice (Figure 2-6). You can write the configuration files either to a diskette or to one of your disk partitions. This operation is *perfectly safe* and does not format your drives.

 Tip If you are coming from the Windows world, the concept of named partitions such as in Figure 2-6 (e.g., /mnt/hda1) may seem a bit odd. Partitions are still common to your old OS, but you are probably used to thinking of them as drive letters.

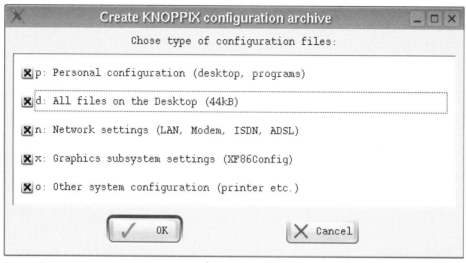

Figure 2-5   Tell Knoppix what settings you want to save.

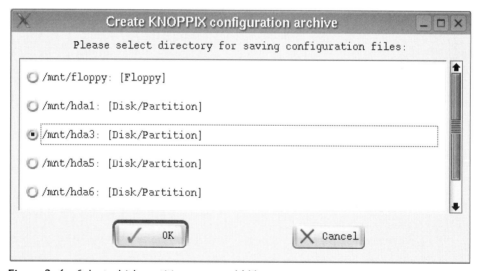

Figure 2-6   Select which partition you would like to use to save your settings.

If you choose to save to a diskette, The next time you boot Knoppix, make sure the diskette is in your drive and enter this command at the boot prompt:

```
knoppix floppyconf
```

If, on the other hand, you chose to use one of your disk partitions, you would flag that in the boot string to restore your settings:

```
knoppix myconfig=/mnt/hda10
```

Should you forget where you stored these settings, you can also type "knoppix myconfig=scan" and Knoppix will look at all your disk partitions and load the appropriate configuration.

The Persistence of Memory

I don't think Salvador Dali had Knoppix in mind when he created *The Persistence of Memory*, one of my favorite paintings, but the title seems appropriate here. If you start saving any amount of data to your knoppix home directory, one of two things will happen. The first is that you will run out of space, since you are writing to a RAM disk, basically just virtual memory. The second is that you'll lose all that information when you reboot. Your digital memories are gone.

To deal with both of these issues, consider setting up a *persistent home directory*. This is a small section of disk, an external drive, or even a USB memory key. The size of this directory is defined either by the size of the partition you choose or as a selected number of megabytes. Here's how you do it.

Head once again to the KNOPPIX menu and choose the Configure submenu. From there, select "Create a persistent KNOPPIX home directory." A short dialog will appear describing the process and asking you if you want to continue. Once you've read it, click Yes. The next dialog will ask you to choose the disk partition (or external storage). It is very similar to the one seen earlier in Figure 2-6.

Once you've selected a partition, a very *important* message appears (Figure 2-7). You are asked whether you wish to format this partition or just create an image on it. I strongly urge you *not* to choose the format option. If you want some dedicated external storage that doesn't share space with your existing partitions, use a memory stick instead.

Important I don't mean to sound repetitious, but it's vital that you make the right choice here. If you don't want to reformat your whole disk to create a persistent home directory, make sure you click **No**.

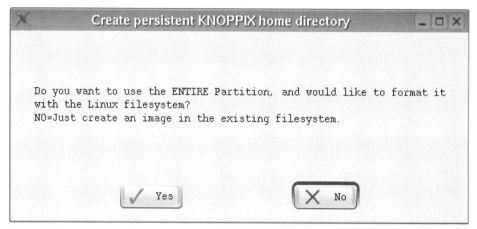

Figure 2–7   Read carefully! Do you want to format your disk or just use a portion of it?

If you chose No, then you will then be asked to enter the size of your persistent home directory in megabytes (Figure 2-8). The default here is 30.

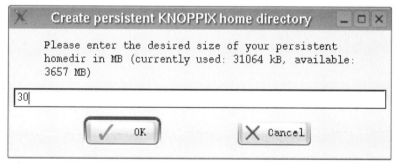

Figure 2–8   Define how much space you would like your persistent home directory to use.

Next you'll be asked whether you want that data encrypted, in which case you will also need to enter a password or passphrase to access that data at boot time. That's the last setting. The persistent home directory is created and you can then access it at boot time. Assuming that I chose my /mnt/ hda10 partition again, here's how I would tell Knoppix to load the persistent home directory:

```
knoppix home=/mnt/hda10
```

(You can also enter "knoppix home=scan".)

To select both my saved settings and the persistent home directory, use the myconf and home flags on boot:

```
knoppix home=scan myconf=scan
```

That's it. One final thought before we move on. The beauty of using the USB memory key is that you can take your WFTL Knoppix disk with you; wherever you go, you have a USB memory key in your pocket and all your configuration and files handy.

Setting Up the Network

Now that I've told you how to save your settings between sessions, let's take a look at one of the more important settings you will configure—your network.

From the Kicker menu, choose the KNOPPIX submenu and then Network/Internet. You'll notice a number of network configuration options, from setting up an ADSL connection to ISDN, wireless, local network card, and more (Figure 2-9).

Let's use the Network card configuration as an example. When you select this, a terminal window will open, followed shortly by a graphical dialog. When the network card dialog appears, it asks whether you want to use a DHCP broadcast to configure the card. Should you choose to manually configure the card, the configuration utility automatically suggests an IP address of 192.168.0.1, which you can override with your own local settings (see Figure 2-10).

With this type of connection, you need to know your local nameserver and gateway. Of course, different network configuration dialogs (e.g., ADSL) will ask different questions. Just follow the prompts and answer the appropriate questions, and you'll be surfing the Internet in no time at all.

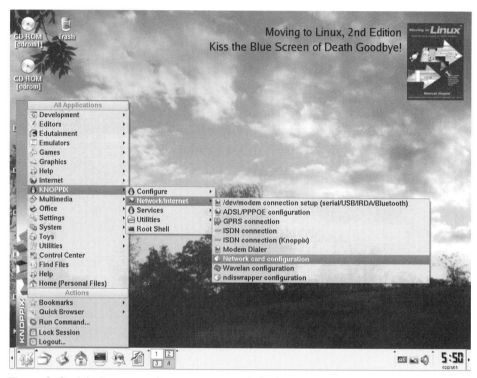

Figure 2-9   It's time to configure your network for Internet access.

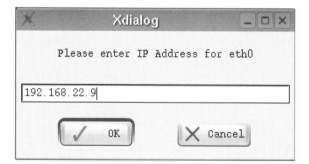

Figure 2-10   Manually setting your IP address.

HELP!

Problems, problems . . . Before we wrap up here, I should take a moment to look at some of the common problems you may encounter and a few questions you may have.

The CD is amazingly good at automatically booting and running on a huge number of systems, but it isn't perfect. There is only so much software you can pack on one CD, and that includes drivers for hardware. That said, most problems with booting Knoppix can be resolved with the right cheat code.

You might have noticed that when the boot prompt came up it said, "Press F2 for help." Pressing F2 will show you some of the more common cheat codes. Pressing F3 will give you even more. One problem you may run into occurs when some systems return an incorrect amount of memory to Knoppix when it boots. This can cause a kernel panic, among other things. Typing the following will inform Knoppix of the computer's real memory:

```
knoppix mem=128M
```

This assumes, of course, that you have 128 megabytes of memory.

Another boot option you might try is the following:

```
knoppix xkeyboard=us
```

This will force the graphical X keyboard to use a standard U.S. English layout (assuming you want standard U.S. English).

I started this discussion of cheat codes by showing you how to get around an unknown graphics card. Knoppix tries to figure out the optimal resolution for your monitor, but this may not be what you want. For instance, if your screen came up in 1024×768 mode and you wanted to use 800×600 instead (perhaps the text appears too small), you would enter the following at the "boot:" prompt:

```
knoppix screen=800x600
```

Similarly, to get 1024×768 resolution, you would type the following:

```
knoppix screen=1024x768
```

A complete list of cheat codes can be found at:

```
http://www.marcelgagne.com/cheatcodes.html
```

What About the Root Password?

The quick answer is "There isn't one." If you need root access, click on the K menu, go up to the KNOPPIX menu, and select **root shell** from the menu. By the way, *root* is the name of the administrator login in the Linux world.

What If My System Can't Boot from the CD-ROM?

There is a diskette boot image included on the WFTL Edition Knoppix CD-ROM should you have a system that won't boot from a CD (this is common with some older BIOS's). If you are currently working from Windows, there's a program called **RAWRITE2.EXE** on the CD-ROM under the KNOPPIX directory. Get yourself a blank diskette, cd (change directory) to the KNOPPIX directory, and execute RAWRITE2.EXE. You'll be asked for a file name (which is **boot.img**). Wait a few seconds while the program writes the boot image to your floppy, and then boot from that floppy (you still need the CD <insert appropriate smiley here>).

From Linux, you can change directory (or cd) to the KNOPPIX directory and create a boot diskette with this command:

```
dd if=boot.img of=/dev/fd0 bs-1440k
```

Either way, after a few seconds, the diskette will be ready.

Can I Install the WFTL Edition Knoppix on My Hard Disk?

Yes, you can install from the CD to your system. I don't recommend the Knoppix disk as the means by which to install Linux because it is *not one of the easiest installs*, certainly not as friendly as picking up a copy of Mandrake or SUSE or Fedora. Knoppix is a great distribution to play with and to get used to working with Linux, but not to install.

That said, there is a script on the CD called "knoppix-installer." Wait until the Knoppix CD is fully booted, jump to the root console (either under the KNOPPIX submenu or by jumping out of the graphical system by pressing `Ctrl+Alt+F1`), and execute the command. The program, which sadly is only so friendly, will walk you through all the steps of installing the Knoppix CD onto your hard drive. Once complete, you can customize your desktop at will and use apt-get (or the graphical Synaptic) to update your system over the Internet.

Remember to Share

Feel free to burn additional copies of this disk and share it with friends.

Resources

The Persistence of Memory at the MOMA

>   http://www.moma.org/collection/browse_results.php?object_id=79018

Knoppix on the Internet

>   http://www.knopper.net/knoppix/index-en.html

3

Ready . . .
Set . . .
Linux!

Ready for some serious fun?

Your Linux adventure is about to begin. You may have chosen to try things out using the bootable Knoppix CD, but at some point (perhaps even now), you may want to do a proper hard-disk install. To really get going, though, you need to deal with two major things. First and foremost, you need to get a copy of Linux.

The second thing we will need to take care of is important only if you have Windows on your system and there is data you need to preserve and migrate. Let's start with the first step.

Getting Linux

This one is actually the easy part.

One way to get Linux is to buy a copy. Head down to your local computer software store and ask for your favorite distribution. Alternatively, visit your favorite vendor's Web site, whether it be Mandrake, SUSE, Red Hat, or any of the many different distributions listed on the DistroWatch (`http://www.distrowatch.com`) Web site, and order one online. Incidentally, Distro-Watch also lists the top ten major distributions at any given time.

 Corporate Name Watch As final edits on this book were already in process, Mandrake had just acquired Conectiva Linux. In doing so, they also changed their name from Mandrake to Mandriva. Since the official release of Mandrake Linux (or Mandriva Linux) was Mandrake 10.1 at the time, I chose to continue using the name Mandrake throughout this book.

Which distribution should you get? Well, every Linux vendor does things a little differently. If you think of this in terms of cars, it starts to make sense. Every single car out there is basically an engine on wheels with seats and some kind of steering mechanism so that drivers can get to where they want to go. What kind of car you buy depends on what else you expect from a car, whether that is comfort, style, the vendor's reputation, or any of a great number of other choices.

 Recommendation You *really* want me to suggest something? Let me start by saying that I think it is a wonderful thing that so many Linux distributions exist. Aside from creating a rich OS landscape, it furthers creativity and fosters innovation in software design. This can only be a good thing. However, if you *push* me for a suggestion and you are *just getting started* with Linux, I would probably suggest Mandrake or SUSE. Both are excellent, well engineered, and beginner friendly. SUSE (now owned by Novell) has a very business-friendly look and feel, whereas Mandrake is perhaps a little more home user friendly.

You might be asking, *If I can get a free copy of Linux, why would I want to pay for one?* As it turns out, that question has more than one answer. The first is that buying a boxed set usually gets you some amount of technical support from the vendor. If you are feeling nervous about your first Linux installation, this might be a good reason. Second, the boxed set usually contains some kind of manual or manuals *specific* to that version of Linux. That will inevitably lead to another question as to what makes this Linux different from that one. Finally, in purchasing a boxed set, you are supporting the company that put leather on the seats or tinted the windows. It's a way of saying, "Thanks for all the hard work."

Because it is possible to get a free copy of Linux, you don't have to shell out the dollars if you don't want to. At most, you'll need a fast Internet connection, a CD burner, and some blank CDs—or a helpful friend who has these.

Getting a Free Copy of Linux

The idea of free software—a free operating system in particular—takes some getting used to, but it happens fast. When you are working with other operating systems, getting and trying new releases involves some kind of cash outlay. In the case of Linux, the most you need is a spare machine on which to play. Consequently, you can load one version of Linux, take it for a spin, then load another and see whether that feels any better to you.

If you have a high-speed Internet connection (and a CD burner), you can visit any of the vendors' sites listed at the end of this chapter and download their latest and greatest. Remember, though, that although you may download their latest Linux free of charge, technical support may still be an extra cost.

If you don't like the idea of visiting each and every one of those sites, a visit to LinuxIso.org (`http://www.linuxiso.org/`) may be in order. This site provides a one-stop shop for the more popular Linux distributions with ISOs (CD-ROM images) available for download.

Package Managers and Updates

Package managers often have a great deal to do with what people end up choosing in terms of a distribution. In this book, I'll be talking about installing software using RPM, and every distribution I mentioned earlier uses RPM as the package manager, so the information you take with you will work with any of these releases. I have also developed a great respect for the power and simplicity of Debian's apt-get program. In fact, you now get apt-get for RPM-based systems.

The method of update is also worthy of consideration. Many vendors now provide an option for updating and patching your system online. As long as you have a fast Internet connection, you are all set. Finally, here's the great disclaimer of the decade: Linux, like all dynamic, living things, is evolving and changing. It is a moving target, and, consequently, the details of a specific distribution will change over time. In Appendix B, I cover four major distributions and their installation procedures to give you an idea of what you can expect to see. For now, let's talk about what you are going to need in preparation for getting Linux on your system.

Dual Booting

As much as I would like to think that each and every one of you is more than ready to say goodbye forever to your old operating system and hello to Linux, I know that for many this is a *very big* jump. If you are still feeling a little insecure about simply breaking free and running Linux, I'm here to tell you that you can get the best of both worlds. It is called *dual booting*.

Dual booting refers to the technique of making a home for both operating systems on your machine. When you start your computer, a small program called a *boot loader* offers you a menu of choices from which you can decide to boot Linux or whatever other operating system you have installed. That boot loader, for the most part, is called *Grand Unified Boot Loader* (GRUB). A second and still very common boot loader is called *LILO*, the Linux Loader.

When you load Linux on a system that already has Windows installed, your new system is smart enough to recognize the existence of this other operating system. You'll find that an entry for both of your operating systems will magically appear in your boot loader menu.

Preserving Your Data

When you've been using a computer for a long time, you amass a lot of data. Forget software—*the data is the most important thing on your system*, and you need to get it backed up. Whether you dual boot or not, I want to stress that you are going to be doing some major changes to your hard disk. Please don't take any chances with your data. Make a backup.

Because Windows backup programs aren't necessarily going to be helpful in getting your data onto a Linux system, you should copy the various word processing documents, spreadsheets, graphics (all those pictures you took with your digital camera), music files, and anything else you will want later onto some kind of media, whether it is a ZIP drive, diskettes, flash memory cards, or a CD.

If you have large amounts of data, it might make sense to keep a Windows partition around long enough to copy from one to the other. Most of the major Linux distributions will not only notice the existence of your Windows partition, they will also provide you with an icon on your desktop so that you can easily access that data. Although this may seem like a great way to avoid backing up your data, *please* don't ignore this step. In fact, if you haven't been backing up your system, your system has been *living* on borrowed time. *If in doubt, back up*.

A Linux-Only System

This is by far the easiest alternative because you don't have to worry about keeping an intact copy of something else on the system. This represents quite the leap because there is no going back (without reinstalling from scratch). If you go down this road, you have access to all your disk space, and Linux uses disk space more efficiently. You can also kiss those proprietary licensing issues goodbye (not to mention the Blue Screen of Death).

When you are ready to install, simply choose the option that will over-write the entire system. The installation process will take care of the rest for you. It's that simple.

Windows on Linux

Under Linux, it is possible to run a number of Windows applications without having Windows installed at all. This is done with Wine. I'm not talking about the fermented beverage some of us are quite fond of, but a package that runs on Linux. Allow me to paraphrase from the Wine Web site . . . *Wine Is Not an Emulator*. Wine is a compatibility layer, a set of APIs that enable some Windows applications to operate on a Linux system running the X window system (the Linux graphical environment).

Wine will not run every Windows application, but the number of applications it is capable of running is increasing all the time. Some commercial vendors have ported certain Windows applications to Linux by making some of the code run in Wine. This has sped up the normal production cycle and made it possible for them to get their programs to Linux users faster. If you really need to run a Windows application under Linux and you would like to go this route, the commercial Wines tend to be a better approach.

Wine Tip When it comes to Wine (the software), younger is most definitely better. A well-aged Wine (the software) will not be as good at running your Windows software as a brand new Wine. As for wine (the beverage), aging is certainly a good thing, but there are limits. As a rule, reds can age longer than whites, but it all depends on the variety. Consult your local wine vendor or pick up a good book on the subject.

Many Linux distributions include a version of Wine on the CDs, and some let you select Windows compatibility applications as part of the installation procedure. Keep in mind that the newer your Wine, the better. For the latest and greatest on Wine development, visit the Wine web site (http://www. winehq.org/). A great deal of Wine development is being done at CodeWeavers (http://www.codeweavers.com/). Its version provides an installation wizard to guide you through the installation and configuration process for Wine. It makes the whole process extremely simple.

VMware

The Wine project has done some impressive work, but it will not run all Windows applications. Sometimes you just need to run the whole shebang, and that means a *full* copy of Windows. Because you don't want to boot back and forth between Linux and Windows, it would be great if you could run Windows entirely on your Linux machine. This is the philosophy behind VMware—and it doesn't stop there.

VMware enables you to create virtual machines on your computer. Complete with boot-up BIOS and memory checks, VMware virtualizes your entire hardware configuration, making the PC inside the PC as real as the one you are running. Furthermore, VMware enables you to run (not emulate) Windows 95, 98, 2000, NT, FreeBSD, or other Linuxes. For the developer or support person who needs to work (or write code) on different platforms, this is an incredible package. Yes, you can even run another Linux on your Linux, making it possible to test (or play with) different releases without reinstalling on a separate machine. VMware knows enough to share your printers, network cards, and so on. You can even network between the "real" machine and the virtual machine as though they were two separate systems.

All this capability comes at a price, however. Aside from the dollars that you spend on this package (and it can be well worth it), there is a considerable price in performance. VMware is a hungry beast. The more processor power and memory you have, the better. A Pentium III with 128 or more megabytes should be your starting point. Unlike Wine, you do need a licensed copy of Windows (or whatever OS you are installing) to run.

VMware comes in a variety of packages and price points. Visit the VMware Web site (`http://www.vmware.com/`) for details.

Win4Lin

Another alternative still requires a licensed copy of Windows. Win4Lin, formerly Netraverse (`http://www.win4lin.com`), sells a package called (you guessed it) *Win4Lin*. This is a package designed to let you run Windows on your system but, unlike VMware, *only* Windows. The classic Win4Lin product only supported Windows 95, 98, and ME, but with the introduction of Win4Lin Pro, Windows 2000 and XP are also supported. It is, however, somewhat less expensive than VMware. Once again, remember that because you aren't *emulating* Windows but actually running a copy, you still need that licensed copy of Windows.

Win4Lin's magic is performed at the kernel level. Consequently, this requires that you download a patched kernel equivalent to what you are currently running or that you patch and rebuild your own. If you have compiled custom drivers into your kernel, you are going to have to go through the process again to get Win4Lin going. This whole process is no longer necessary if you choose to purchase Win4Lin Pro.

What I have found interesting is that Windows installs and loads much faster under Linux than in native mode. Win4Lin works very well indeed and requires surprisingly little in terms of resources. I have run Windows 95 and 98 on Win4Lin using a Pentium 233 notebook with 64MB of RAM and found that it was reasonably peppy. Obviously, the requirements for Windows 2000 and XP are going to be somewhat higher. You do take a performance hit, but it feels minor and should not distract you under most circumstances.

Breaking Free!

You may not need to go through any of these hoops to preserve your old operating system. As you go through this book, you may find that all of your needs are met just running Linux. There are plenty of applications as slick and as capable as anything in the Windows world.

Why go back and forth when you can just go forward? In Appendix B of this book, I cover the installation process of some of the more popular distributions. When you are ready to install Linux for good, take a look there. In the meantime, and until you feel comfortable, you can always try out Linux without installing by using the WFTL Edition Knoppix CD-ROM included with this book.

Resources

CodeWeavers

> http://www.codeweavers.com

Debian

> http://www.debian.org

DistroWatch (for a great distribution roundup)

> http://www.distrowatch.com

Fedora Project

> http://fedora.redhat.com

Linux.org

> http://www.linux.org

Mandriva/Mandrake

> http://www.mandriva.com

Red Hat Software

> http://www.redhat.com

Slackware Linux

> http://www.slackware.com

SUSE Linux

> http://www.novell.com/linux/suse/index/html

VMware

http://www.vmware.com

Win4Lin

http://www.win4lin.com

WINE Project

http://www.winehq.org

Chapter

4

Getting Your Hands Dirty

Welcome to the multiuser, multitasking, multieverything world. Linux is designed to run multiple users and processes concurrently. What that means is that your system is capable of doing many things, even while it appears to be idle. This is the reason so many businesses and organizations use Linux as a Web server, e-mail server, file server, print server . . . well, you get the idea.

From the perspective of the individual user, this means that all users in your family (or office) can have desktop environments that are truly theirs and theirs alone. Your desktop can be configured and modified to let you work the way you want to, with different backgrounds, icons, colors, or themes, depending on your mood. It also protects your personal information from others, meaning that the kids can totally change their desktops and reorganize things but you won't be affected in any way when you log in.

I'll have you logging in very shortly, but for the moment I want to say a few words about your new desktop.

Getting to Know You . . . KDE

Linux is extremely flexible. Linux makes it possible to run in a number of different desktop environments. The plus side of this is that *you* decide how you want to work. Your system works the way you want it to and not the other way around. The downside is exactly the same. Let's face it, being told what to do is often easier, even if it means getting used to working in a way that you may not particularly like at first—not necessarily better, but easier.

On that note, at some time when you've gotten comfortable with your Linux system running the KDE desktop, I'm going to ask you to be brave and experiment with some of these other environments, whether it be GNOME, WindowMaker, IceWM, or one of the many other desktop environments available to the Linux user. You may find yourself totally taken with a different way of doing things. All your programs will still work as they did, but the *feel* of your desktop—the *experience*, if you prefer—will be all yours. For now, we'll stick to KDE.

KDE is the most popular desktop environment in the Linux world, and deservedly so. It is beautiful, slick, mature, powerful, and easy to use. It is also loaded with great applications for e-mail, surfing the Web, playing movies, burning CDs, writing documents, working with spreadsheets, and so on. KDE also features a great collection of games that should keep you busy for some time.

A Few Words about X

In a few seconds, when I start showing you around your desktop, what I am telling you now will fade into the background of your memory, but I still think you should know. KDE, that great-looking desktop system, is the friendly face that rides above your Linux system's real graphical engine. That engine is called the *X window system*, *X.Org*, or simply *X*. What KDE, your desktop environment, does is provide control of windows, borders, decorations, colors, icons, and so on.

Historical Note You may also hear of this graphical engine referred to as XFree86. In January of 2004, X.Org came into being as the body that develops and builds on the X window system code base for Linux. Prior to the emergence of X.Org, Linux systems used XFree86. Within a few months, however, most of the large Linux distributions had switched to the X.Org code base.

When you installed your system, you went through a graphical desktop configuration step of some kind. What you were setting up at that time wasn't KDE or GNOME, but X. X is what the desktop—and every graphical program you run—*really* runs on.

Logging In

In most cases, your workstation will boot up to a graphical login screen. You will likely see the names of users you set up during the installation of your system, with a box for the username and another for the password. Remember that both the username and password are case sensitive, so you must type both as they were created. You can always change the password at a later time. (I tell you about it just a little later in the chapter.)

This graphical login screen is known as the *login manager*. Depending on the installation, it may appear different from system to system. The KDE login screen will look something like the one shown in Figure 4-1, which

Figure 4–1   First face of a graphical login manager.

comes from a Mandrake Linux system. Login managers, like so many things on your system, can be configured to take on different looks and styles. As a result, the companies that provide Linux distributions will often customize them to suit their needs. What they will all have in common is a place for your login name, your password, and an option for selecting your desktop environment (KDE, GNOME, etc.).

Start by logging in with the *non-root* user you created when you installed the system. For session type, make sure you choose KDE. If this is your first time logging in, you may be presented with the KDE Personalizer. I say *may* because some distributions will log you in to a default desktop with a given look and feel that you can then change to suit your needs and tastes, something we talk about in detail in Chapter 6.

Quick Tip If you don't see the KDE personalizer after logging in, you should still take a few minutes to read through this section, because it does introduce you to some basic concepts. You can always run the KDE personalizer with the command "kpersonalizer" by clicking the button in the bottom left-hand corner of your screen and selecting "*Run command.*" Simply type kpersonalizer and press <Enter>. You may also find it in the K menu under Settings. It is listed as "Desktop Settings Wizard." Even so, all of these settings can be changed using the tools I describe in Chapter 6. The kpersonalizer information only applies to first-time logins.

When kpersonalizer runs, you'll first be asked for your country and language of choice (Figure 4-2). Aside from the obvious usefulness of the language setting, this sets some intelligent defaults for you based on that decision; for instance, currency and date format.

The next screen, *System Behavior*, is particularly interesting (Figure 4-3). If you are coming from the Windows world, you are by now used to double-clicking on desktop icons to make things happen. Not so in the Linux world. A single click on an icon activates your program. If you like the double-click, choose Windows for system behavior, or stick with the single-click KDE default.

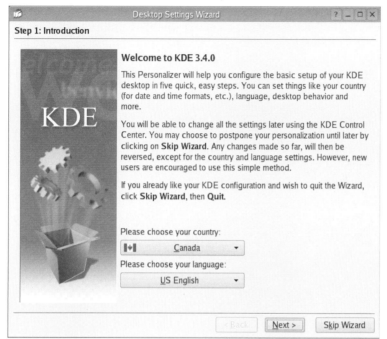

Figure 4–2
Setting your
country
information.

Figure 4–3
Changing
system behavior
(single vs.
double-click,
etc.).

Before we move on, I want to mention one other thing. Notice the Window activation item? This is sometimes referred to as *focus*. On a windowing system, it is possible to have many application windows on your screen at the same time. Sometimes they overlap. When you want to start using a particular window, you click on that window to bring it forward. That's *focus on click*. Aside from the KDE and Windows behaviors, you could also choose UNIX, which has an interesting method of focus. Simply moving your mouse cursor over the background window brings it forward. This is referred to as *focus follows mouse*. It takes some getting used to, but some people, particularly those with large monitors, may find it useful.

The next step brings up the *Eyecandy-O-Meter* (Figure 4-4). If you have a powerful, fast machine, you might want to just crank the slider to the maximum. What you will get are animated icons, sound themes, and special effects of various types. Click on the Show Details button to find out just what you get for your processor and memory buck.

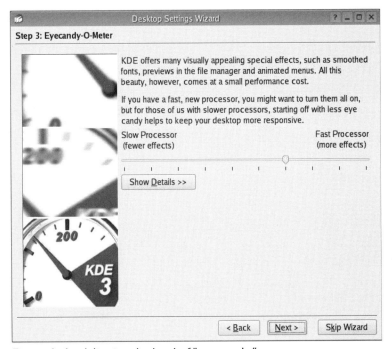

Figure 4-4   Adjusting the level of "eye candy."

Hot on the heels of this screen is even more eye candy—this time in the guise of a desktop theme (Figure 4-5). What kind of style would you like for your desktop? Pick one and click Next, and your desktop style will change automatically. If you don't like the choice, hit the Back button and try again. *For the time being, I highly recommend that you pick the Plastik theme.* That's because the look and feel of the windows I'm going to describe will be affected by the theme you choose, and since Plastik is the default theme for KDE 3.4, that is what I will be using. I revisit this subject in the Chapter 6, at which point you can go wild.

Finally, kpersonalizer offers to load up your panel with some default settings and icons. For now, just accept the default, click Next, and you are done setting up your desktop.

Figure 4–5 Setting the default theme.

Click Here! Click Here!

A quick note on clicking before we continue. Everything is pretty much launched with a single click of the *left mouse button*. As I mentioned earlier, you can change that to a double-click if you prefer, but I suggest that you try to get used to the single click (for the moment, anyhow). I think you will like it.

Clicking on the *right mouse button* almost anywhere will bring up a menu of available options.

The *middle mouse button* (if you have one or have configured your two-button mouse to emulate a three-button mouse) serves a number of purposes, based on the application. The best one, to me, is pasting text from one application to another.

Becoming One with the Desktop

The bar at the bottom of your screen is the panel, also called *Kicker* (Figure 4-6). Among other things, notice the large *K* icon in the bottom left-hand corner. This is the *Application Starter*, similar to the Start button on that other OS. Clicking the big K will bring up a menu of menus, a list of installed applications that you can run with a single click.

Figure 4–6   The KDE panel, also known as the Kicker.

Speaking of running things, Kicker also has a taskbar embedded in it. When you start an application, you'll see it listed in the taskbar. This not only shows you what you have running on your desktop, but it also provides a quick way to switch from process to process. Just click on the program in the taskbar. Alternatively, you can press <Alt+Tab> to switch from one running program to another. The taskbar can be configured to list all processes from all desktops, group similar processes together, or simply show you what is on your current virtual desktop.

Did he just say *virtual desktop*?

Yes . . . virtual desktop. This is one feature you are going to absolutely *love*! On the default installation, you'll also notice four little squares labeled (strangely enough) 1, 2, 3, and 4 (some distributions start you with just two). This is your desktop switcher, allowing you to switch between any of the four virtual desktops with a mouse click. Think of it as having a computer monitor four times as large as what you already have, with each desktop running different things. You can leave each one the way you want it without having to minimize things anytime you want to use them. It gets better: You can have four, five, six, or even more virtual desktops if you find that four aren't enough for you (Figure 4-7).

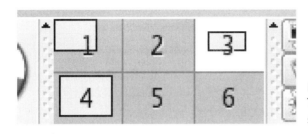

Figure 4-7
The desktop pager with six virtual desktops.

Another way to switch virtual desktops is by pressing <Ctrl+Tab>.

Kicker also has a number of icons to the right of the big K. To find out what each of these is, move your mouse over each one and pause. Context-sensitive bubble help, or "tooltips," will appear showing you what each icon is for. Clicking on any of these icons will launch the program it represents. One you might want to take note of right now is the life preserver icon (which you can also find by clicking the big K and looking for Help). This opens up your desktop documentation and help files.

Let's move to Kicker's far right. You might notice an embedded clock and some smaller icons: a clipboard, a calendar, or a speaker icon. These also represent programs—but *running* programs. These applications have been *swallowed* by the panel and can be called up with a click. That mini-icon area is called the *system tray* (Figure 4-8).

Figure 4-8   *System tray icons.*

Finally, notice the two little icons sitting together vertically. One looks like a lock and the other like a power button. On my desktop, the lock is blue and the power button is red. The lock button will lock your desktop and activate the screensaver. To unlock your desktop, you move the mouse (or hit a key), after which you will be prompted for your password. The power button logs you out and returns the system to the login manager so that you or someone else can log in. I cover screensavers in the Chapter 6.

Your First Application

It's time to really get into this, nail down some terminology, and get you working with the system. Starting a program or opening up an application is as simple as clicking on an icon. Let's do that. In fact, let's open up *the* great KDE application, *Konqueror*.

You'll be using Konqueror a lot. This is the KDE file manager that lets you work with files and folders. Konqueror makes it easy to create folders (or directories, as they are known in the Linux world), copy, delete, and move other folders and files around by dragging and dropping from one to the other. Konqueror is also a Web browser, from which you can surf the Internet, as well as a universal file viewer, so you can view and organize your photo collection, preview documents, and much, much more.

 Quick Tip This is a good time to let you in on a *secret*. While you will find KDE under RedHat, Mandrake, SUSE, and others, the menus may vary somewhat. What this means is that things on your menu may not be in *exactly* the same place as on my menu. Menu organization is only so important, in that multimedia applications like the CD player will be under a menu that sounds like multimedia (it might say "*Enjoy music & video*"), whereas a Web browser might be under the *Internet* menu or something that says "*Use the Internet.*"

What will be consistent is the command's name. For that reason, I will be telling you how to call a program by name throughout this book.

Down in your Kicker panel, notice the icon that looks like a folder with a little house in front of it. The tooltip that pops up when you hover your mouse over it says *Home*. This will open Konqueror as a file manager in your home directory. Click it, and you should get something that looks like Figure 4-9.

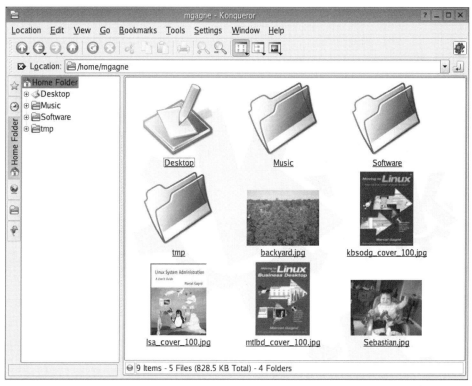

Figure 4–9   Introducing Konqueror, the all-purpose file manager and browser.

On the left, Konqueror shows a tree view of your home directory. This is the *navigation panel*. Pressing <F9> will hide (or bring forward) the navigation panel. The tabs let you switch between a view of your home directory to bookmarks for the Web, a history of places you've visited on the Internet, connected services (such as printers), ftp archives, and so on. On the right, the contents of the current location are displayed. If this is a directory (like your home directory), the various directories will appear as folder icons. Depending on how Konqueror is configured, images in your folders may appear as little thumbnails. Would you like to see the full-sized image? Just click on the thumbnail, and Konqueror will do the rest.

Quick Tip I've made the icons large, which makes the thumbnail images easy to view. To change the icon size, click View on the menu bar and then Icon Size, and select the size you prefer. Just what is the menu bar? Read on.

Konqueror is flexible, powerful, and definitely worth your time to get to know. In fact, it will likely become your most used desktop application. I give Konqueror the focus and consideration it deserves in the next chapter. For the moment, leave Konqueror where it is and read on as we discuss windows—and I don't mean the operating system.

Windows, Title Bars, and Menus, Oh My!

Each graphical program that runs on your desktop will have certain common characteristics. Have a look at the top of your Konqueror window, and you will see something like Figure 4-10.

Figure 4–10   Most windows will have a title bar as well as a menu bar.

The Title Bar

The top bar on a running program is called the *title bar*. Depending on the application, it may display a program name, the name of a document you are working on, a location on the Web, or a nice description explaining what you are running. Left-clicking on the title bar and dragging it with the mouse will move the program window around on your desktop.

Quick Tip Most modern desktops assume a fairly sizeable monitor running at least 1024x768, and a number of applications assume this to be a universal truth. This plays havoc when your monitor is smaller than this (say, 800x600) and the buttons you need to click are off screen. Clicking the title bar and dragging the window gets you only so far.

Don't despair. By pressing the <Alt> key and left-clicking on a window, you can drag it anywhere you wish, including beyond the boundaries of your desktop. This is particularly handy if you need to get at a hidden OK button.

Double-clicking on the title bar will *shade* your program—the application will appear to *roll up* like a window blind. Now move your mouse pointer to the title bar, and the application unrolls. Move off the application completely, and it rolls up again. Double-click on the title bar again, and the application will *unroll* and stay unrolled. Doing this with a number of running applications is an interesting phenomenon that takes some getting used to, kind of like someone reading your mind.

The title bar also has a number of small icons. Pause your mouse cursor over them, and a tooltip will inform you of their functions. Starting at the left-hand corner of the title bar, there are two icons of interest. The far left one brings up a small drop-down menu that makes it possible to move the program to another virtual desktop and to minimize or maximize the application (among other things).

You may also have a pushpin (or a circle) icon beside the menu icon—this makes a window *sticky*. Clicking it again makes it *unsticky*. Try this. Click on one of your other three virtual desktops. If you haven't already excitedly opened dozens of other programs on each one, you should find yourself with a nice, clean desktop. Now go back to your first virtual desktop. Click the pushpin icon. Now jump back to virtual desktop 2. Konqueror is there. Click on desktop number 3, and it is there also. In fact, if you had 10 virtual desktops, Konqueror would be waiting for you on all of them.

Here's a cool bit of information, however. You are still running only *one* instance of Konqueror. It's just that it is available to you on every desktop. Finally, if you stuck the window on virtual desktop 1 and you unstuck it on virtual desktop 3, it will stay on desktop 3.

Before we move on to other things, we need to look at the buttons on the right-hand side of the title bar. You use the icon that has a *minus sign* (it could also be a *dot*) in the center to minimize (or iconize) a window (remember that you can pause over the top with your mouse button to get the tooltip). The icon with a *square* in the center maximizes a window, causing it to take up every bit of space on your desktop except for Kicker's panel. Finally, the *X* does pretty much what you would expect it to. It closes a running application.

On to the Menu Bar

Directly below the title bar is the *menu bar*. The menu bar will generally have a number of labels (such as *File*, *Edit*, and *View*), each grouping the various things you can do into some kind of sensible order.

Every program will have a different set of menu options, depending on the nature of the application. Clicking on a menu label will drop down a list of your options for that function (see Figure 4-11).

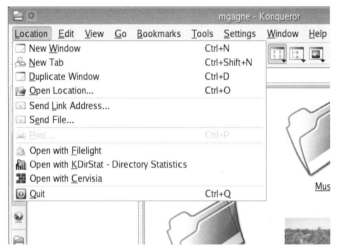

Figure 4–11   Drop-down menus.

Resizing Windows

The last thing you should know is that (for the most part) you aren't stuck with the default window size. By grabbing any of the corners of an application window, you can drag that corner and stretch the window to a size that is more comfortable for you. The same applies to the top, bottom, and sides of a program window.

As you position the cursor on a corner or a side, you'll see the cursor change to a double-headed arrow. Just drag the side or corner to where you want it, and you are done.

Command Central

Sometimes if you know the command, it is just as easy to type that command and tell the program to run without having to work your way through all those menus. On your old system, you would have clicked that Start button, selected Run, and typed something in, usually *setup*, because that is when you tended to use the Run option. On your Linux system, you can do the same thing by clicking the big K and selecting the *Run command*. You can also simply hold down the <Alt> key and hit <F2> (Alt+F2). A nice dialog box will appear asking you to type the name of the program you want to run.

Are you wondering what those programs are called? Let me give you a hint: Click on the big K, select the Multimedia menu, and start the CD player. Now look at the title bar at the top of the player. See that *KsCD*? That's the name of the program—almost. It's the name in mixed case. To run it, forget all those capital letters and just type the command in lowercase—kscd is the name of the program that runs the KDE CD player.

To recap, pressing <Alt+F2>, typing kscd in the dialog box, and hitting <Enter> is the same as going through the menus. Have a look at Figure 4-12 for an example.

Figure 4–12   Running a command with <Alt+F2>.

A Polite Introduction to the Command Line

In your line of Kicker icons is something that looks like a screen with a shell in the lower right-hand corner. If you move your mouse over it and pause for a second, the bubble help will tell you that this is called *Konsole*. This is your command prompt. In Windows-land, you might have thought of it as the DOS prompt.

The reason there is a shell in front of the icon is because Konsole is your access to the Linux command line, known as the shell. There are many types of shells, each of which works similarly (e.g., all allow you to run commands), but each may have different capabilities. The default on Linux is called bash, the *GNU Bourne-Again Shell*.

The shell is powerful, and learning about its capabilities will make you a wizard of the Linux world. Become one with the shell, and nothing can stop you. The shell is the land of the Linux systems guru and the administrator. For the most part, you can do just about anything you need to do by staying and working with the X window system and your KDE desktop. Still, from time to time, I will ask you to do something from the shell prompt. As time goes on, you too will *feel the power* of the Linux shell.

Give Me More!

For those of you who get to the end of the chapters in this book and find yourselves wanting to know *more* about the shell, check out Appendix C.

Here's our polite introduction. Click the Konsole icon. The Konsole will appear, with a Tip of the Day window in front of it (Figure 4-13). Early on in your Linux experience, you might want to leave these tips on. You can even walk through them by clicking on the Next button. When you've had enough

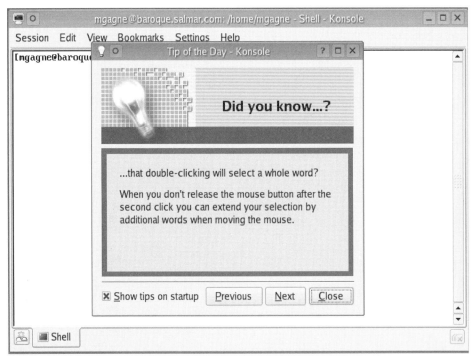

Figure 4–13   Konsole (shell) with Tip of the Day.

of these tips, you can banish them by unchecking the box to Show tips on startup and clicking Close. If you find yourself missing the tips later on, click Help on the menu bar and select Tip of the Day.

When you do click Close, you'll be left with an open Konsole and your cursor sitting beside a dollar sign prompt. This is the shell prompt. Whenever you find yourself at a shell prompt, the system is waiting for you to type in a command. Remember the CD player from earlier? You could type kscd here and have it start up just as easily. For now, type date at the shell prompt and then hit the <Enter> key.

```
[marcel@mypc marcel]$ date
Sat Apr 9 20:56:59 EDT 2005
```

Aside from learning the date and time that I wrote this paragraph, you'll also get your current date and time when you try it. That's what date is, a command that displays the date and time. You'll also find yourself back at the shell prompt as your system patiently awaits your next command. Type exit and press the <Enter> key. The Konsole disappears. That's it.

We use the shell again as we go through this book, but for now your polite introduction to the shell ends here.

Changing Your Password

It is good security policy to change your password from time to time. Under your K menu, you'll find an option for changing your password (most likely under the Settings submenu). You can also run the command, as in our earlier CD player example, by using your <Alt+F2> run sequence and typing the command kdepasswd. A window will appear (Figure 4-14) asking for your current password.

Figure 4–14
Using kdepasswd to change your password.

Notice that, like the login manager, your password is not visible. Instead, each key you press is echoed as an asterisk. When you have successfully entered your password, the system will ask you for a new password. Then you'll be asked for the new password again, this time for confirmation. That's it. Be sure to remember your new password. You'll need it next time you log in.

 Shell Out You can easily change your password from the command line as well. Just open a shell prompt and type this command:

```
[marcel@mysystem marcel]$ passwd
Changing password for user marcel.
Changing password for marcel
(current) UNIX password:
New UNIX password:
Retype new UNIX password:
passwd: all authentication tokens updated
    successfully.
```

While the steps are essentially the same, the wording of the actual password change dialog can vary slightly from system to system.

Speaking of passwords . . .

User Security

As I mentioned earlier in the book, Linux is a multiuser operating system, meaning that one or more users can work on it at the same time. What this *also* means is that each person using your system is an individual, with his or her own home directories, files, menus, and desktop decorations. By creating a login for each member of your family or office, you not only protect the files that belong to each user, but you also protect yourself. If little Natika deletes all her icons or changes the desktop to a *garish green and purple*, it doesn't affect you. Similarly, this is a great opportunity to create a play world for the kids.

Each user is referenced by a username. Each username has a user ID (UID) associated with it and one or more groups. Like usernames, group names are represented by a numeric identifier, this time called a *group ID* (GID). A person's UID is unique, as is a group's GID.

Adding users requires that you operate as root, so when you launch the KDE User Manager (command name `kuser`), you will be asked for the root password. When the program starts, a window will appear like the one in Figure 4-15. There will be two tabs, one for Users and the other for Groups.

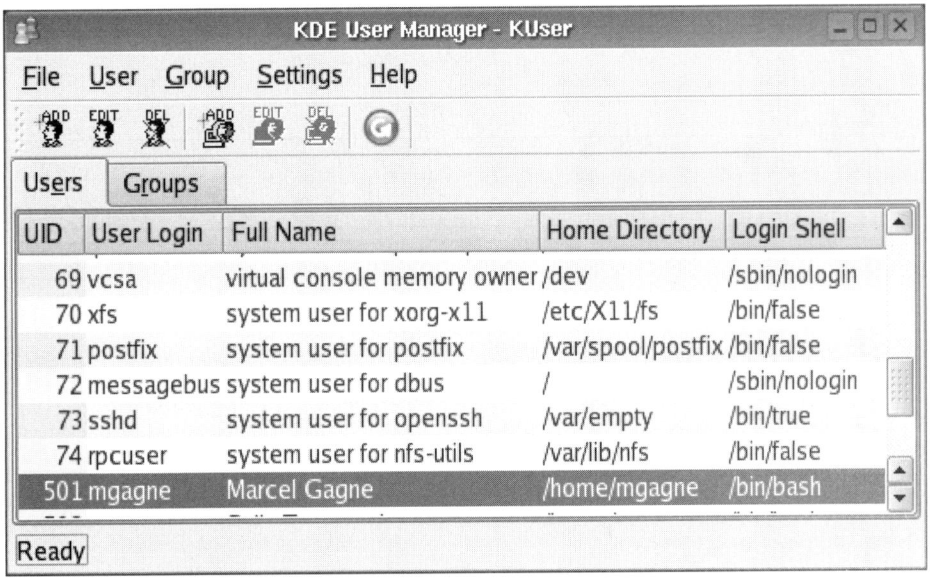

Figure 4–15   The KDE user management tool.

To add an additional user, click User on the menu bar and select Add (you can also click the add user icon below the menu bar). A new window will appear asking you to enter the name of the new user. This username should be in lowercase, with a minimum of five characters and a maximum of eight characters.

When you press <Enter>, a new window will appear, the User Properties dialog (Figure 4-16). You don't really need to add anything new here, but there are fields provided to further identify the person for whom you are creating the login. For instance, you can choose to enter his or her full name, office location, or home address.

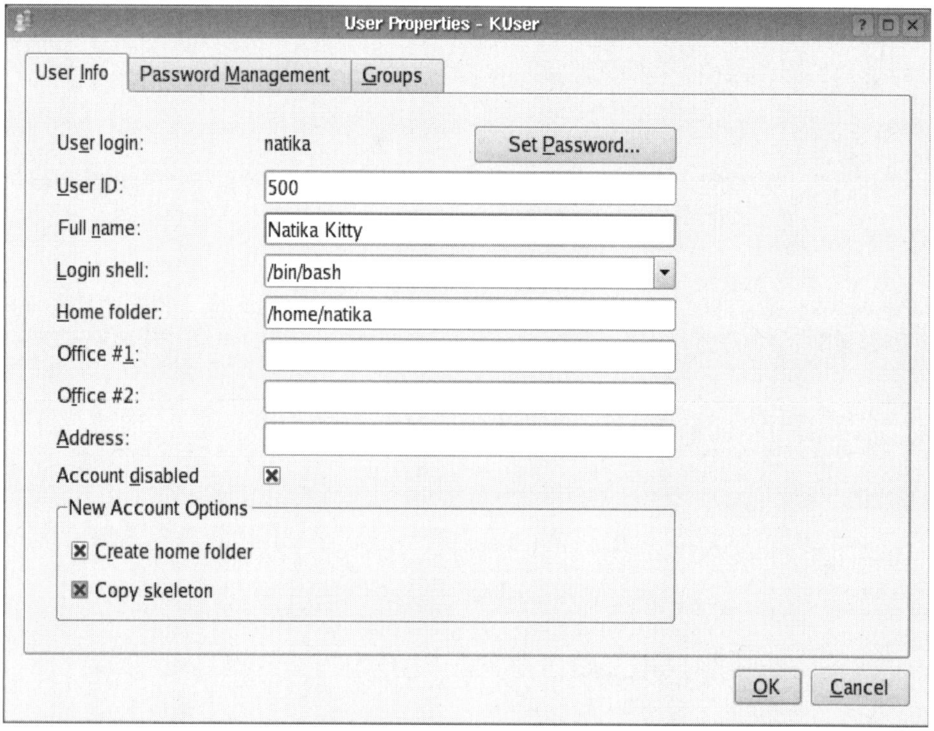

Figure 4–16   Setting user properties.

The most important item on this window is the Set Password button. Click that and you will be asked to enter a password (Figure 4-17). In fact, you will be asked to enter it twice, once for verification. Note that when you do enter the password, you won't actually see it, but rather stars will echo your keystrokes. When you are done, click OK.

This takes you back to the User Properties screen, where you can simply click OK to finish. When you are done adding users, just close KUser.

I Need More Help!

Way back in the introduction to the book, I gave you a list of places you might look to for help, some online and others in the community. As it turns out, your desktop has a very handy and fairly impressive collection of help, right at your fingertips.

Figure 4–17   *Setting a user password.*

The KDE Help Center (command name `khelpcenter`) is usually fairly obvious in a default installation. Look down in your Kicker panel, and you will likely see an icon that looks very much like a life preserver. Another place to look for the KDE Help Center is in your K menu. On my notebook's K menu, the option is labeled "Help". On another system I have here (running Mandrake), it is found under More Applications in the Documentation submenu. When the Help Center opens, you'll see something similar to Figure 4-18.

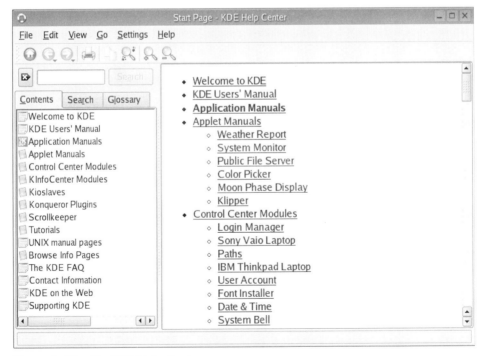

Figure 4–18   The KDE Help Center.

The left-hand pane lists the various documentation categories from KDE user manuals to various modules, tutorials, and more. Most of the entries have a small plus sign to the left. Click this to expand the list of titles within each category. In the larger, right-hand pane (although you can resize these to suit you), you'll find the actual text. Reading anything here is very much like reading in a Web browser. Click on links to go to highlighted sections, or click the forward and back arrows to navigate the documents.

Konqueror and man Pages

Before we wrap up this chapter, I'll show you one last cool trick with Konqueror to assist you with online help. You may have noticed that the KDE Help Center does let you browse *man* pages. man pages (short for "manual") are the classic Linux command documentation.

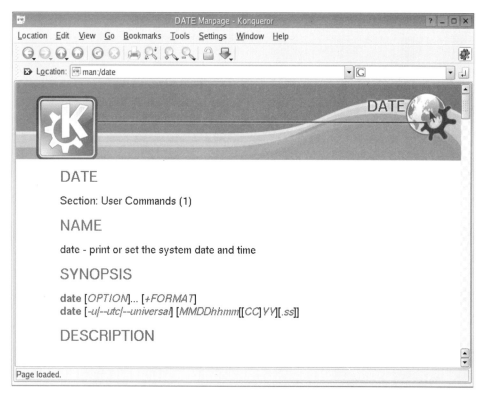

Figure 4–19   Using Konqueror to view man pages.

To view a man page in Konqueror, enter the command name, preceded with the "#" symbol in the Konqueror Location field. For example, to look up the date command I showed you earlier, you would enter "#date". This will be translated to "`man:/date`". You could, of course, just enter that instead, as in Figure 4-19.

Konquest of the Desktop

Now that you and your system have been *properly* introduced, it is time to do some exploring. In the next chapter, you are going to learn to wield Konqueror to navigate, work with, and otherwise unlock the mysteries of your Linux system. Ready? Then, let the Konquest begin.

Resources

X.Org

http://www.x.org

Chapter

5

Konquering Your World

Anyone who has ever had a system crash without a handy backup of his or her files knows that nothing is more important than data. Other than playing games (and even there), computers are about storing and dealing with information. That's why getting a good hang of working with that data— moving, copying, renaming, and deleting it—is vitally important to getting comfortable in your Linux world.

That means it is time to revisit your new old friend, Konqueror.

Files, Directories, and the Root of All Things

There's a saying in the Linux world that *"everything is a file"* (a comment attributed to Ken Thompson, the developer of UNIX). That includes directories. Directories are just files with lists of files inside them. All these files and directories are organized into a hierarchical file system, starting from the root directory and branching out.

 Note Folders and directories are the same thing. The terms can be used interchangeably, but I will be calling them directories. If you are more comfortable thinking of them as folders, don't worry. Depending on the application, you'll see both terms used.

The root directory (referred to as *slash*, or /) is actually aptly named. If you consider your file system as a tree's root system spreading out below the surface, you start to get an idea of just what things look like.

Under the root directory, you'll find folders called usr, bin, etc, tmp, and so on. Open up Konqueror by clicking on the icon in your taskbar that has a house in front of a folder. This brings up Konqueror in file manager mode (remember that Konqueror is also a Web browser). If your navigation panel isn't up (Konqueror's left side panel), press <F9> to open it (Figure 5-1). To either the right or left of the navigation panel (this is all configurable, remember), you'll see a row of tabs. Click on the root directory tab, the one that looks like a small folder. *Here's a hint:* If you move your mouse over the tabs and pause, a tooltip will pop up to let you know you are in the right place. When the file system tree appears (over on the left side), click on the top folder, Root Directory, and then look at the names of those folders.

These are all system directories, and they will contain all the programs that make your Linux system run, including documentation, devices, and device drivers. For the most part, you aren't going to be touching these files. Accidentally changing things around in this part of your system probably isn't a good thing, which is why everyone logs in with his or her own account.

One of the directories under the root is called home, and inside that directory you'll discover other directories, one for each login name on your system. These are the individual home directories, where you'll find your *personal* files and directories. If you want to store personal documents, music files, or pictures, this is the place. Once in Konqueror, you can jump to your home directory by clicking the house icon or clicking Go on the menu bar and selecting Home URL. This is your $HOME.

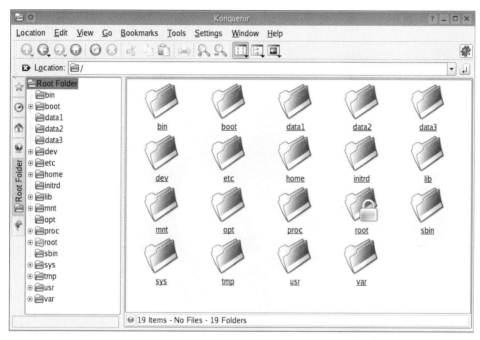

Figure 5-1   Konqueror's file manager view with navigation panel (left) open.

Quick Tip My use of $HOME isn't just to be silly. The system can recognize some things based on environment variables, symbolic names that can refer to text, numbers, or even commands. In the DOS/Windows world, you had similar things, for instance, the PATH in your AUTOEXEC.BAT file. $HOME is an environment variable assigned to every person who logs in. It represents a person's home directory. If you want to see all the environment variables assigned to your session, shell out and type the following command:

```
env
```

Try this. Over on the left side of the tree view, you'll see a little *plus sign* beside the home directory. Click on the plus sign, and the tree view will expand to show your own personal directory. Notice that the plus sign has become a minus sign. If you click it again, the directory view collapses. With the home directory expanded, click on your personal directory. You should see a few items appear in the right side view, including one icon labeled *Desktop*. For an example, see Figure 5-2. On the left side, /dev is expanded, and the right side view shows the same directory collapsed.

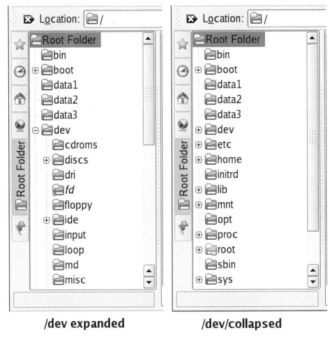

/dev expanded   **/dev/collapsed**

Figure 5–2   Expanding and collapsing directories.

Before you do anything else, I want you do look down in your taskbar, at the bottom of the screen. Do you see the desktop icon there, just to the right of the big K? It looks like a desktop blotter with a lamp above it. Move your mouse cursor over it, and the tooltip will display *Show Desktop*. Click it, and your desktop appears, free of windows. Click it again, and everything returns to normal.

Quick Tip If the Show Desktop icon isn't there, you can easily add it. Right-click on the big K, and select Panel Menu | Add | Special Button | Desktop Access. The button will appear in your taskbar.

I am having you do this because I want you to take note of what icons are on your desktop. Now go back to your Konqueror session and click on the Desktop icon in the right (or main) window. All the icons on your desktop show up there. Why is that, you ask? Because even those icons on your desktop are files or directories. Cool? Let's move on.

Shell Out Open a Konsole by clicking the terminal icon in your panel (the one with the shell). At the shell prompt, type `ls Desktop`. The ls command will list the contents of your Desktop directory. Compare what you see there with the icons currently on your graphical desktop. Do the names look familiar? When you are done, type `exit` to close the Konsole.

Directories (and subdirectories) will usually show up as folders, although this isn't a hard-and-fast rule because you can customize this. Nevertheless, some directories have different icons right from the start—the Desktop icon you just visited and the Trash can being two notables.

Wherever You Go . . .

To move from directory to directory, you can simply click on an icon, whether in the right tree view or in the left expanded view. You can also move the directory tree around by using your *cursor keys.* You'll see the highlight bar move from directory to directory. To see the contents in the main window, move to a folder and press <Enter>. To go up a level in the directory tree (rather than folder by folder), press <Alt+Up Arrow>. Substituting the down arrow for the up arrow will take you to the other directory.

There's another way as well. If you look up at the menu bar, you'll see an up arrow, a left-pointing arrow, and a right-pointing arrow (Figure 5-3). Right next to that is an icon of a house. Clicking that house icon will always take you back to your personal home directory. Clicking the up arrow will move you up the directory tree, and the left arrow will take you back to whatever directory you were last visiting.

Figure 5–3   Konqueror's main navigation toolbar.

The quickest way to navigate your file system (assuming you know the directory you want to be in) is simply to type it in the location bar. Clicking that little *X* on the black arrow to the left of the location bar (where it says *"Location"*) will clear the field. That saves you having to select the text and erase it. From here, you can just type in whatever you want there, for example, `/home/marcel`.

Navigating the Navigation Panel

We should spend a couple of minutes looking at that navigation panel (the left side panel you open and close with <F9>) because it is quite important. You've already seen how to use it to navigate your file system, but wait (as they say on television), there's more. Look at those tabs on the right side of the navigation panel. If you move your mouse over any of them, the tooltips will identify them. Click on them, and you'll switch to whatever view they offer. Click on them again, and the navigation panel will slam shut, leaving only the tabs behind and giving you more viewing space in the main Konqueror window.

Now, about those tabs . . . The first is a *bookmark tab*. When we talk about using Konqueror as a Web browser later in the book, you'll be using the bookmark feature a lot. For now, you should probably know that you can bookmark locations on disk. If you use a particular directory a lot (your music collection, for example), you'll want to bookmark that for easy access. You can also get to the bookmarks (or add them) by clicking Bookmarks on the menu bar.

After the bookmark tab, you'll see the *history tab*. Clicking it will show you a tree view listing various places on your disk (files and directories) or sites you've visited recently.

The tab with a house on it is a direct link to your personal home directory. Next to it is the KDE media player tab. You'll recognize it by the image of a little blue speaker with what appears to be music pouring out. We cover that later when we talk about multimedia. Below that is an icon with a globe of the Earth. That's the *network tab*, which provides you with a quick link to the KDE download areas (FTP sites) and Web pages. For these to work, you must be connected to the Internet. This is another area we cover later in the book. Local network browsing may also be available under the Network tab.

The second-to-last tab accesses your system's root directory, as discussed earlier in this chapter. That leaves only one tab, the *services tab*. This tab lets you zoom in on network services, such as printers or shared directories on other machines or your local CD-ROM device for playing audio tracks. Once again, this is something we discuss later in the book. For the moment, I just wanted you to get a feel for what's there when you open Konqueror.

Enhancing Konqueror

Konqueror is an amazingly powerful tool, and some of its features may be lying dormant and unconfigured. When you ran kpersonalizer, you had the opportunity to select your favored level of eye candy. Keeping in mind that more toys means more demands on your system, some features that are fun but CPU-intensive may have been turned off if you selected anything other than "give me the works."

One of these features has to do with file tips. Try this. In an open Konqueror session, move your mouse over a file or directory and pause there. If you don't see a tooltip pop up describing the file type, its size, and other properties, I'm going to have you turn that feature on now.

Click Settings on Konqueror's menu bar and select Configure Konqueror. Konqueror's configuration dialog will appear (Figure 5-4).

To the left is a panel with the various setting groups that are available under Konqueror (e.g., File Associations, Fonts). For the time being, click on Behavior (there are two behavior icons; the first is for the file system, while the second is for the Web browser view—we want the first). Now, look to the right, under Misc Options. Check the Show file tips option, but leave the Show previews in file tips option unchecked. Click Apply, and then click OK to close the Settings dialog. We'll be using that file tips feature very shortly.

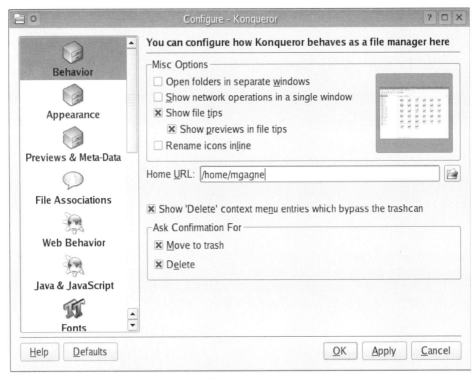

Figure 5–4   Configuring Konqueror's file tips.

In just a moment, I'm going to tell you all about selecting, copying, and moving files. Before we move on, however, I should tell you about another really cool Konqueror trick that makes this whole copying and moving process a whole lot easier. Click on Window on the menu bar and select Split View Left/Right. Suddenly, Konqueror will have two main windows instead of just one (Figure 5-5).

The trick is in trying to remember which window you are working in at any given time. Look in the bottom left corner of one of your split windows. Do you see that little *green* light? It indicates the *active* window, and its pathname will be in the location bar just under the menu bar. Now click on the other window, and you'll see the green light jump to that window. You'll also see the location bar change to that location, which immediately makes you think, "Hey, I can just type in the pathname for the active window in the location bar, and my active window will take me there!" And you are right.

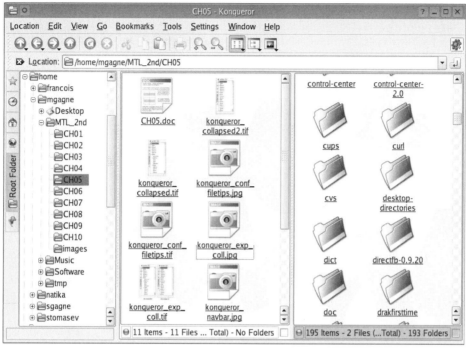

Figure 5–5   Konqueror with a two-panel split view.

Uh, Roger, Copy That . . .

You can create, copy, move, rename, and delete files and directories by using Konqueror. But before you can do any of these things, you need to *select* a file or directory. Selecting files is something you will be doing a lot, so let's start with that. Place your mouse cursor just outside one of the icons of your choosing. Now drag the cursor across the icon and notice the dotted-line box you are creating as you drag the pointer. You'll know a file is selected because it becomes *highlighted*. Right-clicking also selects a file but in a somewhat different way, bringing up a menu dialog that will then ask you what you want to do with that file.

Don't forget your cursor keys either. Moving left, right, up, or down will highlight whatever file or directory you happen to be sitting on. You can then click on Edit in the menu bar (or press <Alt+E> to get to the edit menu) and decide what it is you want to do with the file. I'll talk about those decisions in a moment.

Sometimes one just isn't enough—you need to *select multiple files*. The easiest way of all is with the mouse. Left-click to the top and left of the icon you want to start with, and then drag your cursor across a series of icons. Notice again the dotted-line box that surrounds the files and directories you select. Perhaps you just want a file here and a file there. How do you pick and choose multiple files, you ask? Simply hold down the <Ctrl> key and drag with the mouse. Let's say you have selected a group of four files and that you also want one further down in your directory. Let go of the mouse button (but keep holding down the <Ctrl> key), position your mouse to the top and left of the next group of icons, and select away. As long as you continue to hold down the <Ctrl> key, you can pick up and select files here and there at will.

It is also possible to do all these things with the cursor keys by simply moving your cursor over the file you want to start with, holding down the <Shift> key, and moving the cursor to the left (or whatever direction you like). As you do this, you'll notice file after file being selected. Try it for yourself. For nonsequential selection, use the <Ctrl> key as you did with the mouse. Select (or deselect) the files by pressing the spacebar. When your cursor is sitting on the file you want, press the spacebar, and your files will be highlighted.

Finally, and probably quite important for the future, you can also select by extension. Let's say that you want to select all the files in your directory with an .mp3 or .doc extension. Click Edit on the menu bar, and then click Select. A small window will pop up asking you for an extension. If you wanted all the .mp3 files, you would enter *.mp3. The .mp3 extension will limit your selection to a certain type of file, whereas the asterisk says "give me everything" that matches.

Creating New Folders

If you aren't already running Konqueror, start it up now and make sure you are in your personal home directory. In the main Konqueror window, right-click on any blank area and look at the menu that pops up. Move your mouse pointer over the top item (Create New), and you'll see a secondary menu appear. The first item is Folder, as in "Create new folder." Click here, and the system will prompt you for a folder name. This can be pretty much anything you like. If this folder will house your music files, perhaps its name should be *Music*.

Just remember that you can create folders inside folders, and you can start organizing things in a way that makes sense. For instance, you might want to create folders called *Rock, Jazz, Hip Hop,* and *Classical* in your Music folder.

"I've Changed My Mind," or Renaming Files

You created a folder called *Classical,* and you really meant *Opera.* You could delete the folder or you could simply rename it. To rename a file or directory, select it, right-click to get the menu, and then choose Rename. The name will be highlighted under the appropriate icon—just type the new name and press <Enter>. Alternatively, select it and choose Rename from the Edit menu in the menu bar. The easiest way of all is to press <F2> after you have selected the file or directory.

 Shell Out Open a Konsole and type ls to see your directories. Renaming a file or directory from the shell is easy. Type mv oldname newname and press <Enter>. For instance, to change your Classical directory to Opera, you would type the following command:

```
mv Classical Opera
```

Copying Files and Directories (and Moving, Too!)

Ah! This is where you learn another great trick with Konqueror. An easy way to copy a file from one directory to another is to fire up two versions of Konqueror. In the first, you find the file (or files) you want to copy. In the second Konqueror window, you locate the directory to which you want those files copied. Simply drag the file from one window into the other. A little menu will pop up asking you whether you want to copy the file here or move it here (Figure 5-6).

An interesting question, isn't it? That's because copying and moving files are done in pretty much the same way. Both involve a copy. The difference is in what happens *after* the copy is done. In one case, you copy the file and keep the original, thus giving you two copies of the same file but in different places. A move, on the other hand, copies the file and deletes the original from where it was.

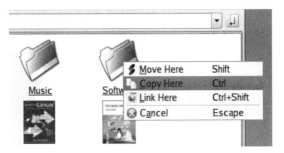

Figure 5–6   Confirmation when moving or copying files.

One easy trick is to select the file you want, right-click to get the menu, and then click on Copy. Now go into the directory where you would like this file to appear, right-click somewhere on a blank space of Konqueror's main window, and click Paste from the pop-up menu. You can also specify the Copy and Paste options from the menu bar under Edit.

Shell Out The Linux command to copy is cp. If you wanted to copy a file called *big_report* to *notsobig_report,* you would type the following command:

```
cp big_report notsobig_report
```

Wait! What about Links?

If you're following along, you probably noticed that the pop-up menu for dragging and dropping a file offered a third option, Link Here. Links are a kind of copy that don't take up much space. In the world of that other OS, you probably thought of them as *shortcuts*. Links let you create a pseudo-copy of a file or directory that doesn't take up the space of the original file. If you wanted a copy of a particularly large file to exist in several places on the disk, it makes more sense to point to the original and let the system deal with the link as though it *were* the original. It's important to remember that deleting a link doesn't remove the original file, just the link.

Speaking of links, if you know the pathname to something, you can create a link in any directory at any time. You might remember that I said your desktop itself was a directory—in fact, you saw it in Konqueror when I had you navigating your personal home directory. Anyhow, by right-clicking in Konqueror's active window, you can choose Create New (like you did to create a directory) and select Link to Location (URL) from the menu.

A pop-up window will appear with the words *New Link to Location (URL)* and a blank box for you to enter a location. In this case, you have to know the name of the location that you are linking. For instance, your system comes with a number of sample wallpapers (which we talk about in the next chapter). If for some reason I wanted to have a copy of one of these wallpapers in my home directory, I might link to it as Figure 5-7 shows. Enter the full pathname and press <Enter>. That's it.

Figure 5–7   *Creating an icon link to a URL.*

When the icon shows up on your desktop, the full path to the file will be the name. If you would like to see something different, right-click on the link you just created and select Properties. A dialog box will appear with three tabs (Figure 5-8): General, which is the link name; Permissions, which represents security-related information; and URL, the path to the file itself. Once created, you probably shouldn't need to change the URL.

On the General tab, you should see an icon next to the name of the file you are linking to. You can change that icon by clicking on it and selecting a new one from the list that pops up (you'll find hundreds). Furthermore, you can change the name of the link you just created to something that makes more sense to you. When you first open the Properties dialog, the file name is already highlighted. Just type the new name and hit <Enter>.

The middle tab, Permissions, lets you change who gets access to a file or directory and what kind of access they get.

Figure 5–8   Desktop icon properties.

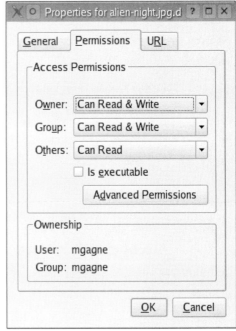

Figure 5–9   File permissions in Properties dialog.

Which Brings Us to Permissions

This is your first look at Linux security, this time at the file (or directory) level. Under that Properties tab, you'll see a list of access permissions (Figure 5-9).

This is how you would go about changing permissions. There is, however, another way to identify file permissions that doesn't involve opening up a properties dialog for every file. Remember those file tips I had you configure for Konqueror? Well, we are going to use those now.

Move your mouse pointer so that it hovers over any file. A file tip dialog will pop up (Figure 5-10) telling you the type of file, the size, the last modification date, and the permissions.

There are actually ten columns describing permissions for a file. For the most part, you'll see either a hyphen or a d in the first column—this would represent a directory. The next nine columns are actually three sets of three columns. Those other nine characters (characters 2–10) indicate permissions for the user or owner of the file (first three), the group (second group of three), and others or everyone else (last three). If you look at an image and see -rw-rw-r--, you'll see that the user and group have read and write permissions. All others have *read-only* permission, the same permission everyone else has.

Shell Out Want to see the permissions at the shell prompt? Simply add -l to the ls command, like this:

```
ls -l directory_name
```

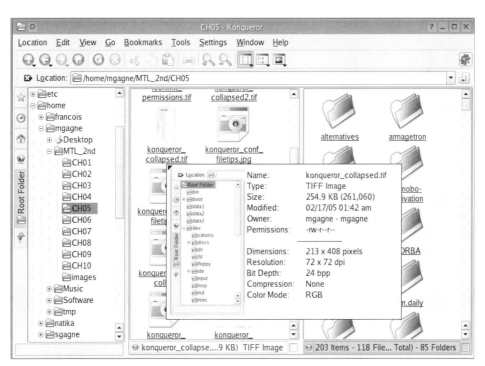

Figure 5–10   *File tips displaying permissions in Konqueror.*

From time to time during your Linux experience, you will have to change permissions, sometimes to give someone else access to your directories or files or to make a script or program executable. By using the Permissions tab, you can select read, write, or execute permissions for the owner (yourself), the group you belong to, and everyone else by selecting the permissions in the appropriate drop-down list under the Access Permissions section.

Deleting Files and Directories

Every once in a while, some file or directory has outlived its usefulness. It is time to be ruthless and do a little cleaning up on the old file system.

As you've no doubt come to expect, there are several ways to get rid of an offending file or directory. The friendliest and safest method is to drag the file from Konqueror to the *trash can icon* on your desktop. For the novice, this is a safer method because items sent to the trash can be recovered—until you take out the trash, that is. Until that time, you can click on the trash can icon and (*you guessed it*) a Konqueror window will appear showing you the items you have sent to the trash. These items can then be moved (or copied) back to wherever you need them. To remove files from the trash permanently, right-click on the trash can icon and click on Empty Trash Bin.

Note Once you empty the trash bin, those files are gone forever.

I did say that there were other ways of deleting a file. From Konqueror, you can select a file or directory, right-click, and select Move to trash. Notice that there is another option on the menu, labeled simply *Delete*. If you are absolutely sure you don't want this file hanging around (even in the trash bin), select Delete from the menu or press <Shift+Delete>. The file will be gone for good.

Note To really and truly delete something, *shred* it. You do this by selecting a file and pressing <Ctrl+Shift+Delete>. This writes random bits of garbage over the file before deleting it.

My World, My Way

I'm hoping that you are walking away from this chapter impressed with some appreciation for the power and flexibility of the tools you have at your disposal. Konqueror may well become your most important application by the time you are finished reading this book. I've barely touched on the some of its capabilities. Never fear, you'll see more of Konqueror when you get to Chapter 10.

Before we move on to the next chapter, I have a special treat for the power users among you. You know who you are because you were getting excited every time I had you shell out. Click Window in Konqueror's menu bar and select Show Terminal Emulator. Just like that, a shell prompt opens up at the bottom of your Konqueror window (Figure 5-11).

From there, you can type all your Linux commands. When you are done, simply type exit, and the window will close.

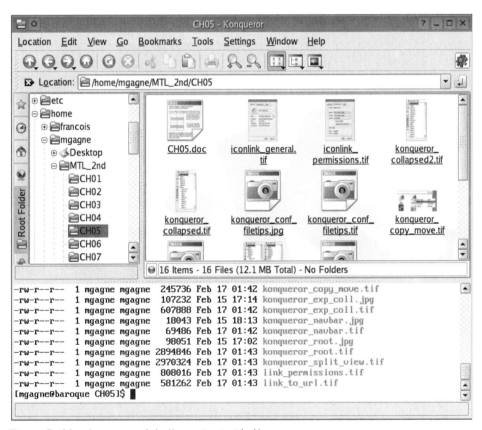

Figure 5–11   A command shell running inside Konqueror.

Making Your Home a Home

By now you're starting to feel like this isn't so difficult after all. In fact, it's probably starting to feel pretty familiar. For one thing, there are many similarities in desktop environments, and working with KDE isn't like working in a totally alien environment. Well, it's time to make your new virtual home even more of a home. It is time to personalize your desktop experience.

In the next chapter, we talk about changing your background, adding icons, setting up a screensaver, and all those other things that help make your desktop yours and yours alone.

Chapter

6

Customizing Your Desktop (or Making Your World Your Own)

After having taken the first steps into the Linux world, you are probably thinking, "Hey, this is pretty easy" and "I wonder what the fuss was all about." For what it's worth, I'm thinking the very same thing. Now that the fear of dealing with a new operating system is gone, it's time to get really comfortable.

In this chapter, I show you how to make your system truly your own. I show you how to change your background, your colors, your fonts, and anything else you'll need to create a desktop as individual as you are. Would you like some icons on your desktop, perhaps some shortcuts to programs you use on a regular basis? No problem. I cover all those things, too.

I Am Sovereign of All I Survey . . .

As I've already mentioned, working in the Linux world is working in a *multi-user* world. What this means is that everyone who uses your computer can have his or her own unique environment. Any changes you make to your desktop while you are logged in as yourself will have no effect on little Sarah when she logs in to play her video games. If she happens to delete all the icons on her desktop or changes everything to a garish purple and pink, it won't affect you either.

Let's start with something simple. The first thing most people want to change is their background. It's sort of like moving into a new house or apartment. The wallpaper (or paint) that someone else chose rarely fits into your idea of décor. Same goes for your computer's desktop. Let's get you something more to your liking.

Changing the Background

Start by right-clicking somewhere on the desktop. From the menu that appears, choose Configure Desktop and the Configure dialog will appear (see Figure 6-1). On the left side of that dialog is a sidebar that allows you to change various settings. One item is called *Background*. Click on that, and you will be able to modify your background settings.

Over on the right side, a display shows you a preview of what your new desktop will look like. Right at the top is a drop-down list labeled *Setting for desktop*—this gives you the opportunity to change your settings for all your virtual desktops or each individually. When you start feeling *particularly creative*, you can play around with creating a unique identity for every virtual desktop, but for now leave the setting at the default, which is *All Desktops*.

To change the background image, make sure the *Picture* radio button is selected. To the right of the *Picture* label is a drop-down list with the default system backgrounds. You'll find that quite a few are already installed. Scroll down the list, highlighting titles as you go, and notice that a preview of your new background appears in the small monitor image. To find images in something other than the default directory, click the directory navigator icon to the right, and a Konqueror-like file manager will pop up, allowing you to navigate the disk in search of your personal images. When that file dialog opens, make sure you click on the icon directly beside the drop-down navigation bar. Those are the navigator settings, and one of them is *Show Preview*, which, as the title implies, turns the image preview on. You'll definitely want it *on*. Pressing <F11> has the same effect.

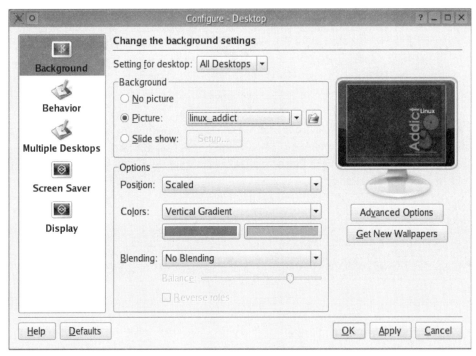

Figure 6–1   Choosing a background image for your desktop.

When you see something you like, click on either OK or Apply to make it official. The difference between the two is that OK will exit the configuration program, whereas Apply will change your background but leave the settings program running (in case you are feeling particularly indecisive).

It is also possible to configure multiple backgrounds. What this does is provide you with a means of picking several wallpapers that you can set to automatically switch at whatever interval you decide on (the default is 60 minutes). Click on the *Slide Show* radio button instead of Picture. The *Setup* button will become active. Click here, and you'll be asked to select the time interval for the images to rotate. There's a checkbox here to turn on random mode instead of the default sequential display. I happen to like random. Now click Add, and that Konqueror-like file manager will pop up so that you can select the images you want to use in the random rotation. Select as many or as few as you like, click OK to exit the various dialogs, and you are done.

Directly below the Background selection area is an area labeled *Options*. One of these options is *Position*. This tells the system how to treat the image you select. Some images are only small graphic *tiles*, designed to be copied over and over until they fill your screen. For these, you would change the mode to Tiled. If the image you are using is a bit small for your screen, you might consider Centered Maxpect, which will grow the image as much as possible while retaining the relative width and height. If you just want the image to fill your screen and you don't care what it looks like, go for Scaled. Play! Experiment! These are *your* walls.

Incidentally, you don't *have* to have a background. You can create a nice, plain background by selecting the *No picture* radio button. Then, in the Options section, you would select different patterns, color schemes, and different ways of blending those colors.

Save My Screen, Please!

Okay, screensavers don't really do much screen saving these days. The idea, once upon a time, was to protect screens from phosphor burn-in. Old-style monochrome screens were particularly bad for this. In time, the letters from your menus (we were using text in those days) would burn in to the phosphor screen. Even when you turned off the monitor, you could still see the ghostly outline of your most popular application burned into the screen itself. As we moved to color screens and graphics, that changed somewhat, but the problem continued to exist for some time, partly due to the static nature of the applications we were using.

Time passed, and some bright light somewhere got the idea that if you constantly changed the image on the screen, that type of burn-in would not be as likely. What better way to achieve this than to have some kind of clever animation kick in when the user walked away from the screen for a few minutes (or hours). Heck, it might even be fun to watch. The screensaver was born. Modern screens use scanning techniques that all but banished burn-in, but screensavers did not go away. Those addictive fish, toasters, penguins, snow, spaceships, and so forth have managed to keep us entertained, despite the march of technology. Let's face it, we are all hooked.

Depending on your distribution, your screensaver may or may not already be active by default. Getting to your screensaver setup involves the same first steps as changing your background. Right-click on a clear part of the desktop and choose Configure Desktop. The desktop Configure dialog will appear. On the left side of that window is an item called *Screen Saver*. Click away.

Like the background manager before this, you get a nice little preview window over to the right that gives you an idea of what your screensaver will look like (Figure 6-2). The first thing you will want to do is check the box that says *Start automatically*, assuming, of course, that it isn't already checked. Under that checkbox is the length of inactivity you want to allow before the screensaver starts. The default is 3 minutes. Now pick a screensaver from the list and watch the results on the preview screen. To see the real thing in action, click the Test button. To go back to the configuration screen, press any key. Some screensavers can be modified, which is why you also have a Setup button. For instance, the *Rock* screensaver, which simulates flying through space, lets you change the number of rocks (or asteroids) flying toward you and whether your spaceship moves or rotates through the mess.

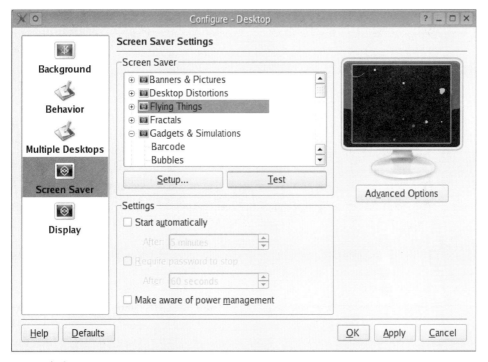

Figure 6–2 Selecting a screensaver.

Before you click OK, you may want to change the default time before your screensaver kicks in. Mine is set for 5 minutes. In an office environment (or a busy household), you will probably want to password-protect your screen when you walk away. To do this, check the box for *Require password to stop*. When the screensaver starts, you will need to enter your login password to get back to your work. Always remember that your password is case-sensitive.

Moving Things Around

If you haven't already done this, click on an icon (hold the click) and drag the icon to some other spot on the desktop. Easy, isn't it?

The taskbar is something else you may want to move. Just drag the panel and drop it to one of the four positions on the desktop (top, bottom, left side, or right side). The location, by the way, can also be changed by right-clicking on the taskbar and selecting Configure Panel. On the card that appears (Figure 6-3), you can select the location, the size of the panel and its icons, and the length you are willing to allow the panel to extend on your desktop. For instance, you might decide you don't want a panel with a lot of blank space, in which case, a centered Kicker that takes up only 80% of the screen might look better to you. If you do go for a shorter panel, make sure you click the *Expand as required to fit contents* checkbox.

 Semantics Technically, the taskbar is that portion of the *panel* that shows your open programs, letting you quickly click from one to the other. That said, you may find that some people speak of the taskbar and the panel interchangeably.

On that customization card, you can lock in on some taskbar-specific configurations. For instance, by default, your taskbar will *Show windows from all desktops* you have open on your desktop, regardless of which virtual desktop you opened them on. Some people like this feature, but I am not one of them. This is something I leave unchecked because I want to see only the programs on the virtual desktop I am currently running on. Remember, these settings are a personal thing.

The *Show window list button* checkbox option provides a small pop-up right next to the taskbar. This pop-up shows a quick list of all windows on all desktops—handy if, like me, you turned off the first option. *Group similar tasks* is another very personal option. Let's say you opened up three Konsoles.

If you have this option set, only one task group will show up in the taskbar—a small black arrow on the task will let you know that there are more like that. If you click on the Konsole task (in the taskbar), you'll see all three. This option is configurable so that you can elect to have this grouping occur never, always, or only when the taskbar is full.

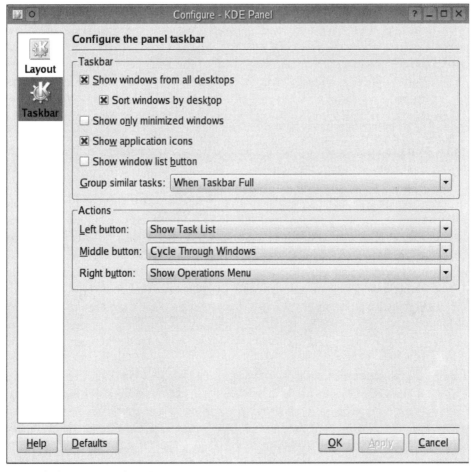

Figure 6–3 Panel and taskbar settings.

Is That a Theme or a Motif?

I'm referring not to a musical theme but to a desktop theme. A *theme* is a collection of buttons, decorations, colors, backgrounds, and so on, preselected and packaged to give your desktop a finished and coherent look. Some themes even incorporate sounds (for startup, shutdown, opening and closing program windows, etc.) into the whole package. It can be a lot of fun.

Then we have *styles*, which are sort of like themes but are not as all-encompassing. Styles tend to concentrate on window decorations and behavior as well as *widgets*. Widgets are things like radio buttons, checkboxes, combo boxes (drop-down lists), sliders, tabs, and so on.

All right, I know you want to get to it and change your theme a time or two, but first I'm going to tell you something rather important. Most (if not all) of the things I've shown you so far on customizing your desktop can be done through the *KDE Control Center*. You'll find it by clicking on the big K and looking for Control Center. If you are having trouble locating it, remember that you can bring it up by pressing <Alt+F2> and typing in `kcontrol`, its program name.

As soon as the KDE Control Center loads up, it displays some capsule information about the system, its hostname, and the version of Linux running on it. Over on the left side, an index page covers a number of items that can be either viewed or modified on the system. I say *either* because some of what you see here is just information and cannot be changed. One of these items is *Appearances and Themes*. Click the plus sign beside it, and you'll get a list of options for changing your desktop environment's look and feel (Figure 6-4).

Almost everything you could possibly ever want to do to alter your desktop experience is here. Change the background, colors, fonts, icons, screensaver . . . you name it. It is all here! That includes your themes and styles. Go ahead: Click on Style and select a style from the Widget Style list. As you click, the preview window will show you how it affects the overall look. If you just want to see it in action but you don't want to commit yet, click Apply. When you know you can live with the changes, click OK.

Let's look at a couple of those look and feel changes and see how they affect what you do and how you work.

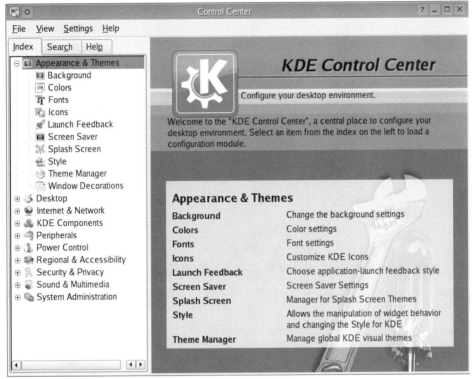

Figure 6–4   Changing the look and feel in KDE's control panel with Appearances and Themes.

Window Decorations

This is also your opportunity to undo something I had you change back in Chapter 4. When you ran kpersonalizer, I had you select the Plastik style so that we could all be on the same page (so to speak) in terms of what you see in your title bar. Figures 6-5 through 6-7 show the KDE2 (Classic), Plastik, and Keramik window decorations, respectively.

If you would like to use something else, you can make that change now. Just remember that things may look a little different than what I show you in the book from here on. With that little disclaimer in place, you may now express your individuality.

Figure 6–5   KDE 2 Classic window decoration.

Figure 6–6   Plastik (KDE 3.4 default) window decoration.

Figure 6–7   Keramik (KDE 3.3 default) window decoration.

Themes and Styles

Themes and styles are essentially collections of look and feel changes. A style is a collection of definitions affecting primarily widgets (buttons, tabs, etc.; see Figure 6-8). A theme, on the other hand, might encompass changes in

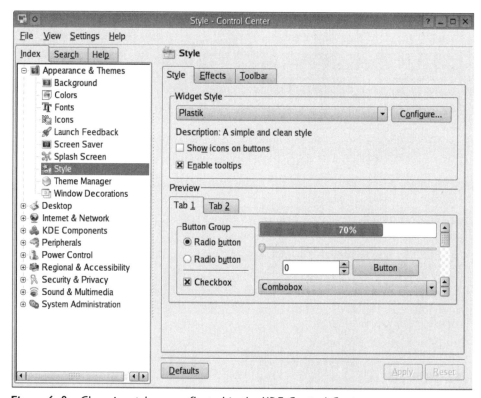

Figure 6–8   Changing styles are reflected in the KDE Control Center.

window decorations, wallpaper, colors, and icons to create a cohesive, integrated desktop experience, whereas a change in window decoration would affect only the window decoration itself.

The theme manager (Figure 6-9) is similar. Under the heading *Choose your visual KDE theme*, you'll see a list of the installed themes, with a preview window to the right. Below is a list of buttons that allow you to override the settings that come with a particular theme. If you don't like the theme's default background (but you like everything else), click the Background button and make your changes. You can even create your own themes if you feel the creative urge.

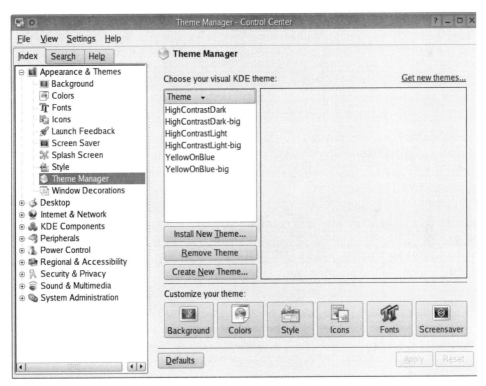

Figure 6–9   Theme manager options in the Control Center.

The fashion slaves among you will quickly grow tired of the themes and styles your system comes with—there are quite a few, but not nearly enough for those surfing the edges of what's hot today. That's why you should keep this little Web site in mind:

```
http://www.kde-look.org
```

This site has tons of themes, styles, alternative wallpapers, and icons—
enough to keep you busy for a long, long time. Now, I know we haven't talked
about getting on the Net yet; we still have a few things to cover. If you just
can't wait, then jump ahead to Chapter 9, "Connecting to the Internet." Just
make sure you come back here. You wouldn't want to miss anything.

Adding Icons and Shortcuts to Your Desktop

I covered this topic somewhat in the last chapter, but it is time to look at this
in detail. While working with Konqueror, you might recall that you had a
directory called *Desktop* and that this directory actually *was* your desktop. If
you wanted to get a file onto your desktop, you could just drag and drop
(copy or link) a file there. A good reason for doing this is that it puts things
you use on a regular basis (a business spreadsheet perhaps or a contact list)
right where you can quickly get to them.

  The single most useful icon you will want to add to your desktop is a link
to a program on your system (*Link to Application*), something you might have
called a *shortcut* under your old OS. Maybe you need to have your word processor or your CD player handy. Whatever it is, you would like it there in
front of you.

  The second most useful link is a Uniform Resource Locator (URL) to a
regularly visited Web site. We already looked at creating a Link to Location in
the last chapter because a URL can point to a file just as easily as a Web site.
Instead of the path to a file, simply type in the URL to your favorite site. I
cover surfing the Net in greater detail later in this book. Let's continue by
adding a program to your desktop.

  What you need to understand is that you won't really be putting the program there but rather a link to it. Right-click on the desktop, move your
mouse cursor over *Create New*, and then select *Link to Application*. The dialog box or card that opens has three tabs. The first, *General*, lets you choose a
name for the program. Notice that the words *Link to Application* are highlighted. You can just type a name that makes sense to you here. For instance,
if you are putting a link to the CD players, whose program name is `kscd`, you
might just want to enter "CD Player" for the icon's name. To the left of the
name is a square with a gearlike icon. Clicking this square brings up a large
collection of icons from which you can select whatever happens to take your
fancy (Figure 6-10).

Figure 6–10   *Selecting an icon for your new shortcut.*

Once you have chosen an icon, skip over to the third tab, *Application*. The field labeled *Command* is where you enter the program's real name. For example, if you wanted a link to the calculator, you would enter /usr/bin/ kcalc. Another way to get there is to click the Browse button and navigate your way to the application. The *Permissions* tab lets you decide whether others can see, modify, or execute the icon. (Remember that it is possible to create these links in other directories, including public directories.) If you are creating an icon for your personal home directory, you can pretty much ignore this.

When you are happy with your changes, click OK. Your new program link (which you can launch with a single click) should appear on your desktop.

Shell Out To create a shortcut icon for a command, you first have to know what the command is and where it is. To be honest, a command or program (such as the KDE calculator, kcalc)

could be almost anywhere on the disk. For the most part, programs tend to be in one of the "bin" directories, /bin, /usr/bin, or /usr/local/bin. You can also use the whereis command to tell you exactly. For instance, in order to know where the kcalc program is, I would do the following at the Konsole shell prompt (the "$" sign):

```
[mgagne@mysystem mgagne]$ whereis kcalc
kcalc: /usr/bin/kcalc
```

In some cases, you may see more than one file associated with a program's name, but the actual executable to use is in /usr/bin. The bin, in this case, stands for "binary"—in short, a program.

Miscellaneous Changes

Now that I have shown you how to find all these things, I'm going to let you explore the Appearances and Themes menu on your own. Check out the Fonts dialog if you would like different desktop fonts than what is set by default. You might find it interesting to note that different icon sets are available than the ones you currently see. Click Icons and go wild. If you do change the icons, just *be aware* that those I describe when pointing to the panel or to various applications may look a little different than what you now see.

Let me give you one final *treat* before I close this chapter. Still working from the KDE control center, look for Keyboard Shortcuts (under *Regional and Accessibility*), and you'll discover lots of interesting keyboard shortcuts to do things such as switching from one application to another, switching from one desktop to another, opening and closing windows, getting help, taking a desktop screenshot (in case you want to share your fashion sense with others), and so on.

Resources

KDE-LOOK.org

http://www.kde-look.org

Chapter
7

Installing New Applications

The average Linux distribution CD comes with several gigabytes of software. SuSE, for one, delivers several CDs in a boxed set with enough software to keep you busy for weeks, maybe months. I'll tell you how to install that software, easily and without fuss. Despite all that your distribution has to offer, sooner or later you will find yourself visiting various Internet sites, looking for new and updated software. Where will you find this stuff, and will installing be the same as getting it from your CDs?

Before we get into finding, building, and installing software, I'd like to address a little myth. You have no doubt heard that installing software on Linux is difficult and that it is inferior to what you are used to in the Windows world. Nothing could be further from the truth. In fact, software installation under Linux is actually superior to what you are leaving behind in your old OS.

Security Note When you install software and software packages, you must often do so as the root, or administrative user. As root, you are all powerful. Linux tends to be more secure and much safer than your old OS, but that doesn't mean disasters can't strike. Know where your software comes from, and take the time to understand what it does. When you compile software (which I cover later in this chapter), it might even be a good idea to get into the habit of building as a nonroot user and then switching to root for the installation portion. Don't worry—I'll explain.

Linux and Security

When it comes to installing software, security is something we should talk about. I've already said that you should know where your software is coming from, but that is only part of the consideration. That's why I'm going to clear up some bad press Linux gets when it comes to installing software.

In the Windows world, it is frighteningly easy to infect your PC with a virus or a worm. All you have to do is click on an e-mail attachment, and you could be in trouble. With some e-mail packages under Windows, it does the clicking for you and by being so helpful, once again, you could be in trouble. You won't find many Linux packages provided as simple executables (.EXE files and so on). Security is the reason. To install most packages, you also need root privileges. Again, for security reasons. Linux demands that you be conscious of the fact that you might be doing something that could hurt your system. If an e-mail attachment wants to install itself into the system, it will have to consult the root user first.

Package managers, such as `rpm` (the RPM Package Manager) and Debian's `dselect` and `apt-get`, perform checks to make sure that certain dependencies are met or that software doesn't accidentally overwrite other software. Those dependency checks take many things into consideration, such as what software already exists and how the new package will coexist. Many of you are probably familiar with what has been called DLL hell, where one piece of software just goes ahead and overwrites some other piece of code. It may even have happened to you. Blindly installing without these checks can be disastrous. At best, the result can be an unstable machine—at worst, it can be unusable.

Installing software under Linux may take a step or two, but it is for your own good.

The Many Faces of Software Installation

Because most packages are either RPMs or DEBs, knowing how to install them primarily involves knowing how to deal with that particular type of package. In truth, it isn't that complicated, but there can be stumbles along the way, particularly when it comes to dependencies. Some packages will require the presence of another package before it can be installed. Sometimes it may require several packages. Going through a process of trial and error to get all your dependencies resolved can create quite the headache.

Every major Linux vendor wants to make the Linux experience as wonderful as possible, particularly when it comes to installing software packages. Consequently, almost everyone has a software installation tool that they have tweaked to make the user experience as simple as possible, a tool that deals with package dependencies easily. For instance, SuSE provides YaST2. Mandrake has Rpmdrake (or the command-line `urpmi`). Lindows has its Click-N-Run service. The new RedHat/Fedora distribution uses Yum. Slackware uses installpkg. Using the software installation tools provided by your vendor is almost always the easiest approach.

When you just can't get what you want through the vendor's packages, or if you can't find the appropriate package, sometimes going back to the source is your best approach. Yes, I'm talking about source code. Compiling from scratch really isn't all that difficult either, and I show you how at the end of this chapter.

Let's start by looking at a couple of vendor-specific software installation tools, beginning with SuSE and their YaST2 installer.

SuSE Software Package Installs

An SuSE boxed set comes with thousands of applications, so much so that you may not have to look anywhere for some time. SuSE software installations as well as software updates are handled through the YaST interface (command name `yast2`). When the YaST control center comes up, select Install and Remove Software. A second window will open, from which you can search for a particular package. Let's say you wanted to install a video conferencing application, but you didn't know what the application was called. Enter the word *video* in the search field, and all of the packages that have video in either their package name or description will appear in the window to the right (you can specify other search criteria on the page).

Click on a package name, and a description of the software will appear in the tabbed "Description" window in the right lower half of the screen (Figure 7-1). If this is the package you want, check the box next to the package name and then click the Accept button in the bottom right-hand corner. Should there be dependencies associated with the package you chose to install, a pop-up window will appear informing you of this fact. Click Continue and the installation will proceed. That's all there is to it.

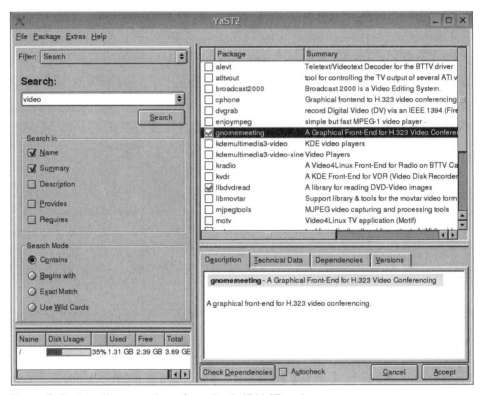

Figure 7–1   Installing a package from the SuSE YaST tool.

For those times when you know the package name, you call the YaST installation module directly. For example, let's say I wanted to install Kover, a package that makes it easy to create CD jewel case covers. In a Konsole command shell, type the following:

```
/sbin/yast2 -i kover
```

Mandrake's `urpmi`

Installing software with Mandrake is done with the `urpmi` command. Like Debian's apt-get (which I discuss shortly), urpmi takes care of all that nasty checking for prerequisite software. When installing an RPM package using urpmi, you will sometimes be told that other packages are needed and asked whether you want urpmi to automatically install them. The right answer is almost always yes. But I'm getting ahead of myself.

Most people running directly from the desktop will see urpmi through the Mandrake Control Center (command name `drakconf`). When the Control Center starts up, click on Software Management (in the left-hand sidebar). This gives you four choices. You can install software packages, remove packages, search for and install updates (very important for security and bug fixes), or add new software installation sources. When you choose to install or remove software, you are actually running another program, called Rpmdrake (command name `rpmdrake`).

When the Rpmdrake window comes up (Figure 7-2) you'll be able to search for packages. At the top of the Rpmdrake window is a small search

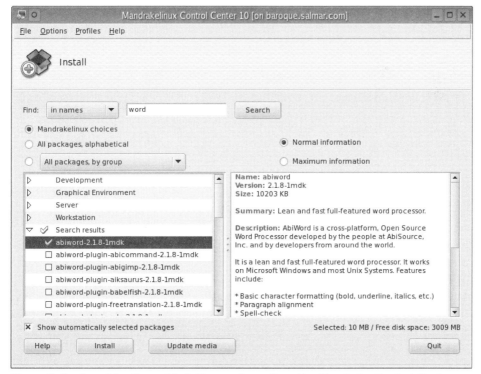

Figure 7–2   Searching for and installing packages from the Mandrake Control Center.

field with the default search criteria set to "in names." The example in Figure 7-2 shows a search for *word* that found, among other things, the abiword package. You can also search more broadly by selecting "in descriptions." That may actually take a little longer, but it gives you a more flexible search, particularly if you don't know the package name.

When you have found a piece of software you are looking for, click the checkbox next to the name. If additional packages are required, Rpmdrake will inform you of it. When you have everything picked out that you want, click *Install*.

If you knew what package you wanted to install, you could easily do it from the command line (as root) like this:

```
urpmi abiword
```

Mandrake's urpmi Made Even Easier

Those of you running Mandrake know that adding a package is as easy as typing "urpmi package_name" and letting the program do the rest. The urpmi program (or rpmdrake if you go graphical) will even go out to the right place (an update site, for example) and download what you need. In doing so, it will alert you to any dependencies that it needs to address. You may also even know that other sites offer Mandrake RPM repositories. So where are these sites, and how do you add urpmi repositories to your system?

Start by visiting the Easy URPMI site at the Penguin Liberation Front (more on them shortly):

```
http://easyurpmi.zarb.org/
http://www.urpmi-addmedia.org/index2.php
```

Once there, just fill in the form, identifying your Mandrake release level (10.1, 9.2, etc.), whether you are interested in regular distrib packages, updates, contribs, and so forth. Upon processing, the form will tell you what to type at the root prompt to get these sources added to your system. It's easy, and you'll be extending the number of available packages you can easily install on your system. Ah yes, the PLF. Some packages may not be legal in your part of the world, most notably DVD decryption libraries in the United States. If you are in the United States, you should not add the link to the PLF repository while on the page. If you do, you will be able to install packages that may not be legal in your jurisdiction, such as the aforementioned DVD decryption libraries.

Searching for Common Ground

As you can see from the examples of installing software under Mandrake, SuSE, Debian, and Fedora, there are many alternatives. I'd like to follow this up by trying to be as release-*agnostic* as possible and show you a tool that should be in almost any distribution running KDE. That tool is KDE's own package manager, *kpackage*. Depending on the distribution, you may have to install kpackage from your distribution CDs (remember what I said about a particular distribution preferring that you do it their way). It is usually called `kdeadmin-kpackage`.

Kpackage

KDE's package tool, kpackage, uses a graphical interface to allow for easy installation or removal of packages. When you first start up kpackage (which you can quickly call by pressing <Alt+F2> and typing `kpackage`), you'll get a two-panel display, with the installed packages on the left and an information window on the right. Click on an installed package (such as *tar* in Figure 7-3),

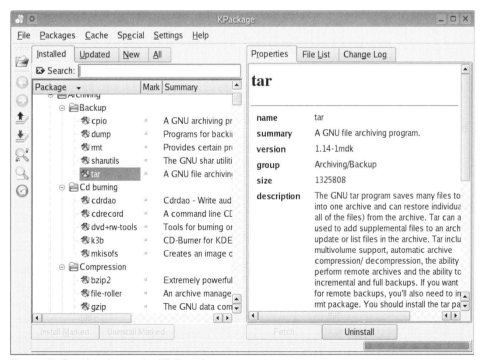

Figure 7–3   Kpackage, the KDE package manager.

and you'll get to know all about that package in the right-hand window's Properties tab.

Click on the File List tab, and you'll get a listing of every file that makes up this package and where these files live on your system. This is actually a great way to get to know the packages installed on your system, and I highly recommend walking through the list and getting a feel for what comprises your Linux system.

Notice as well that all of the packages in that tree view to the left are in a category hierarchy, based on what kind of package they are.

To remove (or uninstall) a package, just click on the Uninstall button at the bottom of the screen (Figure 7-4). A warning screen will appear listing the package (or packages) you are looking to uninstall. If this is really what you want to do (and by the way, this is just an example—I do not recommend that you uninstall tar), click Uninstall. A report of the uninstall process will appear in the right-hand-side information window.

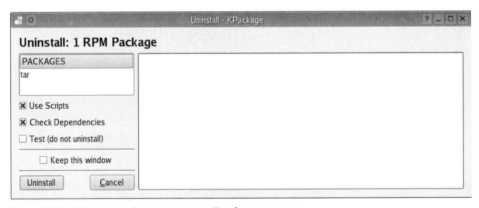

Figure 7–4   Using kpackage to uninstall software.

Installing Packages

To install a package, we first need to identify one, and there are many ways of doing this. Using Konqueror, you can surf over to your favorite software repository (such as RpmFind at `http://www.rpmfind.net`) and search for a package. When you find something compiled for your particular Linux distribution, click on the package file. Konqueror recognizes this as an RPM package and offers to bring up Kpackage, the installation tool. You can also right-click on the package, click Open with from the menu, and select or type *kpackage*.

Another way to do this is to define package sources. These sources could be on a CDROM, on your hard drive, or at a location somewhere on the Internet. To add a package source, click Settings on the menu bar and select Configure Kpackage. A dialog will appear from which you can decide what kind of package source you want to add (Figure 7-5). These could be Debian APT, RPM, Slackware, and others. For this example, I clicked the *Location of Packages* RPM button.

In the case of each of these possible package types, you have a lot of room for entering data sources (Figure 7-6). Each of the seven tabs is an opportu-

Figure 7–5
Selecting sources for package installation.

nity for entering six different package locations. Enter the path to the directory containing the RPM packages you wish to install from and then click the Use checkbox to the left of the path. If this is a network location, make sure you enter the path to the directory in proper URL format (`ftp://ftp.server.dom/path/to/packages`).

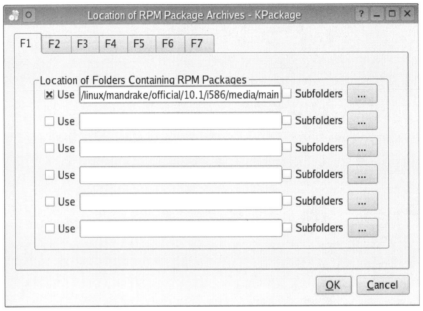

Figure 7–6   Selecting the path to a software installation source.

 Quick Tip You'll see many different types of packages in these listings. Pay particular attention to the last two suffixes in the package name, for example, `.i386.rpm`. This references a package built for the Intel (x86) architecture. An `.i586.rpm` would indicate a package that will not work on anything less than a Pentium architecture (no 486 for you). Another you may see is `.alpha.rpm`. This one represents the PowerPC architecture. If you see `.src.rpm`, this represents a source package. It is non-binary and would have to be built on your system before you could use it (*more on this a little further on*).

Dealing with Dependencies

Installing a single package without dependencies is easy. Select the package, then click Install Marked. If the package has dependencies, it requires additional steps. Let's pretend we want to install Gnumeric, a spreadsheet package that makes an excellent replacement for Excel. The first step is to find the package in the list from my new package archive. We can either scroll down the list until I find the package, or we can take a shortcut and do a search for it.

To search for a package, either click the *Find Package* icon on the left-hand button bar or press <Ctrl+F> to bring up the search dialog. With gnumeric located, we can download the package by clicking the Fetch button on the bottom right-hand side (Figure 7-7).

Figure 7–7   *Searching for and fetching a package with Kpackage.*

After fetching the gnumeric package, we are suddenly presented with quite a bit more information, including a list of unsatisfied dependencies. In my Gnumeric example, two packages are missing: libgda2 and libgnome-db2.

Over on the left-hand side, we still have my listing of all the packages from our software repository.

One by one, I fetch the remaining packages. By the way, it isn't necessary to wait until one package is downloaded before fetching the other. After clicking Install Marked, the installation dialog will appear (Figure 7-8) with a few last-minute options: Upgrade, Replace Files, Replace Packages, Check Dependencies, and Test (which doesn't actually do an installation).

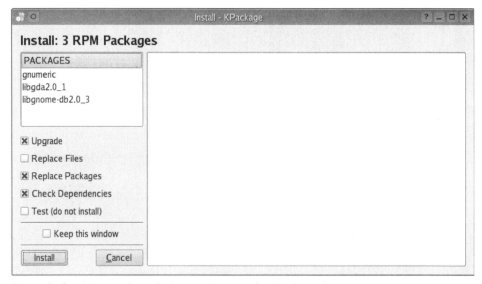

Figure 7–8   *All set to launch the installation of multiple packages.*

You can safely accept the default options, which are to upgrade, replacing old packages as well as checking dependencies. When you are ready to do the install, select your package (listed to the left) and click Install. You will now be asked for the root password. Enter it and press <Enter>.

After a few seconds, the package installation will complete, and kpackage will display the status of the new package, along with its description.

Quick Tip There's another way to install using kpackage, and this is particularly good if you are installing more than one piece of software (or if you are a big fan of drag-and-drop computing). After finding a package with Konqueror, simply drag the rpm package onto a running kpackage and follow the steps.

RPMs, the Shell Way

Would you like a very fast and easy way to install RPM packages? You may find this hard to believe, but at times opening up a shell and typing commands can be much faster than going through all those graphical steps. I'll show you how it is done in this *extended Shell Out session*. Let's pretend you have just downloaded some great package, and now the RPM file for it is sitting in one of your directories. Using a hypothetical package of my invention, let's install that package with command-line rpm:

```
cd /directory_where/package_lives
rpm -ivh ftl-transport-2.1-1.i386.rpm
```

The only thing you need to be aware of here is that package installation needs to be done as the root user. The command that does all the work is called rpm. The flags that I am passing to it tell rpm to install the package (the -i flag), to be verbose (the -v flag), and to print out little hash marks while it does its work (the -h flag). Note that you do not have to have a dash before each letter option (-i -v -h)—you can combine them instead (-ivh):

```
# rpm -ivh ftl-travel-2.1-1.i386.rpm
ftl-travel        #####################################
```

If you want to know everything that is happening, drop the -h flag and add two more v's. The results are pretty wordy, but you do get to see what is happening during the various stages of the installation as well as what files are being installed and where.

Note Commands in the Linux world are case sensitive. The hypothetical command makecoffee would be different than MakeCoffee. The same is true for command-line parameters such as in the earlier RPM example; options and flags such as -U mean different things than -u.

Upgrading an existing package is just as easy. As part of the process, older versions of files will be replaced, and the package's default configuration files may be moved or renamed to preserve the originals (you will usually see appropriate messages if this occurs). Upgrading is more or less the same as installing except that you use the `-U` flag on the command line instead of the `-i` flag:

```
rpm -Uvh matter_transporter-1.2-1.i386.rpm
```

To erase a package, use the `-e` flag instead:

```
rpm -e matter_transporter
```

Notice that when I delete the package, I don't add the release number extensions (the `-2.1-1.i386.rpm` type of suffix).

A full-blown Linux installation will have a lot of packages installed. If you are curious, you can list every single package by typing the following command:

```
rpm -qa | sort | more
```

That shell command is actually three in one. The `rpm -qa` portion tells rpm to *query* the RPM database and list *all* the packages. The bar that you see is called the *pipe* symbol. It literally means to pipe the output of the first command into the second command. The second command in this case is `sort`. After the packages have been listed and sorted, we pipe that output one more time into the `more` command. In other words, show me a screen full of information, and then pause before showing me more. To see the next page, press the spacebar. To quit the listing, type the letter q by itself.

RPM can tell you a lot about the packages you have installed. To find out what version of the `fileutils` package you have on the system and what it is, use the `-q` flag along with the `-i` flag:

```
$ rpm -qi fileutils
Name        : fileutils               Relocations: (not relocateable)
Version     : 4.1.11                       Vendor: MandrakeSoft
Release     : 5mdk                     Build Date: Wed 28 Aug 2002
08:39:42 AM EDT
Install date: Sun 20 Oct 2002 10:00:04 AM EDT     Build Host:
ke.mandrakesoft.com
Group       : File tools              Source RPM: fileutils-4.1.11-
5mdk.src.rpm
Size        : 2344533                    License: GPL
Packager    : Thierry Vignaud <tvignaud@mandrakesoft.com>
URL         : ftp://alpha.gnu.org/gnu/fetish/
Summary     : The GNU versions of common file management utilities
Description :
The fileutils package includes a number of GNU versions of common and
```

```
popular file management utilities.  Fileutils includes the following
tools: chgrp (changes a file's group ownership), chown (changes a
file's ownership), chmod (changes a file's permissions), cp (copies
files), dd (copies and converts files), df (shows a filesystem's disk
usage), dir (gives a brief directory listing), dircolors (the setup
program for the color version of the ls command), du (shows disk
usage), install (copies files and sets permissions), ln (creates file
links), ls (lists directory contents), mkdir (creates directories),
mkfifo (creates FIFOs or named pipes), mknod (creates special files),
mv (renames files), rm (removes/deletes files), rmdir (removes empty
directories), sync (synchronizes memory and disk), touch (changes file
timestamps), and vdir (provides long directory listings).
```

Using -l instead of -i will list all the files in the package. You can even do a sort of reverse file listing by asking rpm to look in its database to identify what package a particular file belongs to. To find out what package a file belongs to, use the -f flag. For example, in my /sbin directory is a file called sysctl. If I want to know where this file came from and what package it belonged to, I use this command:

```
# rpm -qf /sbin/sysctl
procps-2.0.7-14mdk
```

To discover all the things the rpm command can do for you, type man rpm, and you will be able to read the manual page related to that command. As you can see, it really isn't all that complicated to work from the command line. If you prefer the graphical tools, then by all means use them. But don't be afraid of using the shell when you have the opportunity.

Look, Use the Source . . .

Once you've downloaded that new software, you'll no doubt be anxious to take things out for a spin. The truth is that there is an *amazing* amount of software available for Linux. If trying out new things is exciting for you, I can pretty much guarantee that you won't get bored anytime soon.

Much of this software is available as source—not surprising because the GPL (under which much of the Linux software out there is distributed) requires that you distribute source along with the programs. There are also open source projects that have no relation to the GNU projects that employ the license as a means of copyright. Then there are other open source projects that use BSD-style licensing, artistic licensing, postcard licensing, and many others; all distribute their programs in source format.

At first glance, this may appear to be nothing but a nuisance, yet source makes software portable. The number of platforms on which a single package can be compiled tends to be much higher because the applications can be built using your system at your operating system level with your libraries. It means that if you are running VendorX 8.1, you don't need to go looking for the VendorX 8.1 package.

Here's another reason: It takes developers time to provide packages compiled and ready to run on multiple platforms—time they may not have, particularly if they are doing development without pay. Consequently, developers sometimes have source code available that is much more recent than the pre-compiled packages they offer. Why? Because they haven't found the time to build the packages for all those platforms. Here's a plus side you may not have considered: If at some point you decide that you want to try your hand at programming, open source means that you too can get into the game.

 Note As crazy as it may sound, building from source is not all that complicated, and many of the steps required are common across most source distributions. At first it may sound difficult, but no more so than any of the myriad things you've learned how to do with your computer over the years. I admit that compiling from source isn't as straightforward as downloading an RPM package and installing it, but it does open up *thousands* of possibilities.

Here's an added bonus—if you can build one software package, you can pretty much build them all.

The Extract and Build Five-Step

The vast majority of source packages can be built using what I call the *extract and build five-step*. I suppose that step 1 could also involve the downloading of the software, but I'll pretend you've already found and downloaded something, a hypothetical little package called *ftl-travel*, and that you are now anxious to take it for a ride. I'll give you the five steps; then I will discuss them in more detail.

```
tar -xzvf ftl-travel-2.1.tar.gz
cd ftl-travel-2.1
./configure
make
su -c "make install"
```

Easy, isn't it? Now you can just type `ftl-travel` and be on your way. Now that you've seen a source package installation, let me give you some details.

Step 1: Unpacking the Archive

Most program sources are distributed as *tarballs*, meaning that they have been stored using the tar archiving command. In the name just listed (`ftl-travel-2.1.tar.gz`), the `ftl-travel` part of it is the name of the program itself. The `2.1` represents the version number of the package, and the `tar.gz` tells us that this package is archived using the tar command and compressed using the `gzip` command.

You can, therefore, extract the archive with this command:

```
tar -xzvf ftl-travel-2.1.tar.gz
```

The x means extract. The z tells the tar command to use the `gunzip` command to extract. The v says that tar should show us a list of the files it is extracting—in other words, be verbose. Finally, the f identifies the file itself, the one you just downloaded.

Sometimes the extension `.tar.gz` will be shortened to `.tgz`. There are a few other extensions in use out there. For instance, the package may have a `.tar.Z` extension instead, meaning that the file has been compressed using the compress command. To extract the source from this tarball, you first uncompress the file using the uncompress command. Then you continue with your tar extract:

```
uncompress ftl-travel-2.1.tar.Z
tar -xvf ftp-travel-2.1.tar
```

To make life even easier, you could also just shorten the whole thing to:

```
tar -xZvf filename.tar.Z
```

Every once in a while (if the package is very large), the extension will be .bz2, otherwise known as a *bzip2 archive*. To open this one, you perform essentially the same steps you did with compress. Use the command

```
bunzip2 ftl-drive-1.01.tar.bz2
```

to uncompress the file; then extract using the standard `tar` command.

Steps 2–5: Building Your Programs

Once you have extracted the program source from the tar archive, change directory to the software's distribution directory. That's step 2. Using my current ftl-travel example, type `cd ftl-travel-2.1`. From there, I build and install my software, like this:

```
./configure
make
su -c "make install"
```

 Quick Tip Most programmers will include a `configure` script. But if it is missing, make sure you read the README and INSTALL files provided in the installation directory.

The `./configure` step builds what is called a `Makefile`. The `Makefile` is used by the next command, `make`. In building the `Makefile`, the `configure` step collects information about your system and determines what needs to be compiled or recompiled in order to build your software. This brings us to the next step, which is to type `make`. You'll see a lot of information going by on your screen as programs are compiled and linked. Usually (after a successful compile), you follow the make command by typing `su -c "make install"`. This will copy the software into the directories defined in the `Makefile`.

 Quick Tip The reason I have you type `su -c "make install"` is that the final step of an installation usually needs to be done by the root user. Because we don't want to be running as root on a regular basis (for security reasons), the `su -c` step lets us quickly jump into root user mode for one command (where you will be prompted for the root password) and just as quickly jump back out.

A number of programmers also provide a make uninstall option, should you decide you do not want to keep the program around.

 Note If you are an open source programmer (or plan to be one) and you want to make people happy, *always* provide an uninstall option.

README, Please!

If you are like me, you tend to want to just install and run that software, which is partly why I jumped ahead a bit and skipped a very important step. You generally do not have to do this, because 95% of installs are the same, but . . . just before you go ahead with your final three steps, you should consider pausing in the source directory and typing *ls* to list the files in the directory. What you would see are numerous files, something like this:

```
CHANGES   README       Makefile      Makefile.in  configure
INSTALL   ftl-travel.h  ftl-travel.c  engine.c     config.h
```

The first thing you want to do is read any README and INSTALL files. The next step is almost always going to be the ./configure step I mentioned as part of my extract and build the five-step, but there may be details you want to know about in those files. There may also be some prerequisites you should know about or some personal options you may want to set. It takes only a few minutes, and it may be extremely useful.

Getting Your Hands on Software

Way back when, at the beginning of this chapter, I mentioned that there was plenty of software available for your Linux system. Finding it isn't difficult, and there are many ways to start your search. One way is to join a Linux User Group or chat with other Linux enthusiasts or users. That's a surefire way of getting your hands on the latest, greatest, and coolest software.

Another way is to visit some of the more popular Linux software repositories. These include search engines for both packaged software (RPMs) and source (tarred and gzipped files). My favorites in this arena are pbone.net and TuxFinder (I list all of these in the Resources section). Take a moment as well to visit the monster archive at ibiblio.org. For Debian packages, you can also take a look at packages.debian.org.

You might also want to look at the project and review sites. My favorites in this group are Freshmeat, SourceForge, and Linux TUCOWS.

At this rate, you'll never run out of software to try out!

Resources

Debian package search

http://packages.debian.org

Easy URPMI

http://easyurpmi.zarb.org/

Freshmeat

http://www.freshmeat.net

Ibiblio.org

http://www.ibiblio.org

Rpmfind

http://www.rpmfind.net

Pbone.Net

http://rpm.pbone.net/

SourceForge

http://www.sourceforge.net

TUCOWS Linux

http://linux.tucows.com

TuxFinder

http://www.tuxfinder.com

8

Printers and Other Hardware

Ah, hardware . . . "I hate hardware!"

Part of the personal computer experience seems destined to be an eternal battle in getting your current system to talk to the latest and greatest devices. There's always a new, hyperfantastic, 3D video card; mind-blowing stereo sound system; or hair-trigger game controller out there. Then there are more mundane things, such as modems, scanners, and printers. Getting all these devices to work with your system is something that has caused us all grief over time, regardless of what operating system we were running.

We are used to assuming that anything works with Windows, but even that isn't true. From time to time, even Windows users must visit hardware vendors' Web sites to download a driver. I personally spent several hours looking for and downloading an accelerated video driver for my little niece's Windows computer so she could run a Barbie ice-skating program. (She is my niece—I couldn't really let her down.)

In this chapter, I provide the tools you need to deal with common issues and give you some tips on avoiding problems in the first place.

Yes, It Runs with Linux!

Device support under Linux is excellent. No, really. The sheer number of things that will work "out of the box" without your having to search for and install drivers is impressive and, quite frankly, beats your old OS. That doesn't mean all is rosy, however. Let me be *brutally* honest here. Some devices have been written to work with Windows and only Windows . . . or so it seems. One of the great things about this open source world is that developers are constantly working to write drivers to make it possible to run that faster-than-light communications card.

That said, if you haven't already bought that new gadget, there are a couple of things that you should do. For starters, if you are in the store looking at that new printer, pull the salesperson aside and *ask* whether it runs with Linux. If the person doesn't know (which is sometimes a problem but less so as time goes on), take a few minutes to check out the excellent Hardware HOWTO document. You can always find the latest version by surfing on over to the LDP Linux Hardware Compatibility HOWTO page:

```
http://www.tldp.org/HOWTO/Hardware-HOWTO/index.html
```

If you don't find what you are looking for there, check out the hardware compatibility guide on your Linux vendor's site.

 Quick Tip Red Hat's hardware catalog is worth the visit, regardless of what version of Linux you are running. However, keep in mind that things do change on Web sites. If you don't find it there, just go to Red Hat's Bugzilla site at the following address:

```
http://bugzilla.redhat.com/hwcert
```

Although Linux is Linux, different releases of different vendors' products may be at different levels of development. Consequently, at one time or another, Red Hat may have slightly more extensive support for hardware than the others, and a month later SUSE may have the widest range of support.

As Linux gains in popularity, you'll find that hardware vendors are increasingly interested in tapping into this ever-growing market. I've had the experience of being on site, adding hardware to a customer's system (Ethernet cards come immediately to mind), and finding that the system did not have the drivers. I quickly visited the Ethernet card manufacturer's Web site and found precompiled drivers ready and waiting for me.

Plug and Play

For the most part, adding a device to a Linux system is simply a matter of plugging it in. If you don't want to configure it manually, a reboot will force hardware detection, and the device should be recognized by the system and configured. USB devices tend to be even easier because of their hot-plug nature. In other words, you don't need to reboot the system in order to have a USB device recognized, and you can unplug it while the system is running.

Getting a device recognized is only part of it, though. Just because your system knows about the device doesn't necessarily mean that it is configured for your applications.

Going back to the driver issue, you may still have to install a driver, as you sometimes had to do in the Windows world. I wouldn't be fair to you if I simply ignored this little tidbit, so I won't.

Getting Familiar with Your Hardware

Meeting new people isn't always easy. Sociologists will tell us that there is a complex interplay that takes place whenever we meet someone new, much of it subconscious. Although it is possible to meet someone and instantly like him or her, it is more likely that you become comfortable enough to develop a friendship only after having been around a person for some time—in other words, after you've gotten to know a person better.

Now, what the heck does this have to do with hardware and your Linux system?

Well, it's like this . . . For most, the computer we use is a black (or beige) box with a few things plugged into it and some magic happening inside that makes it possible to surf the Internet. Anything that falls outside the small subset of applications we use makes us uneasy. That's why the notion of trying something new may be intimidating. The best way to get over that is to become comfortable with what you have.

The KDE Info Center (Figure 8-1) is the perfect place to start for getting to know what makes up your system. You'll find it by clicking on the big K and looking for *Info Center* (usually in the System submenu) or by clicking on the

Kicker panel. If you are having trouble locating it, remember that you can bring it up by pressing <Alt+F2> and typing in `kinfocenter`, its program name.

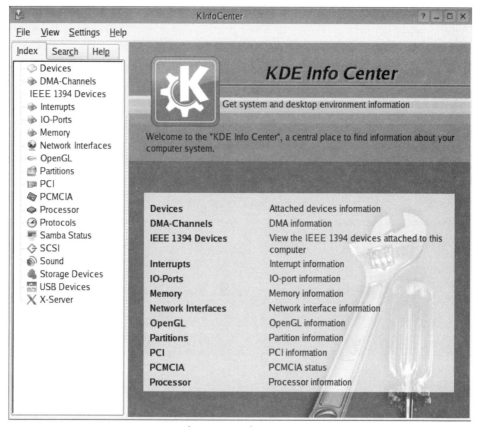

Figure 8–1   The KDE Info Center (kinfocenter).

As soon as the KDE Info Center loads up, it displays some capsule information about the various system features on which it can display information. The descriptions in the main window to the right correspond to the various categories in the left-hand sidebar.

Would you like to know just how fast your processor really is? Click on Processor in the category list. You might be surprised. How about memory? Just click on Memory, and you'll know where every bit of RAM and swap is allocated. For a look at your X window configuration, click X-Server. There is a lot to it, isn't there? Why don't you take a few minutes to explore this hardware landscape? When you are ready to continue, I'll spend a little time on some specific areas, starting with PCI devices.

PCI Devices

Adding a PCI device definitely requires a reboot because we are talking about internal devices. These are cards that fit in the slots inside your computer. When you reboot the machine, Linux should be able to scan for these cards and identify them without any problem. When you click on PCI in the Control Center Information category, you'll get a detailed list of every device known to the system (see Figure 8-2).

 Shell Out You can also run the command /sbin/lspci for a more succinct list.

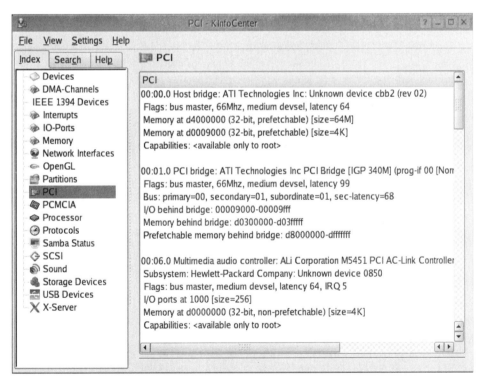

Figure 8–2   Using KInfoCenter to list PCI devices.

If the Linux kernel has the appropriate device drivers available as modules, they will be automatically loaded, and nothing else need be done to make the device available. The reason this information is useful has to do with those times when you do not have a driver handy or directly available. Being able to get the details on the troublesome device in this way is the first step toward getting it working.

A classic example of this is the *Winmodem*, so called because it was designed to work specifically with Windows. If you have one of these modems and it was not automatically configured by the system, never fear. I talk about Winmodems in more detail later in the chapter. For the moment, let's talk USB.

USB Devices

The whole idea behind USB was eventually to replace all those different connectors on the back of a computer. That includes serial ports, parallel ports, and mouse and keyboard connectors. The acronym stands for *Universal Serial Bus*. To get a list of USB devices, click on the USB Devices information category. On any USB system, there will be at least one USB hub and whatever devices are attached. If you look at Figure 8-3, you'll see three USB controllers (one is a USB 2.0 port), a generic webcam, a Canon S10 digital camera, and a mini USB mouse for my notebook, all connected to my system.

Trivia Time I casually mentioned that my notebook computer had both USB and USB 2.0 ports. It's worth noting, because not all systems will have both, and there is a difference between the two. The new USB 2.0 uses an identical connector to the original USB 1 port, but the hardware supports a much faster rate of information exchange. This is particularly useful for devices that must transmit a large amount of information, such as a digital video camera. USB 1 has a speed of 12 megabits per second, while the new USB 2.0 can transmit data at 480 megabits per second.

The sheer number of USB devices available is phenomenal, to say the least, and the list is growing. Many of these devices use a standard set of drivers, which means that a number of things can literally be plugged in and used—no need to mess with loading drivers because it is all being done for you.

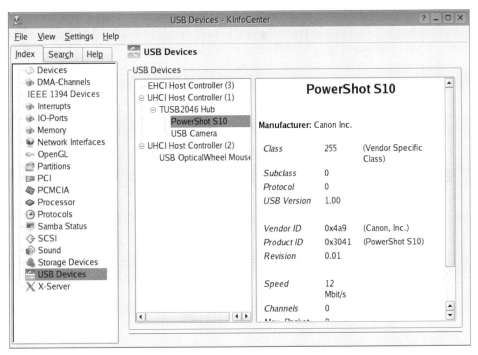

Figure 8–3   Info Center USB device list.

You noticed the word *many* in that last sentence, right? Keeping track of what works (*and what doesn't*) and providing access to drivers that aren't included in current distributions is the *raison d'être* of the *Linux USB Device Overview* Web site. If you find yourself looking at a new webcam and you aren't sure whether it is supported under Linux, look here first:

```
http://www.qbik.ch/usb/devices/
```

The site is organized into sections, depending on the device type (audio, video, mass storage, etc.). Each device is assigned a status identifying just how well a device is supported, from *works perfectly* to *works somewhat* to *don't bother*.

Printers and Printing

This might seem like a silly thing to mention, particularly if your printer was automatically detected, configured, and tested at boot time. Nevertheless, there are things that you might want to do with your printer, and we should probably cover some of these now. Furthermore, *printing is one of the most important functions* a personal computer can perform. It's good to get it right. On that note, I'm going to spend a little time talking about printers and printing. *Trust me*, it's going to be lots of fun.

Printing under Linux works on the basis of *print queues*. At its simplest, this means that whenever you send something to the printer, it is queued in a directory where it awaits its turn at the printer. This de-queuing is known as *spooling*. Consequently, the process that sends the print jobs from the queue to the printer is called the *spooler*. That spooler can be one of a small handful of programs, all of which are transparent to you when you print from applications. Here's a quick roundup of the more popular spoolers.

CUPS, the Common Unix Printing System, is designed to be a platform-independent printing system that works across a great number of UNIX flavors, including Linux. CUPS uses the Internet Printing Protocol (IPP), a next-generation printing system designed to allow the printing of any job to any printer, anywhere. At this point, CUPS certainly looks like the spooler of the future. Most modern Linux distributions include CUPS, and KDE will use it transparently.

The second most likely spooler you will run into is LPD, the classic UNIX spooler. LPD has been around for a long, long time and continues to be distributed with pretty much every Linux out there. I mention it mostly for historical reasons. It's there, but you won't likely be using it.

Whether it is CUPS or LPD, KDE handles printing beautifully. Adding, configuring, or removing a printer is done through the KDE Control Center. After kcontrol has been activated, click on the plus sign in the left-side category window, select Peripherals, then Printers from the list.

We'll start by adding a printer. Because adding hardware, like adding software, is an administrative function, start by clicking the Administrator button at the bottom of the Printing Manager window. A window will pop up asking you for the root password (Figure 8-4).

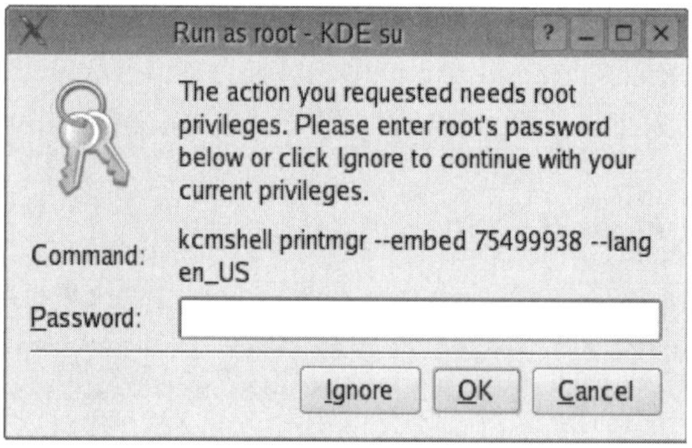

Figure 8–4
Accessing the printer configuration requires the root password.

When you have entered the password, you'll be looking at the same interface, but things will be a little different. For starters, the window to the right is now surrounded by a *red border*. Furthermore, some of the icons have gone from being grayed out to being active. If the toolbar and icons are not visible, right-click in the printer list window (at the top of the printer configuration window). A pop-up menu will appear (Figure 8-5), from which you should select View Toolbar or View Menu Toolbar. Both have the same menu options but are presented somewhat differently.

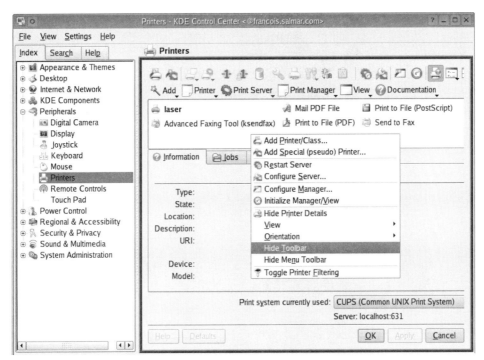

Figure 8–5   Toolbar menu options in the KDE printer configuration manager.

One of those is the Add printer/class icon. Clicking that icon brings up the KDE Add Printer wizard (see Figure 8-6).

Click Next through the welcome screen, and you can select the type of printer and whether it is connected directly to your PC with a parallel or USB cable or via the network in some way. Network-connected printers could be good old LPD printers, Microsoft Windows-connected and -shared printers (SMB), CUPS, HP JetDirect, IPP, or others. Click on the one you are looking to connect and click Next. In my example, I was hooking up an Epson Stylus Photo 820.

When you click Next after selecting your connection, you'll face different choices, based on whether the printer is local or on the network. For a local printer, your choice is parallel port, serial port, or some kind of USB connection.

Figure 8–6   The KDE Add Printer Wizard.

After you click Next, the wizard will load its printer database. Select your vendor and model from the list (Figure 8-7) and click Next.

This brings us to the Printer Test screen. The information regarding your new printer will be displayed, and you'll have the option of sending a test page to the printer. I *strongly recommend* that you do print a test page before moving on.

At this point, you can also click the Settings button and personalize certain defaults, for instance, the default page size (U.S. letter, A4, etc.), margins, print quality, or (in the case of a color inkjet like mine) how ink cartridges are accessed and used. If everything looks as you expect it to on your test page, click Next one more time. You'll be looking at the banner selection screen. Simply put, would you like a banner page before or after your print job has completed? Unless you are in an office with many people trying to keep their jobs straight, you probably don't want to waste the extra paper. Luckily, no banners of any kind is the default.

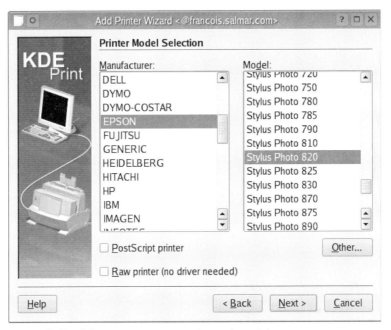

Figure 8–7   Selecting a printer vendor and model.

Click Next and you'll be looking at the Printer Quota Settings (Figure 8-8). You might be asking what a printer quota is and why you should care. Once again, if this is your home printer, you can just click Next and completely ignore it. In some office environments, it may be practical (or necessary) to limit the number of jobs any single user can print to a printer in a given time period. The time period can be per hour, per day, or per week—even per minute. The size of job can be based on the number of pages or the amount of data sent.

Click Next, and it is time for the user access settings, where you can decide who can and can't use your printer. You can specify either a list of *Denied users,* where everyone can use your printer except those listed, or a list of *Allowed users,* where only those listed can use the printer. It is at times like this that Linux reminds you it is a *multiuser* system.

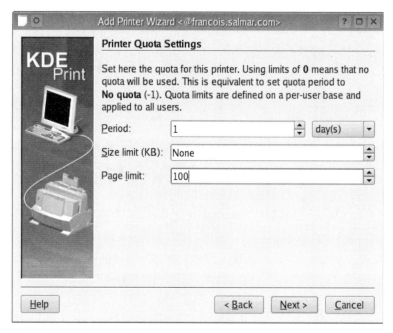

Figure 8–8   You can add restrictions on printer use.

After making all these decisions, we come to the general information, or summary, screen. Enter a name for this printer (a one-word name is best), followed by a location and a description. In reality, the only thing you need to enter is a name for the printer. Click Next, and you'll have a final opportunity to review the choices you've made up to this point. At this point or at any point before now, you can still click Back and make different choices. If you are happy, click Finish, and you are done. Congratulations, you've added and configured a printer.

Let's have a closer look at the Print Manager (Figure 8-9). Take a moment to move your mouse slowly over the various icons at the top and take note of the tooltips. You can do a lot in terms of printer modification and administration here. If you are looking to share your Linux printer with Windows workstations in the office (or home), you can even export the driver for use. Notice the tabs, as well—Information, Jobs, Properties, and Instances.

Information is just that, basic information about your printer, such as its name and location. Under the Jobs tab, you can see all the jobs currently waiting in your print queue.

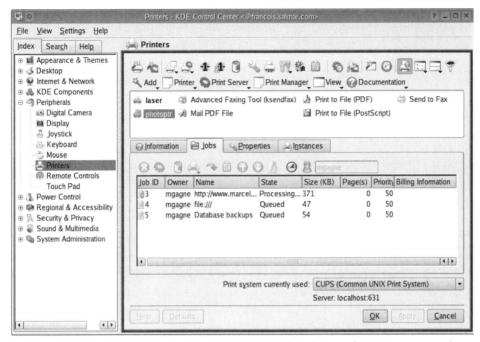

Figure 8–9 The Control Center Print Manager provides all the information you need.

Let me tell you about a great way to work with printers, monitor print jobs, and so on. For quick access to your printing subsystem, right-click on the application launcher (the big K), select Panel Menu | Add | Special Button, and click on Print System. A *new icon* will appear in your Kicker panel. Click on that icon, and all your printers will appear in a pop-up list (along with quick access to other print system tools). Click on the appropriate printer icon, and a window will appear with a list of jobs waiting to be printed (Figure 8-10).

From the jobs list, you can delete jobs, change the order in which they print, or redirect them to another printer if yours is particularly busy. Using the *Properties* tab, you can change some of the characteristics you assigned to your printer when you configured it, such as quotas and banner pages (just make sure you are in Administrator mode).

Quick Tip You might have noticed that the title on that window is "KJobViewer." If you want, you can also just run the command `kjobviewer` or call it up using your <Alt+F2> shortcut.

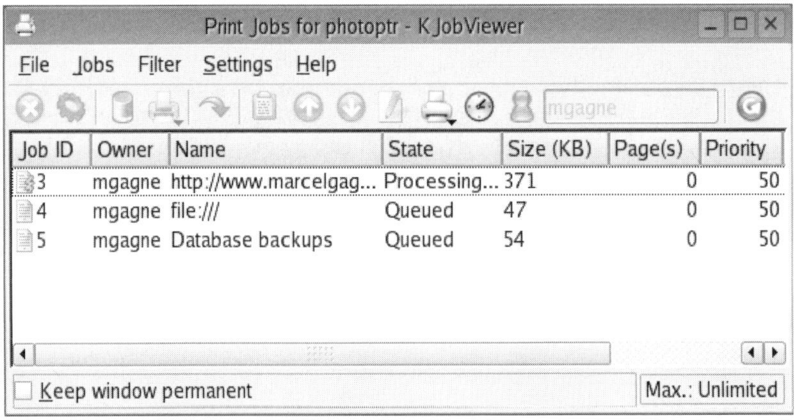
Print Jobs for photoptr - KJobViewer
File Jobs Filter Settings Help
mgagne
Job ID Owner Name State Size (KB) Page(s) Priority
3 mgagne http://www.marcelgag... Processing... 371 0 50
4 mgagne file:/// Queued 47 0 50
5 mgagne Database backups Queued 54 0 50
Keep window permanent
Max.: Unlimited

Figure 8–10 Checking on queued print jobs.

That brings us to *Instances*. Each printer you create will have at least one instance, the default instance. The idea behind this is that you can create multiple instances of the same printer. Let's pretend we are talking about a color printer and that you often switch between a high-quality color mode (for photographs) to a lower-quality draft mode when you want to conserve that expensive colored ink. Just add another instance of the same printer but with different characteristics.

Now that you have added a printer (or printers), configured it, and given yourself supreme power over all print functions, it is time to print something. Luckily, this is the easiest part of all. Whenever you print from any KDE application (Kmail, Konqueror, and so on), you'll be presented with a common printer dialog (Figure 8-11).

From that window, you can select the printer of your choice or click Properties and change the number of copies, the paper size, and a number of other settings associated with that particular printer and that particular job. If you want to see those details up front, click on the Expand button for a somewhat more *panoramic* view. Finally, you can even start from here to add yet another printer. Notice that little icon to the left of the Properties button, the one that looks a bit like a magic wand. Clicking this fires up the Add Printer wizard.

Yes, we've come back around to where we started.

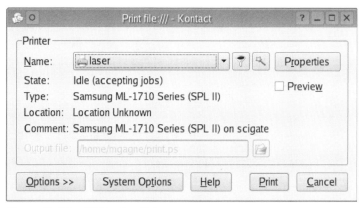

Figure 8–11   KDE print dialog.

Kprinter

Part of the KDE print system includes a tool that doesn't get anywhere near enough attention. That tools is `kprinter`, a universal KDE printing front end that you can call from anywhere (or by using your <Alt+F2> shortcut). Check out Figure 8-12 for an idea of what it looks like.

What I like about kprinter is that you can manually add a list of files you would like to have printed by navigating your directories (see the Files tab). Then, modify your job by selecting number of copies from the Copies tab and so on.

You can also substitute `kprinter` for simple commands like `lpr` in scripts where you would like to have a nice graphical pop-up for the user. Being able to use the command in this way just provides an added layer of flexibility to the print system.

```
kprinter /path_to/some_file
some_command | kprinter
```

Modems versus Winmodems

Way back when, in the introductory chapter, I mentioned Winmodems as one of the few minuses of running Linux. You'll recall that Winmodems are modems designed to work only with Windows. They are sometimes referred to as *software* or *controllerless* modems and tend to be less expensive than controller-based modems.

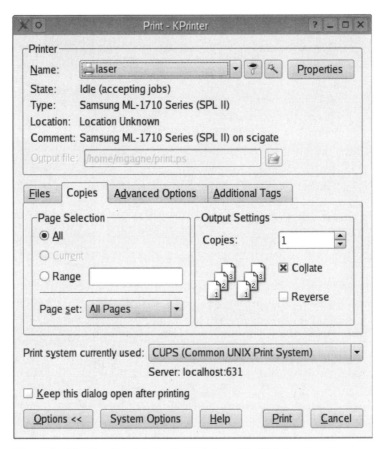

Figure 8–12   *Sending jobs to the printer with KPrinter.*

If you are running a Winmodem, all is not lost. The Linux community is nothing if not resourceful. Even when manufacturers are slow to notice Linux users, the same isn't true the other way around. As more and more people run Linux, this becomes less and less of a problem. In time, hardware manufacturers may be building for Linux first and Windows second. In the meantime, check out the *Linmodems.Org* Web site at http:// www.linmodems.org and you should be up and running shortly.

So just how do you transform a Winmodem into a Linmodem? Well, let me give you an example.

Among the more common Winmodems out there are those based on the *Conexant* chipset; these are starting to be very well supported. For the latest driver, just head over to Linuxant's Web site (not related to Conexant) at `http://www.linuxant.com`. Not only can you get source drivers, but precompiled packages are available for a number of popular Linux distributions.

Identifying the Winmodem is your first step. You can use the KDE Info Center to get a listing of your PCI hardware, where you will get a lot of detail. You can also *shell out* and use the `lspci` command for a quick list of all the PCI devices found on your system. Here's what it looks like:

```
$ lspci
00:00.0 Host bridge: VIA Technologies, Inc. VT8367 [KT266]
00:01.0 PCI bridge: VIA Technologies, Inc. VT8367 [KT266 AGP]
00:06.0 Communication controller: Conexant HSF 56k Data/Fax/
Voice/Spkp    (w/Handset) Modem (WorldW SmartDAA) (rev 01)
00:08.0 Ethernet controller: Realtek Semiconductor Co., Ltd.
RTL-8139/8139C (rev 10)
00:11.0 ISA bridge: VIA Technologies, Inc. VT8233 PCI to ISA
Bridge
00:11.1 IDE interface: VIA Technologies, Inc. Bus Master IDE
(rev 06)
00:11.2 USB Controller: VIA Technologies, Inc. USB (rev 18)
00:11.5 Multimedia audio controller: VIA Technologies, Inc.
VT8233 AC97    Audio Controller (rev 10)
01:00.0 VGA compatible controller: nVidia Corporation NV11
[GeForce2 MX DDR] (rev b2)
```

In some cases, you will find precompiled driver packages. These are the RPMs, as we discussed earlier. Some are specific to your release, and others will be generic. In the case of my Conexant-based Winmodem, I downloaded the RPM package and installed it.

Per the instructions that followed the RPM install, I typed the following command:

```
/usr/sbin/hsfconfig
```

A short dialog followed asking me for the country (Canada, in my case), after which the program compiled and installed the driver for me. It even linked the newly created device, `/dev/ttySHSF0`, to `/dev/modem`. I was ready to use my modem without a care.

Shell Out From the shell prompt, I can verify the location of my modem with this command:

```
$ ls -l /dev/modem
```

The system then responds with this information:

```
lr-xr-xr-x   1   root    root    8 Sep  9   11:23  /
dev/modem  -> /dev/ttySHSF0
```

This listing is all one unbroken line.

The Winmodem/Linmodem Roundup

Clearly, none of this whole Winmodem problem applies if you are using an *external* modem or happen to be among the lucky ones using a cable modem connection or high-speed DSL access from your local phone company. For others out there, it can be a bit more complicated. I've already given you the address of the Conexant Web site, and I will give you more right here.

Remember, *many of these modems* can be made into useful and productive members of Linux society with a visit to the right Web site. On that note, here's my roundup.

Conexant Modems (HCF and HSF)

http://www.linuxant.com

Smart Link Modems

http://www.smlink.com

Lucent Modems

http://www.physcip.uni-stuttgart.de/heby/ltmodem/

PCTel Modems

http://linmodems.technion.ac.il/pctel-linux/

What? More Devices?

We've covered a lot of ground here, but we are by no means finished. Those things we attach to our PCs aren't much good if we don't put them in context with the tools we use them for. Those tools tend to require a somewhat more in-depth examination. For instance, burning CDs isn't just about creating collections of your favorite songs. People use them for backups as well, or to make collections of digital photos for sharing with the family.

The same is true of scanners. These gizmos are incredibly handy devices for the home or office. Aside from converting nondigital pictures to place on your Web site, you can use your scanner as a photocopier and as a way to send faxes when the pages require your signature (you can fax from a word processor, after all).

We cover all those things in the chapters to come.

Resources

Linux Hardware Compatibility HOWTO

> http://www.tldp.org/HOWTO/Hardware-HOWTO/index.html

Hardware Catalog at Red Hat

> http://bugzilla.redhat.com/hwcert

Linmodems.org (Winmodems under Linux)

> http://www.linmodem.org

LinuxPrinting.org (Linux Printer Database)

> http://www.linuxprinting.org

Linux USB Device Overview

> http://www.qbik.ch/usb/devices/

Chapter

9

Connecting to the Internet

I'm going to start this chapter with a little Networking 101. It will be fun—really. Those of you who already know everything about TCP/IP and how IP networks operate can skip ahead a few paragraphs.

Communication over the Internet takes place using something called the TCP/IP protocol suite. TCP/IP actually stands for Transmission Control Protocol/Internet Protocol, and it is the basic underlying means by which all this magic communication takes place. Everything you do on the Net, whether it is surfing your favorite sites, sending and receiving e-mails, chatting via some instant messaging client, or listening to an audio broadcast—all these things ride on TCP/IP's virtual back.

TCP/IP is often referred to as a protocol suite, a collection of protocols that speak the same language. Essentially, this comes down to the transmission and reception of IP packets. Those packets have to get from place to place, and that means they need to know how to get there. IP packets do this in exactly the same way that you get from your house to someone else's house. They have a home address from which they go to a remote address.

Each and every computer connected to the Internet has a unique address called an *IP address*, four numbers separated by dots (e.g., 192.168.22.55). Some systems that are always online (banks, Web sites, companies, etc.) will have a *static* address. Dial-up connections for home users tend to be shared—when you aren't connected, someone else may be using the same address—which is referred to as a *dynamic* IP address.

You may be wondering how a symbolic Web site address such as www.marcelgagne.com translates to the dotted foursome I just mentioned, and that would be an excellent question.

Consider the real world again. We think of our friends not as "136 Mulberry Tree Lane" or "1575 Natika Court" but rather by their names. To find out where our friends live, we check the phone book (or ask them). The same holds true in the digital world, but that phone book is called a *domain name server* (DNS). When I type a symbolic (i.e., human-readable) address into my Web browser, it contacts a DNS (assigned by my Internet service provider [ISP]) and asks for the IP address. With that IP address, my packets almost know how to get to their destinations.

Almost?

To reach an address in the real world, you drive your car out of your driveway and enter some road to which all other roads are connected. If you drive long enough, presumably you get to Rome (having often been told that *all roads lead to Rome*). Before you can get to Rome, you enter your default route, namely, the street in front of your house. The same principle exists in the virtual world. For your IP packages (an e-mail to your mother, for instance) to get to its destination, it must take a particular route, called a *default route*. This will be the IP address of a device that knows all the other routes. Your ISP will provide that route.

That concludes Networking 101. Not particularly complicated, is it?

Before You Begin

Connecting to the Internet is one of those things you set up once and then forget about. Still, you do need to get some information from your ISP up front. The basics are as follows:

- Your user name and password
- The phone number your modem will be dialing to connect
- The IP address of the DNS (name servers—described earlier)

- The IP address of your SMTP and POP3 e-mail hosts
- The IP address of your news server (optional)

All of this information likely came with your contract when you first signed up with your ISP. Armed with this information, you are ready to begin.

Getting on the Net

As I write this, there are three very popular methods of connecting to the Internet, notwithstanding your own connection at the office. These are cable modem, DSL service from the phone company, and good old-fashioned dial-up modem. The first two are usually referred to as *high-speed* or *broadband* connections, and dial-up access is usually made fun of.

With all the press and hype about high-speed service, you would think this is all people run. Think again. As I write this, the majority of people in North America are still connecting through a dial-up connection. Make no mistake—as Mark Twain might have remarked, the rumors of dial-up access's demise are greatly exaggerated. You may be among the majority who are still using dial-up; I cover that in detail shortly.

Before we get started, make sure you have all the information provided by your ISP. At bare minimum, this will consist of a username, a password, and a number to connect to. You will likely also be given a default route, a DNS address (possibly two), and the addresses of your mail server. If you are ready, let's begin.

Connecting to the Net with a Modem

Most ISPs provide dial-up access through the Point-to-Point Protocol, or PPP. The KDE program that gets you connected to the Internet with a modem is called kppp. On a standard KDE setup, you'll find it, under Kicker's big K, by choosing the Internet menu and then clicking Internet Dialer. On Mandrake, look under Networking and then Remote Access; Red Hat has it under Extras and Internet. You can always just start the application with the command kppp & from an X window terminal session or by using your old friend, the <Alt+F2> combo—once again, just type kppp.

Tip You may have noticed in the preceding paragraph that I added an ampersand (&) to the end of the kppp command. When you start a command from a shell prompt, it normally runs in the foreground. What this means is that you can't start another process at the shell until the current one finishes (you could, of course, open up another shell). The ampersand tells the shell to put the process in the background so that you can run other things.

When KDE's Internet connection tool comes up for the first time (Figure 9-1), there isn't much to see because nothing has been configured. You'll see a blank Connect to list as well as blank Login ID and Password fields.

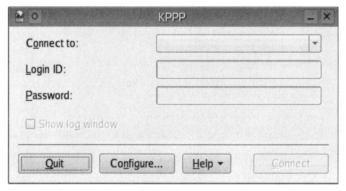

Figure 9–1   First time with KPPP.

To get started, click the Configure button. This will take you to the KPPP Configuration screen.

I realize that the Accounts tab is the first, but I want to talk about the Device tab for a moment. I covered devices back in Chapter 8, specifically the issue of modems, and it is particularly relevant here. If you click on that tab, you'll notice that the modem device is set to /dev/modem, which is a symbolic link to the actual port for the modem. That might be /dev/ttyS0, but it could be many other things as well.

If you find yourself having problems here when you dial out, it may be that the link wasn't set properly. Never fear, click on the drop-down list, and you will see a number of potential devices. After choosing a device, click on the Modem tab and choose Query Modem. If kppp successfully sees your modem, you should see something similar to Figure 9-2.

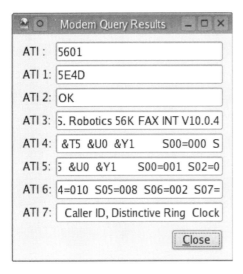

Modem Query Results	
ATI :	5601
ATI 1:	5E4D
ATI 2:	OK
ATI 3:	5. Robotics 56K FAX INT V10.0.4
ATI 4:	&T5 &U0 &Y1 S00=000 S
ATI 5:	5 &U0 &Y1 S00=001 S02=0
ATI 6:	4=010 S05=008 S06=002 S07=
ATI 7:	Caller ID, Distinctive Ring Clock
	Close

Figure 9–2 Modem query results.

Let's get back to the Accounts tab now. As you can probably infer from this screen, it is possible to configure and maintain several dial-up accounts from here. Most people will probably use just one, but you can also use it to set up multiple profiles of the same account. If you happen to be a road warrior or globe trotter with a notebook, you can create profiles for the various cities you visit.

From the Account setup window, click New to create a new account. Skip by the Wizard option (which tends to be for European sites) and choose the Dialog Setup instead. You'll be asked for a connection name, a phone number for your ISP, and the authentication type (see Figure 9-3). This defaults to PAP authentication (which most ISPs today use). If your ISP still has you go through some kind of authentication script (known as an *expect/ send dialog*), choose Script-based from the list.

Notice that you have some additional tabs on the menu. The IP tab enables you manually to enter the IP address provided by your ISP. Because most dial-up accounts use dynamic addresses, that is the default selection, and you probably don't have to change anything there. The same goes for the next tab, the Gateway tab. This is usually set for you as you connect. Once again, you can override this setting by providing a static gateway address if your ISP provides it.

Figure 9–3   New account setup.

The last tab is one you will probably need to worry about—the DNS tab. In all likelihood, you will want to configure an address here as indicated by your ISP. Click the Manual button. Enter the DNS address you were given into the DNS IP Address field, and then click Add. If you have a second address, enter it in the same way.

Of course, the most work you may have to do comes under the Login Script tab, where you may have to provide your dial-up configuration with the appropriate dialog for a connection. This is also something your ISP should have supplied you with. This requirement tends to be rare these days.

When you click OK, you'll find yourself back at the configuration screen. Click OK one final time and you return to the initial Kppp window, with one difference. In the Connect to connection list, your new connection should be visible (see Figure 9-4). Enter your login ID and password, click Connect, and you are on your way.

Figure 9–4 Ready to connect to your ISP.

Before I move on, notice the Show log window checkbox. If you find that you are having problems connecting, checking this box will show you a login script window as the connection takes place. This can help you debug any problems you might have with the connection.

Cable Modems and High-Speed DSL

For the most part, if you installed your Linux system with the cable modem connected, this is probably already working, and you have nothing left to do. If, however, you are already up and running and you are just now getting a cable modem, it is probably time for a few pointers. Quite frankly, these days (with a modern Linux distribution), there isn't much to it.

To begin with, cable modems aren't modems in the classic sense. The so-called modem is connected to your cable TV service on one side and to an Ethernet card inside your PC on the other. High-speed access through your phone company's DSL service is similar, in that they will provide you with an external, modemlike device (in many cases, it is really a router) that also connects to an Ethernet card.

The Ethernet card (which should be automatically detected by your system) gets an IP address from the cable modem via the Dynamic Host Configuration Protocol (DHCP). Although this address may appear permanent, in that it rarely (if ever) changes, it is nevertheless dynamic, because your actual Ethernet card gets its address whenever it connects.

The process of getting your system configured varies a little bit from distribution to distribution, but only cosmetically. When you install your new Ethernet card (for access through the cable modem), it will be autodetected by the system on reboot. As part of that process, the system will ask whether you want to configure the card. The answer is yes, of course. Next, the system will ask whether you want to supply an IP address or have it autoconfigure via DHCP. With a cable modem, as with DSL, autoconfiguring is what you want.

Now that I've shown you how incredibly *easy* it is to do this, I'm going to mention that there are many different providers of high-speed cable and DSL access. What this means is that if your system doesn't autorecognize and configure your connection, you may need to do one of these things. For cable modems, the answers vary, but start by checking out the Cable Modem HOWTO at `http://www.tldp.org/HOWTO/Cable-Modem/index.html` for details on your particular geographic location.

If you are on a phone company DSL service, look on your distribution disks for the `rp-pppoe` package (PPP over Ethernet) and install it (many distributions will have it installed by default since DSL is so popular). You can also get the package from Roaring Penguin at `http://www.roaringpenguin.com/pppoe/`, but you probably have it on your CDs. Make sure you check there first.

Once the package is installed, open a shell (Konsole) and switch to the root user. Do this by typing "`su - root`" at the shell prompt. You'll be asked for the root password. One you have entered it, type this command:

```
adsl-setup
```

This is basically a fill-in-the-blanks session. Your phone company will have assigned you a username and password, along with some connection information, and will have provided you with this. Answer all of the questions (the information is case sensitive, so be careful entering it). When you have answered everything, type the following at your shell prompt:

```
adsl-start
```

That's it. You have no doubt guessed that there is also an `adsl-stop` command as well as `adsl-status` (which, among other things, will tell you your IP address). If you install the RPM package from your distribution, `adsl-start` will run automatically when you reboot your system, so you don't need to worry about it each time.

Okay, I'm Connected. Now What?

Good question. For starters, you have everything the Internet has to offer. You can surf the Web (which I cover in Chapter 10), send e-mail (Chapter 11), and find and download software, music, and video. The Internet is a vast cornucopia of news, information, conversation, sights, sounds, and a thousand other things. When looking at all this, it is easy to forget that it really all comes down one thing—*communication*.

The Internet was born on communication; e-mail specifically was the tool that drove its development into the globe-spanning network that it is today. That's why I devote all of Chapter 11 to electronic mail.

These days, however, a new kind of communication has evolved—call it "mini e-mail." The one-liner. The short and sweet message. The *instant message*. People in our Net-connected society have grown to love those quick, always-on means of sending one another information. My own parents (who live in another Canadian province) send me a daily one-line weather report via their Jabber instant messaging client. If you are coming from the Windows world, there's a good chance you already have one of these accounts, either with Yahoo!, AOL, MSN, or Jabber.

Why Jabber?

There are several reasons aside from the two I just mentioned (open source and open protocol). The Jabber *protocol* doesn't belong to any one in particular, so there is no company driving its destiny (although there are companies using Jabber). Jabber uses a decentralized approach, so the system is more robust. In fact, anyone can run a Jabber server if he or she wants to. This is a boon to companies that may want to run a *private*, *secure* instant messaging network.

Whether you choose to run Jabber, Yahoo!, MSN, or something else, the ideal instant messaging client is a multiprotocol client, one that lets you talk to all these services without having to run a client for Jabber, one for AOL, one for Yahoo!, one for . . . well, you get the idea. Let's look at KDE's Kopete, a superb Linux instant messaging client with great multiprotocol support and IRC as well.

Kopete

Kopete is a powerful multiprotocol instant messaging system. It supports a plugin-based architecture, making it possible to extend the package with a variety of additional features. Some of the existing features include history, translation tools, text effects, and cryptography, among others. Because it is part of KDE, it fits nicely into the desktop and docks into the system tray when not in use. It uses both sound notifications and passive text alerts that let you continue working.

You'll find Kopete under your Internet submenu in the program launcher. It's program name is kopete, which means you can launch it from the shell or with your <Alt+F2> keyboard shortcut. The first time Kopete starts, the configure window pops up along with the main (currently empty) Kopete window (Figure 9-5).

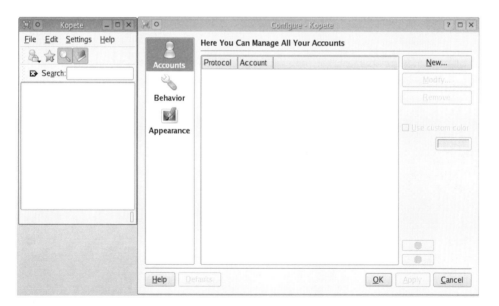

Figure 9–5   First time out with Kopete.

Time to create a new account. On the Configure Kopete dialog, make sure Accounts is selected in the left-hand sidebar (this is the default), and click the New button on the right. The Add Account wizard will appear. Click Next, past the introductory screen to the protocol selection screen (Figure 9-6). You'll be presented with a list of the protocols supported by Kopete: AIM, Gadu-Gadu, Novell GroupWise, ICQ, IRC, Jabber, MSN, SMS (telephone text messaging), and Yahoo!.

Figure 9–6 Kopete supports a number of popular instant messaging protocols.

When you click Next, the Account Information setup window will appear. There are three tabs here, one for Basic Setup, one for Connection information, and the other for File Transfer (Figure 9-7). Let's start with the Basic tab. For a Jabber ID, enter a screen name that appeals to you. Keep in mind that you may have to try this more than once to make sure you get something unique (or you could just start with something unique). To avoid having to enter your password each and every time you connect, make sure the *Remember password* checkbox is checked. Then, directly below, enter your password.

Figure 9–7   Creating a new Jabber account.

The other important thing on that tab is listed as Exclude from connection. By default, accounts connect automatically when Kopete starts up (in earlier versions of KDE, the default was the opposite). This is strictly personal preference, and you may choose to override it by clicking the checkbox, but an automatic login is a feature I find handy.

Tip In my example, I used a screenname@jabber.org ID on the main Jabber public server. There are others, however, that may be closer to you or that offer additional services. You can find out about them on the Web by paying a visit to the Jabber.org site:

```
http://www.jabber.org/network/
```

Each site listed on that page includes details as to what features they support. For instance, some feature free group chat or secure communications using SSL. Pick one that suits your needs.

Time to click the Connection tab (Figure 9-8). This one is pretty simple, but there are a couple of things to watch out for. Both deal with the information in the preceding tip. I mentioned that there are other Jabber servers out there and that some of them support SSL. If that is the case and you desire encrypted communication, set the checkbox accordingly. Then there's the server address itself. The address you registered under the Basic Setup tab assumes you will use the same server hostname. If, for some reason, that isn't the case, you can change it here by clicking the checkbox labeled Override default server information. The Server field will then be available for you to enter the correct address.

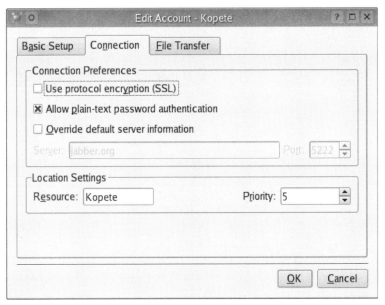

Figure 9–8 Setting up the Connection information for your new account.

Finally, we have the File Transfer tab. While you are engaged in a Jabber chat session, it's possible to transfer files to your friend. Imagine that you are having a chat about your new baby. You could, during the chat, send a picture to show just how cute the baby really is. The other item on this tab deals with whether or not your company goes through a proxy (including whether it requires authentication) and so on. This will vary based on the server you register with and with the security requirements in your own company. Home users generally don't need to worry about this.

After entering all your information, go back to the Basic Setup tab and click *Register New Account*.

A successful account registration at this point should mean that you can now connect using the account you just created. In the main Kopete window (Figure 9-9), you should see a little light bulb icon in the bottom right-hand corner of the main Kopete window. Click on the icon, and a menu of options associated with that account will appear, including "Online." Click Online, and the light bulb icon will flicker and come on when the connection is established.

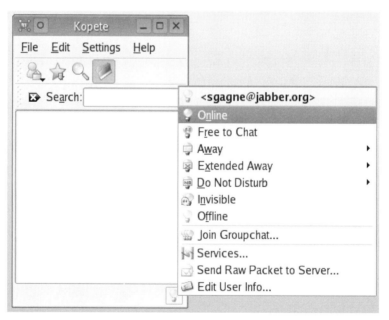

Figure 9–9   Kopete's account connection menu.

Tip The account icons vary depending on the service you choose. MSN accounts have a butterfly, Yahoo! has a Y with a smiley, ICQ has a flower, and so on.

Adding Kopete Contacts

Before you can chat with anyone, you need to add contacts to your Kopete account (or they need to add you). Click File on the menu bar, and select Add Contact (you can also click the appropriate icon). Since Kopete is actually a KDE application, there are some interesting benefits. One of these has to do with adding contacts (sometimes referred to as *buddies*). When the Contact Addition Wizard appears, it asks you whether you want to use the KDE address book to enter this contact. What this means is that you can either search for someone already in your address book or create a new entry as you add the individual to your Kopete contact list. At the bottom of this first window is a checkbox for this option. If you don't want to use the address book, just uncheck it.

Click Next to continue, and you will be asked to enter the Display Name and Group. At the top of the screen, enter a display name for the person you want to add. This isn't that person's account name or screen name, but what you want it to look like in your contact list (e.g., Elizabeth in sales). Below that field is a list of group names. By default, there is only a Top-Level group, but you can choose to create a new one here (e.g., Sales, Customers) by clicking the *Create New Group* button. Make sure you put a check by the group you want to use and click Next. The next screen is where you enter the actual Jabber account information (e.g., userid@jabber.org). Click Next, then click Finish on the final screen, and you have added your contact. After you accept your new contact, that individual will get a message asking for confirmation, following which the new contact name will appear in your main Kopete window (Figure 9-10).

To start a chat, double-click on the contact name and type a message in the bottom part of the chat window (Figure 9-11). If someone contacts you for a chat, a passive alert will appear near the Kopete icon in the system tray (bottom left of your desktop). Click View to answer the call, or click Ignore to pass.

Figure 9-10   Kopete with an active contact list.

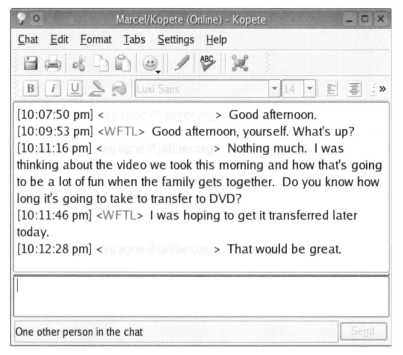

Figure 9-11   Holding a Kopete conversation.

Tip The conversation shown in Figure 9-11 is presented in a chat style called XChat. This look and feel (font, colors, layout, etc.) can be modified to suit your tastes. Click Settings on the Kopete menu bar and select Configure Kopete. Next, click Appearance from the sidebar and select the Chat Window tab. You'll see a number of different styles there, such as Gaim (another popular Linux instant messaging client), Keramik, iChat, MSN, and XChat, among others. Click one, and you'll see a preview of the chat style in the window to the right. When you're happy with your choice, just click OK to close the configuration dialog.

I'm going to leave things here. But before we move on, take a moment to go through some of the other Kopete settings. Just click Settings on the menu bar, and select Configure Kopete or Configure Plugins. You'll find options to configure the chat window, set tabbed messaging windows, configure history, encryption, and much more. It's worth checking out, and it can greatly enhance your Kopete experience.

Resources

Cable Modem HOWTO

 http://www.tldp.org/HOWTO/Cable-Modem/index.html

GAIM Instant Messaging

 http://gaim.sourceforge.net

Jabber Software Foundation

 http://www.jabber.org

Kopete

 http://kopete.kde.org

Chapter
10
Surfing the Internet

When it comes to Web browsers on the desktop, Linux users are faced with an embarrassment of riches, with plenty of alternatives to choose from. For those who are looking for a screaming-fast browsing experience and can do without the graphics, Linux offers a number of text-based browsers. (I talk about these at the end of the chapter.)

In the graphical world where most people will spend their browsing time, a new program has set the browser world on fire. It's called Firefox. In just a few short months, it has reignited the browser wars and done what no one thought possible—taken a substantial market share away from the security-problem-plagued Internet Explorer. Thanks to the incredible popularity of Firefox and its multiplatform support (it is also available for Windows), Internet Explorer's browser market share had dipped to below 90% in the first five months following Firefox's release. This is quite a feat, considering that Internet Explorer had commanded something around 95% of the market before Firefox. Better security and advanced features were drawing millions of users away from Microsoft's browser. Firefox is an exciting program, and I show you how it works in this chapter.

Then we have KDE's own browser, Konqueror. Besides being a great browser, Konqueror is a powerful file manager (as you discovered earlier in the book). I should tell you that I myself move back and forth between browsers. In fact, I tend to be a two-browser guy, flipping between Firefox and Konqueror (although I do favor Konqueror these days). If you are running KDE, you won't need to download Konqueror. It's part of the whole KDE environment. Exploring Konqueror's Web browser *persona* is where I begin this chapter. Then I move on to Firefox. Compare the features and decide for yourself what will define *your* browsing experience.

Konqueror

To start surfing the Net with Konqueror, you'll need to connect to the Internet—it's a good thing we covered that in Chapter 9. Starting Konqueror as a browser is the same as starting Konqueror any other way. Most distributions, however, have an icon, either on the desktop or on Kicker itself, to start up Konqueror as a browser. The difference is that in the browser configuration, you generally set a home page (more on that later).

Konqueror does pretty much anything you expect from a graphical Web browser and some things you don't. You can go forward and back, save bookmarks (click Bookmarks in the menu bar), download files, and print pages. Because I am assuming that you have all used a browser before, I'll concentrate on the things that I think you will want to know. When you start Konqueror for the first time, there won't be any kind of home page set. What you will see is an introductory screen (Figure 10-1) that offers you some interesting choices and destinations.

Some of those options hint at the very powerful features that Konqueror offers. You might want to click on each of them and explore a little bit. For instance, clicking on Storage Media (`media:/` in the Location field) lets you navigate your hard disks or CD- and DVD-ROMs. Choosing Applications (`applications:/` in the Location field) allows you to navigate the various menus and types of programs on your system. You can even run programs from there by clicking on them. For instance, click Toys and then Kodo to fire up a strange little program that places an odometer on your desktop whose entire purpose is to measure how far your mouse travels as you go through your day. Want to explore your system's settings? In Chapter 5, I introduced you to the KDE Control Center (`kcontrol`). Click Setting (`settings:/` in the Location field) and you'll discover another way to explore your Linux system's secrets. There's more, but for now I'd like to tell you about surfing the Internet.

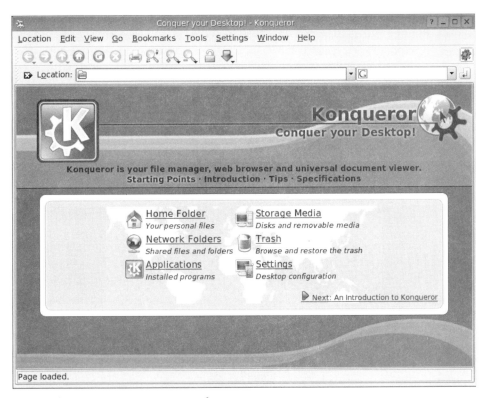

Figure 10–1 Konqueror as seen on first use.

To start surfing the Net, this is all you have to do: Fire up Konqueror, enter your favorite Web site's URL into the Location: bar window, and press <Enter>. In a few seconds, your Web site's page should appear.

Quick Tip Notice the black arrow with an x through it, to the immediate left of the Location label. Clicking this will automatically clear the Location field. No need to select or backspace over the last URL.

Page Home for Me . . .

Setting your home page is easy. Simply visit the site of your choice, drag the Konqueror browser window to the size you want, and then click *Settings* in the menu bar and select *Save View Profile "Web Browsing."* This brings up the Profile Management dialog (Figure 10-2), where you can save this as your default Konqueror Web view.

Notice the two checkboxes at the bottom. Make sure you click them both if you want to preserve the size of browser window you specified as well as the link to your home page. Click Save, and you are done. Next time you fire up the Konqueror browser, you'll head straight to your home page.

Figure 10–2   Saving your Konqueror browsing profile.

You might wonder what the point of creating a profile just to set your home page might be. Profiles are interesting because you can create custom Konqueror views for yourself as desktop icons. When you start any other browser, you have one home page. Sure, you could put links on your desktop that go to a specific site simply by right-clicking on the desktop, choosing Create New, and selecting Link to Location (URL). But what if you wanted one browser to be a certain window size as well? What if on some sites you wanted the navigation panel on, and on others off? Profiles let you do this.

Here's how it works. Start by creating a new profile. You do this by clicking Settings on the menu bar and selecting Configure View Profiles. Enter a name where it says Profile Name, and then click on Save. Now click on Settings one more time, select Load View Profile, and select the profile you just created. Surf over to the site of your choice, size the windows as you would like them to be, open (or don't) a navigation panel, and so on. When you are happy with your new *starting point*, click Settings and click on Save View Profile YourProfileName.

Almost there. The last thing we need is a desktop icon that automagically loads this profile. The easiest way to do this is to click on the big K, open the Internet menu, and find Konqueror. Click and drag the Konqueror icon onto the desktop. You'll be asked whether you want to Copy, Move, or Link the program. Choose Copy. Now right-click on the new icon and select Properties. As before, you can choose an icon that suits you, and you probably want to pick a name for the newly created icon. The real work here is done on the Application tab (Figure 10-3). Notice that under Command, it says "kfmclient openProfile webbrowsing." That represents the default profile. You want to replace the word *webbrowsing* with whatever you called your profile. A word of caution: If you used spaces in your profile name (I created one called My Daily News), you will need to surround the profile name with quotes. For example:

```
kfmclient openProfile "My Daily News"
```

Click OK to save your icon, and you are done.

Personal Note I routinely use profiles as a quick way to move files from my own notebook to my Web site and other Web sites. Profiles let me open split-screen browsers already logged in to the remote sites. It's a great time saver.

Cool Konqueror Tricks

I am going to show you a few things to try with Konqueror that you may find quite handy. As you read the next couple of pages, you will learn some great tricks, shortcuts, and otherwise fun things to do with your KDE browser.

Figure 10–3   Creating a new browsing profile.

Split Views

Remember all the things you learned when using Konqueror as a file man-ager? They still apply. For instance, you might remember that you could split your Konqueror window to provide multiple views. Let's say you wanted to look at two Web sites simultaneously, with the top half of the browser dis-playing one site and the bottom half displaying another. Try this: Open Kon-queror and surf over to the site of your choice. Now click on Window in the menu bar and choose Split View (either top/bottom or left/right). You should have two copies of the same site open in two separate views. You can close either view by clicking on Window and then clicking on Remove Active View.

As when you used Konqueror as a file manager, the active window will have a little *green light* on in the bottom left-hand corner. Click that bar on either window to switch from one to the other. You can now enter a new address into the Location field to open a new Web site.

Super-Speedy Searches

Ah, shameless alliteration . . . Let's say you wanted to search on Linux media players in Google. Normally, you would enter `http://www.google.com`, wait for the site to load, type in *Linux media players*, and click to start the search. With Konqueror, a number of quick search shortcuts have been defined that make searching feel so much easier. To search Google for our media players, you could simply type the following in the Location field:

```
gg: Linux media players
```

Konqueror automagically feeds the search terms to Google. You can do a rapid-fire search of the Google *Usenet groups'* archive as well. Pretend you are having problems with an FTL3D VR card for your system:

```
ggg: FTL3D VR card setup Linux
```

There are other great shortcuts. For instance, typing `fm:` will let you search the Freshmeat software archives, and `rf: package_name` will search RPMfind.net for RPMs of your favorite software. Here's a list of others you may want to try:

`av:`	Use the AltaVista search engine
`ad:`	Acronym Database lookup
`ggn:`	Search Google News
`ggi:`	Search Google Images
`hb:`	Search HotBot
`sf:`	Look through SourceForge
`imdb:`	Internet Movie Database search

You can check all these out for yourself by clicking on Configure Konqueror in the menu bar under Settings. Then choose Web Shortcuts from the sidebar on the left, and you will get a nice long list of these shortcuts. One of my favorite shortcuts of all time is the *online dictionary* search. Using the `dict:` shortcut, Konqueror will search through the *Merriam-Webster Dictionary*, and the `ths:` shortcut will look things up in the online thesaurus:

`ths:`   thesaurus

You know, there really is no synonym for *thesaurus*.

 Quick Tip You can add your own Web search shortcut. When looking through the shortcuts under Web Shortcuts, select one, click Modify, and follow the example to create your own.

Go for the Big Screen

Nothing beats looking at the virtual world through a big screen. As much as I would like to, I can't increase the size of your monitor, but I can help you with the next best thing. When you are busy surfing the Internet and you want as much screen as possible, why not try Konqueror's full-screen mode?

At any time while viewing a page, you can click Window on the menu bar and select Full-Screen Mode. The title bar will disappear, as will Kicker and all other border decorations. When the switch happens, pay attention to the icon bar (just below the menu bar). A *new icon* appears to the right of all the others. On my system, it looks like a little screen with four red arrows pointing in (Figure 10-4). Clicking on that icon will return your Konqueror session to normal. You can also quickly toggle back and forth by pressing <Ctrl+Shift+F>.

Figure 10–4   A new icon appears allowing you a one-click way to exit full-screen mode.

Yum . . . Cookies

Not that kind of cookie. Cookies are simply small text files transmitted to your browser (or system) when you visit a Web site. The original idea behind cookies was that a server would give you a cookie as a marker to indicate where you had previously visited. That cookie might store a username and password to access a particular Web site or other information related to your visit, such as an online shopping cart. When you next visit the site, the server would ask your browser whether it had served you any cookies, and your browser would reply by sending the cookies from before. In this way, the Web site would recognize you when you next visited, and certain useful defaults would be set up for you. Cookies can be very good.

The problem with cookies is that they can also be shared within larger domains, such as advertising rings. Using these shared cookies, advertisers can build a profile of your likes and dislikes, tailoring and targeting advertising to you specifically. Many people object to this method of building user profiles and consider the use of cookies to be quite unethical, an invasion of privacy. The dilemma then is to find a way to accept the cookies you want and reject the others. Konqueror lets you do just that.

Click on Settings, and then select Configure Konqueror. From the side panel, click on Cookies. Under the Policy tab, make sure you have cookies enabled with the checkbox. Then, using the checkbox below that, select Ask for confirmation before accepting cookies. You may also want to *only accept cookies coming from originating server*, another checkbox item.

The first time a site offers you a cookie, a dialog box will appear asking whether you want to accept or reject that cookie (Figure 10-5). Best of all, it asks you whether you want to reject them now or always. Choose All cookies from this domain before you click Reject, and that ad site will never store another cookie on your computer.

Figure 10–5   Do you accept or reject this cookie?

Ban the Pop-Ups Forever!

Honestly, I can't think of a single person who likes to visit a Web site, only to have that site throw up annoying pop-up window ads. Konqueror lets you turn off this *feature* that certain sites provide. Once again, click Settings | Configure Konqueror, and choose Java & JavaScript from the sidebar. Select the JavaScript tab, and click whichever radio button suits your taste (Figure 10-6).

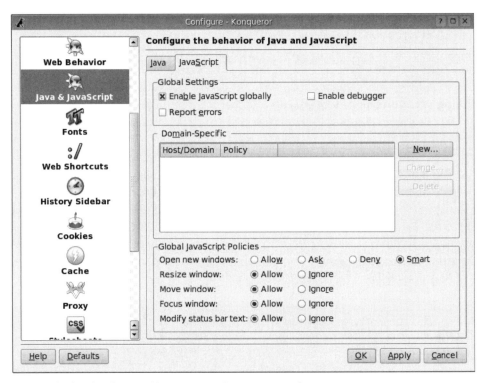

Figure 10–6   Configuring Konqueror to ban pop-up ads.

I've found that Smart is indeed pretty smart and that it generally takes care of deciding whether to allow pop-ups. You can also decide to have Konqueror ask you each and every time a site tries to open a pop-up, or you can simply Deny everything.

Keeping Tabs on the Web

Konqueror sports a great feature called *tabbed browsing*. Here's how it works.

Sometimes when you are viewing Web sites, you want to keep a particular site open while moving to another place on the Web. Normally, you would click File and select New Window. This is fine, except that if you keep doing this, you'll wind up with however many versions of a browser open on your desktop. Switching from one to the other involves doing a little digital juggling. Tabs make it possible to bring a nice, clean air of sanity to what could otherwise become a very cluttered taskbar (or desktop).

To open new tabs, click Window on the menu bar and select New Tab or simply press <Ctrl+Shift+N> (pressing <Ctrl+T> works as well). You can also open a new tab from a link in the current Web page by right-clicking on that link and then selecting Open in New Tab. Take a look at Figure 10-7 to see Konqueror's tabs in action.

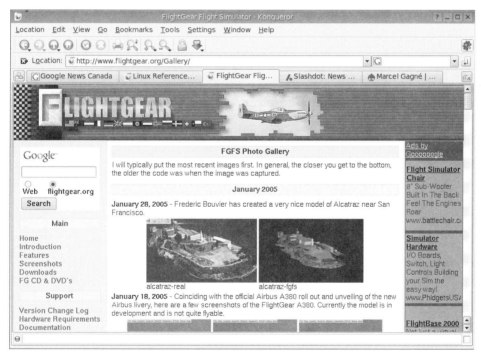

Figure 10–7 Konqueror does tabbed browsing.

Mozilla Firefox

As I mentioned in the introduction, these days I find myself switching back and forth between Mozilla Firefox (Figure 10-8) and Konqueror. Actually, it used to be just plain Mozilla and Konqueror, but times have changed and Mozilla's little sibling, the Firefox browser, has set the world on fire.

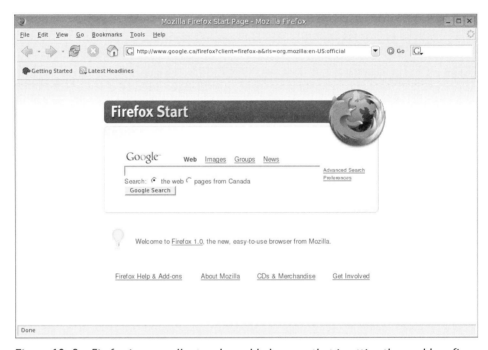

Figure 10–8   Firefox is an excellent and capable browser that is setting the world on fire.

So what's the difference between Mozilla and Firefox? The actual Mozilla browser is more like the Swiss Army knife of browsers. It includes an e-mail package and IRC client, is ideal for reading newsgroups, and comes with an HTML editor. Firefox, on the other hand, is strictly a Web browser. To get the equivalent stand-alone e-mail package, you would download Thunder-Bird. (I cover e-mail packages in Chapter 11.) Right now I'd like to concentrate on Firefox, so let's get started.

To start Firefox, click on Kicker's big K, select Internet, and choose Firefox from the list. If Firefox isn't installed, you can get the package at

```
http://www.mozilla.org/products/firefox
```

or simply get it off your distribution CDs.

Working from Home

When you first start Firefox, it will take you to its home, currently a Google/ Firefox welcome and search page. Getting to a Web site and navigating Firefox is much the same as in any other browser you have used, particularly if you were using Netscape (or Mozilla) with your old OS. All you do is type the URL of the Web site you want to visit into the location bar, and away you go. If you would like to start each time on a personal home page, this is easily done.

Click on Edit in Firefox's menu bar and select Preferences. The Preferences window opens up with a left-hand Category panel, from which you select the part of Firefox you want to modify. By default, it opens up to the General category (Figure 10-9). Over on the right side, in the Home Page section, are three buttons. The first button, *Use Current Page*, will enter into

Figure 10–9   Setting your home page in Firefox's Preferences window.

the Location field as your home page whatever URL (or page) you are currently visiting. The middle button, *Use Bookmark*, brings up a dialog with your current bookmarks. Clicking the *Use Blank Page* button will start Firefox on a blank page. You could, of course, just type in the URL into the Location field, click OK, and be done.

 Quick Tip Before closing the Preferences dialog, notice that the Location field actually says Location(s). That's right, it could be plural. If you have multiple tabs open (which I cover next), the *Use Current Page* button becomes *Use Current Pages*. When you click the Home icon, Firefox will open tabs to all your favorite pages. If you want to manually enter a list of pages into the location bar, just separate each page with the pipe symbol, or " | " (usually found on the backslash key on your keyboard).

Firefox Does Tabs, Too

Before I tell you how tabs work in Firefox, it seems only fair to tell you that Firefox's older sibling, the Mozilla browser, had tabbed browsing before Konqueror did (particularly because I gave Konqueror first billing). The concept behind tabbed browsing in Firefox is the same as in Konqueror, but the keystrokes are a little different.

Start by visiting a site of your choice. Now click on File, select New, and choose New Tab from the drop-down menu. You can also use the <Ctrl+T> keyboard shortcut to do the same thing. Notice that Firefox now identifies your sites with tabs just below the location bar (Figure 10-10). Add a third or a fourth if you like. Switching from site to site is now just a matter of clicking the tabs on your single copy of Firefox.

While in tab mode (as shown in Figure 10-10), you can right-click on a tab to bring up the tab menu. From there you can close or reload the current tab (or all tabs) and even open new tabs. Another way to close the active tab is to click on the X just to the right of the tab list.

Still Don't Like Pop-Up Ads?

I have to mention this again because it is one of the things that make some of these Linux browsers so wonderful—the ability to stop unwanted pop-up

Figure 10–10 Firefox showing off its tabs.

window ads. Like Konqueror before, Firefox lets you do this easily. Actually, Firefox has pop-ups blocked by default, but you may want to alter that behavior for some sites. Here's how.

Start by bringing up the Preferences menu again (click Edit on the menu bar and choose Preferences). From the category list (Figure 10-11), choose Web Features. You'll see a checkbox labeled *Block Popup Windows*. Next to that is a button labeled Allowed Sites. Clicking this button allows you to specify sites where pop-ups may be desirable. When you are satisfied with your configuration, click OK to close the Preferences menu.

When Firefox intercepts a pop-up, it displays a message like the one in Figure 10-12. Clicking the bar as indicated offers you three choices. You can allow the pop-up or edit the pop-up blocker options. You also have the option of choosing never to see the message when pop-ups are blocked.

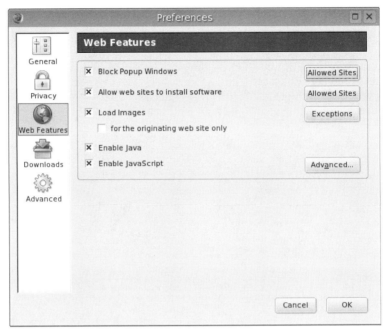

Figure 10–11   Firefox lets you specify sites where pop-ups are okay.

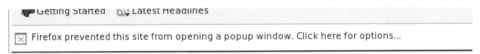

Figure 10–12   Firefox has blocked a pop-up. What would you like to do?

Controlling Cookies

Firefox is also very versatile in its handling of cookies. Before you excitedly turn off all cookies, do remember that they can be useful, particularly with online services such as banks and e-commerce sites. That said, you may very much want to curb cookie traffic as much as possible.

From the Preferences menu, open up the Privacy category submenu (Figure 10-13). Over on the right, you'll see *Cookies* in the list. Click the plus sign next to it to open your options.

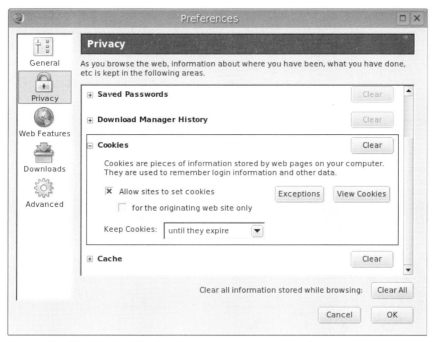

Figure 10–13   Back to Firefox's Preferences menu to configure cookie policies.

Unless you really want to refuse all cookies, leave the *Allow sites to set cookies* checkbox checked. Then, from the *Keep Cookies* drop-down box, choose *Ask me every time*. Click OK, and resume your surfing. When you visit a site that tries to set or modify a cookie, an message will pop up alerting you to the cookie and asking you how to proceed. If you decide to deny a cookie and you never want to see another cookie from that site, check *Use my choice for all cookies from this site* before clicking Deny (Figure 10-14).

Figure 10–14   A pop-up allows you to allow or deny a cookie.

The Firefox Sidebar

The Firefox sidebar is a quick way to get to your information, in this case browsing history and bookmarks. You can have one or the other at your side by clicking View on the menu bar and selecting the sidebar submenu. One quick way to activate the bookmarks sidebar is by pressing <Ctrl+B>. The same keystroke will banish the sidebar.

You may already know that your system keeps a history of Web sites you have visited. By default, that history goes back nine days. The amount of history can be set by clicking Edit on the menu bar and selecting Preferences. You'll find the History settings under Privacy, just as you did with Cookies.

To activate the history sidebar, choose it from the View menu (under Sidebar) or press <Ctrl+H>, and the sidebar will appear (Figure 10-15). The sidebar makes searching for a site you visited in the last few days easy. At the top of the sidebar, you'll see a search field. Just type your search keywords in the location bar and press <Enter>. Click on any link displayed and you will instantly be transported to that site.

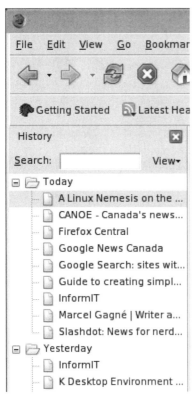

Figure 10–15   The Firefox history sidebar—it's just a jump to the past.

Wrapping Up

I started this chapter by telling you that Linux has many browsers available. If you like Firefox, you might also want to look at Mozilla as a full-featured browser suite featuring an e-mail client, HTML editor, and more. Find it at

```
http://www.mozilla.org/products/mozilla1.x/
```

On the GNOME side, we have *Epiphany*, which is based on Mozilla's rendering engine. If you installed support for both the KDE and GNOME desktops, you should have it already installed. Epiphany can be downloaded from

```
http://www.gnome.org/projects/epiphany
```

Another browser worth a look is *Opera*, an excellent, very fast, lightweight graphical browser that is distributed using an interesting model. The freeware version of the browser serves up small banner ads in the upper part of the browser as you use it; you can also purchase an ad-free version (which additionally gets you an Operamail account and support). To take Opera for a spin, you will have to head to the Opera Web site at `http://www.opera.com` and pick up a copy.

We can't stop there. Most Linux distributions come with several browsers, including some text-only browsers such as *lynx* and *links*. If these aren't already installed on your system, they are very likely on your distribution CDs.

 Shell Out When you feel like seeing the World Wide Web without its clutter of images, why not give lynx or links a try? Just open a Konsole shell and try the following:

```
lynx http://www.marcelgagne.com/
links http://www.marcelgagne.com/
```

You may be amazed at the speed and performance of nonflashy Web.

Resources

Epiphany, the GNOME Web Browser

http://www.gnome.org/projects/epiphany

Firefox

http://www.mozilla.org/products/firefox

Konqueror Web Site

http://www.konqueror.org

Links Text Web Browser

http://links.twibright.com

Lynx Browser

http://lynx.isc.org/

Mozilla

http://www.mozilla.org/products/mozilla1.x/

Opera

http://www.opera.com

Chapter

11

Electronic Mail Clients

These days, it seems that when we think about the Internet, we think about Web browsers first. To those of us who have been on the Net for more years than we care to admit, that always seems a bit strange. The chief medium of information exchange on the Internet has always been electronic mail, or e-mail. Although the perception has changed, e-mail is probably still the number-one application in the connected world.

For a powerful, graphical e-mail client, you need look no further than your KDE desktop. Its e-mail package is called KMail, and I'm going to tell you all about it. KMail can be run as a solo application, but it is also tightly integrated into the new and powerful Kontact groupware suite. Users coming from Outlook or similar clients will be familiar with the handy accessibility of multiple functions such as address books, calendars, and to-do lists. Keep reading, though. In just a few keystrokes, you'll be sending and receiving mail like a Linux pro.

I'm also going to talk about an alternative package called *Evolution*. Those of you who are coming from that other OS and who might be pining for the look and feel (and the integration) of Outlook are going to be pleasantly surprised. Evolution integrates many powerful features, including a contact manager and a well connected organizer.

Be Prepared . . .

Before we start, you will need to have some information handy. This includes your e-mail username and password as well as the SMTP and POP3 server addresses for sending and receiving your e-mail. All of this information will be provided for you by your Internet service provider (ISP) or your company's systems administrator.

Kontact

In the first edition of this book, I mentioned a great e-mail package for KDE called KMail. I'm still going to cover KMail, but in the last couple of years that story has taken on a number of interesting new chapters. KMail is still available as a stand-alone application, but you are most likely to first be introduced to it as part of the fantastic new Kontact personal information management suite.

Kontact is a full-featured and powerful information center. You'll most likely find Kontact in the Office submenu of your program launcher (the big K) or as a stand-alone icon in your Kicker panel. You can also start it by running the program name, `kontact`.

First Kontact

When the program runs for the first time, you'll be presented with an introductory menu from which you can read the Kontact manual, visit the Kontact Web site, or configure Kontact as a groupware client. Home users probably won't be interested in this feature. But if you are working in an office with a number of users and an existing groupware server, this is definitely something you'll be interested in (Figure 11-1).

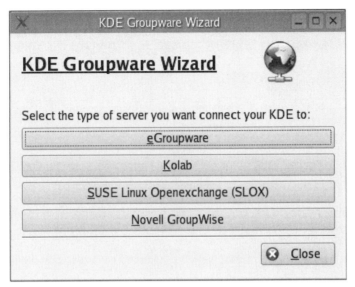

Figure 11–1   Business users will be very interested in the Kontact groupware integration.

If you prefer to skip the groupware configuration section, just click on the "Skip this introduction" link on the intro page and you'll be transported to the Kontact summary page. The Kontact suite is presented in a single-panel window with a sidebar on the left (Figure 11-2). That sidebar contains a lists of icons representing the components that make up the Kontact suite. By default you have a summary page, the KMail e-mail client, an address book for your contacts, a calendar and organizer, a to-do list, a daily journal, little yellow notes, a new aggregator , and a synchronization tool. Important dates like holidays and birthdays (from the entries in your address book) are also displayed.

Choosing what sort of information makes it onto the summary screen is simple. Click Settings on the menu bar, and select Configure Summary View from the list. The status of your mailbox isn't enabled by default, so this is one you may wish to turn on. Looking at Figure 11-2, you might have noticed a list of news stories from KDE Dot News. This is just a sample of a number of news sources you can add to the summary screen. Just click News Sources in the configuration sidebar and you are on your way.

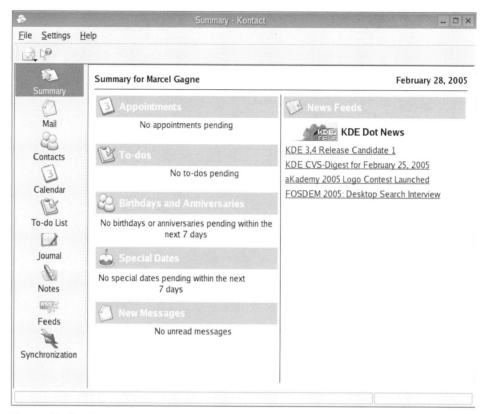

Figure 11–2 Kontact opens with a configurable summary screen.

Next time you start Kontact, you may not be looking at that summary screen. That's because the default behavior is to open whatever application you were last using, whether that is your e-mail, your address book, or your organizer. If you would like to see that summary screen each time you start Kontact (handy for those upcoming birthdays), click Settings on the Kontact menu bar and select Configure Kontact from the drop-down menu.

The resulting dialog lets you configure each of the individual components that make up the Kontact suite. In particular, look at the Kontact entry right at the top in the left-hand sidebar (Figure 11-3). To the right is an entry labeled "Always start with specified component," with a checkbox to the left. Make sure that box has been checked, and then select Summary from the drop-down list. Click Apply or OK to save your changes.

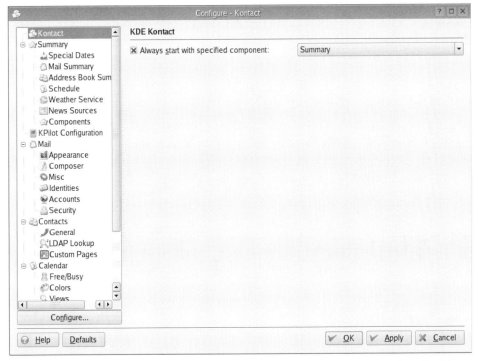

Figure 11–3   You can define which Kontact component you want at start time. In this case, the Summary screen is selected.

I cover the address book later in this chapter and the calendar and organizer application in Chapter 12. Let's move on to KMail now.

KMail

On a default installation of the KDE desktop, you'll find an icon for Kontact already sitting in your Kicker panel. The icon design will vary (mine is a globe with an envelope and a calendar page on top), but moving your mouse over the icons will reveal tooltips that will help you identify the application. Kontact, as I mentioned, is usually under the Office submenu. It's also possible to start KMail without Kontact by clicking the big K, looking into the Internet submenu, and selecting KMail from there.

Shell Out If you wish to start KMail from the shell, just type its command, `kmail &`, at the shell prompt. Alternatively, you can press <Alt+F2> and type the command there. For the remainder of this chapter, I'm going to work with KMail as it is represented in the Kontact personal information manager suite.

To run KMail from Kontact, simply click the Mail icon in the left-hand sidebar. You should see a window similar to that in Figure 11-4. The very first time you run KMail, it will create a number of default e-mail folders for you: inbox, outbox, sent-mail, trash, and drafts.

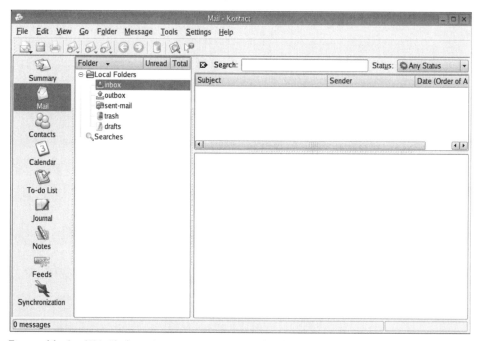

Figure 11–4   KMail's first-time screen as seen within Kontact.

Notice the folders listed down the left side. On the right is the mail window, where you'll read your messages. The top pane lists your messages, while the bottom pane displays the contents of those messages. Of course, before we can do any sending or receiving of e-mail, we need to tell KMail a little about ourselves.

Click Settings on the menu bar and select Configure KMail. Immediately after the Configure dialog starts (Figure 11-5), you will have to go through a little question-and-answer session. The sidebar has a list of icons labeled for their various sections: Identities (secret or otherwise), Accounts, Appearance, Composer, Security, and Misc.

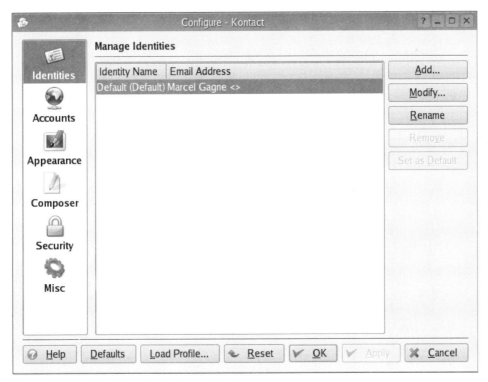

Figure 11–5 *Creating a default user identity.*

To the right, in the main Configure window, is a default identity waiting to be modified. Most people will only need to configure one identity, but you can have as many as you like. This is particularly handy if you use different signatures or return addresses for work and home. For now, we'll just stick with the default identity. Click Modify to continue.

The Edit Identity dialog is actually fairly simple, despite the five different configuration tabs: General, Cryptography, Advanced, Signature, and Picture (Figure 11-6). The information in the General tab is pretty self-explanatory. Enter your name, the name of your business or organization (you can leave this blank if you wish or enter something like "What organization?"), and your e-mail address.

I'll skip the Cryptography tab (where you can configure your OpenPGP or GnuPG encryption key) and head straight to the Advanced tab. The most important thing on this tab is the Reply-To address. Ninety-nine percent of the time, this is the same as your e-mail address. You may, however, want your contacts to reply to your e-mails using a different address than the one you use for outgoing mail. In my case, I enter the same address as my e-mail address and continue on. I should mention that you can specify different sent-mail and drafts folders here rather than going with the defaults used by KMail. You may wish to do this if you are using different identities.

If you would like a signature to be automatically added when you send mail, click on the Signatures tab and enter the information there. Note that you will have to click the Enable signature checkbox, after which you can enter what you would like to have appear at the end of your e-mails. There is also a drop-down list so that you can specify a text file with your signature or

Figure 11–6 What's your identity? It's time to tell KMail about yourself.

a program (or script) that automatically generates some sort of (no doubt, very clever) text dynamically.

Finally, should you choose to do so, the Picture tab allows you to configure a picture to include with e-mail messages that you send out. This can be a picture of yourself (or anything else for that matter). If you choose to do this, you might want to keep the picture small. There are still people using dial-up out there, and a large image attached to every message isn't necessarily the nicest thing to do. When you are done, click OK to close the Edit Identity dialog.

The Importance of Being Networked

Now that KMail knows who you are and what kind of wittiness you like to provide at the end of your communication, you are no doubt anxious to send and receive some mail. For that you need a little network configuration. Click on the Accounts icon in the Configure KMail dialog sidebar, and you'll wind up with two tabbed windows on the right-hand side—one for Sending and one for Receiving (Figure 11-7). Let's start with Receiving tab, since it's usually the easier of the two to set up.

Figure 11–7 Setting up network accounts in KMail.

You can actually specify different transports here, as well as different hosts to use for outgoing mail. Click Add to create a new account. A small dialog box will appear asking you to specify a Transport. Your choices are SMTP and Sendmail, with SMTP selected by default. *Sendmail* (as well as Postfix and others) is an industrial-strength mail server used by businesses who run their own domains. Your Linux system is quite capable of acting as its own mail server. That said, most ISPs I know of don't allow home users to pass sendmail traffic through their servers. That makes the default choice of SMTP the only choice for most people.

Choosing SMTP will bring up the Add Transport dialog (Figure 11-8), where you will specify a name for this connection (this is just a name that means something to you, such as "My ISP"), the mail Host (which your ISP or office will provide), and a Port number. Although technically your ISP could run an SMTP host on something other than port 25 (the default), this will likely never happen. Accept the default of 25, click OK, and you are ready to send. That means we are halfway there.

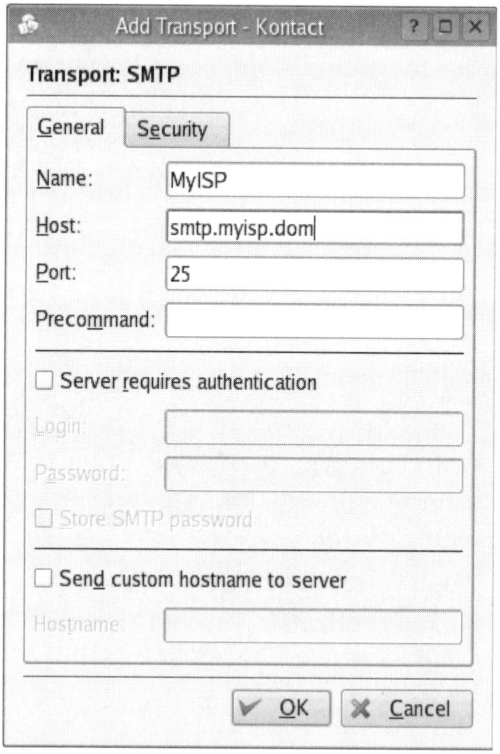

Figure 11–8
SMTP server configuration.

Click on the Receiving tab to prepare Kmail for your incoming mail, and then click on the Add button on the right. A small box will appear asking you for the type of account you want to set up. Your choices are Local Mailbox, POP3, IMAP, Disconnected IMAP, and Maildir mailbox. Most ISPs are still using POP3 as the default mail delivery protocol, but this is something you should make sure of. If you are setting up your PC in an office environment, you are likely going to use either IMAP or POP3. Again, check with your systems administrator. When you are happy with your choice, click OK, and you should be presented with the dialog box shown in Figure 11-9.

Figure 11–9   Setting up a POP3 mail account.

The Add Account dialog window will appear, and this is where you configure your account. Please note that you can configure a number of different accounts, and all of them can be accessed through KMail (just as you could configure many identities).

Start by filling in the Account name: field. Once again, this is just a name that makes sense to you, so it can be anything you like. The Login, Password, and Host information will be provided by your ISP or system administrator. As with the SMTP port 25 discussions earlier, although it is *unlikely* that your ISP could use something other than port 110 for POP3 (or 143 for IMAP), it's still *possible,* so you might want to check. For the most part, you can safely leave those settings as the default.

Before you go clicking OK in all this excitement, there are a couple of other options you should consider. Notice the checkbox on the window that says *Store POP password.* Unless you want to be asked for your password each and every time you check your mail, it is probably a good idea to check that box here. You probably also want to make sure that *Leave fetched messages on the server* is unchecked.

The last thing I want to point out is near the bottom of the window, the Destination folder option. Most people will want to have their new mail arrive in their inboxes. But for those of you who are going to configure multiple accounts and identities (there's a joke there somewhere), this is where you will specify different folders for each of those accounts and personalities—uh, I mean *identities.*

Before we wrap on creating a POP3 (or IMAP) mail account, take a moment to look at the *Extras* tab. If your ISP or company uses encrypted mail downloads or an alternate method of authentication, you may need to set it here. There is a button on the *Extras* tab that allows you to *Check What the Server Supports.* Usually, you'll choose whatever your ISP or systems administrator has prepared for you. When you have entered all the information, Click OK, then click Apply, and then click OK once more to leave the configuration settings.

 Note If at this point the system presents you with the KWallet, select Basic setup and click Next. On the screen that follows, enter a master password (you can leave it empty, but this is very insecure), and click Finish. You'll then get a message telling you that Kontact has requested access to the wallet. Click *Allow Always.*

For more details on the KWallet system, see the following document on my own Web site at this address:

`http://www.marcelgagne.com/cwl042004.html.`

That's all there is to it. If you are connected to your ISP or through your company LAN, you can start sending and receiving mail. For those who configured an IMAP account, you'll notice a folder with that account's name in your folder list. When you click on the plus sign beside the folder, KMail will connect to your IMAP server and show you the rest of your folders. Take a look at Figure 11-10 for a look at a new KMail window.

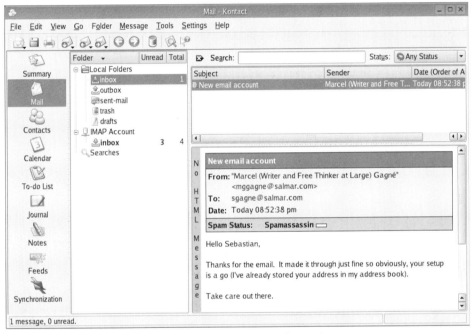

Figure 11–10   KMail with one IMAP account in the folders list.

Now that your e-mail account, including the incoming and outgoing mail servers, is configured, it's time to send some mail.

Let's Communicate!

Sending messages is easy. Click on the New Message icon—it's the first one at the top left, just below the File menu. If you like the idea of keyboard shortcuts, press <Ctrl+N>, and you'll achieve the same result. The KMail composer window (Figure 11-11) will appear, and you can start typing your message.

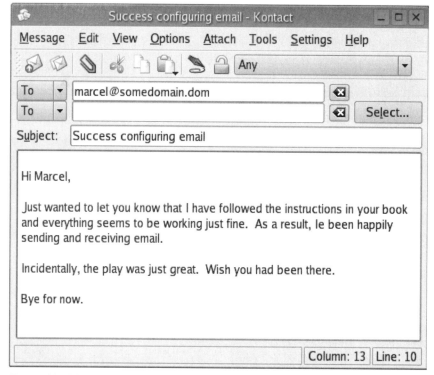

Figure 11–11   Writing an e-mail message in the composer window.

I'm working on the premise that you have all sent e-mail at some point; I'll let you take it from there. Fill in who the message is going to and the subject of your message, and then start writing. When you are ready to send the message, click the Send Message icon (directly under the Message menu on the KMail composer menu bar). For the keyboard wizards out there, try <Ctrl+Enter>.

Receiving Mail

To pick up your mail, click File on the menu bar and select Check mail. You can also use a <Ctrl+L> keyboard shortcut or the Check Mail In icon (Figure 11-12). It is usually fourth from the left in the icon bar.

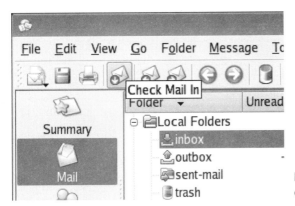

Figure 11–12
Checking for mail with a click.

Your Little Black Book

All you ladies and gentlemen reading this book have by now wondered when I was going to talk about address books. After all, e-mail implies some kind of socializing, whether it be e-mail or personal. When composing an e-mail message (as in Figure 11-11), notice the *Select* button at the end of the *To:* field. Clicking this button will bring up a simplified list of e-mail addresses from your address book, from which you can select who you would like the message to go out to.

The only problem is that you probably don't have anything in the address book at this moment. Assuming you are starting from scratch, look in the Kontact sidebar and you'll see an icon labeled Contacts. When KDE's address book opens up, click on File and select New Contact, or click the icon directly beneath the File menu. The keyboard wizards can press <Ctrl+N>. You will see the dialog box shown in Figure 11-13.

When the Entry Editor appears, add whatever information is appropriate for the contact. The person's name and his or her e-mail address are sufficient if these are all you need. When you are done entering information, click OK. You can add as many names as you want in one sitting. To save your address book as you go, click that little diskette icon in the toolbar. When you do close, your changes are saved automatically.

Another way to add names to your address book (and by far the *easiest*) is to take the address from a message that has been sent to you. While you are viewing someone's e-mail to you, right-click on the e-mail address in the From field. Click Add to Address Book, and you are done. A small pop-up menu will appear (Figure 11-14).

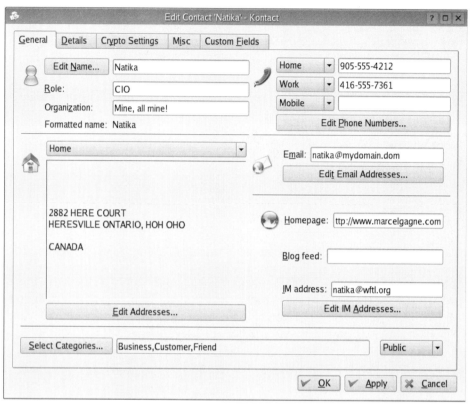

Figure 11–13   New contact address book information.

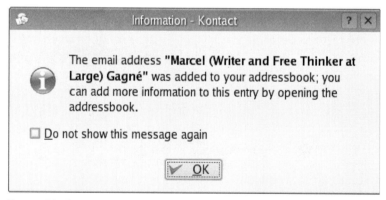

Figure 11–14   Right-click an address from KMail to quickly add it.

Explore The KDE address book (Contacts under the Kontact suite) is a very powerful piece of software. I've only given you the basics, but there is a lot more to explore. Click *View* on the menu bar and select *Add View*. Perhaps a Rolodex-style card view is more to your liking.

Attached to You . . .

As you sit there writing your letter to your old high school friend, it occurs to you that it might be fun to include a recent picture of yourself (with your spouse and new baby). After all, you haven't seen each other in 20 years. To attach a file, click on the paper clip icon directly below the menu bar. If you have a Konqueror file manager window open, you can also drag an icon from Konqueror into your composer window. In fact, if you have an icon on your desktop, you can drag that into your composer as well, and the images (or documents) will be automatically attached.

If you prefer the menu bar, click on Attach and select Attach File. The Attach File dialog window appears, giving you the opportunity to navigate your directories to find the appropriate file. Directly to the left of the navigation bar is an icon that lets you turn the preview mode on and off. This is handy when you are trying to find the right picture to attach. Figure 11-15 shows this dialog in use.

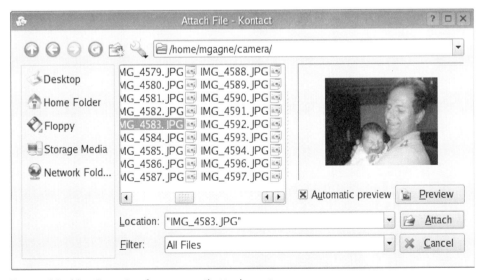

Figure 11–15   Browsing for an e-mail attachment.

Once you have attached a file, it will show up in a separate attachments pane in your composer window. From there you can select those attachments and change your mind. Right-click on the attachment and select Remove.

Send Now or Later

People who aren't online all the time may find that it makes more sense to queue messages rather then to send them immediately. When the time is more convenient (or you are online), you can send all of the queued messages. To do this, write your message as always. When you are ready, click Message on the menu bar and select Send Later; the messages will be transferred to your outbox folder. You can also click the icon directly to the right of KMail's Send icon (on the default KDE theme, it looks like stacked envelopes). To actually *send* the messages, dial up to your ISP, click File on the menu bar, and select Send Queued Messages. Note that this menu option will be grayed out if there are no messages in your outbox.

Convenient timing affects more than just when you are online; it also influences when you can finish an e-mail message you happen to be working on. Let's say that you are composing a rather long message to Aunt Sybil, who lives in Australia. After about an hour of typing, you realize that you were supposed to be at your brother's wedding. Looking at your watch, you note that you only have 10 minutes to get to the wedding, and Aunt Sybil's e-mail will certainly take another hour. Because you've already done all this work and you don't want to risk losing it, consider saving your e-mail in your drafts folder.

From the composer window, click Message on the menu bar and select Save in Drafts Folder. When you are ready to resume your e-mail (after the wedding, of course), click on the drafts folder and double-click on your e-mail in process.

Evolution

What's hard for some people moving to Linux is saying goodbye to certain familiar applications. Two of the most commonly used e-mail packages in the Windows world are Outlook and its cousin, Outlook Express. Those users will feel right at home on their new Linux desktops when they fire up *Evolution*. Figure 11-16 will no doubt seem extremely familiar. In fact, Evolution looks and feels like Outlook, but with some very important improvements.

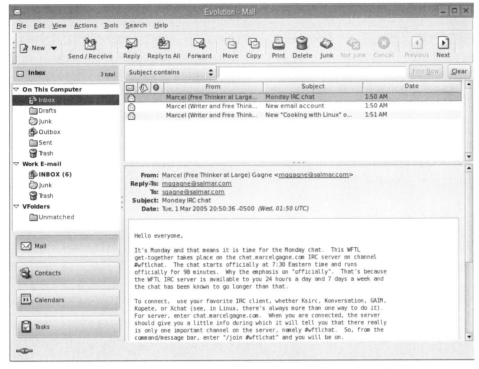

Figure 11–16 Evolution will make Microsoft Outlook users feel right at home.

Once again, it is likely that you will find Evolution on your distribution CD. Another way to get a copy is to head over to

```
http://gnome.org/projects/evolution/
```

the Web site for the Evolution package.

Clarification Evolution was originally Ximian Evolution. Ximian was bought by Novell, which still distributes and contributes to Evolution. Evolution is also a GNOME project, and you can also download the package from there. Novell Evolution and GNOME Evolution are the same thing, but you can get it from two different locations, and both are listed in the Resources section.

Upon starting Evolution for the first time, you will be presented with the Evolution Setup Assistant to take you through the various preparatory steps. After clicking Forward through the introductory window, you'll be asked for your default identity. This is where you enter your full name and e-mail address, along with other options, such as a Reply-To address (Figure 11-17).

Figure 11–17   Evolution's Setup Assistant.

When you are done, click Forward, and it will be time to enter information for receiving mail. You start by selecting a Server Type. For most users, this will be POP or IMAP, as with KMail. Evolution allows you to set up other servers as well, including Novell GroupWise and USENET news. Now enter the hostname of the POP3 or IMAP host (as provided by your ISP) as well as your username. If you don't want to enter your password each and every time Evolution checks for mail, you should click the *Remember password* checkbox. When you click Forward, you'll have the opportunity to decide whether Evolution checks for mail automatically (the default is to check every 10 minutes). Don't set this unless you are always connected; otherwise you can choose whatever interval suits you. Click Forward again, and you will be able to configure your outgoing mail.

The default Server Type for sending is SMTP, and that is almost certainly what you will need. Enter the hostname as provided by your ISP (or system administrator), and click Next. The Account Management screen follows, with your new e-mail account listed as it will be displayed in Evolution. You could change this to be a name rather than an e-mail address if you prefer. When you are done here, click Forward.

You are almost done. The final step is to select your time zone. Select an area on the map (preferably near to where you live) to narrow down your search. The map will zoom in to the area you clicked, allowing you to fine-tune your selection (Figure 11-18). Make your final selection (you can use the drop-down box to aid in your selection), click Forward again, then Apply, and you are done.

Evolution starts up with a list of resources "On This Computer" high-lighted in the left-hand sidebar. The most notable of these resources is, of course, your e-mail (see Figure 11-19). Like the Outlook package in Windows, a set of icons runs down the left-hand sidebar, giving you access to your Calendar, Tasks, Contacts, and e-mail.

Sending and Receiving Mail

To send a message, start by clicking on the Inbox icon (under the Shortcuts sidebar), and then click the New button just below the menu bar. By default, Evolution creates a new Mail Message, but notice as well that there is a drop-down arrow just beside the word New. Click that arrow, and you can create an appointment (more on that in Chapter 11), a contact, a task, and so on. To create a new mail message, you can also click File on the menu bar and select New and then Mail Message from there. Evolution's compose window will appear (Figure 11-20).

As with KMail, this is pretty standard stuff. Fill in the person's e-mail address in the To: field, enter a Subject, and type your message. When you have completed your message, click the Send button on the compose window (or click File on the compose window's menu bar and then select Send).

Figure 11–18   Evolution's Setup Assistant zooms in to help in selecting your time zone.

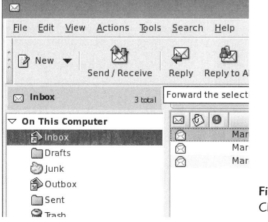

Figure 11–19
Close-up of "On This Computer."

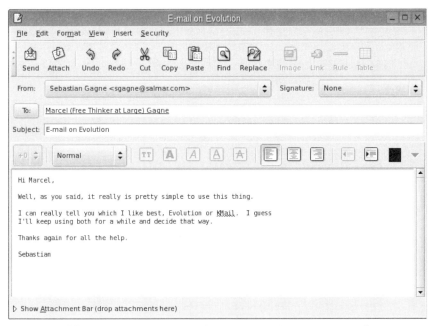

Figure 11–20   Sending a message with Evolution—the compose window.

To pick up your e-mail, make sure once again that you have the Inbox button selected; then click the Send/Receive button (Figure 11-21) at the top of Evolution's main window (or click Actions on the menu bar and select Send/Receive).

Figure 11–21   Click Send/Receive to check for and send e-mail.

The first time you pick up your mail, Evolution will pause and ask you for the password (Figure 11-22). You have an interesting choice to make here. Beside the words *Remember this password* is a checkbox that lets you lock in the information. If you choose not to record your password with Evolution, you will have to enter your password each time you check for mail.

Figure 11–22   Remember the password?

Like Microsoft Outlook, Evolution is an integrated contact management, e-mail, and scheduling system all in one. Aside from basic e-mail functionality, you can plan your day, set alarms, keep a contact list, and more. I discuss some of those capabilities in more detail when I cover ways to stay organized in the next chapter.

What to Use?

As to whether you use KMail or Evolution (or some of the other options I mention in a moment), this is something you will have to experiment with in order to decide. Personal preference is a huge factor here. I, for one, enjoy the fact that I can run KMail on its own. Historically, I'm not a big fan of integrated clients, but that is strictly a personal preference and one that may change. Others can't imagine using anything other than Evolution, for reasons that are exactly opposite to the one I mentioned. It's your system and your choice. The best way to discover what you want is to try things out.

Other Options

In this chapter, I've introduced you to KMail and Evolution. By no means should you look at these as your only options. If you are used to working with Mozilla mail in the Windows world, these very options are available with Linux, and they work exactly the same. Currently, there is a new addition to the Mozilla lineup for e-mail, and it is well worth looking into. It's called Thunderbird, and it's taking the Windows and Linux world by storm, along with its older sibling, the Firefox Web browser.

Graphical clients aren't the only things available either. Some people find they prefer to work with text-only clients. After all, e-mail is primarily about writing and reading words and less about attached files. The average Linux distribution installs a handful of very nice, text-only e-mail clients. Notable among these are *mutt* (http://www.mutt.org) and *pine* (http://www.washington.edu/pine/). In both cases, check your distribution CDs before you download.

Resources

KMail Homepage

http://kmail.kde.org

Mozilla Thunderbird

http://www.mozilla.org/products/thunderbird/

Novell Evolution

http://www.novell.com/products/desktop/features/evolution.html

GNOME Evolution

http://gnome.org/projects/evolution/

Chapter

12

Getting Organized

It is sometimes hard for me to fathom as I look at the piles of papers, books, cables, devices, and toys scattered across my desk that computers have helped in getting us more organized. No, it's true. Work with me here.

Once upon a time, I made appointments, scribbled down the information, and hoped that I'd find it again later. Maybe it wasn't an appointment, but somebody's birthday. Either way, if I got lucky and managed to find my paper planner (or scrap of paper) in time, I might just make it to where I was supposed to be. My friends will tell you that I was always 20 minutes late. These days, I'm only 5 minutes late. The reason? My personal digital assistant. Currently, it is a Palm Zire 72, but I have had others. There's nothing like an alarm going off to remind you that, yes, you do have something planned.

I keep my PDA backed up and synced to the notebook computer on which I do my writing. My notebook also has a copy of the calendar, complete with all its appointments, in a great little piece of software called KOrganizer (part of the Kontact personal information management suite I told you about in the introduction to Chapter 11). Now if I happen to leave my PDA in another part of the house, a second piece of software is ready to warn me when I'm supposed to return a phone call. My life is far from being perfectly organized, but, trust me, its organization has improved dramatically. In time, I aim to be only 2 minutes late.

I start this chapter with a look at KOrganizer. After that, I give you a tour of Evolution and its organizer tools. Ready? Great. Let's synchronize those watches.

KOrganizer

KOrganizer is included as part of your KDE desktop. It is a feature-packed time management system and electronic organizer that could become one of the most important tools on your desktop. Besides the obvious calendar and schedule capabilities, KOrganizer features group scheduling, to-do lists, import and export of calendar data (e.g., holidays), and sharing of free/busy lists, to name just a few of its features.

Start KOrganizer by clicking on the K menu and launching Kontact. If you would prefer to launch KOrganizer on its own, look under Office applications in the K menu. For now, I'm going to look at the package as part of the Kontact suite. When Kontact starts, click Calendar in the left-hand sidebar.

 Shell Out If you wish to start KOrganizer from the shell, just type its command, `korganizer &`, at the shell prompt. Alternatively, you can press <Alt+F2> and type the command there.

Okay, let's jump right in and have a look at the KOrganizer window as seen through Kontact (Figure 12-1). You may want to adjust or maximize the display to suit your viewing preferences.

Along the top is the familiar menu bar, and directly below that is the icon bar. The icon bar in this case is highly geared to navigating the calendar. Pausing over each button with the mouse pointer will bring up a tooltip identifying

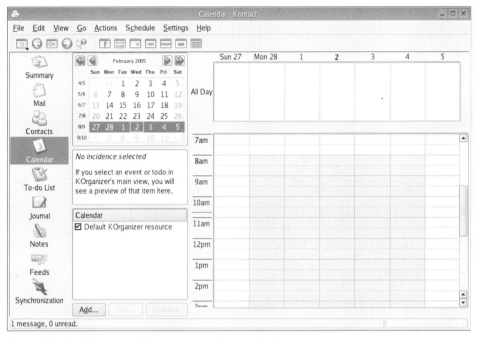

Figure 12–1   The main KOrganizer window under Kontact.

that button's function. With a single click, you can switch from a single-day view, a seven-day week (as well as a five-day workweek), a three-day view, or a full month. Previous versions of KOrganizer let you enter to-do items here, but this new version breaks to-dos into a separate application under Kontact (look for it in the sidebar). You can also switch views by clicking *View* on the menu bar and choosing the display you would like to see. If, after moving around in the calendar, you want to find yourself back at today, click *Go* on the menu bar and select *Go to Today*.

The left-hand side of the screen provides a small calendar (known as the *Date Navigator*) that lets you jump quickly to any day, month, or year. Below that is a small window that will display a preview of any event or to-do items you select. Before we start adding things to our calendar, have a look at the final window on the bottom left, the one labeled "Calendar." When you started KOrganizer, you loaded up the default calendar (labeled Default KOrganizer resource on my system), which makes sense since we are starting with a clean slate. Over on the right-hand side, taking up most of the screen real estate, is the main window. This is where most of the action takes place.

Adding an Event

Let's just jump right in and add an appointment. Using the Date Navigator, choose an appropriate date. If you want your appointment to be on the same day, you can quickly jump to that day by clicking *Go* on the menu bar and selecting *Go to Today*. Start an appointment by double-clicking in a chosen time slot on the main window. Another way to start a new event is to click *Actions* on the menu bar and select *New Event*. I'll choose 10:00 am for this example. You should now be looking at the New Event dialog (Figure 12-2).

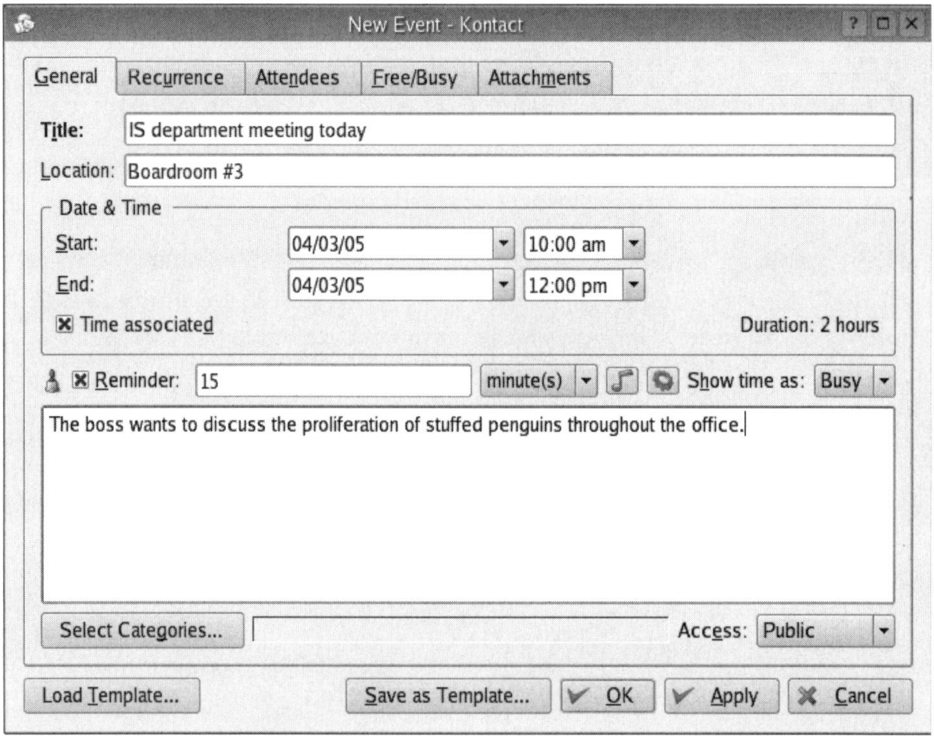

Figure 12–2   Adding an event in KOrganizer.

There is a lot we can do in terms of describing an event. The five tabs at the top hint at some of those possibilities. For the moment, let's keep this first example simple and stick to the information in the *General* tab. Enter a Title (e.g., IS department meeting today) for the event and a Location (e.g., Boardroom #3). The default duration time of 2 hours can be changed by clicking on the drop-down box for the Start and End times. Speaking of start times, this is one meeting we don't want to miss, so click on the checkbox next to the bell icon and just to the left of *Reminder*. Usually, it's good to have something more than a 1-minute reminder, so change this to 15 minutes.

Take a look to the right of the reminder time, specifically the drop-down list that currently says "minute(s)." You'll see two icons there. The first icon has a musical note on it. This is so you can set some kind of sound file to go off when the alarm pops up. You might not be at your desk but still within hearing range, or perhaps you want to annoy your coworkers. Clicking this icon will start the Open File dialog, from which you can select the appropriate wav format file. You'll find sounds for various applications in numerous places on your system. Some sounds are included with the KOrganizer application, and you'll find those under

```
/usr/share/apps/korganizer/sounds
```

The `alert.wav` file is particularly attention-getting. The second icon (directly to the right of the musical note) lets you set a program. Perhaps 5 minutes before the meeting is a great time to have the system automatically start a game of solitaire or patience (`/usr/bin/kpat`).

We're almost done entering our first event. That large box just below the reminder bell lets you enter more detailed notes on the event. Below the comment box and to the left, click on the button labeled *Select Categories*. KOrganizer provides a handful of useful preset categories (Figure 12-3), but

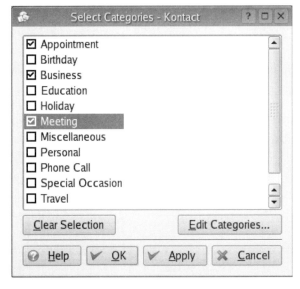

Figure 12–3
Selecting categories to assign to your event.

you can easily add more by clicking the *Edit Categories* button. Make your selection (or make several), and then click *OK*.

You'll find yourself back at the Edit Event dialog. Click OK to close the dialog and you are done! When the alarm time appears, you'll see a pop-up box similar to Figure 12-4. To acknowledge the alarm, click OK. You can also press the equivalent of a snooze button by setting a *Suspend duration* time, in minutes, and clicking the *Suspend* button.

Figure 12–4   It's alarming! Time for that meeting.

We'll get back to looking at more complex events shortly. For now, let's take a look at entering a to-do item.

So Much To Do . . .

To-Do items in KOrganizer can be added in a similar fashion to adding events, but they have some very different properties. To start a new to-do item, click *Action* on the menu bar and select *New To-do*. You can also start a new to-do by clicking and holding down the New Event icon at the upper right. If you hold the mouse click, you'll find that a drop-down list appears from which you can create an e-mail message, a contact for your address book, an event, a to-do item, a journal entry, or a note. Whichever method you choose, once you've elected to create a new to-do item, the New To-do dialog will appear (Figure 12-5).

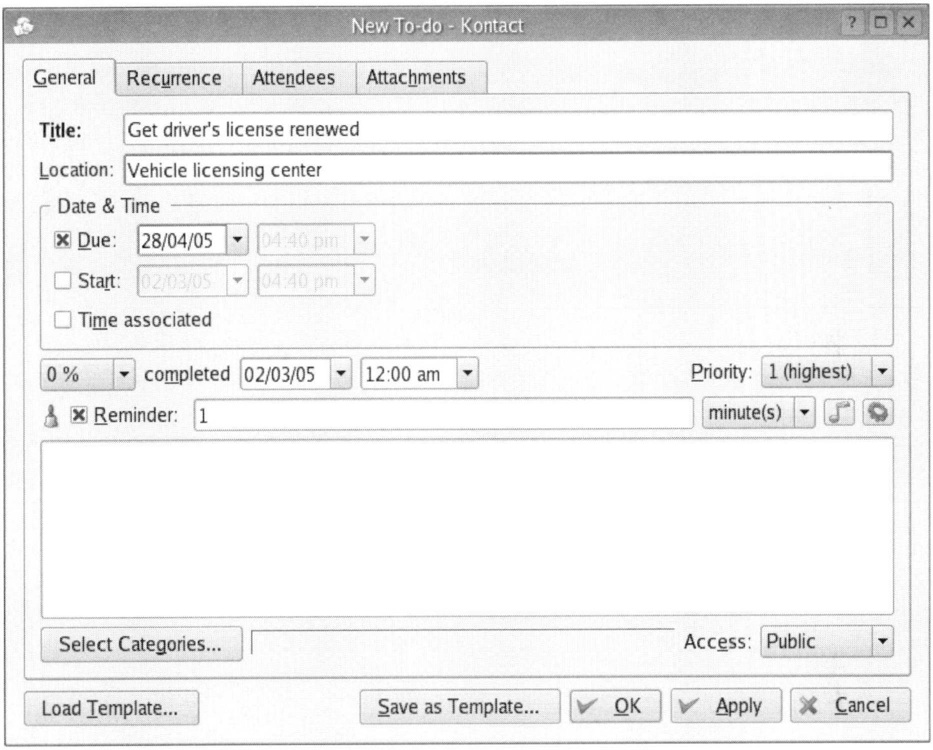

Figure 12–5   Entering a new to-do item.

Along the top of the New To-do dialog are four tabs: General, Recurrence, Attendees, and Attachments. For the first part of this example, I'm going to concentrate on the General tab. Much of what you see here is quite similar to what you saw when entering an event. Start by giving your to-do or task a Title (e.g., Get driver's license renewed). Then, if necessary, enter a Location (e.g., Vehicle licensing center).

Many times, a to-do item is something that needs to get done, sometimes with a due date in mind, and sometimes it just needs to get done *sometime*. If the item does have a due date, click the *Due* checkbox. For items that have a specific date associated with the start of your task, click *Start* and enter a start date and time. For instance, I might need to have my license sticker by April 28, but I might want to start working on it a couple of weeks earlier than that. If the task in question has a specific time associated with it, click the *Time associated* checkbox and enter that information as well.

Below the Date & Time information is a section regarding the status of the to-do item. Since tasks may be worked on over several days or weeks, you can update the to-do item from time to time by adjusting the percent completed value. Obviously, in the case of my license sticker, it is either done or it isn't. However, a report to a customer or a long-term project you are working on is just such an item. Furthermore, tasks and to-dos often have a priority associated with them. By default, everything has a priority value of 5. Priorities can be adjusted from 9 at the low end to 1 for the highest priority. You can also choose an *unspecified* priority.

Just a little over halfway down the page, below the *Reminder* settings, is a large area for entering additional detail about this current task. As you did when entering information for an event, it is possible to assign categories to the to-do items. When you have everything entered, click *OK*.

If your to-do item did not have an associated time, it will appear not directly in the calendar view, but above it as an all-day item. You can also see a complete list of to-do items and get a more detailed view by clicking the To-do List icon in the Kontact sidebar. The results will be displayed in a nice, tabular format, as in Figure 12-6. To return to the normal KOrganizer view, click the Calendar icon in the Kontact sidebar once again.

> *Tip* To enter a superquick to-do item, click inside the box just above the to-do list in the Kontact To-do List view. You'll see a field with the words "Click to add a new to-do" in gray. Enter your few words of information and press <Enter>. A to-do item will be created without a specific date and with a priority of 5.

Printing Your Calendar

Paperless society aside, there are times when nothing beats hard copy. Printing the day's calendar is easy to do. Select the day you want to print (you might find it easier to switch to a one-day view for this), click File on the menu bar, and select Print. KOrganizer's print dialog will appear (Figure 12-7), with a list of options. Click the appropriate radio button to select either a sin-

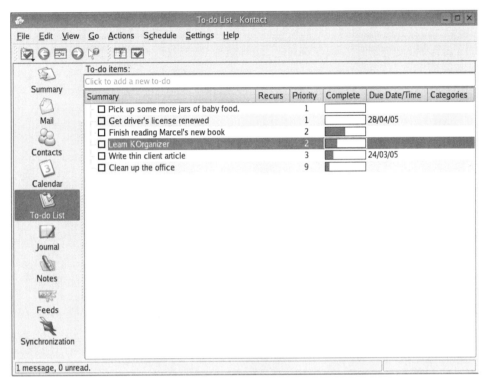

Figure 12–6 Viewing your list of to-do items in Kontact.

gle day, a week, a month, or your to-do items. You have the opportunity here to select a different day or a range of days, depending on the type of report you want. Before you go and click that Print button, select "Print week" if you haven't already done so. A "Type of View" dialog will appear on the print window to let you select the style of printed page—Filofax style, timetable, or split week view. When you are happy with your settings, click *Print*. Note that these are all single-page views (one day per page, one week per page, etc.), with the exception of the split week view.

Wow! Déjà Vu: Recurring Events

If that Monday morning IS status meeting is something you have to attend every two weeks, it doesn't make sense to enter the event over and over. That's the whole point of recurrence, and it's the first advanced event configuration I want to look at. Double-click on the Monday (or whatever day you

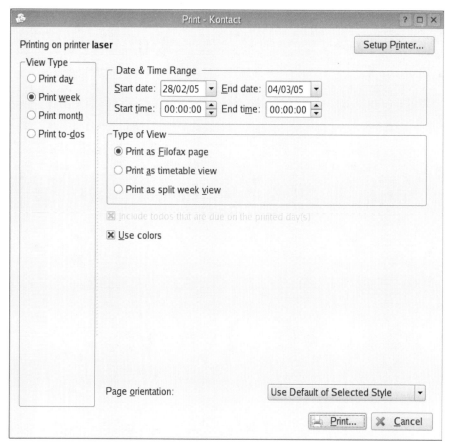

Figure 12–7   Getting ready to print your calendar.

chose) meeting you created earlier (or create a new entry). When I had you enter your first event, I concentrated my attention on the *General* tab. There are four other tabs in the KDE 3.4 version of KOrganizer: *Recurrence, Attend-ees, Free/Busy,* and *Attachments.*

To activate a recurring event, click on the Recurrence tab (Figure 12-8), and start by clicking on the Enable recurrence checkbox. Directly below the checkbox, you will see the initial information relating to the event you cre-ated. Below that is the Recurrence Rule. Click the radio button that matches the kind of recurrence you want to assign to that event. For our IS meeting, I would click Weekly. To the right of that, I have the option of selecting whether this weekly recurrence is every week or the second, third, or fourth week. In ths example, I've set the meeting up for every 2 weeks.

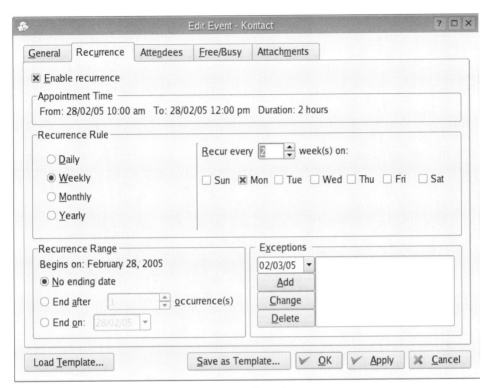

Figure 12–8 *Setting an event to recur every 2 weeks.*

Perhaps this meeting relates to a project that is currently under way and, therefore, the recurrence will end in another couple of months. That's the idea behind the *Recurrence Range* (bottom left). Select a date for the termination of the recurrence, or specify a fixed number of occurrences.

Finally, look to the right. You'll see an area for entering exceptions to the rule you are creating (perhaps you get a few of those weekly meetings off for good behavior). Click the drop-down box, and a small calendar (like the Date Navigator) will drop down. Select the date you want, and the calendar retracts. Click Add, and you have your exceptions. When you are happy with your changes, click *OK*.

Inviting Others to an Event

Meetings would not be a lot of fun if only one person attended. All right, maybe they would be fun, but a one-person meeting is a contradiction. In a moment, we'll create (or update) an event so that it isn't too lonely. Before we do that, however, I'd like you to configure a small piece of groupware functionality in KOrganizer. You'll see why in a few minutes, when we start inviting people to our meetings.

When I introduced you to Kontact, in the preceding chapter, I mentioned that Kontact could integrate with a number of groupware servers. The setting I'm talking about isn't on that level, but it is important for group scheduling. Start by clicking Settings on the menu bar and selecting Configure KOrganizer. When the Configure dialog appears, click Group Scheduling in the left-hand sidebar (Figure 12-9).

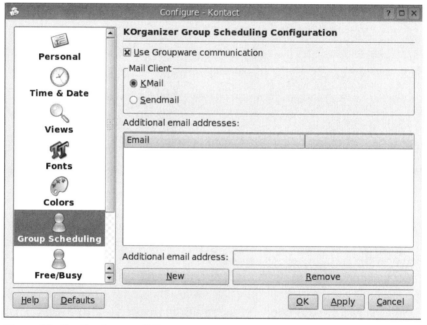

Figure 12–9   Configuring KOrganizer to use groupware communication.

Look in the right-hand side pane at the top and you'll see a checkbox labeled Use Groupware communication. Make sure that is checked on. The mail client default should stay as KMail. Now click OK, and we are ready to continue with our big meeting.

Either double-click on an existing event or start a new one. After making sure you have the information you need in the *General* tab, click on the *Attendees* tab (Figure 12-10).

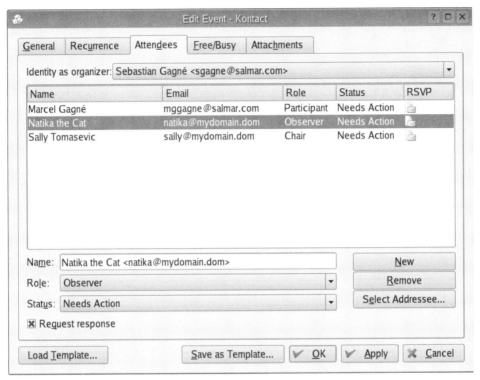

Figure 12–10 Adding and defining the role of attendees to an event.

In the beginning, there will be no entries on the page. There are two ways to enter information. The first is to click *New* and then to enter a name in the *Name* field and an e-mail address in the *Email* field. You can also choose from a list of names in your address book by clicking the Select Addressee button. A dialog box will appear with a list of names currently in your address book. Select a name by clicking on it, and then click the OK button to add it. That's all there is to it.

Look below the *Email* field and you'll see a drop-down box for *Role*. From this list, select what role the attendee will have in this event. You can select from Participant, Optional Participant, Observer, and Chair. Below the *Role* selection we have *Status*. This is the status of the attendee, as selected from Needs Action, Accepted, Declined, Tentative, Delegated, Completed, and In Process. In all likelihood, you'll want confirmation from those people invited to your meeting, so click the *Request response* checkbox. A small e-mail icon will appear to the right of the attendee's information. Should no response be necessary, a red X will appear instead.

Now that we have our event scheduled, recurrence information taken care of, and our list of attendees defined, we can click OK to close and save this entry. If, as in this case, attendees are associated with the event, a dialog box will pop up informing us of this and asking whether an e-mail should be sent to those people (Figure 12-11). This is the reason we activated the group-ware feature a few paragraphs back. The correct answer here is probably Yes. A KMail message will be created with the list of attendees in the To: field. Review the message and click the Send icon (or press <Ctrl+Enter>).

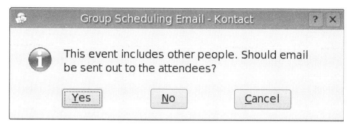

Figure 12-11   Should attendees be sent an e-mail invitation?

What Happens When You Get Invited?

The invitation e-mail goes out with an iCal attachment (the attachment will have a an extension of .ics). That means that any iCal-compliant organizer software will be able to import the item (as I discuss in just a moment). You can save the attachment to your folder or directory and import it manually.

Those running Kontact, however, will find this just too easy. The message will have an attachment with the words Accept, Accept cond., and Decline at the end of the event information. If the meeting time and date are okay with you, click Accept, and the meeting will automatically be entered into your KOrganizer. It's that easy!

Importing Calendars

Do you find that there's just not enough penciled in to your calendar? This little tip can help you out. KOrganizer can import iCal-format files to supplement the current list of information in the default calendar. This can be someone else's calendar (or your old iCal files). But as it turns out, a number of sites on the Internet provide downloadable calendar files that cover local holidays, television schedules, historical events, concert tour dates, and a whole lot more. Using Konqueror, pay a visit to www.icalshare.com for plenty to choose from. Given the truly impressive list of calendars on the site, you are bound to find something you *need*.

Importing a calendar is easy. Find something you like (a calendar of astronomical events, for instance) and save it to your home directory. Then, from KOrganizer, click *File* and then *Import*. When the file selection dialog appears, navigate to where you downloaded your iCal file and click <OK>. A final dialog will appear offering you some interesting choices (Figure 12-12).

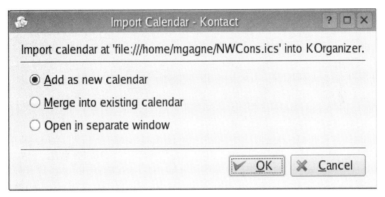

Figure 12–12   When importing calendars, consider your options.

 Warning! All right, this is not all that scary, but the more calendars (iCal files) you import and merge into your KOrganizer, the more cluttered things will start to appear. Keep that in mind as you populate your calendar with all sorts of interesting events. This is a good argument for adding calendars rather than merging them into your existing calendar. That way you can turn them on and off with a mouse click.

Evolution

In the preceding chapter, I mentioned that Evolution was a great e-mail client for those coming from the Windows world, particularly if they were used to working with Outlook. This is equally true when working with Evolution's calendaring applications.

Take a look along the top of the application, just below the menu bar (Figure 12-13). The icons to the left let you quickly create appointments, send and receive e-mail, print, and so on. The icons to the right represent five calendar views: a day, a workweek (five days), a full week, a month, and a straight list of events. Clicking any of those buttons will change the calendar view in the main window below.

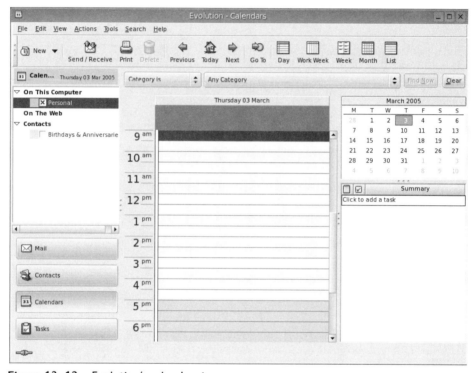

Figure 12–13   Evolution's calendar view.

The main window is divided into three sections. To the left of the main window (centrally located) is your main calendar view. To the right of that, you have a small calendar showing the current month. Clicking a date in that smaller calendar lets you jump right to that date. Still in the right-hand section, but below, you'll find a quick summary of your to-do items. Finally, a set of icons runs down the left-hand sidebar, providing you with quick access to Mail, Contacts, Calendar, and Tasks.

Tip To select any number of days (and create your own view), just highlight a sequence of days in the minicalendars to the right. The main calendar view will update with your selection.

Creating Appointments

Where KOrganizer calls these *events*, Evolution uses the term *appointment* or *meeting*.

Note Meetings and appointments are, in many ways, essentially the same thing, but the differences are substantial as well. An appointment is a personal event blocked on your calendar. A meeting can involve others and require group scheduling functions. In the Add dialog, appointments have only two tabs, *Appointment* and *Recurrence*. Meetings add a *Scheduling* tab and an *Invitations* tab.

The idea is the same. To create a new appointment in Evolution with a single click, move your mouse pointer to the *New* button and click there (or press <Ctrl+N>). Notice the down arrow beside the New button (Figure 12-14). Clicking on the arrow brings up a number of additional choices, from composing a mail message to creating a contact in your address book. If you like, you can always take the multiclick route by clicking *File* on the menu bar, selecting *New*, and then selecting *Appointment*. If you will be inviting others to this event, choose *Meeting*.

Another way to do this is to double-click on the time you want in the main calendar view. As soon as you do this, the new *Appointment* dialog will appear. Start by entering your *Summary* information (e.g., Poker night) and a *Location* (e.g., Jake and Michelle's house). A *Start time* will have been entered as well as an *End time*, but you may have to fine-tune those. Clicking on the down arrow beside the date pops up a small calendar, from which you can quickly pick the date. The drop-down list associated with the time is divided into half-hour intervals.

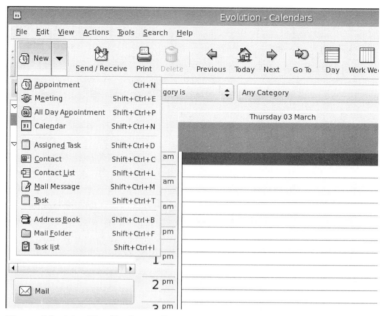

Figure 12–14 The Evolution *"New"* dialog.

Quick Tip Look to the right of the start and end time drop-down lists (you need to uncheck "All day event"). See that little icon? Clicking here brings up a world map, from which you can select the time zone in which the appointment will take place. Click on one of the dots, and the map zooms in to let you fine-tune your choice.

An appointment can also be set as an all-day event by clicking the All day event checkbox. Doing this will blank out the start and end times but not the dates.

If this is an important appointment, you will likely want to be reminded of it. Click on the *Alarm* checkbox. There are three default reminders to the right of that button. Unless you change the settings, the message will appear 15 minutes before the appointment. The other settings are 1 hour before and 1 day before the appointment. If this isn't specific enough, click the Customize button. Your default alarm will appear (the 15-minute one) with an option to Add new alarms or Remove the current one. Remove the current alarm (or click Add if you want multiple alarms), and the Add Alarm dialog will appear (Figure 12-15).

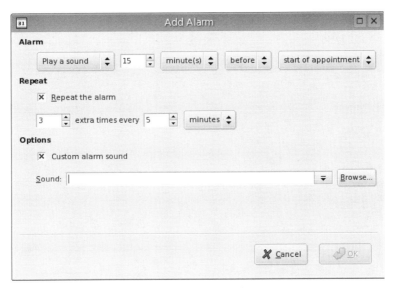

Figure 12–15   Evolution can remind your of your appointments in many different ways.

In order to create a different type of alarm, click on the *Pop up an alert* button (under the *Alarm* label) and change it to either *Play a sound* or *Run a program*. You can set a custom pop-up message and even specify a repeat for the alarm. Another way to look at it is *how often do you want to be nagged?*

When you are done with the new alarm, click OK. To add more alarms, all you have to do is click the *Add* button once. Now you get the idea.

Let's Do That Again: Evolution Recurrence

Before we move on to making this more than a one-person appointment, let's look at recurrence. If the gang meets for that poker game every week or every month at the same place and time, it just makes sense to enter the appointment once and have the system do the rest for you. Click on the *Recurrence* tab (Figure 12-16).

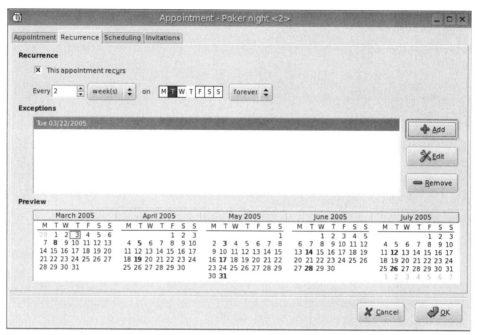

Figure 12–16 *Setting recurrence information for an Evolution appointment.*

Activate recurrence by clicking the *This appointment recurs* checkbox. Choose how often you want this appointment to occur and with what frequency (e.g., every 2 weeks on Tuesday). Directly below is the *Exceptions* dialog. Clicking on the down arrow to the right of the *Add* button will pop up a small calendar. Select those days that don't apply to the standard recurrence (e.g., your holidays) and click *Add*. You can specify as many exceptions as you like. When you are happy with everything, click the *OK* button. The new appointment will appear in your main calendar view.

The Makings of a Meeting

For your meeting to be truly a meeting and not just an appointment, you'll need some people to invite. As I mentioned earlier, meetings have two additional tabs along the top, labeled *Scheduling* and *Invitations*.

Click on the *Invitations* tab. The first thing you should see (if you created this appointment) is that you are listed as the *Organizer* of the meeting. This is something you can override. But if you created the meeting, it probably makes sense to leave it as is. Below that is a large window labeled *Attendees*. Click the *Add* button to the right, and a field will open in which you can add the person's e-mail address. (You can also click the *Contacts* button and choose attendees from your address book.)

Under the *Type* heading, you can define whether that attendee represents an individual or some other resource. Next, under the *Role* heading, select whether the individual will act as chair, a participant (required or not), or an optional-participant (i.e., an observer) or whether you are specifying a resource. Under the next heading, *RSVP*, decide whether or not the attendee should confirm his or her attendance. Finally, under *Status*, you may define whether the attendee has already accepted, declined, or whether their attendance is tentative. By default, entries are listed as *Needs Action*.

Finally, we have the *Scheduling* tab (Figure 12-17). This is another way to select individuals, but one that allows you to check free/busy information. Near the bottom of this window, you'll see the word *Autopick* by a drop-down box. To the right and left are buttons with double arrows on them. Click these, and Evolution will automatically select the next block of time (either before or after your initial attempt) in which all invitees are free, based on their published free/busy information. When you click *OK*, your attendees will be sent an e-mail message in which they can choose to accept or decline the invitation to attend.

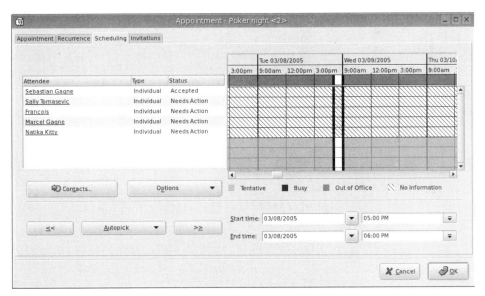

Figure 12–17   *Scheduling a meeting with free/busy information.*

Tasks and Other To-Dos

In Evolution, your to-do items are called *tasks*. Looking at Evolution's main calendar display, you'll see a summary task list in the lower right-hand pane. Adding a new task is as easy as clicking the field labeled *Click to add a new task*. Type a brief description of your task, and press <Enter> when you are done. For a task-only list, click the Tasks button in the left-hand sidebar. That will provide you with a much larger view and another quick-entry field.

Double-click on any field, and a dialog will appear offering you a much more detailed view of the task in question (Figure 12-18). The new window features two tabs, labeled *Task* and *Status*. These allow you to enter a description of the task, assign a completion date and time, and indicate priority and status information, such as whether the task has been started and its percentage of completion.

One last, and fairly important, feature is the ability to delegate this task to someone else. Right-click on the item you want in the task list. Select *Assign Task* from the drop-down list. A new tab will appear, labeled *Assignment,* from

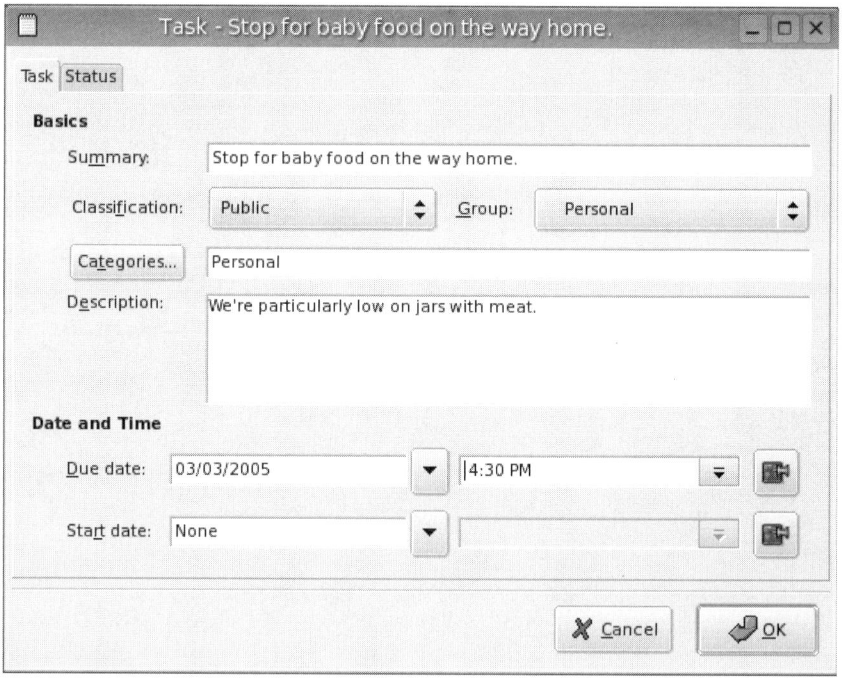

Figure 12–18   A more complete task dialog.

which you can select an individual to carry out the task. When you have entered the information, a window will pop up asking whether the assigned task should be sent. The correct answer is, of course, *Yes*.

Other Tools

We've come a long way from the yellow sticky notes on your desktop to the modern, connected organizers of today. Or have we?

One of the really cool applications under the KDE desktop is *Knotes* (program name `knotes`). This program lets you write electronic versions of those little yellow notes, which you can then scatter across your desktop, where they vie for your attention. Knotes docks nicely into your icon tray and remembers past notes and your changes. There's more than a paper replacement here, though. You can e-mail these notes, print them, or change the color. You can also view these notes in a more compact manner by clicking on the Notes icon in your Kontact sidebar.

Furthermore, both Kontact and Evolution let you synchronize with your Palm PDA.

Another program worth your time is KArm (program name `karm`). This is a small-event timer. Let's say you are on the phone with a customer and want to track how long the call takes. Use KArm to start a new task, and then click the *Start clock* button. A timer will start keeping track of how long you spend on that call. KArm also lets you create subtasks, pause timing, resume (so you can track multiple events through the course of a day), and, if necessary, print the results.

Resources

Kontact Web site
http://kontact.kde.org

Kontact Groupware Information
http://kontact.kde.org/groupwareservers.php

Korganizer Web site
http://korganizer.kde.org

GNOME Evolution
http://gnome.org/projects/evolution

13

Word Processors (It Was a Dark and Stormy Night . . .)

Sorry, but at some point I just had to use that famous opening from Edward George Bulwer-Lytton's "Paul Clifford" (written in 1830). Those famous words "It was a dark and stormy night" were made even more famous (infamous?) by Charles M. Schulz's Snoopy, that barnstorming, literary beagle. It just seems fitting, considering this chapter's topic—word processors.

Word processors run the gamut in terms of complexity, from simple programs that aren't much more than text editors to full-blown desktop publishing systems. Users coming from the Microsoft world are most likely to use OpenOffice Writer, part of the OpenOffice.org suite.

OpenOffice.org is actually the free sibling of the commercial StarOffice suite. When Sun Microsystems decided to open the source to StarOffice, it became another boon for the open source community, not to mention the average user. OpenOffice became the free version of this powerful word processor, spreadsheet, and presentation graphics package, and StarOffice became the corporate choice. Both of these are full-featured office suites, and users familiar with Microsoft Office will feel right at home with the similarities.

You might well be wondering what differences exist between these two sibling suites. The great difference is the price. For anyone with a reasonably fast Internet connection (or a helpful friend), OpenOffice is *free*. StarOffice, on the other hand, will cost you something for the boxed set. Included with StarOffice is documentation and support as well as additional fonts and clip-art. That said, you'll find that it is still *far less expensive* than the Windows alternative.

If you are following along and using the KDE desktop, you probably also have *KWord* at your disposal. Then, as I hinted, there are the others. We'll talk about a few of them at the end of this chapter.

 Trivia Time It may interest you to know that this book was written using OpenOffice.org 1.1.3 as well as the beta release of OpenOffice.org 2.0.

OpenOffice.org Writer

Start Writer by clicking on the big K, scrolling up to the OpenOffice.org menu (in some distributions, check under the Office menu), and clicking on OpenOffice.org Writer. The first time you start Writer, the welcome wizard will appear, with a few questions as it sets up your work environment.

Move past the introductory screen by clicking Next, and you'll be presented with the OpenOffice.org license agreement. Scroll down as you read by pressing the Scroll down button. When you get to the end, the grayed-out Accept button will be available. Click Accept to move to the next screen. Here you will enter your name and initials (Figure 13-1). This information is used in the Properties dialog to identify documents you create. Fill this in and click Next.

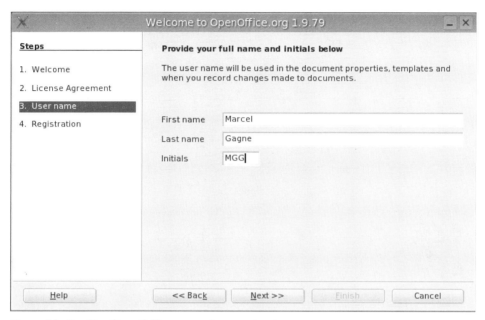

Figure 13-1 The OpenOffice.org welcome wizard.

On the last screen, the wizard asks whether you wish to register as an OpenOffice.org user. This is entirely up to you, and there's no need to register if you don't want to. However, registration does add to the official OpenOffice.org numbers, and it provides a means by which the development team can inform you of interesting changes or updates with the package. Click Finish and you are done.

Shell Out To run OpenOffice.org Writer from the command line (or via your <Alt+F2> shortcut), use the command `oowriter` (think OpenOffice.org Writer). Please note that some distributions may still use `swriter` (the StarOffice version of the command).

OpenOffice.org Writer starts up with a blank page, ready for you to release that inner creative genius (Figure 13-2). At the top of the screen, you'll find a menu bar where commands are organized based on their categories, including the friendly-sounding Help submenu (more on that shortly).

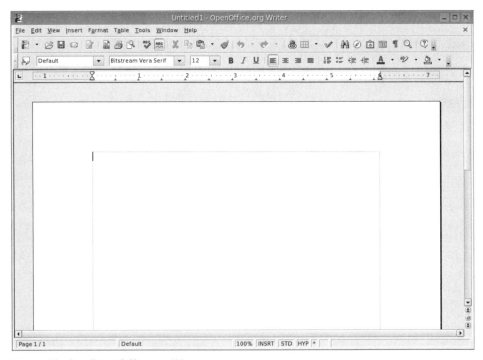

Figure 13–2   OpenOffice.org Writer on startup.

Write Now!

At this point, Writer is open and you are looking at a blank screen. Let's write something. As any writer will tell you, nothing is more *intimidating* than a blank page. Because I opened this chapter with a reference to the famous line *It was a dark and stormy night*, why don't we continue along that theme? That line is often pointed to as an example of bad writing, but the paragraph that follows is even worse. Type this into your blank Writer page, as shown in Figure 13-3.

Paul Clifford, by Edward George Bulwer-Lytton

It was a dark and stormy night; the rain fell in torrents—except at occasional intervals, when it was checked by a violent gust of wind which swept up the streets (for it is in London that our scene lies), rattling along the house-tops, and fiercely agitating the scanty flame of the lamps that struggled against the darkness. Through one of the obscurest quarters of

London, and among haunts little loved by the gentlemen of the police, a man, evidently of the lowest orders, was wending his solitary way. He stopped twice or thrice at different shops and houses of a description correspondent with the appearance of the quartier in which they were situated—and tended inquiry for some article or another which did not seem easily to be met with. All the answers he received were couched in the negative; and as he turned from each door he muttered to himself, in no very elegant phraseology, his disappointment and discontent.

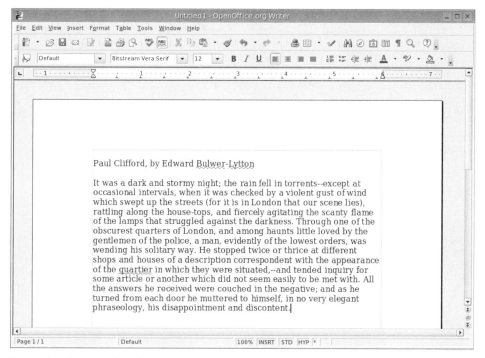

Figure 13–3 Your first document, dark and stormy.

Okay, you can stop there. Isn't that wonderful stuff? If you feel the need to read more, I've got links to the story and the famous Bulwer-Lytton fiction contest at the end of this chapter.

The Hunt for Typos

For years, I've been including in the signature section of my e-mails the tag line *This massagee wos nat speel or gramer-checkered.* Given that I continue to use this line, I am obviously amused by it. But never running a spell-check is far from good practice when your intention is to turn in a professional document.

OpenOffice.org Writer can do a spell-check as you go without actually correcting errors. With this feature, words that don't appear in the dictionary will show up with a squiggly red line underneath them, which you can then correct. Many people find this a useful feature, but some, like myself, prefer to just check the whole document at the end of the writing session. This feature is activated by default, but you can deactivate it if you prefer. Here's how.

Click Tools on the menu bar and select Options. This is a multipurpose dialog that allows you to configure many of OpenOffice.org's features (Figure 13-4). For the moment, we'll concentrate on the auto-spell-check. To the left of the dialog is a sidebar with many categories. You want Language Settings. Click the plus sign beside it. This will drop down a submenu from which you will choose Writing Aids. Now look to the left, and you'll see a section called Options and at the top of that a checkbox beside the words *Check spelling as you type*. To turn off the auto-spell-check feature, uncheck this box, and then click OK to close the dialog.

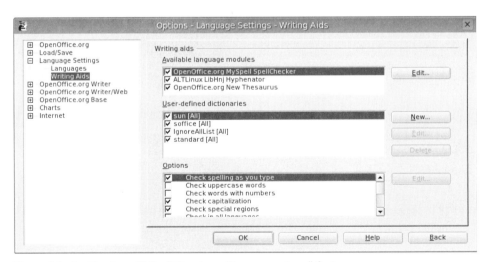

Figure 13–4   Turning off the "Check spelling as you type" feature.

To start a full-document spell-check, click Tools on the menu bar and then SpellCheck. You can also just press <F7> at any time to start a spell-check.

What Language Is That?

OpenOffice.org supports many different languages, and, depending on where you picked up your copy, it may be set for a different language than your own. To change the default language, click Tools on the menu bar and then Options, Language Settings, and Writing Aids. Look familiar?

The dialog box that appears (Figure 13-4) should have OpenOffice.org MySpell SpellChecker checked on. You can then click the Edit button next to it and select your language of choice under the Default languages for documents drop-down box. When you have made your choice, click OK to exit the various dialogs.

Saving Your Work

Now that you have created a document, it is time to save it. Click File on the menu bar and select Save (or Save As). When the Save As window appears (Figure 13-5), select a folder, type in a filename, and click Save. When you save, you can also specify the File type to be OpenOffice.org's default Open-Document Text format (.odt), RTF, straight text, Microsoft Word format, or a number of others. You can even save in Palm doc format so that you can take it with you on your Palm device.

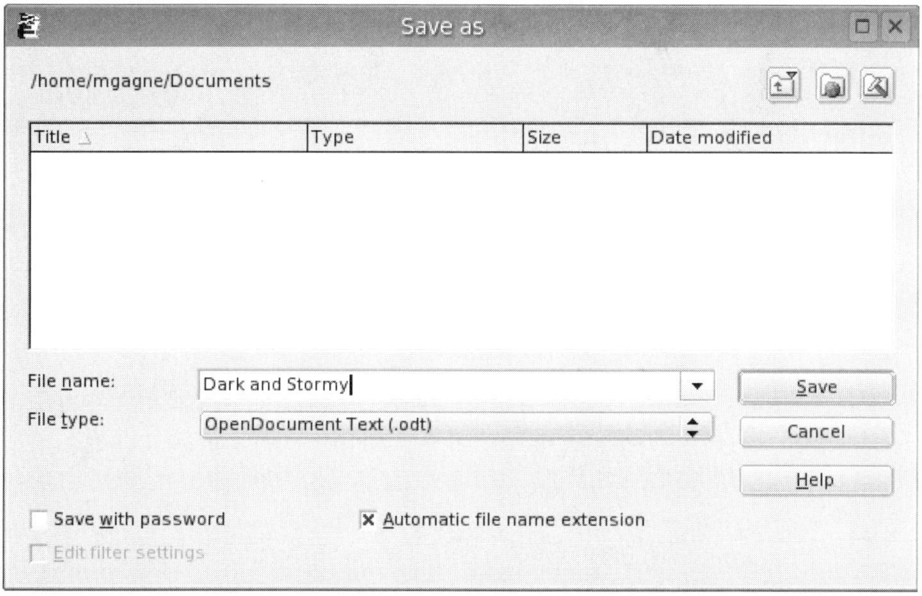

Figure 13-5   It is always good to save your work.

If you want to create a new directory under your home directory, you can do it here as well. Click the icon that looks like a folder with a star or globe in front of it (the middle icon near the right-hand corner), and then enter your new directory name in the Create new folder pop-up window.

Should you decide to close OpenOffice.org Writer at this point, you can always return to your document at a later time by clicking File on the menu bar and selecting Open. The Open File dialog will appear, and you can browse your directories to select the file you want. You can specify a file type via a fairly substantial drop-down list of available formats. This gives you a chance to narrow the search to include only text documents, spreadsheets, or presentations. You can also specify a particular document extension (e.g., only *.doc files) or a particular pattern.

Printing Your Document

Invariably, the whole point of typing something in a word processor might be to produce a printed document. When you are through with your document, click File on the menu bar and select Print.

The Print dialog (Figure 13-6) has several options. The easiest thing to do after selecting your printer is just to click OK. The print job will be directed to your printer of choice, and in a few seconds you'll have a nice, crisp version of

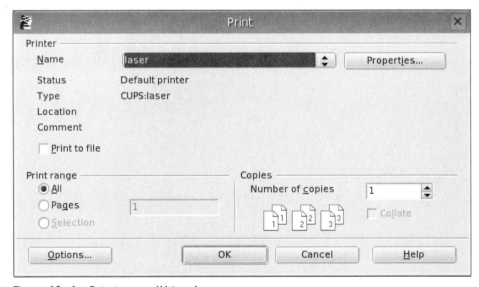

Figure 13–6   Printing your Writer document.

your document. You can select a page range, increase the number of copies (one to all your friends), or modify the printer properties (paper size, landscape print, etc.).

You can also print to a file. By default, this generates a PostScript document, a kind of universal printer language. A number of tools can view PostScript documents, including Konqueror, by using the KGhostView embedded viewer.

You can also save to PDF, something I cover a little later in the chapter.

Toolbars of Every Kind . . .

Now that you are feeling comfortable with your new word processor, let's take a quick tour of the various toolbars, icons, and menus in Writer.

The icon bar directly below the menu bar is called the *Standard bar*, and it contains icons for opening and creating documents, cutting and pasting, printing, and other functions. The Standard bar is common to all the OpenOffice.org applications (Writer, Calc, Impress, etc.).

Below the Standard bar is the *Formatting bar*. It provides common editing options, such as font selection, bolding, italics, and centering. Select words or phrases in your document with the mouse (hold, click, and drag across the desired text), and then click *B* for bold or *I* for italics. This bar will change from application to application, depending on what type of formatting is most needed.

At the bottom of the editing screen is the *Status bar*. What you'll see there is the current page number, current template, zoom percentage, insert (or overwrite) mode, selection mode, hyperlink mode, and the current save status of the document. (If the document has been modified and not saved, an asterisk will appear.)

In all cases, pausing over each of the icons with your mouse cursor will make a tooltip appear describing the functions of the individual icons.

Help!

Under the Help heading on the menu bar, you'll find plenty of information. By default, tooltips are activated so that when you pause your mouse cursor over an item, a small tooltip will be shown. These tips are terse, usually no more than a couple of words. It's also possible to get a little more information by turning on Extended tips. Before I tell you how to do that, take a look at

Figure 13-7 for a sample of the difference. The upper image shows the default tip for the Paste icon, while the lower image shows the extended tip for the same function.

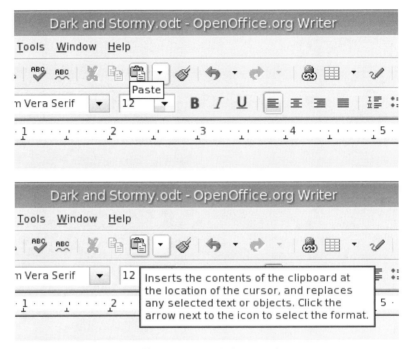

Figure 13–7   What a difference extended tips makes.

For that little extra help, click Tools and select Options. Under the Open-Office.org menu on the right, you'll find a subsection labeled General. Click there and then look over on the right. You'll see a checkbox for Extended tips right near the top. Turning that on will give you slightly more detailed tooltips.

If you are looking for help on a specific topic, there's always the included manual. Click Help on the menu bar and select OpenOffice.org Help (you can also press <F1>). The various tabs at the top left of the help screen let you search for topics by application with the Contents tab, alphabetically using the Index tab, and by keyword using the Find tab. You can even set bookmarks under the Bookmarks tab for those topics you regularly access.

To Word or Not to Word?

Ah, that is the question indeed. OpenOffice.org's default document format is the OASIS OpenDocument XML (eXtensible Markup Language) format, an open standard for document formats (it is saved with an .odt extension). The OpenDocument format is the closest thing to document freedom you will get (short of plain text). The format is vendor and application neutral. You are guaranteed support and portability because it is an open standard. Many organizations, such as the European Commission and the State of Massachusetts, are starting to recommend the OASIS OpenDocument format for the very reasons I've mentioned. For more on this emerging standard, check the Resources section at the end of this chapter.

Alternatively, the main reason for sticking with Word format is, *quite frankly*, that Word is everywhere. The sheer number of Word installations is the very reason that OpenOffice.org was designed to support Microsoft Office format as thoroughly as it does. That said, if you do want to switch to the OASIS OpenDocument format, Writer provides an easy way to do that. Rather than converting documents one by one, the Document Converter speeds up the process by allowing you to run all the documents in a specific directory in one pass. It also works in both directions, meaning that you can convert from Word to OpenOffice.org format, and vice versa. The conversion creates a new file but leaves the original as is.

From the menu bar, select File, move your mouse to Wizards, and then select Document Converter from the submenu. To convert your Microsoft Office documents (you can do the Excel and PowerPoint documents at the same time), click Microsoft Office on the menu, and then check off the types of documents you want. The next screen will ask whether you want both documents and templates or just one or the other. You will then type in the name of the directory you want to import from and save to (this can be the same directory). After you've entered your information and gone to the next screen, the program will confirm your choices and give you a final chance to change your mind. Click Convert to continue. As the converter does its job, it will list the various files it encounters and keep track of the process.

When the job is done, you'll have a number of files in your directory with an .odt extension. If you change your mind, don't worry. Your original files are still there, so you've lost nothing.

If working with Word documents in Word format is important, then read on. Ah, heck. Even if it isn't, you should read on.

Personalizing Your Environment

Every application you use comes with defaults that may or may not reflect the way you want to work, and this is true here as well.

Click Tools on the menu bar and select Options. There are a lot of options here, including OpenOffice.org, Load/Save, Language Settings, OpenOffice.org Writer (including HTML/Web documents), OpenOffice.org Base (the built in database), Charts, and Internet. Each of these sections has a submenu of further options. Because there are so many options here, I certainly can't cover them all; besides, I don't want to bore you. Instead, I'll mention a few things that I *think* are important and let you discover the rest.

The main OpenOffice.org dialog covers a lot of general options regarding the look and feel of the applications. Take a moment to look at the *Paths* settings. If you keep your documents in a specific directory, you'll want to set that here. Under Type, choose My Documents, click Edit, and then enter the new path to your directory of choice.

Let's move on to the very important *Load/Save* settings menu (Figure 13-8). If you are constantly going to move documents back and forth between systems running Microsoft Word and your own, you'll want to pay special attention here. Click the plus sign to the left of it, and then click Microsoft Office.

Click the Convert on Save (and load) checkboxes to on, and your OpenOffice.org Writer documents will be saved in Word format by default while your Calc sheets will wind up in Excel format. We're almost there. Although

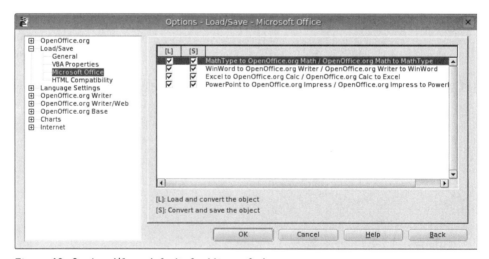

Figure 13–8   Load/Save defaults for Microsoft documents.

the conversion is pretty automatic here, when you try to resave a document you have been working on, Writer may still disturb you with the occasional pop-up message informing you of the *minuses* of saving in Word format.

You get around this with one other change. In the same menu section, click General. Notice where it says *Default file format* (Figure 13-9). For the Document type of Text document, select *Microsoft Word 97/2000/XP* from the Always save as drop-down list to the right. While you are here (assuming you are making these changes, of course), you probably want to change the Always save as format for *Spreadsheet* to be Microsoft Excel, and so on.

Click OK, and you are done.

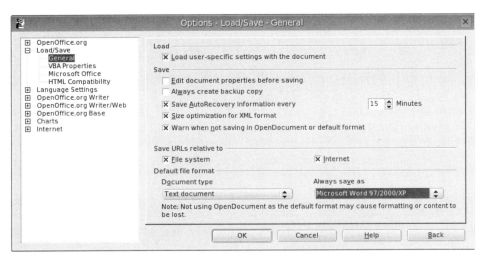

Figure 13-9 Defining the standard file format to be Microsoft Word.

Note I'm not saying that Microsoft's document format is in any way superior. It not only isn't, but you are also trapped in a proprietary standard that may make it difficult to import your data in the future. While there's no guarantee that any document format is going to be *the standard* in the future, it's nice to know that you can always load and read your old documents. That said, if you have to move back and forth from the open document format to Microsoft's proprietary format all the time, you don't want to be bothered with doing a Save as every time. It just gets tedious.

Let's move on to the *OpenOffice.org Writer* category (in the left-hand sidebar menu) for changes related specifically to the Writer application. Whenever you start a new document, OpenOffice.org assigns a default font when you start typing. This may not be your ideal choice, and you don't have to accept it. Sure, you can change the font when you are writing, but why do this with every document when you can change it once? Click *Basic Fonts*, and you'll have the opportunity to change the default fonts your system uses.

When you are done with the Options menu, click OK to return to the OpenOffice.org application.

A Wizard of Words

OpenOffice.org comes with a number of templates that are available throughout the suite. The document Wizards feature helps you choose and walk through the setup of some basic documents. The easiest way to understand what these Wizards can do for you is to dive right in and try one.

On the menu bar, click File, and move your mouse over to Wizards. You'll see a number of document types here, from letters to faxes to presentations. We'll use Letter as an example. When the Letter Wizard starts up (Figure 13-10), it will offer you three kinds of letters: business, formal personal, and

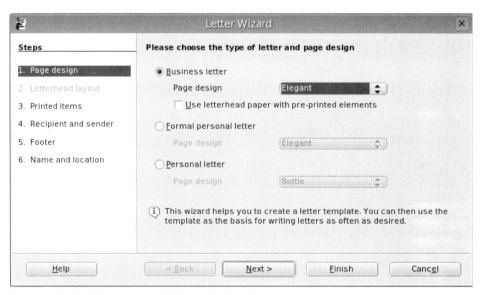

Figure 13-10   Writing using the Letter Wizard.

personal. Each of these may have different styles. As you progress through the various steps, you'll be asked to enter some basic information related to the type of document you chose. In the case of a letter, this would involve an opening and a closing greeting, a sender and recipient name and address, and so on. The Wizard also lets you save the document as a template so that you can use it at a later date.

Navigating Style

With Writer open, click Format on the menu bar, and then select Styles and Formatting; a window labeled *Styles and Formatting* will appear, floating above your document. Pressing F11 will also bring up the stylist. Clicking the x in the corner of the window will banish it. I'd like to give you some idea of how useful this little tool can be in formatting your documents. If you've banished the Stylist, bring it back by clicking its icon or pressing <F11>.

Great Time-Saving Tip Here's a good trick you might want to keep in mind if you start using styles in a big way. Click on the stylist's title bar with your left mouse button and slowly drag the stylist window over to the right edge (or the left edge) of your Writer window. As the stylist starts to go beyond the edge of the Writer window, you should see a gray vertical outline appear under the stylist. Release the mouse button and the stylist will dock into the main writer Window (Figure 13-11).

Whenever you start a new document, it loads with a default style. That style is actually a collection of formatting presets that define how various paragraphs will look. These include headings, lists, text boxes, and so on. All you have to do is select a paragraph, double-click on a style, and your paragraph's look—including font style and size—is magically updated. As an example of how to use this, try the following.

Start by reloading your Dark and Stormy document, and then highlight your title text to select it. At the bottom of your Stylist, it says *Automatic*. With your title highlighted, double-click on Heading 1. The heading changes to a large, bold, sans serif font. Now click the arrow at the bottom of the list, and change from Automatic to Chapter Styles. Double-click on Title, and your title is suddenly centered with the appropriate font applied (Figure13-11).

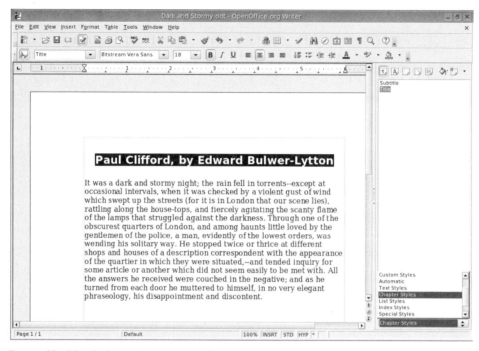

Figure 13–11   *Styles make paragraph formatting easy and consistent. Note that the stylist is docked on the right.*

The Stylist is pretty smart, really. Look back to the bottom of the list at those categories—HTML Styles, Custom Styles, List Styles, and so on. Depending on the document type you are working on, the Stylist will come up with a pretty sane list for that Automatic selection. If you call up an HTML document, HTML formatting will show up in the Automatic list.

Quick Undo Tip To remove a docked Stylist, just drag it out of its dock and drop it above the document itself. It turns back into a floating window. You can also press <F11>, and it will promptly vanish from the dock. The great thing about doing it with the function key is that the Stylist remembers where it was. If it was docked when you pressed <F11>, it will be when you press it again.

Navigating the Rivers of Text

The second floating window is called the *Navigator*. This is a great tool for the power user or anyone who is creating long, complex documents. When you start up the Navigator by clicking Edit and then Navigator (or by pressing <F5>), you'll see a window listing the various elements in your document (Figure 13-12). These will be organized in terms of headings, tables, graphics, and so on.

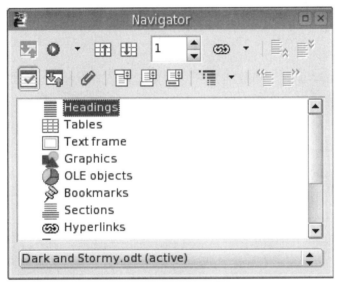

Figure 13–12 The Navigator gives you access to all your document elements.

 Quick Tip You guessed it! Just like the Stylist, the Navigator can be dragged to either edge of the document and docked into the main Writer window. Just make sure you drag it far enough so that it isn't another vertical window next to the Stylist, but rather sits above or below it.

What makes this a great tool is that you can use it to navigate a document quickly. Let's say that (as in this chapter) there are a number of section headings. Click on the plus sign beside the word *Headings*, and a treed list of all the headings in the document will be displayed. Double-click on a heading, and you will instantly jump to that point in the document. The same goes for graphics, tables, and other such elements in your document.

Speaking of Document Elements . . .

Take a look over at the far right of the Standard bar. See the little icon that looks like a picture hanging on a wall? That's the *gallery* of graphics and sounds, decorative elements that can be inserted in your document. When you click the picture (or select Gallery from Tools on the menu bar), the gallery will open up, with a sidebar on the left listing the various themes.

Wander through the collection until you see something that suits your document, and then simply drag it into your document, just as I did with that rather bright rule below the "Paul Clifford" title in Figure 13-13. To banish the gallery, just click the icon again.

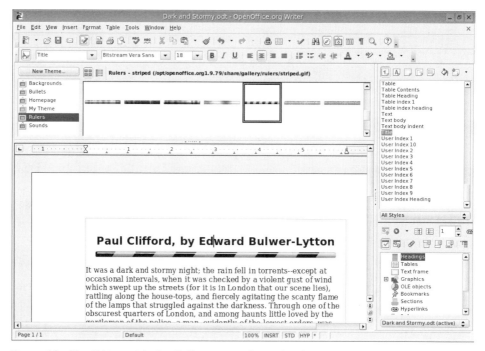

Figure 13–13   Writer with the Gallery open above the document and with a docked Stylist and Navigator to the right.

While you were using the Gallery, did you notice the words *New Theme* . . . at the top of the category sidebar? Click those words (which is really a button), and you'll be able to create a new category of images, clipart, or sounds. If you've got a directory of images you've collected, enter the path to that directory, pick a name for this collection, and you are done. Next time you bring up the Gallery, you can select from your own custom collection.

More! Give Me More!

OpenOffice.org comes with a limited number of templates, graphics, and icons. The fuller complement of these that comes with its commercial (non-free) cousin, StarOffice from Sun Microsystems, is one of the advantages of StarOffice. However, if you find yourself in need of more templates or a richer gallery than you already have, take careful note of the following Web site. It's called *OO Extras*, and it may be the answer to your prayers:

```
http://www.ooextras.org
```

In addition to individual macros, icons, and templates, the goal of this Web site (created by Travis Bauer) is to provide downloadable packages to enhance OpenOffice.org's suite. As of March 2005, the download bundle contained some 200 different templates. It's well worth a look.

Other Options

I've concentrated on OpenOffice.org Writer perhaps because it is the real contender to Microsoft Office and the one that most people moving to Linux from the Microsoft Office world are likely to want to use. That's not to say that this is your only choice. For instance, the KDE suite comes with its own word processor, part of the KOffice suite, called *KWord*. Furthermore, KWord is one of the word processors that can deal with the new OASIS OpenDocument format.

KWord is a frame-based word processing package. People used to working with desktop publishing packages such as FrameMaker will find this a familiar environment, just as those coming from Microsoft Word will experience somewhat of a learning curve. What KWord does is make it possible to create extremely precise documents where the layout of text and graphics must be accurate.

Another excellent word processor worth your consideration is *Abiword*. You can probably find Abiword on your distribution CDs, but you can always get the latest version on the Abisource Web site (`http://www.abi-source.com`). What Abiword really has going for it is size and performance. This is a lightweight application that will perform well even on slower machines. It starts up fast and is excellent at what it does.

What KWord and Abiword have going against them (at least at the time of this writing) are compatibility issues with Microsoft Word documents. Both read the documents fairly well, but they do not export quite as well. As development in import and export filters continues, this may not be an issue for long.

Resources

Abiword

http://www.abisource.com

Bulwer-Lytton Fiction Contest

http://www.bulwer-lytton.com

KDE's KWord

http://koffice.kde.org/kword/

OASIS OpenDocument Format

http://www.oasis-open.org/committees/office/faq.php

OpenOffice.org Web Site

http://www.openoffice.org/

Sun Microsystems StarOffice

http://www.sun.com/software/star/staroffice/

Chapter

14

Spreadsheets (Tables You Can Count On)

A spreadsheet, for those who might be curious, allows an individual to orga-
nize data onto a table made up of rows and columns. The intersection of a row
and a column is called a cell, and each cell can be given specific attributes,
such as a value or a formula. In the case of a formula, changes in the data of
other cells can automatically update the results. This makes a spreadsheet
ideal for financial applications. Change the interest rate in the appropriate
cell, and the monthly payment changes without your having to do anything
else.

The idea of a computerized spreadsheet probably existed before 1978, but it
was in that year that Daniel Bricklin, a Harvard Business School student,
came up with the first real spreadsheet program. He called his program a vis-
ible calculator and then later enlisted Bob Frankston of MIT (Bricklin names
him as co-creator) to help him develop the program further. This program
would come to be known as VisiCalc. Some argue that with VisiCalc, the first
so-called killer app was born.

Now that we have the definitions and history out of the way, let's get back to your Linux system and have a look at OpenOffice.org's very own spreadsheet program. It is called *Calc*—an appropriate name, given what spreadsheets tend to be used for.

Starting a New Spreadsheet and Entering Data

There are a few ways to start a new spreadsheet. If you are already working in OpenOffice.org Writer (as I am right now), you can click File on the menu bar, move your mouse to the New submenu, and select Spreadsheet from the drop-down list. Another way is to click the application starter (the big K) and select Calc from the OpenOffice.org or Office menu. When Calc starts up, you'll see a blank sheet of cells, as in Figure 14-1.

Directly below the menu bar is the *Standard bar*. As with Writer, the icons here give you access to the common functions found throughout Open-Office.org, such as cut, paste, open, and save. Below the Standard bar is the

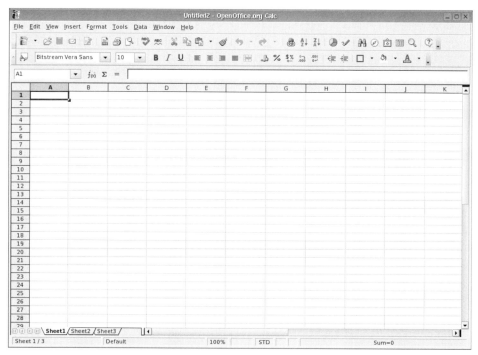

Figure 14–1   Starting with a clean sheet.

Formatting bar. Some features here are similar to those in Writer, such as font style and size, but others are specific to formatting content in a spreadsheet (percentage, decimal places, frame border, etc.).

Finally, below the Formatting bar you'll find the *Formula bar.* The first field here displays the current cell, but you can also enter a cell number here to jump to that cell. You can move around from cell to cell by using your cursor keys or the <Tab> (and <Shift+Tab>) key or simply by clicking on a particular cell. The current cell you are working on will have a bold black outline around it.

Basic Math

Let's try something simple, shall we? If you haven't already done so, open a new spreadsheet. In cell A1, type *Course Average*. Select the text in the field, change the font style or size (by clicking on the font selector in the Formatting bar), and then press <Enter>. As you can see, the text is larger than the field. No problem. Place your mouse cursor on the line between the A and B cells (directly below the Formula bar). Click and hold, and then stretch the A cell to fit the text. You can do the same for the height of any given row of cells by clicking on the line between the row numbers (over to the left) and stretching these to an appropriate size.

Now move to cell A3 and type in a hypothetical number somewhere in the range of 1–100 to represent a course mark. Press <Enter> or cursor down to move to the next cell. Enter seven course marks so that cells A3 through A9 are filled. In my example, I entered 95, 67, 100, 89, 84, 79, and 93. (It seems to me that the 67 is an aberration.)

What we are going to do now is enter a formula in cell A11 to provide us with an average of all seven course scores. In cell A11, enter the following text:

```
=(A3+A4+A5+A6+A7+A8+A9)/7
```

When you press <Enter>, the text you entered will disappear, and instead you'll see an average for your course scores (Figure 14-2).

An average of 86.71 isn't a bad score (it is an A, after all). But if that 67 really was an aberration, you can easily go back to that cell, type in a different number, and press <Enter>. When you do so, the average will automagically change for you.

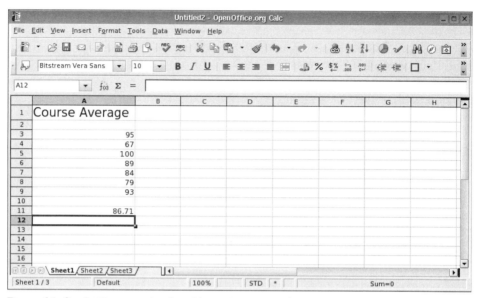

Figure 14–2 *Setting up a simple table to determine class averages.*

Calculating an average is a simple enough formula. But if I were to add 70 rows instead of 7, the resulting formula could get *ugly*. The beauty of spreadsheets is that they include formulas to make this whole process somewhat cleaner. For instance, I can specify a range of cells by putting a colon in between the first and last cells (A3:A9) and using a built-in function to return the average of that range. My new, improved, and cleaner formula looks like this:

```
=AVERAGE (A3:A9)
```

Incidentally, you can also select the cell and enter the information in the input line on the Formula bar. I mention the Formula bar for a couple of reasons. One is that you can obviously enter the information in the field as well as in the cell itself.

The second reason has to do with those little icons to the left of the input field. If you click into that input field, you'll notice that a little green checkmark will appear (to accept any changes you make to the formula), and to its left there will be a red *X* (to cancel the changes). Now look to the icon furthest on the left. If you hold your mouse over it, it should pop up a little tooltip that says *Function Wizard*. Try it. Go back to cell A11, and then click your mouse into the input field on the Formula bar. Now click on the Function Wizard icon. (You can also click Insert on the menu bar and select Function.)

On the left side you'll see a list of functions, with descriptions of those functions off to the right. For the function called *AVERAGE*, the description is *Returns the average of a sample*. Because this is what we want, click the Next button at the bottom of the window, after which you will see a window much like the one in Figure 14-3. This is where the Wizard starts to do its real work.

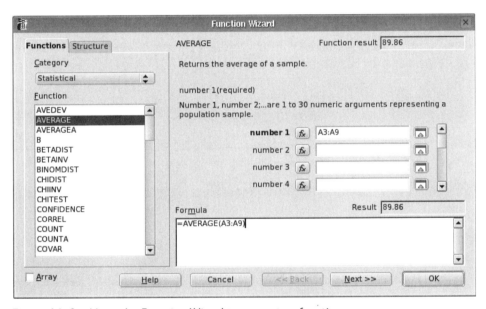

Figure 14–3   Using the Function Wizard to generate a function.

Look at the window labeled *Formula* at the bottom of the screen. You'll see that the formula is starting to be built. At this point, it says *=AVERAGE()* and nothing else. Near the middle of the screen, on the right side, are four data fields labeled *number 1* through *number 4*. The first field is required, whereas the others are optional. You could at this point enter *A3:A9*, click Next, and be done. (Notice, while you are here, that the result of the formula is already displayed just above the Formula field.) Alternatively, you could click the button to the right of the number field (the tooltip will say *Shrink*), and the Function Wizard will shrink to a small bar floating above your spreadsheet (Figure 14-4).

Figure 14–4   The Function Wizard in a more compact format.

On your spreadsheet, select a group of fields by clicking on the first field and dragging the mouse to include all seven fields. When you let go of the mouse, the field range will have been entered for you. On the left-hand side of the shrunken Function Wizard is a maximize button (move your mouse over it to activate the tooltip). Click it, and your Wizard will return to its original size. Unless you have an additional set of fields (or you wish to create a more complex formula), click OK to complete this operation. The window will disappear, and the spreadsheet will update.

Saving Your Work

Before we move on to something else, you should save your work. Click File on the menu bar and select Save (or Save As). When the Save As window appears (Figure 14-5), select a folder, type in a file name, and click Save.

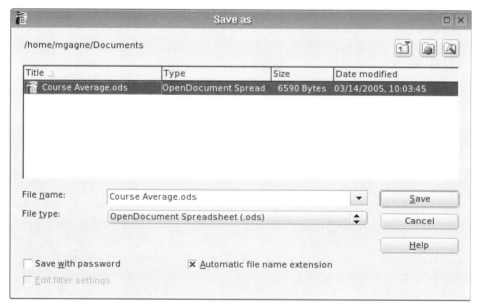

Figure 14–5   Don't forget to save your work.

When you save, you can also specify the File type to be OpenOffice.org's default format, OpenDocument, DIF, DBASE, Microsoft Excel, and other formats.

Should you decide to close OpenOffice.org Calc at this point, you could always go back to the document by clicking File on the menu bar and selecting Open.

Complex Charts and Graphs, Oh My!

This time, I'll show you how you can take the data that you enter into your spreadsheets and transform it into a slick little chart. These charts can be linear, pie, bar, and a number of other choices. They can also be two- or three-dimensional, with various effects applied for that professional look.

To start, create another spreadsheet. We'll call this one *Quarterly Sales Reports*. With it, we will track the performance of a hypothetical company. In cell A1, write the title (Quarterly Sales Reports); in cell A2, write the description of the data (in thousands of dollars). Now, in cell A4, write the heading *Period*, and then enter *Q1* in cell A6, *Q2* in cell A7, *Q3* in cell A8, and *Q4* in cell A9. Finally, enter some headings for the years. In cell B4, enter *2000*, then enter *2001* in cell C4, and continue on in row 4 right up to *2004*. You should have five years running across row 4, with four quarters listed.

Time to have some virtual fun. For each period, enter a fictitious sales figure (or a real one if you are serious about this). For example, the data for 2001, Q2, would be entered in cell C7, and the sales figure for 2003, Q3, would be in cell E8. If you are still with me, finish entering the data, and we'll do a few things.

Magical Totals

Let's start with a quick and easy total for each column. If you used the same layout as I did, you should have a 2000 column that ends at B9. Click on cell B11. Now look at the icon in the middle of the sheet area and the input line on the Formula bar. It looks like the Greek letter epsilon. Hold your mouse pointer over it, and you'll see a tooltip that says *Sum*. Are you excited yet? Click the icon, and the formula to sum up the totals of that line, =SUM(B6:B10), will automatically appear (see Figure 14-6). All you need to do to finalize the totals is to click the green checkmark that appears next to the input line.

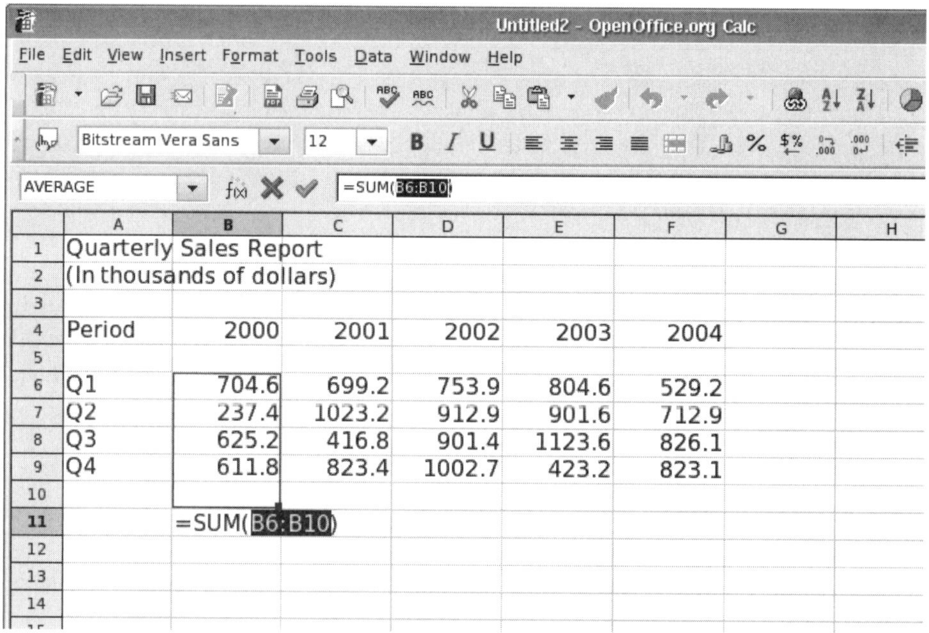

Figure 14–6 Select a series of cells, and Calc will automatically generate totals for you.

Because a sum calculation is the most common function used, it is kept handy. You can now do the same thing for each of the other yearly columns to get your totals. Click on the sum icon, then click your beginning column, and drag the mouse to include the cells you want. Click the green checkmark, and move on to the next yearly column.

Nice, Colorful, Impressive, and Dynamic Graphs

Creating a chart from the data you have just entered is really pretty easy. Start by selecting the cells that represent the information you want to see on your finished chart, including the headings. You can start with one corner of the chart and simply drag your mouse across to select all that you want.

Warning If there are some empty cells in your table (in my example, row A3), you will want to deselect them. You can do this by holding down the <Ctrl> key and clicking those cells with the mouse. In the case of my example, I am referring to that empty row 5.

Once you have all the cells you want selected, click Insert on the menu bar, and select Chart. This window (Figure 14-7) gives you the opportunity of assigning certain rows and columns as labels. This is perfect because we have the quarter numbers running down the left side and the year labels running across the top. Make sure the boxes for *First row as label* and *First column as label* are checked.

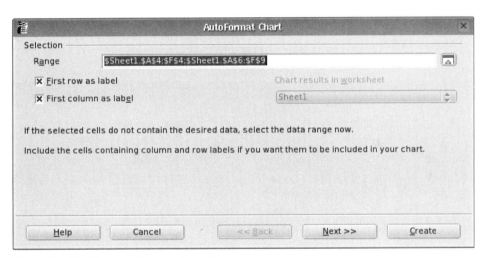

Figure 14–7 The AutoFormat chart dialog.

Before you move on, notice the drop-down list labeled *Chart results in worksheet*. By default, Calc creates three tabbed pages for every new worksheet, even though you are working on only one at this time. If you leave things as they are, your chart will be embedded into your current page, though you can always move it to different locations. You have a choice at this point to have the chart appear on a separate page (those tabs at the bottom of your worksheet). For my example, I'm going to leave the chart on the first page. Make your selection, and then click Next.

Note There is also an Insert Chart icon up on the Standard bar. If you click that icon (instead of clicking Insert and then Chart from the menu bar), the software automatically assumes you want the chart in the worksheet. Furthermore, your cursor will change to a small chart icon. Click a location on the document where you want the chart to appear, and the AutoFormat Chart dialog will appear.

The next window (Figure 14-8) lets you choose from chart types (bar, pie, etc.) and provides a preview window to the left. That way, you can try the various chart options to see what best shows off your data. If you want to see the labels in your preview window, click on the checkbox for *Show text elements in preview.*

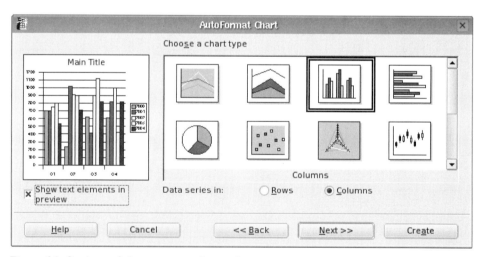

Figure 14–8   Lots of chart types to choose from.

You can continue to click Next for some additional fine-tuning on formatting (the last screen lets you change the title), but this is all the data you actually need to create your chart. When you are done, click the Create button, and your chart will appear on your page (Figure 14-9).

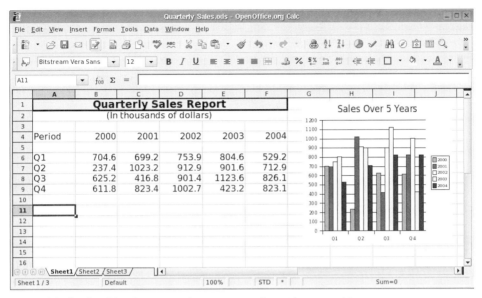

Figure 14–9 Just like that, your chart appears alongside your table.

To lock the chart in place, click anywhere else on the worksheet. You may want to change the chart's title as well—double-click on the chart, and then click on the title to make your changes. I'm going to call mine *Sales Over 5 Years*. If the chart is in the wrong place, click on it and then drag it to where you want it to be. If it is too big, grab one of the corners and resize it.

What's cool about this chart is that it is dynamically linked to the data on the page. Change the data in a cell, press <Enter>, and the chart will automatically update!

Final Touches

If you select (highlight) the title text in cell A1 and click the "center" icon, the text position doesn't change. That's because A1 is already filled to capacity, and the text is essentially already centered. To get the effect you want, click on cell A1, hold the mouse button down, and drag to select all the cells up to F1. Now click Format on the menu bar and select Merge Cells. All six cells will merge into one, after which you can select the text and center it.

For more extensive formatting of cells, including borders, color, and so on, right-click on the cell, and select Format. (Try this with your title cell.) A

Format Cells window (as in Figure 14-10) will appear, from which you can add a variety of formatting effects.

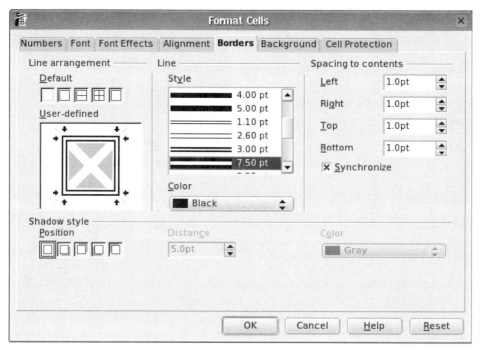

Figure 14–10   Adding borders and fill to cell.

A Beautiful Thing!

When you are through with your worksheet, it is time to print. Click File on the menu bar and select Print. Select your printer, click OK, and you'll have a product to impress even the most jaded bean counter. While you are busy impressing people, keep in mind that you can also export this spreadsheet to PDF with a single click, just as you did with Writer in the last chapter.

Alternatives

Because OpenOffice.org is such an obvious and excellent replacement for Microsoft Office (including Word, Excel, and PowerPoint), it's easy to forget that there are other alternatives. One of the great things I keep coming back to when I talk and write about Linux is that we do have alternatives, some costing no more than the time it takes to download and install them.

When it comes to spreadsheet programs, your Linux distribution CDs likely came with a few spreadsheet programs. The primary candidates are *Gnumeric*, *KSpread*, and the program we just looked at, OpenOffice.org's *Calc*.

Both Gnumeric and KSpread are certainly worth a look, but I've found Gnumeric to be particularly good when it comes to working with Excel spreadsheets.

Resources

Gnumeric

http://www.gnome.org/projects/gnumeric/

KSpread

http://www.koffice.org/kspread/

OpenOffice.org's Calc

http://www.openoffice.org/

Chapter
15

Presentation Graphics (For Those Who Need No Introduction)

Once upon a time, even a simple business presentation could be quite a costly affair. The person putting together a presentation would create it using a word processor (or pen and ink) and then transfer all this to a business graphics presentation tool. Alternatively, a special design service might be hired to take that next step. But eventually, the whole thing would be sent to yet another service that would create 35mm slides from the finished paper presentation.

On the day of the big meeting, the old carousel slide projector would come out, and the slides would be painstakingly loaded onto the circular slide holder. Then the lights would dim, and the show would begin. With any luck, the slides would all be in the right order and the projector would not jam up.

These days, we use tools that streamline this process, allowing us to create presentations, insert and manipulate graphical elements, and play the whole thing directly from our notebook computers. The projectors we use simply plug into the video port of our computers. There are many software packages to do the job under Linux. The most popular (and the one I cover here) is part of the OpenOffice.org suite. It is called Impress. For those of you coming from the Microsoft world, Impress is very much like PowerPoint. In fact, Impress can easily import and export PowerPoint files.

Getting Ready to Impress

After having worked with OpenOffice.org's Writer and Calc, you should feel right at home when it comes to using Impress. Working with menus, inserting text, spell-checking, and customizing your environment all work in exactly the same way. The editing screen itself is probably more like Calc than like Writer in some ways. The Impress work area will have tabbed pages, so you can easily jump from one part of the presentation to another. Each page is referred to as a *slide*. Given the history of business presentations—specifically, the making of these 35mm slides—it's probably no wonder that we still use the same terms when creating presentations with software like Impress.

To start Impress, click on your application starter (the big K), select OpenOffice.org (or Office), and click on OpenOffice.org Impress in the submenu. You can also start a new presentation from any other OpenOffice.org application, such as Writer or Calc. Just click File on the menu bar, select New, and choose Presentation from the submenu.

When you start up Impress for the first time, the Presentation Wizard will appear, where you will be presented with a number of choices. You can start with an empty presentation (Figure 15-1), work from a template, or open an existing presentation. Incidentally, some earlier versions of OpenOffice.org started with a blank page. You have the opportunity to select this behavior by clicking the checkbox labeled *Do not show this wizard again*.

 Quick Tip At the time of this writing, OpenOffice.org was shipping with only a couple of Impress templates. As I've mentioned before, one of the differences between OpenOffice.org and StarOffice (its commercial sibling) is that StarOffice comes with a number of templates. That said, you can still download some free templates for OpenOffice.org from www.ooextras.org.

Figure 15–1   Starting a new presentation with the Presentation Wizard.

The Presentation Wizard allows you to select from existing presentations as well as templates. For the moment, I'm going to stick with the very basics. Leave *Empty Presentation* selected, and click Next. Essentially, this starts us with off with a blank slide. Step 2 (Figure 15-2) gives us the opportunity to select a slide design. You may find a few options for slide design here (these would be your templates). Choose *<Original>*. Before you click Next, pause and look at the options for output medium. By default, Impress creates presentations designed for the screen (or a projector connected to your PC).

Step 3 (Figure 15-3) lets you define the default means for slide transition. You've all seen these presentations; as someone shows a presentation, slides dissolve to show the next one, or fly in from the left, or drop like a trap door closing. At this stage of the game, pick one of these effects from the drop-down box labeled *Effect*, and then choose the Speed of that transition. On the right-hand side is a preview window that will show you what the effect looks like when you select it.

Directly below the slide transition selection, you will select the presentation type. Your choices are Default and Automatic. By default, transition from slide to slide is accomplished by pressing a key, whether it be <Enter> or the spacebar (you can define this). Presentations can also run without any intervention from the person giving the presentation. By selecting Automatic,

you can define the amount of time between slides or even between presentations. Accept the default setting here, and click Create to start building your
presentation.

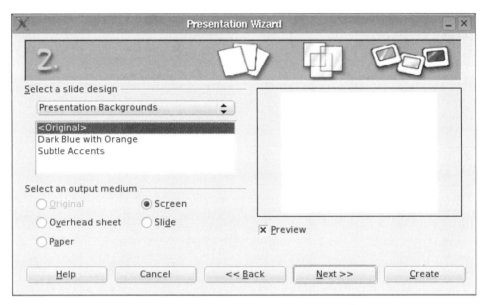

Figure 15–2   Impress defaults to creating presentations designed for the screen.

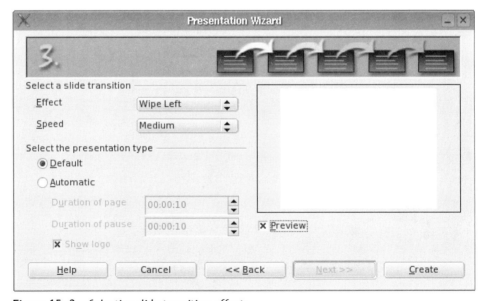

Figure 15–3   Selecting slide transition effects.

We now have everything we need to start working on our presentation. Impress opens to a blank page that is divided into three main panes, or frames (Figure 15-4). Over on the left, small previews of all your slides are displayed (just a single blank slide at this moment). As you work, you can quickly move to any slide you wish by scrolling down the lists and clicking on the slide. Below each preview is the slide's title. By default, the title is *Slide*, followed by the slide's number, in sequence. If you don't like this naming convention, you can easily override it by right-clicking on the title and selecting Rename slide.

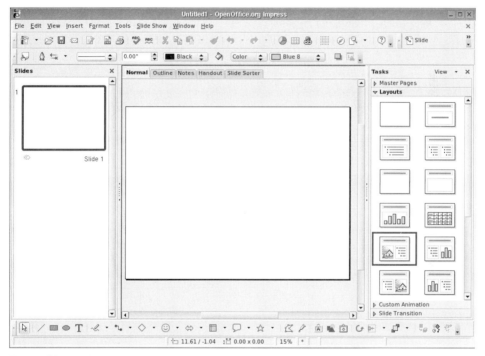

Figure 15–4 *Selecting your slide layout.*

Over to the right, another pane is visible, with a number of potential slide layouts having small preview images. This is the Tasks pane, and it is further divided into four sections: Master Pages, Layouts, Custom Animation, and Slide Transition. By default, the Layouts section is open. From here, you can decide on the appearance of the slide, the number of columns, title locations, and so on. If you pause over one of the images with your mouse cursor, a tooltip will appear telling you a little about the layout format.

Finally, there's a rather large central pane with five tabs, labeled Normal, Outline, Notes, Handout, and Slide Sorter. The Normal view is where you do most of your work, creating and editing slides. The Outline view is a kind of bird's-eye overview of the whole presentation. You can reorder slides, change titles, and so on. The Notes view does pretty much what you expect—it provides an easy way to add notes to the slides. The Handout tab is, I think, very handy. Sometimes when you are doing a presentation, you are expected to provide printouts of the slides for those in attendance. With Handout, you can define how those printouts look and how many slides will fit on a single page. Finally, we have the Slide Sorter, which is just a larger version of the Slides preview pane on the left. With a larger area, sorting slides is made just that much easier. For now, we will be working with the Normal view.

Finally, you'll notice that the various toolbars and menus have some resemblance to those of both Writer and Calc (discussed in the preceding two chapters). The menu bar sits just below the title bar, and the Standard bar is directly below that. You'll notice that the formatting bar has a number of different options unique to working in the Impress environment. Along the bottom is the Drawing bar, which provides quick access to objects, drawing functions, 3D effects, and so on.

So let's jump right in and create a presentation. From the Tasks pane, select the Layout section, if it isn't already open. Choose the *Title, Clipart, Text* layout by clicking on it, and it will instantly appear in the main work area in the center (Figure 15-5).

At any point, you can start the slide show by clicking Slide Show on the menu bar and selecting Slide Show. Pressing <F5> has the same effect. There won't be much to see at this point, but you can do this from time to time to see how your presentation is coming along.

To start editing your slide, click (or double-click for images) the section you want to change. Make your changes by typing into that area. For the title, you might enter *Introducing Linux!* When you are happy with your changes, just click outside of the frame area. Over on the right, in the frame that says *Click to add an outline*, insert these bulleted points:

- What is Linux?
- Is Linux really free?
- What can it do?
- Advantages?
- Disadvantages?

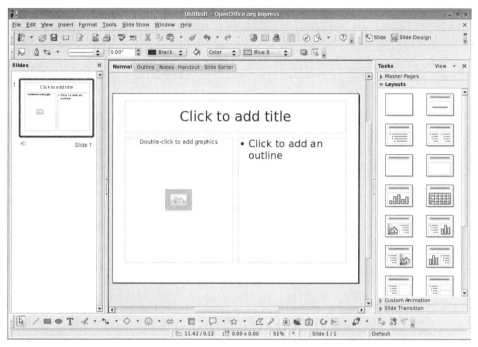

Figure 15–5 Having chosen a slide design, we are now ready to start editing that slide in the central work area.

As you might have noticed, this outline serves as talking points that mirror some of the topics I covered in the first chapter of this book. Now, over on the left-hand side, double-click on the frame (as instructed on the default slide) and insert a graphic. The Insert Picture dialog will appear (Figure 15-6), allowing you to navigate your folders and look for the perfect image.

You can use any image you like here. For my image, I used Konqueror to surf over to Larry Ewing's Web site (`www.isc.tamu.edu/~lewing/linux`), where I picked up my Tux graphic from the source. (I'll tell you more about Tux at the end of this chapter.) You may choose another image if you prefer. When you have your image selected, click Open, and it will replace the default text in the left-hand frame.

 Quick Tip Another option is to single-click the default image and press <Delete>. Then you can click Tools on the menu bar, select Gallery, and drag one of the included images onto your slide.

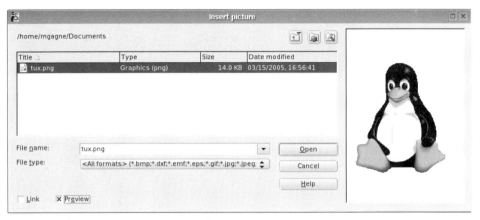

Figure 15–6 Inserting a picture into the presentation.

That's it. Your first slide is done. You might want to pause here and save your work before you move on. (Masterpieces must be protected.) Click File on the menu bar, select Save As, and then enter a filename for your presentation. I used *Introducing Linux* as my title. Now click Save, and we'll continue building this presentation.

Inserting Slides

At the right-hand end of the Standard bar is a button labeled Slide. Clicking this button will insert a new slide after whatever slide you happen to be working on. You can also click Insert on the menu bar and select Slide. Once again, you will be presented with a blank slide, ready for your creative vision (as in Figure 15-4). Over in the left-hand frame, a new blank slide appears below the preview of the completed first slide.

For this second slide, let's select a new slide design. Go back to the Layouts section of your Tasks frame and select the slide design called *Title, Text* (Figure 15-7).

Because we had five points (after our introductory slide), let's do a quick add of the next four slides by just clicking the Slide button on the Standard bar. You should now have preview images labeled *Slide 1* through *Slide 6*.

Now click on the preview image for Slide 2, and then click the top frame, where it says *Click to add title*. Enter the first bullet point from Slide 1. Then repeat the process for the next four slides, inserting the appropriate bullet point as the title.

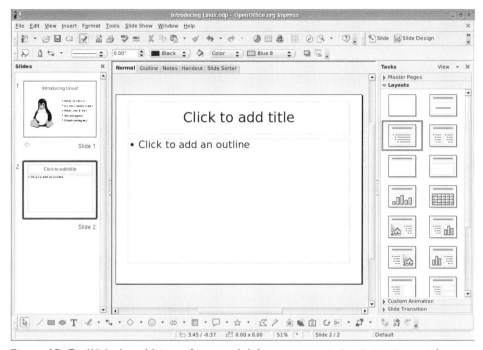

Figure 15–7   With the addition of a second slide, our presentation is starting to take shape.

Quick Tip You can give those slide labels more useful names by right-clicking on them and selecting Rename Slide.

As to what to enter in the text area of each slide, that I will leave either to your imagination or to your memory of Chapter 1. When you have finished entering all the information you want, save your work. I'm going to show you how to dress up those plain white slides.

Adding Color

Right-click on your slide (not on the text), and select Slide from the pop-up menu. Now click on Page Setup (Figure 15-8).

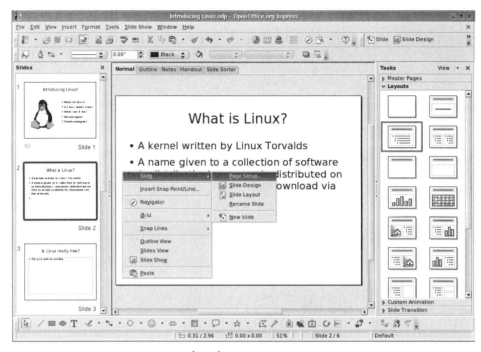

Figure 15–8   Modifying the page (slide) setup in preparation for color.

What you will see is a two-tabbed window (one tab says *Page* and the other says *Background*) (Figure 15-9). Click on the Background tab. Notice the five radio buttons. Each provides an option for background selection, whether it be plain white, colors, gradients, hatching, or bitmaps. Click on each to see the choices it offers.

For example, you might choose the Linear blue/white gradient (a very business-looking background) or perhaps the Water bitmap. The choice is yours. When you click OK, you'll be asked whether you want this background setting to be for all slides. For now, click Yes.

All right. You've done a lot of work, so save your work. Click File on the menu bar and select Save (or Save As) from the menu. If you choose Save As, you will have the opportunity to select the presentation format, whether native OpenOffice.org OpenDocument or Microsoft PowerPoint format.

Now it's time to see the fruits of your labor. Click Slide Show on the menu bar and select Slide show. You can also use the <F5> keyboard shortcut. The slides will transition with a touch of the spacebar or a mouse click. You can exit the presentation at any time by pressing the <Esc> key.

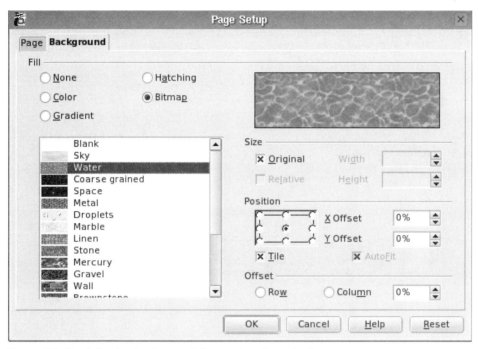

Figure 15–9 Selecting background decorations from the Impress page setup.

Printing Your Presentation

As with the other OpenOffice.org applications, click File on the menu bar and select Print—you can also click the small printer icon on the Standard bar. The standard OpenOffice.org print dialog will appear, from which you can select your printer of choice.

Instant Web Presentations

Here's something you are going to find incredibly useful. Impress lets you export your existing presentation to HTML format. The beauty of this is that you can take your presentation and make it available to anyone with a Web browser. Best of all, the export functionality takes care of all the details associated with creating a Web site, including the handling of links and forward and back buttons.

To create an instant Web presentation in OpenOffice, here is what you do. Make sure your current Impress presentation is open and that your work is saved. Click File on the menu bar and select Export. The Export dialog will appear. Because all the generated pages will appear in the directory you choose, it might make sense, before entering a filename, to create an empty directory into which to save your files. That filename, by the way, is the HTML title page, normally called index.html. If you would like a different name, choose it here, minus the .html extension (e.g., Linux_Intro), and click Export. A new window will appear. This is the HTML Export dialog (Figure 15-10).

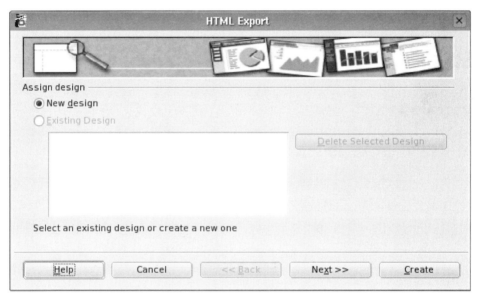

Figure 15–10   The HTML Export dialog on first run.

If this is your first HTML export, you only have one option on the first screen, and that is to create a new design. Click Next and you'll be presented with a few additional choices (Figure 15-11).

You are given the choice of several publication types. The default choice (and probably a very good one) is Standard HTML format. You can also decide to create an HTML publication with frames if you prefer. If you want to be totally in control of what your audience sees, you can also elect to create an automatic slideshow (using HTML refresh times of whatever length you choose) or a WebCast. When you have made your choice, click Next.

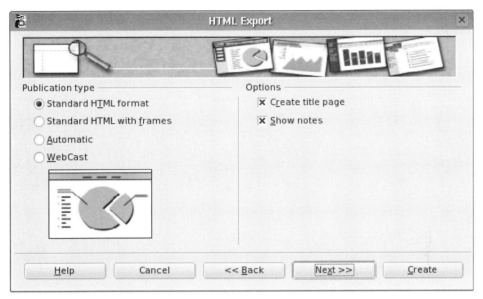

Figure 15–11   It is time to choose the format of your HTML presentation.

On the next window (Figure 15-12), you must decide the *resolution of the images* created for your Web publication. The default is to use JPG images at 75% compression. You can elect to set this all the way up to 100% for the best quality possible, but be aware that the higher the quality, the larger the images and the slower the download time. If this presentation is meant to be viewed on your personal office network, it probably doesn't matter.

You are also asked to choose the *Monitor Resolution*. This is an excellent question that is probably worth more than a few seconds of configuration. At some point in your history of surfing, you must have come across a Web site where the Web page is larger than your browser window. To view the page and read the text, you needed to move your horizontal slide bar back and forth. Although we are used to scrolling up and down to read text, left-to-right scrolling is somewhat more annoying. If you want to be as inclusive as possible for your audience, use 640×480. That may be going overboard, though. Most personal computer monitors these days will handle 800×600 without any problem, and many people run 1024×768 displays. Is there a right answer? Probably not. Consider your target audience, make your decision based on that consideration, and click Next.

One last thing before we move on. Notice the checkbox under the label *Effects*. I'm not a big fan of Web pages that play sounds when I do things. You can choose to export sounds whenever slides advance. The best way to decide what you like is to try both. It's all for fun, anyhow.

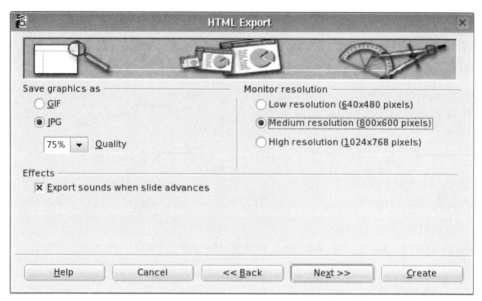

Figure 15–12   *Select your image quality and monitor resolution.*

On the next window that appears, fill in *title page information* for the Web presentation. This is the author's name (yours), your email address, and a link back to your own Web site if you wish. Click Next, and you'll then have the opportunity to decide on the graphics you wish to use for the forward and back buttons. If you don't want to use graphical buttons, you don't have to. In fact, the default is to use Text only, so to use a particular button style instead, make sure you uncheck the checkbox (Figure 15-13), select your button style, and click Next.

We are almost there. The final window lets you decide on the *color scheme* for the presentation. The default is simply to use the colors from the original Impress publication, but you can override this as well as the default color for hyperlinks and the default Web page background. Make your choices and click Create. One last window appears, asking you to name the HTML design. This is a free-form text field. Enter a brief description, and click Save.

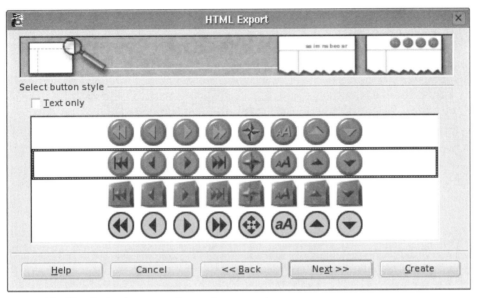

Figure 15–13   Pick a button style, any button style.

The process of exporting your presentation may take a few seconds or a few minutes, depending on the speed of your machine and the complexity of your presentation. To view the presentation, open your browser and point to the title page. That's all there is to it.

How About a Little Flash? Shocking!

Before we wrap up, let's revisit that Export dialog one more time. Click File from the menu and select Export. When the Export dialog appears, have another look at the File format selection box, just below the File name field. The default is to export to an HTML document, but there are other options. For one, we have a PDF export—the one-button export is common to Impress as well.

Notice that you also have a Macromedia Flash export capability. Isn't that interesting? Enter a filename for your presentation (no need to add the swf extension). With a single click of the Export button, your presentation will be saved to Macromedia's Flash format. Now your presentation is viewable from any browser with a Macromedia Flash or Shockwave plugin. The advantage of this over the HTML export is that all your animated slide transitions are preserved. Visitors to your site can view the presentation as it was intended.

So What's with the Penguin?

Having made you run off to Larry Ewing's site for a copy of Tux, I suppose I should take a moment to answer one of the most frequently asked questions in the Linux world. After all, every time you look at a Linux book, boxed set, or Web site, you stand a good chance of coming face to face with a fat, smiling penguin. You may well be wondering what Linux has to do with this penguin (Figure 15-14). Well, for starters, his name is *Tux*, and he is the Linux mascot. The most famous version of Tux (and there are many) is Larry Ewing's design.

Figure 15–14
Tux, the Linux mascot.

The story behind Tux is the stuff of legend now and, like most legends, a little hard to pin down. Linus Torvalds was asked what he envisioned for a mascot. The answer from Linus was "You should be imagining a slightly overweight penguin (*), sitting down after having gorged itself, and having just burped. It's sitting there with a beatific smile—the world is a good place to be when you have just eaten a few gallons of raw fish and you can feel another 'burp' coming."

There is also another story, in which Linus claims he was attacked by a killer penguin at the Canberra zoo, where he contracted "penguinitis," a disease whose main symptom is that you "stay awake at nights just thinking about penguins and feeling great love towards them."

That's the thing about legends. They tend to get strange over time.

> Some people have told me they don't think a fat penguin really embodies the grace of Linux, which just tells me they have never seen an angry penguin charging at them in excess of 100 mph. They'd be a lot more careful about what they say if they had.
>
> *– Linus Torvalds*

Extra! Extra!

Before we move away from the classic office applications, I would like to take another moment to address the issue of templates. Although StarOffice, the nonfree commercial sibling of OpenOffice.org, comes with a number of templates for word processing, spreadsheets, and presentation graphics, OpenOffice.org is still quite *light* in this area. As I mentioned earlier, the Impress package has no included templates at all.

To resolve this issue, the *OO Extras* Web site was born (see the Resources section at the end of this chapter). Travis Bauer has put together a great site with a number of community-created and -distributed templates for the OpenOffice.org suite. The site is laid out so that you can look for things specific to your application of choice, and screenshots are provided so that you can get a preview of what the document will look like. Because OO Extras has become an international affair, these extras come in different languages as well.

A visit to OO Extras is well worth your time. Perhaps someday you too will contribute to this growing body of work.

Alternatives

In the preceding two chapters, I mentioned that the KDE office suite, KOffice, offers similar components that you may want to consider. These include KWord for word processing and KCalc for spreadsheets. There's also an alternative for presentation graphics and that is KPresenter. In all of these cases, the advantage is one of performance and tight integration into the KDE desktop. That, in itself, makes the KOffice suite extremely attractive.

Resources

KPresenter

http://koffice.kde.org/kpresenter/

Larry Ewing's "Tux" (the Official Linux Penguin)

http://www.isc.tamu.edu/~lewing/linux/

Linux Logo Links at Linux.org

http://www.linux.org/info/logos.html

OO Extras

http://ooextras.org

16

Digital Photography

Then we have digital cameras. In the world of your old OS, you needed special software to work with your particular camera. In the Linux world, you can do it all with a single interface. In fact, if you've come this far in the book, you probably already know almost everything thing you need to know to work with your camera at a basic level. We won't stop there, however. Once I cover the basics, I introduce you to a fantastic digital photography package called digiKam.

Finally, I cover another of piece of graphical magic when I show you how to use a scanner with your Linux system, from capturing your old photos to capturing and interpreting text.

Ready? Then smile!

Working with a Digital Camera

Behind the fancy graphical front end that takes photos from your camera and lets you work with them on your Linux system is a little package called *gPhoto2*. This package is actually a back end used by various other graphical programs, including, as you will see shortly, Konqueror.

A number of digital cameras are supported through gphoto2, 436 of them as I write this chapter. To discover whether your camera is supported directly, shell out and type the following command:

```
gphoto2 --list-cameras
```

You should see output similar to the following shortened, example list.

```
Number of supported cameras: 436
Supported cameras:
        "AEG Snap 300"
        "Agfa ePhoto 1280"
        "Agfa ePhoto 307"
        "Argus DC-2000"
        "Argus DC-2200"
        "Barbie"
        "Benq DC1300" (TESTING)
        "Canon Digital IXUS"
        "Canon PowerShot Pro70"
        "Canon PowerShot S10"
        "Canon PowerShot S40"
        "Epson PhotoPC 700"
        "Epson PhotoPC 850z"
        "Panasonic Coolshot NV-DCF5E"
        "Panasonic DC1580"
```

If your camera is not listed, don't despair. A visit to the gPhoto Web site for an updated version of the software may be all you need:

```
http://gphoto.sourceforge.net
```

 Quick Tip Here's another way to get pictures off an unsupported camera. Just get yourself a USB media reader from your local computer store. They are extremely inexpensive, and many will support multiple formats, such as Smart Media, Compact Flash, and more. The USB reader mounts as just another directory or folder on your desktop. Click on it with Konqueror, and then drag and drop your photos to where you want them.

Picture-Perfect Konqueror

Getting images from your USB digital camera is not at all difficult. Connect your camera to your Linux system via a USB cable. Every camera is a little different, but all will have some kind of switch or setting to turn them on and allow transfer to the PC. Mine has a little jagged line with arrows at either side to represent a connection. Check your camera's manual for details.

Depending on your Linux distribution, you may find that a camera icon appears on your desktop when you plug in the camera. Click on that icon; Konqueror will open, and your camera's internal directories will be there for you to see. If such an icon doesn't magically appear, it's time for your old friend, Konqueror, to come to the rescue.

Type camera:/ in the Konqueror location field, and press <Enter>. You should see your digital camera listed in Konqueror's main window. On my system and with my USB-connected camera, it shows up as *Canon PowerShot S10*. Click on that icon, and you'll see folders corresponding to the way your camera stores its images. Just navigate down those directories until you get to your photo directories. One by one, preview images of the photos stored on your camera will appear (Figure 16-1).

To move (or copy) your photos into a folder, start by bringing up Konqueror's navigation sidebar by pressing <F9>. Now select the images you wish (or press <Ctrl+A> for all the images) and drag them into a folder in the navigation window on the left-hand side. That is all there is to it.

This method is perfect for casual use. But when you start taking and storing vast quantities of pictures, as happens when you discover digital photography, you'll want something more powerful. That something is digiKam.

Quick Tip If you don't see a preview of your images, click View on Konqueror's menu bar, select Preview from the menu bar, and check off Images in the drop-down list. You should now see little thumbnail images corresponding to the images on your camera.

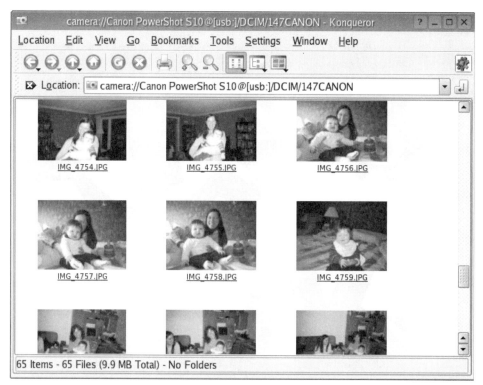

Figure 16–1   Pictures appear as thumbnails in Konqueror.

Picture-Perfect digiKam

digiKam is a complete digital photo management system. Using digiKam, you can create collections and organize your photos (by date, type, and more) in easily searchable albums. Selecting and downloading images from your favorite digital camera is easy and fun. You can add comments to pictures, adjust light levels, fix the dreaded red-eye, collect and e-mail images, burn them to CD, or create a nifty instant calendar. With digiKam, you can do it all. digiKam is now distributed as part of KDE, with the latest and greatest always available at http://digikam.sourceforge.net.

To run digiKam (program name digikam), look for it in your Graphics menu, or use your <Alt+F2> quick launch. If this is your first time with digiKam, you'll be presented with a dialog asking for the location of the directory that will house your photo albums (Figure 16-2). By default, this is a directory called Pictures, directly under your home directory. You can, if you wish, specify an alternate path, but the default is usually fine for most people. Press OK to continue.

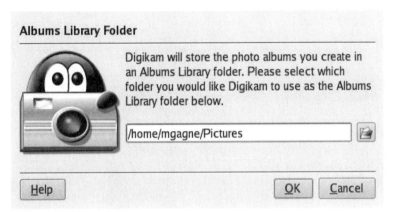

Figure 16-2   On first run, digiKam needs to know where you will store your albums.

When the main digiKam window appears for the first time, things are going to look a little plain (Figure 16-3). The window is divided into two main panes. The left-hand pane lists your albums and your tags. The main window, on the right, is where you will see your pictures, edit them, and so on. Directly below the menu bar, you'll find a number of icons to let you quickly manipulate albums and pictures (pause over each one, and a tooltip will appear describing their function). Don't worry, it will all make sense as we start working with the package.

In order to get anything interesting done, we need at least one album, so let's create one now. Click Album on the menu bar and select *New Album*. You can also click the New Album icon if you prefer. When you do, another window will appear, asking you for the details of this collection (Figure 16-4).

Enter the details, which include the title of the album, the collection it belongs to, some appropriate comments, as well as the date this album represents. You can create albums as you need them or a number of them at once. Each album can be filled with pictures you may already have on your hard disk—my local camera store provides a service where I can have my 35mm pictures burned to a CD. These pictures could, of course, also come from your digital camera. To do that, you need to tell digiKam about your camera.

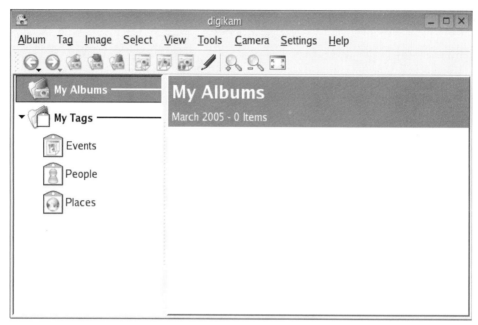

Figure 16–3 digiKam's clean and bare interface on first use.

Figure 16–4
Creating a new digiKam album.

Configuring Your Digital Camera

Click Camera on the menu bar and select Add Camera. The camera Configure dialog will appear, waiting for you to add your particular model (Figure 16-5). On the left-hand side of the window is a series of icons relating to many other things besides the camera itself. That's because the Add Camera option is a shortcut to the camera section of the digiKam configuration utility. You could click the *Add* button on the right-hand side and go through the various steps, but look just below that and you'll see a rather useful *Auto-Detect* button. Make sure your camera is turned on, and then click Auto-Detect. Chances are very good that your particular camera will be detected.

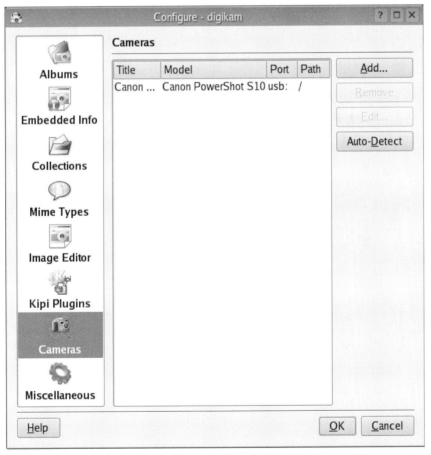

Figure 16–5 The Auto-Detect feature in the digiKam Configure dialog is great.

If the camera isn't detected, it is possible that it is one of the cameras not covered in that list of nearly 450 supported cameras (covered earlier when we talked about gPhoto2). It is also possible that it just wasn't detected at the moment. Click the Add button, and you'll be presented with a dialog from which you can select your camera, identify the port it is connected to, and so on.

Once your camera is properly configured, it's time to look at the pictures you have taken. Make sure your camera is turned on and in the data transfer mode. Most digital cameras have a special setting for downloading to your PC. Next, click Camera on the menu bar, and you'll see your camera listed above the Add Camera menu selection. Click on your camera's name, and the camera dialog will appear. A few seconds after that, thumbnails of all the pictures currently stored on the camera will be displayed (Figure 16-6).

Figure 16–6   Clicking on your configured camera will download thumbnails of the pictures you've taken.

Before you go clicking that Download button at the bottom in all this excitement, I want to tell you about a couple of other interesting features you'll find here. One of those features is under the Advanced button. If you've taken several pictures over many days, it might be handy to have them automatically inserted into subdirectories based on the date the pictures were taken. By clicking the Advanced dialog checkbox labeled *Download photos into automatically created date-based sub-albums of destination album*, you can do just that. This is a great thing to remember next time you take a week of holidays.

The Select button allows you a quick way to select all of the photos, unselect them all, or invert your selection—you may want to exclude two or three photos, and it's easier to select one and invert the selection than to select them all and unselect two or three. Then, under the Delete button, it's possible to delete photos directly from your camera. Just select and delete them.

Finally, there's the real reason we are here in the first place, and that's the Download button. Once you've made your selection, click on the Download button, choose Download All or Download Selected, and you are ready to go. One final dialog will appear, asking you to choose the album into which you want the pictures downloaded (Figure 16-7). Since we only have one album so far, that choice is easy.

That's really all there is to getting images from your camera. I did mention earlier, however, that you might also want to organize all those photos that are already on your computer's hard disk. Create a new Album, and then right-click on the album name. From the pop-up menu that appears, select *Add Images*. The standard KDE file selection dialog will appear. Navigate to where your pictures are located, and add them to your new album.

What About Those Tags?

We now have a couple of albums with pictures in them. The album titles are now listed under My Albums, on the left-hand side, and that all makes sense. Directly below that is another section, though, titled My Tags. So what are these tags?

There is a clue. Notice the three categories: Events, People, and Places. The idea is that you can assign tags to the pictures in your photo albums to make them easier to locate. For instance, say you have a couple hundred travel pictures, of which 30 or so are from your visit to Rome. You could assign all vacation pictures the Places tag, making it simple to call up all your vacation pictures. But how would you find Rome amongst all those vacation

Figure 16–7   Almost done. Select an album and import your digital camera's photos.

shots? The thing to do would be to create subtags under your Places tag and label them according to country, and that is precisely what you can do here. You might want to do the same with your family members. That way, finding the pictures you've taken of Grandma is just a matter of clicking her tag. Let me show you how.

Start by right-clicking on the People tag, and then click on *New Tag*. Enter the name of the tag you are creating. In this case, you might create one for all the people in your family. Now go back into your albums and right-click on an image of your choice. One of the options in the pop-up menu is Assign Tag; below that is a list of the tags you have created. To find pictures of a particular member of your family, click on the tag you created for them, and digiKam will find them, regardless of which album they are stored in (Figure 16-8). To find out which album a particular picture belongs to, pause over the thumbnail with your mouse pointer and an information window will appear.

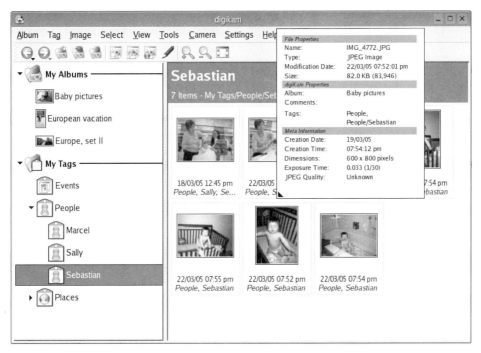

Figure 16–8 Assigning tags to your pictures makes it easier to organize them and to locate them at a later time.

But Wait—There's More!

Unfortunately, I won't be able to cover everything about digiKam here, but I do want to give you a taste of some of its other great features. Click on an image, and the viewer window will appear. This also happens to be the image editor. From here, you can rotate and resave your pictures, adjust the light levels, and fix the evil red-eye.

For a great trip down memory lane, select an album (or a group of photos), click Tools on the menu bar, and select SlideShow. Also under Tools, you can create a calendar with pictures of your favorite memories. Fire up the color printer, run off a collection, and forget about buying calendars ever again.

Want to share those memories? Select a group of photos, right-click Image on the menu bar, and select Email Images. A message is automatically created, using the e-mail client of your choice, with the photos already attached. How about creating a CD or DVD collection of photos? Select the photos you want, click Album on the menu bar, and select Export. From there, it's easy to create that permanent archive collection.

Smile!

Scanning . . .

Many scanner options are available, from old-fashioned parallel port devices to SCSI-connected units. These days, most people will choose a USB scanner for its low price and easy connection to the system. As with all devices, a visit to the Web site for USB devices for Linux will save you time (and money) by helping you select a device well suited to run under Linux. With most modern Linux distributions, your scanner will be detected automatically, so there isn't much you need to do in terms of configuration if yours is a supported model.

What models are supported? The USB devices list I mentioned in Chapter 8 is a great start. Since scanning under Linux is done using a package called *SANE* (Scanner Access Now Easy), that site is one of the best places to check out scanner compatibility. Here's the link:

```
http://www.sane-project.org/sane-supported-devices.html
```

That page also has a link to the Scanner Search Engine. This is a fantastic tool that lets you enter a specific model number to find out if it is supported. You can even put in the name of a particular vendor and it will list all the scanners by that manufacturer.

Scanning under KDE—Kooka

A number of scanning programs exist for Linux, and most are front ends to *SANE*, the program I just mentioned. One such front end is included with your Linux system. *Kooka*, part of KDE, is one such program.

Kooka is both a scan program and an optical character recognition (OCR) program. What this means is that you can use it to scan a document of text and export that text back into some word processing package for further editing.

You'll find Kooka under the main Multimedia or Graphics menu, but you can also start the program from the shell or with your quick launcher <Alt+F2>. The actual program name is kooka. When you start the program, you will see a dialog box similar to that in Figure 16-9. Kooka looks for available scanners and offers you a choice. If you have only one scanner on your system (as is usually the case), check the box labeled *Do not ask on startup again, always use this device* before clicking OK.

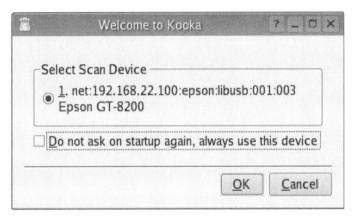

Figure 16–9 Kooka auto-detects your connected scanner.

Once past this point, Kooka's main window will appear (Figure 16-10). Along the top or the larger Kooka window, you'll see a familiar-looking menu and icon bar. The window consists primarily of four areas, or *frames*: two horizontal frames to the left consisting of a navigation window up top and a Scanner Setting window at the bottom. The larger top pane on the right-hand side is a tabbed scan window. The left-hand side tab shows the main scan window, while the right-hand side tab is for scan previews (more on this later). The smaller pane along the bottom is a kind of scanner desktop where thumbnails of final scans are presented. To suit your tastes, you can resize the main window (and monitor size) as well as the individual frames.

Let's start by looking at the scan preview window. There are two tabs here: the *image view* tab (identified by a small folder icon on the tab) and the *scan preview* tab (the one with a magnifying glass icon).

On the left side, near the top you will see a directory and file browser with a default master directory called *Kooka Gallery*. You can create additional folders below this by right-clicking on the directory and selecting Create directory. As with all such dialogs, you can create directories inside of directories to organize your files efficiently. Scanned files will be saved in these directories.

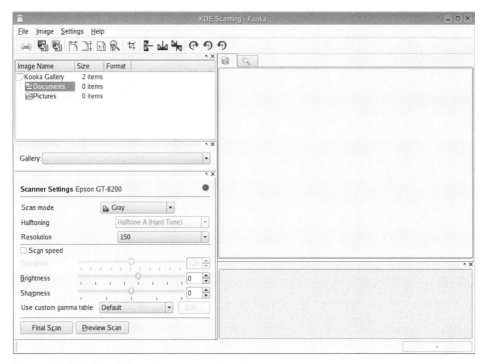

Figure 16–10   Kooka's main screen and work area.

Before scanning your first image, look down at the bottom left-hand window, where your scanner settings are set. What you see there will vary, depending on the model and type of scanner you are running. On my system, I used an Epson GT-8200. You can adjust scan mode (black and white, grayscale, or color) as well as resolution. Keep in mind that although higher resolution generally means higher quality, it also means a *much larger file* in terms of storage space. For Web page purposes, 75–100 dpi is probably ideal.

On my scanner, I can also adjust the brightness, sharpness, and gamma correction. The correct settings are somewhat of a trial-and-error affair. More than one scan may be necessary to decide what works (and looks) best.

Note These settings are scanner-specific, and different scanners may have different settings.

Find a photograph or picture you like, and put it on the scanner. Change the Scan mode from Gray to Color if you prefer, and then click the Preview Scan button in the Scanner Settings window. After the scan is complete, the main window to the right will automatically flip to the Preview tab.

In the image preview window, you can select the scan size to define the actual dimensions of the scanned file. If you want only a small portion of the photo, you can also drag the dotted lines in the preview window (with the mouse) to encompass only the part you wish to save. If you have a small image on a white (or black) background, try using the Auto-Selection mode by clicking on the *"active on"* checkbox and selecting the appropriate background color. When you are happy with the preview, click Final Scan in the settings window.

When the scan is complete, the Kooka Save Assistant will appear (Figure 16-11). The various image formats available will be displayed, along with a description to help you make a decision on whether this is the format you

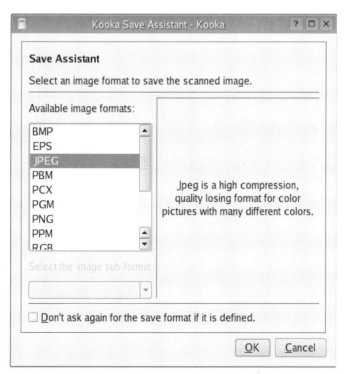

Figure 16–11   The Save Assistant helps you choose the file format.

wish to use. For instance, JPEG is described as "a high-compression, quality-losing format for color pictures with many different colors." If you are always saving in the same format, you can elect to click the checkbox labeled *Don't ask again for the save format if it is defined.* Should you change your mind, click Settings on the menu bar, and select Configure Kooka. Under Image Saving, you can elect to bring back the Save Assistant.

Once you click OK, your scanned picture will appear in the main scan window to the right (Figure 16-12). You may have to click the left-hand scan image view tab. Furthermore, a small thumbnail will appear in the scan desktop pane at the lower right (this gives you an easy, visual means to navigate multiple scans). View options, such as *Scale to width*, *Set zoom*, and *Rotate image clockwise*, can be selected by right-clicking on the image. These view options are also available via the icons just below the menu bar.

Figure 16–12   The final scan.

Saving Your Work

In a strange way, your images are already saved. In your home directory, you'll find another directory, called `.kde`, where your KDE configuration files, Kmail address books, Konqueror bookmarks, and other files live. As it turns out, your scanned images are already saved there, although technically they are still work files, numbered sequentially. In fact, you could quit Kooka right now and come back later and find your images still there. If you want to have a look, check out

```
.kde/share/apps/ScanImages
```

in your home directory. If you created new directories in your Gallery, you'll see them as well.

To *officially* save your work in Kooka, right-click on one of your scanned images in the Gallery frame (the file list window on the top left), and select Save Image. You'll be presented with the standard KDE Save As dialog. Choose a directory and a name for your image, and click Save (Figure 16-13).

Figure 16–13   Now it is time to save your images.

You can now take that image, fire up the GIMP, and modify it at will.

The GIMP? I cover that in the next chapter. I still have a little scanning magic to share with you.

Optical Character Recognition

Before I wrap up this discussion of Kooka, let me tell you about one other very cool thing the program does. Say you have an old document page you want to transcribe. The obvious first choice is to sit it in front of you, open up a word processor, and start typing. Your second option is to pop that page on your scanner, use Kooka to scan it, then run it through OCR.

Here's how you do it. Because most people won't be using OCR, most distributions by default don't install the supporting software. The package is called *ocrad,* and you can find it at

```
www.gnu.org/software/ocrad/ocrad.html
```

Check your distribution CDs first. If you are going to do OCR, Kooka needs to have this installed.

Start by scanning your page as you would any image. Binary scan mode is probably fine for straight text, but this is one case where *the higher the resolution, the better your chances are of an accurate OCR*. When you are happy with the preview, click Final Scan, and you should see your page in the right-hand window. Now click Image on the menu bar, and select *OCR image*. Alternatively, you can click the second icon from the left in the icon bar—it does the same thing.

A window labeled *Optical Character Recognition* will pop up (Figure 16-14) that allows you to specify a handful of settings to tune the character recognition software. Remember: OCR is not perfect by any means, but with some tweaking you can achieve fairly high levels of accuracy. For your first scan, simply leave it at the defaults and click Start OCR. The whole process of character recognition may take a few seconds, so be patient.

After the process is complete, a window will appear showing you the results of the OCR process (Figure 16-15). If you opted to spell-check the results, the spell-check window will appear as well.

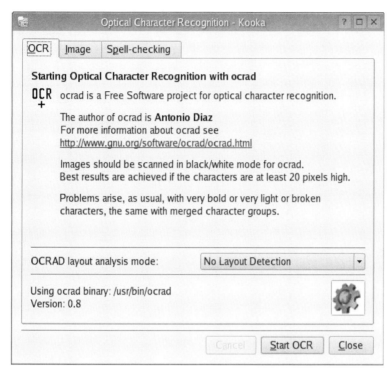

Figure 16–14 OCR settings such as multicolumn layout and spell-checking are handled here.

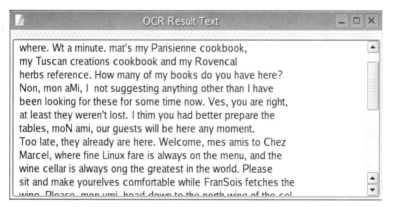

Figure 16–15 Kooka OCR results window.

Remember: The higher your scan resolution, the better your results. The only catch, of course, is that higher resolution requires more disk space and more processing power when you are through. If you want to save the results and edit at will, then copy and paste the text into your favorite word processor or text editor, whatever suits your needs.

 Quick Tip Most Linux distributions also come with another scanning package, called XSane (command name `xsane`).

Resources

digiKam
http://digikam.sourceforge.net

gPhoto Software
http://gphoto.org

SANE–Supported Devices page
http://www.sane-project.org/sane-supported-devices.html

Chapter

17

Digital Art with the GIMP

Oddly enough, applications allowing users to work with graphics are among some of the most highly developed in the world. To see the truth in this rather bold statement, turn your eyes to Hollywood. Blockbusters such as Titanic, Star Trek: Nemesis, Shrek, and others use Linux and Linux clusters to create the complex special effects.

In terms of graphical design and photo editing, your Linux system comes with one of the most powerful, flexible, and easy-to-use packages there is, regardless of what OS you are running. It's called the GIMP. Allow me to introduce you to some of its many features.

The GIMP is one of those programs that has helped create an identity for Linux. Of course, there are plenty of programs out there, as I'm sure I have demonstrated by this point in the book, but the GIMP is special. The Linux community has used it to create images, buttons, desktop themes, window decorations, and more. Even the Linux mascot, Tux the Penguin, whose best-known incarnation was created by Larry Ewing, was a product of the GIMP.

The GIMP is an amazingly powerful piece of software, yet its basic functions are easy to use as well. With a little bit of work, a lot of fun, and a bit of experimentation, anyone can use the GIMP to turn out a fantastic piece of professional-quality art. You doubt my words? Then follow along with me, and in just a few minutes you'll have created a slick-looking logo for your Web page or your desktop. That said, with time, you can also learn to wield the GIMP with the power of a Hollywood special effects master.

Ladies and Gentlemen, Start Your GIMP

Click on the application starter (the big K), scroll up to the Graphics submenu, and click on the GIMP. You can also use your program quick launch by pressing <Alt+F2> and entering gimp into the command field.

If you are starting up the GIMP for the very first time, the GIMP User Installation dialog will appear (Figure 17-1). You'll be asked a number of questions regarding the location of your personal GIMP directory (defaults to a directory called .gimp-version.no under your personal home directory), how much memory you wish to allocate for the GIMP to do its work, and so on. For the most part, you can just accept the defaults by clicking Continue through the various screens.

Once you have entered all this information, the GIMP proper will start up. You will probably get a number of panels aside from the GIMP's main screen. You will also likely get the GIMP Tip of the Day. As with all such tips, you can elect not to have it appear each time the program starts—just uncheck the button labeled *Show tip next time GIMP starts* before you hit Close, and you won't be bothered with it again. What you are likely to see (minus that Tip of the Day) should look a bit like Figure 17-2.

The long window on the right is split into two main areas. At the top is the layers, channels, and paths dialog. The dialog below has three tabs, one for brushes, another for patterns, and another for gradients. If you choose to

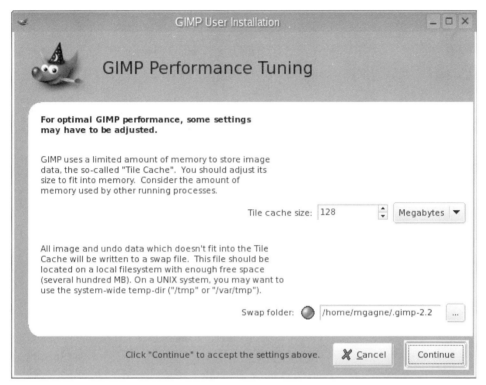

Figure 17–1 When you start the GIMP for the first time, you'll need to adjust a few settings.

close this window, there is no harm done, but you'll end up calling up dialogs as you need them. We visit this again when I cover brushes later on.

The most important of those windows is the GIMP toolbox. That's the window to the left in Figure 17-2. The toolbox itself is the top half (see the close-up in Figure 17-3). The bottom half of the dialog represents the options available to the currently selected tool. If you were using the text tool, you would have a choice of font styles and sizes at your disposal.

Along the top, directly below the title bar, is a familiar-looking menu bar labeled, quite simply, *File, Xtns,* and *Help.* Clicking on these will show you additional submenus. Below the menu bar is a grid of icons, each with an image representing one of the GIMP's tools. I cover all of these things shortly, but first let's take the GIMP out for a spin.

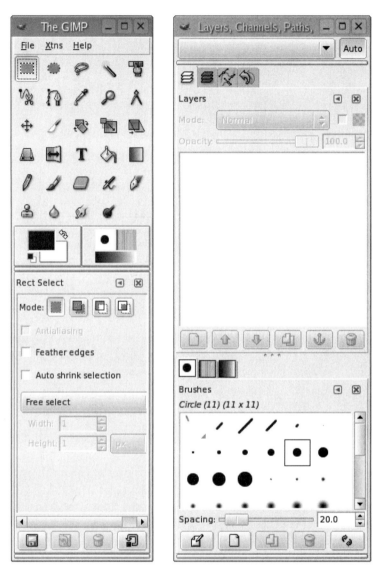

Figure 17–2   First time through, the GIMP will start with the layers, channels, and paths dialog (right) open as well.

Figure 17–3
The GIMP toolbox.

Easy Logos with the GIMP

The nitty-gritty can wait. I think we should do something fun with the GIMP right now. I'm going to show you how to create a very cool-looking corporate or personal logo with just a few keystrokes. If you don't have the GIMP open yet, start the program now. From the main toolbox menu bar, select Xtns and scroll down to Script-Fu; another menu will cascade from it.

Quick Tip Notice that the menus have a *dashed line* at the top. These are menu tear-offs. By clicking on the dashed line, you can *detach the menu* and put it somewhere on your desktop for convenient access to functions you use all the time. In fact, all the menus, including submenus, can be detached.

From the Script-Fu menu, move your mouse to Logos. You should see a whole list of logo types, from *3D Outline* to *Cool Metal* to *Starscape* and more. For this exercise, choose *Cool Metal*.

Every logo has different settings, so the one you see in Figure 17-4 is specific to *Cool Metal*. *Particle Trace* will have a completely different set of parameters. To create your *Cool Metal* logo, start by changing the Text field to something other than the logo style's name. I'll change mine to read *Linux Rocks!* The font size is set to 100 pixels, and we can leave it at that for now.

Figure 17–4   *Script-Fu logo settings for Cool Metal.*

In many of these logos, a default font has been selected for you. You can override the current choice (written on the button itself) and pick something else by clicking on the font button. The Font Selection window shows you the various fonts available on your system and lets you try different font types, styles, and sizes. A preview window gives you an idea of what the font looks like (Figure 17-5).

To create my logo, I'm going to choose a font on my system called *ActionIs* (and just like that, the old Spiderman theme jumps into my brain). You may choose whatever you like. When you have decided on a font, click OK. Then click OK again, this time in the Script-Fu: Logos/Cool Metal window. The result should be something similar to my own logo in Figure 17-6.

Figure 17–5
Script-Fu Font Selection dialog.

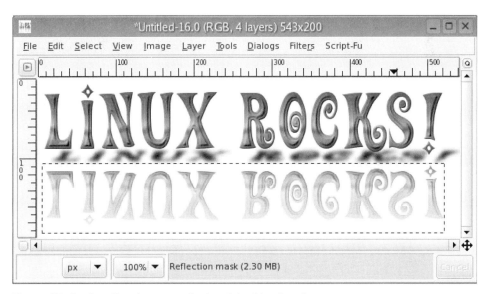

Figure 17–6   Just like that—a professional-looking logo!

If you don't like the results, close the image by clicking the Close button in the corner (usually an X, unless you have changed your desktop theme or style). A warning box will pop up telling you that changes have been made and that perhaps you might want to save your work (more on that in a moment). Your options are *Save, Don't Save,* and *Cancel.* Click *Don't Save,* and it goes away. Then start over with another logo. You might try changing the background color or the gradient this time. You might even want to try a different type of logo altogether.

Saving and Opening Your Work

Now it is time to preserve your masterpiece. It's also a good time to have another look at the image window, in this case your logo. Every image created in the GIMP has a menu bar across the top labeled File, Edit, Select, View, and so on. These menus can also be called up by right-clicking anywhere on the image. To save your work, right-click on the File menu, and select Save As. The Save Image dialog will appear (Figure 17-7).

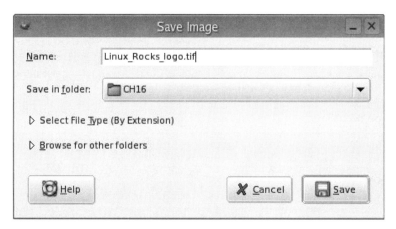

Figure 17–7   It's time to save your creation.

Notice the small arrow beside the words *Select File Type (By Extension)*. If you already know that you want to save your image as a .jpg or a .tif file (or any number of formats), you can simply add it to the filename. The GIMP can figure it out for you. If you would prefer to see a list of available formats, click the arrow; the Save Image dialog will change to display the various formats supported by the GIMP. There's also an arrow beside the label *Browse for other folders*. By default, the GIMP will use the current folder to save your work. To choose another directory, click the arrow; a more comprehensive navigation dialog will appear (Figure 17-8).

Figure 17–8   A more comprehensive folder navigation dialog to save your work.

When you have entered your filename and selected a file type, click OK, and you are done. Opening a file is similar. From the GIMP toolbox menu bar, select Open (or use the <Ctrl+O> shortcut) to bring up the Load Image dialog. The difference between this and the Save Image dialog is that when you click on a filename, you can also click on Generate Preview to display a small thumbnail preview in the Open Image dialog.

Printing Your Masterpiece

You've created a masterpiece. You are infinitely proud of it, and you want to share it with your friends who, alas, are not connected to the Internet. It's time to print your image and send it to them the old-fashioned, snail-mail way.

Okay, perhaps you aren't feeling quite that sharing, but there are times when you'll want to print the results of your work. Simply click File on the image menu bar, and select Print (once again, you can right-click on your image if you prefer). A printing dialog box will appear (Figure 17-9), from which you can specify a number of print options, including, of course, which printer you would like to use.

Figure 17–9   Time to print your masterpiece.

Quick GIMP Trick Want to take a screenshot and open it up to edit in the GIMP? It's easy. Click *File* on the GIMP toolbox menu bar, move to *Acquire*, and click *Screen Shot*. The image size will be the same as your screen (e.g., 1024x768). Since the GIMP will be in the screen shot you take, you may want to minimize it before capturing the image. In order to make that possible, select an appropriate time delay—say, five seconds—from the Screen Shot dialog box that appears. Minimize the windows you don't want to see, and then wait. After the capture completes, a GIMP image window will appear where you can make your modifications.

Tools, Tools, and More Tools

Now that we've had some fun and created some *true art*, it's time to find out what all those icons in the GIMP toolbox do. Before we do this, however, we should look at those two boxes at the bottom of the toolbox, because what they offer affects what the icons do.

The block on the right is the color menu (Figure 17-10). It gives you quick and easy access to foreground and background colors. The black and white squares on the left can be changed to other colors by double-clicking on one or the other. If you click on the arrow between the two, you switch between foreground and background colors.

Figure 17–10
The multifunction color, brushes, pattern, and gradient menu.

The box to the right is a quick dialog menu and really consists of three different tools: a brush selector, a pattern selector, and a gradient selector. Click on any of them to bring up the list of choices each provides. Figure 17-11 shows the brushes dialog. Think back to the introduction to this section and you'll recall that there was a layers and channels dialog in addition to the main

GIMP toolbox. At the bottom of that window was the brushes dialog (as well as gradients and patterns). If you left that window open, then the brushes selection will still be there.

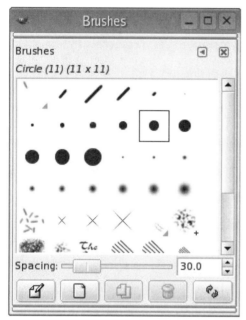

Figure 17–11
The brush selection dialog, on its own.

If you select a different gradient, pattern, or brush from the resulting menus, you'll also see them change on the dialog menu at the bottom of the GIMP toolbox. This gives you a quick visual feedback on what brush, pattern, or gradient is active at the moment.

Now, on to the Tool Icons

In the next few pages, I'm going to cover the GIMP's tools one by one, a row at a time. Each row has five tools, except for the last, which has four. The reason I am mentioning this is because this is the default layout. If you decide to resize the GIMP toolbox by dragging one of the sides out, the toolbox will widen, but the number of tools per row will increase as well, so you could have six or seven tools if you wished. The reverse is true should you decide to shrink the width of the GIMP toolbox.

Start by moving your mouse over the various icons, pausing over each one. Tooltips will appear telling you what tool each of the icons represents. (I go over these in a moment.) If you click on any of these icons, the window below the toolbox will change to present you with that tool's option, as with the Flip dialog in Figure 17-12.

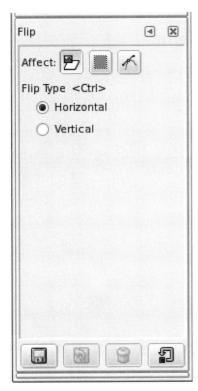

Figure 17–12
Tool options dialog, in this case for the flip tool.

So what are all those icons for? An excellent question. Let's look at them again, one row at a time, starting with—you guessed it—the first row (Figure 17-13).

Figure 17–13   First icon group.

The first icon, represented by a dotted rectangle, lets you select a *rectan-gular* area. Just hold down the left mouse button at whatever point you choose for a starting corner, and drag it across your image. A dotted line will indicate the area you've selected. If you hold down the <Shift> key at the same time as the left mouse button, your selections will always be perfect squares.

Quick Tip To undo changes, press <Ctrl+Z>.

The dotted-circle icon next to it is much the same, except it selects a *circu-lar or elliptical* area. Similar to the rectangular select, you can hold down the <Shift> key along with the left mouse button to select only perfect circles.

Next, we have the *lasso* tool. This is another selection tool, but this one lets you select irregular or hand-drawn regions. Hold down the left mouse button and *draw* your selection around the object.

Quick Tip When you have selected an area on an image, you can right-click, move your mouse cursor over the Edit menu, and select Cut or Copy. You can then Paste your selection back to another part of the image.

Then comes the *magic wand*. This is a strange tool to get used to. It selects an area by analyzing the colored pixels wherever you click. Holding down the <Shift> key lets you select multiple areas. This is a very useful tool but also a little tricky. Double-click on the icon to change the sensitivity.

Finally, we wrap up the first row with the *color picker* tool. Using the color picker feels a bit like the magic wand, but the functionality is based on color rather than on a single area at a time. Select the color picker and click on any colored area, and *all* areas matching this color will be selected.

That wraps it up for the first row of tools. It's time to look at the next set (Figure 17-14).

We start this row with another selection tool, the so-called *intelligent scis-sors*. You select an area by clicking around it. What this tool does is follow curved lines around an object. It does so by concentrating on areas of similar contrast or color. Simply click around the perimeter of the area you wish to select, and watch the lines magically draw themselves. When you join the last dot, click inside the area to select it.

Figure 17–14   *Second icon group.*

The second icon in this row is the *Bezier tool* (also known as the path tool), which, to be honest, takes some getting used to. Once you get used to it, however, you'll be impressed with the flexibility it affords you in selecting both straight and curved areas. Click a point outside the area you want to select, and it creates an anchor point. Click again a little further along your outline, and you get a new anchor point, with a straight line connecting to the original. Click and drag an existing anchor point, and a *bar* will appear with control boxes on either end. You can then grab those control points and drag or rotate them to modify the straight line between the points. Once you have joined the final point, look at your tool options (the pane below the GIMP toolbox) and click the button labeled *Create selection from path*. You'll see an animated dotted line, as with the other selection tools.

The third icon looks like an eyedropper. This is the *color picker*. Choosing an exact color can be difficult (if you need to get the tone just right). But if the color you want is on your existing image, click on that spot, and you've got it (your default active color will change).

The *magnifying glass* does exactly what you might expect. Click an area of the screen to zoom in. Double-click the icon to reverse the zoom. This doesn't actually scale the image, it just changes your view of things. Zoom is usually used to make it easier to work on a small area of the image.

We finish up this row with the calipers, or *measuring tool*. This doesn't actually change anything on your image but instead it reports. Click a starting point on the image, and then drag the mouse pointer to another part of the image. Now look at the bottom of your image window. You'll see the distance in pixels from your starting location to where you let go of the mouse pointer. The angle of the line will also be displayed.

On to row 3 (and Figure 17-15).

The first icon on the third row looks like a cross with arrows pointing in all directions. This is the *move tool*. It is really quite simple. Click the tool, grab the selected area on the screen, and move it to where you want. If you haven't selected an area, you can move the entire image in the window.

Figure 17–15   Third icon row.

On to the knife icon—the *crop tool*. If you start working with digital photography in a big way, this is one you will also truly want to get to know. I use the crop tool all the time when I am trying to get a small part of a larger image. It is what I used to separate the rows of icons from the GIMP toolbox image I captured. Click on a part of the screen, and drag it to encompass the area you want to select. The space around your selection will darken (Figure 17-16).

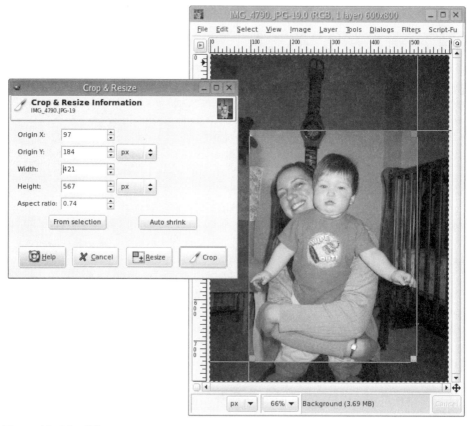

Figure 17–16   When cropping an image, the selected area will be emphasized by a darkening around the rest of the image.

When are satisfied with your selection, click the Crop button. You can also fine-tune the settings (X and Y position, etc.) at this time.

The third icon on this row is the *rotate tool*. Click on an image (or a selection), and small square *handles* will appear at the corners of your selection. Grab one of these handles (or points) and drag the mouse, and the selection rotates. When you have it in a position you like, click Rotate on the pop-up window that appears. The image will lock into place.

The fourth icon, the *scale tool*, is very similar to the rotate tool. Instead of rotating the selected area, you drag the points to resize the selected area. As before, a pop-up window appears so that you can lock your changes. It's also the place to manually enter your changes if you would like finer control than dragging the mouse offers you.

The *shear tool* is the last on this row, and, once again, it acts on a previously selected area. This one looks a lot like the last two in terms of functionality, but the effect is more like taking two sides of an object and stretching it diagonally in opposite directions. A square becomes a parallelogram, which gets longer and thinner as you continue to stretch the image. When you're happy with the changes, click the Shear button on the pop-up dialog.

And now . . . row 4 (Figure 17-17)!

Figure 17–17   Row 4 icons.

We start this fourth row with the *perspective tool*. This is one of those you almost have to try out to understand, but let me try to describe it. Remember your grade school art classes, when you first learned about perspective? A road leading off into the distance compresses to a single point in the distance. With the perspective tool, you can take a selected area and pull the points in whatever direction you want to create the perspective effect. Do that with a person's head, and the top of the head comes together in a sharp little point. As with the last three tools, there's a pop-up where you lock in your changes. Just click Transform.

Next in line is the *flip tool*. By default, it flips the image horizontally. The tool option, in the lower half of the GIMP toolbox, has a checkbox so that you can flip vertically instead.

Tip Remember that if you closed the tool options below the GIMP toolbox, you can always double-click a tool to bring up the options dialog.

The next icon is the *text tool*. That's what the big *T* signifies. Click on your image, and the GIMP Text Editor will appear. This is where you enter your text. In your tools option is the font selector, the same one you used for your logo. Select a font style, size, and color, and the changes will be visible in the image. This makes it easy to change the look and feel on the fly. Type in your text in the Preview section, and click OK. Where the text appears on the screen, the move tool will be activated, allowing you to place the text accurately. The color of the text will be your current foreground color.

And now, in the fourth position, is the paint can. This is the *fill tool*. It can fill a selected area not only with a chosen color but with a pattern as well. To choose between color and pattern fill, double-click on the icon to bring up its menu.

The last item on this line is the *gradient fill tool*. Start by selecting an area on your image, and then switch to this tool. Now click on a spot inside your selected area and drag with the tool. The current gradient style will fill that area. This is another one of those things you almost need to try in order to understand what I mean.

 Quick Tip Would you like a blank canvas right about now? Click File on the GIMP toolbox menu bar and select New.

And now, may I introduce the fifth row of icons (Figure 17-18).

Figure 17–18   The fifth row is primarily drawing tools.

The first icon of this group looks a *pencil*. In fact, this and the next three buttons all work with a brush selection (the bottom right-hand box). This pencil, as with a real pencil, is used to draw lines with sharply defined edges. Try drawing on your image with the different types to get an idea of what each brush type offers.

The next icon is the *paintbrush*. The difference between it and the pencil is that the brush gives softer, less starkly defined edges to the strokes. Double-click the icon to bring up the paintbrush's menu, and try both the Fade Out and Gradient options for something different.

If the next icon looks like an *eraser*, that's no accident. The shape of the eraser is also controlled by the current brush type, size, and style. Here's something kind of fun to try. Double-click on the icon to bring up its menu, and change the Opacity to something like 50%. Then start erasing again.

Now it's on to the *airbrush* tool. Just like a real airbrush, you can change the pressure to achieve different results. Hold it down longer in one spot, and you'll get a darker application of color.

Next we arrive at another drawing tool, the pen, or *ink tool*. Double-clicking the icon brings up a menu that lets you select the tip style and shape as well as the virtual tilt of the pen. The idea is to mimic the effect of writing with a fountain pen.

Which brings us to the sixth and final row of tools (Figure 17-19).

Figure 17–19   These row 6 tools can be thought of as specialized brushes.

We start this final row with the *clone tool* (the icon looks a bit like a rubber stamp). Sheep? No problem! We can even clone humans. Okay, that's a bit over the top. Where the clone tool comes in handy is during touch-ups of photographs. Open an image, hold down the <Ctrl> key, and press the left mouse button over a portion of the image—the tool will change to a crosshair. Let go of both the mouse button and the <Ctrl> key. This is your starting area for cloning. Now move to another part of the screen, click, and start moving your mouse button (the shape of the area uncovered is controlled by the brush type). As you paint at this new location, you'll notice that you are recreating that portion of the image you indicated with the <Ctrl+mouse-click> combination. Start with someone's head or body, and you can have twins on the screen.

The droplet you see in the second position represents the *convolver tool*. Use it to blur or sharpen parts of an image. You switch between the two operations by selecting the mode in the tool options below the toolbox or by double-clicking the icon. Change the rate to make the effect more pronounced.

On to the finger, or the *smudge tool*. Pretend that you are painting. You press your finger on the wet paint and move it around. The smudge tool has exactly the same effect on your virtual canvas.

Finally, the *dodge and burn tool* looks like a stickpin, but those who have worked in a darkroom might recognize it for something different—a stick with an opaque circle on the end of it. It is used to adjust the brightness or shade of various parts of an image (a photograph might have been partly overexposed).

Quick GIMP Trick When you need to zoom in on an image to get some fine work done, just press the plus sign on your keyboard. If you zoom in enough, though, it can get difficult to navigate the larger image. You wind up trying to adjust the scrollbars to locate the area you want. Instead, click on the little crosshair icon in the bottom right-hand side of the image editor window. A smaller version of your image window will appear, with a target area outline that you can move to where you want it (Figure 17-20).

Figure 17–20
The small image icon at the bottom right-hand side of the image editor makes navigating a large image a snap.

Touching Up Photographs

I've mentioned the idea of touching up photographs on a few occasions while I discussed the tools. The GIMP is a wonderful tool for this and more than just a little fun. One of the most common functions I use is changing the light levels on photographs, automagically and instantly. After all, light levels are rarely perfect, unless you are a professional photographer and paying attention to every shot. Here's what I do.

Click Image on the Layers menu bar (or right-click on the image to bring up the menu), move to the Colors submenu, and select Levels. You should see a window like the one in Figure 17-21. Notice the Auto button? That's where the magic is. I've found that more often than not, I can get a nice, dependable reset of levels just by doing this simple operation.

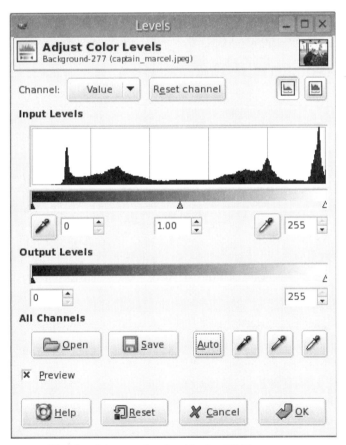

Figure 17–21   Adjusting levels with the GIMP.

Another very common adjustment you will make to your photos, particularly scanned images, is contrast and brightness. You'll find this dialog in much the same place as Levels. Click *Layers* on the menu bar, then *Colors*, and finally *Brightness-Contrast*. To change one or the other, just pull the appropriate slider to the left or right (Figure 17-22).

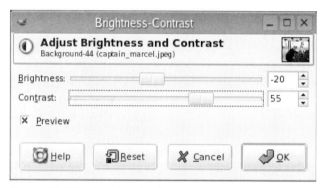

Figure 17–22   To adjust brightness or contrast, just pull the sliders.

There are also the silly and *just plain fun* things you can do. For instance, open an image in the GIMP, perhaps one you scanned in earlier. If you don't have something handy, grab an image from a Web site. This is just something to play with. Now choose Filters from the image menu bar. A submenu will open with even more options. You might want to detach this menu—you'll certainly want to play with what is there.

Try FlareFX under the Light Effects menu. If you've ever taken a flash picture through a window, you'll recognize this effect. Then try Emboss under the Distorts submenu. The effect is that of a metal-embossed picture (Figure 17-23).

Take some time to try the various filter options. When you are finished there, right-click on a fresh image and select the Script-Fu menu. There are other interesting effects available here as well, such as Clothify under the Alchemy submenu. Your image will look as though it had been transferred to a piece of cloth.

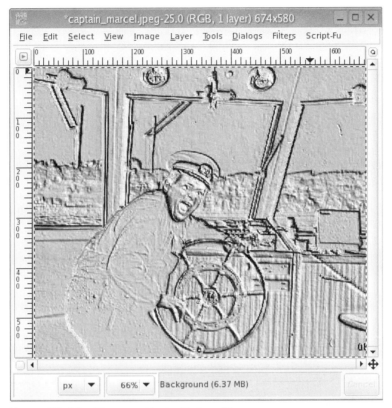

Figure 17–23 Playing with the Emboss filter.

So What Is Script-Fu?

Although it sounds like a strange form of martial arts, Script-Fu is in fact a scripting language that is part of the GIMP. With it, you can create scripts that automate a number of repetitive tasks to create desirable effects. When you created your logo, you might have noticed that a number of things were happening as it was being created. Try another logo and watch carefully what is happening. These steps are part of a Script-Fu script.

The GIMP comes with a number of Script-Fu scripts, and these are used for much more than just creating logos. Click Xtns on the GIMP toolbox, and scroll down to the Script-Fu menu. In addition to logos, you'll see options for creating buttons (for Web pages), custom brushes, patterns, and more. Play! Experiment! Don't be afraid.

Open an image. Then right-click on that image and scroll down to the Script-Fu part of the menu. Another menu drops down with selections such as Alchemy, Decore, Render, and so on. These are all precreated effects that would ordinarily require many repetitious steps. Script-Fu is very much like a command script, where one command follows another. In this case, the commands just happen to be graphical transformations.

Resources

GIMP Web site

http://www.gimp.org

Chapter
18
Linux Multimedia
(If Music Be the Food
of Love . . .)

Playing music on your Linux system is only the beginning of the multimedia experience. After all, multimedia isn't about just music. It represents a cornucopia of sensory experience delivered digitally, comprising text, audio, video, and endless combinations of the three.

Most modern Linux installations offer an impressive selection of programs to satisfy your cravings for the multimedia experience, from audio to video and everything in between. These programs include sound control systems, CD players, recorders, MIDI programs of varying flavors, music synthesizers, video players, music notation programs, and . . . the list goes on.

In this chapter, I cover some of the more popular multimedia tools for your Linux system. So, as old Will Shakespeare might have said, "If music be the food of love, then multimedia must represent the smorgasbord."

Adjusting the Levels

Think back for a moment to those days of old when Mom or Dad would yell into your bedroom to "TURN THAT NOISE DOWN!" Doesn't that bring back memories? In particular, it brings back my memory that sometimes you just have to crank the tunes.

Most music or multimedia players you are likely to use under Linux have some kind of a volume control. Your speaker system likely has one as well. There is, however, a third set of controls you should know about—KMix, the master mixer controls on your system (Figure 18-1).

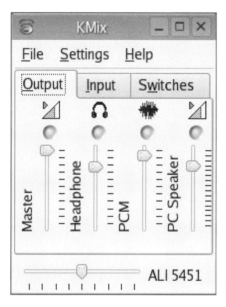

Figure 18–1   KMix controls.

The various sliders correspond to various levels, from that of your CD player itself to the PCM output, microphone inputs, and so on. Pause your mouse pointer over the sliders, and a tooltip will tell you what that slider does. The left-to-right slider at the bottom is for your left-to-right speaker balance.

Note The number of sliders and controls will vary from sound card to sound card. Your KMix likely won't look exactly like mine (unless you have the same type of sound card).

If you close KMix now (click the X in the top right-hand corner), you'll still have quick access to probably the most important item, the master volume control. Look down at the system tray at the bottom right corner of your screen, and you should see an icon that looks like a speaker. Click on that speaker icon, and a simple volume slider will appear (Figure 18-2). This provides a fast means of making volume-level adjustments.

Figure 18–2 A volume control in your system tray.

 Quick Tip If you find that the levels are still a bit low, you may want to check out the global system settings. This is controlled by a program called `aumix`, which you can call from the command line or via your <Alt+F2> quick launch. This is a simple graphical user interface (GUI) from which you can drag the levels to something more to your liking. When you are done, click File on the menu bar, then Save, and then Quit.

Now that you can easily modify the level of *noise* coming from your speakers, it's time to get some music on.

KsCD, the KDE CD Player

You might remember that I mentioned KsCD earlier on in this book, when I was discussing command execution (Chapter 4). This is the default CD player included as part of the KDE desktop (Figure 18-3).

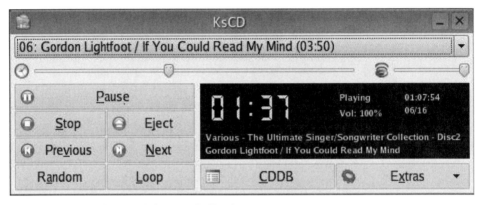

Figure 18–3   KsCD, the default KDE CD player.

If all you want to do is play your CDs and have a simple, easy-to-use interface, look no further. Click the application starter (the big K), and look for KsCD under the Multimedia menu (the command name is `kscd`). Then push the play button, sit back, and enjoy.

Once KsCD is started, look in your system tray. You'll see a small icon that looks like a CD with a musical note across it. Left-click the icon, and the CD player disappears into the panel. Right-click it, and you'll have access to the basic CD player controls (forward, next, stop, play, etc.).

Tip If you've minimized the players, click the KsCD icon to bring it back. Look at the bottom of the player; you'll see a button labeled *Extras*. I'll let you explore the features there, but first I want to direct your attention to something. PCs are sometimes built without a sound cable attached from the CD player to the motherboard. If you aren't getting any sound when you try to play a CD, this might be something to look at. Take out any CD you may have in the drive. Click the Extras button and select Configure KsCD. When the configure dialog appears, make sure you have the CD Player icon clicked in the left-hand sidebar. Now look about two-thirds of the way down, to a section titled CD-ROM device, with a checkbox beside the words *Use direct digital playback*. Click the checkbox, click OK, and try your CD again.

XMMS

XMMS is pretty much the standard Linux media player, but it is much more than a music player. Properly used, it is a spectacular lightshow as well. It supports OGG Vorbis, MP3, and WAV formats. With the right extensions, you can also use it to play RealAudio and even MPEGs. More on that later.

Every major Linux distribution comes with XMMS, so you don't have to go far to find it. If it isn't already part of the installation, look on your distribution CD-ROM. If all else fails, you can always go to the source at `http://www.xmms.org` for the latest and greatest.

An Alternative XMMS I mention XMMS here because your distribution is almost guaranteed to come with it. As I write this, a relatively new music player has come on the scene based on XMMS. The Beep Media Player (BMP, for short) is based on the XMMS code set but uses the more up-to-date GTK2 development libraries. This gives BMP a more modern look when it comes to its menus and file selector. To get a copy of BMP, visit the BMP home page at

`http://www.sosdg.org/~larne/w/BMP_Homepage`

To start the program, look for XMMS under your Multimedia menu, or type xmms & (either from a shell or by pressing <Alt+F2>) and press the <Enter> key (Figure 18-4).

Notice that the figure shows three *components*. If you are starting XMMS for the first time, you are likely to see only one component, the amplifier module at the top left of the figure. Look at the small buttons on the right side of the amplifier, labeled *EQ* (the equalizer) and *PL* (the playlist). Clicking these *buttons* will bring up the two additional modules for your stereo system. The buttons themselves may take some getting used to. They look more or less the same as you would expect on a home system and perform the same functions, but, as you shall soon see, when I explain *skins*, the *look* is very flexible.

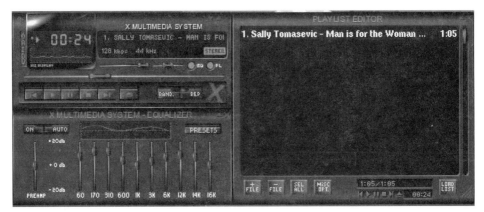

Figure 18–4   XMMS amp, equalizer, and playlist.

Quick Tip Before you try anything with XMMS, I should tell you that each of the three modules can be moved about individually on the screen. The arrangement I'm using, with the amplifier on top of the equalizer on the left and the playlist on the right, isn't the only variation. Consequently, you may find yourself readjusting their positions more often than you care to. The easy way to solve this is by right-clicking on the amplifier module, choosing Options from the menu, and choosing Easy Move. There's a <Ctrl+E> keyboard shortcut as well.

If you want to play songs, click the +FILE button on the playlist editor, and select the songs you want from the file menu that appears. If you hold that button down for a second or two, you'll also have the opportunity to add either a Web link (+URL) to a collection of songs or a directory (+DIR). The button directly to the left of it (–FILE) lets you undo your choices. Once you have made your choices, press the Play button.

XMMS Lightshows

XMMS has extensive plugin support for input, output, and visualization. To get at these, use the Preferences menu (the shortcut is <Ctrl+P). A new window will pop up offering you tabs for various runtime options, fonts, and so on. This is also where you find the control for the various audio I/O, special effects, and visualization plugins (Figure 18-5). If you find yourself having problems with sound when you first start up XMMS, this is the place to start. Look under the audio section and check the output plugin. Running under KDE, you will likely use the aRts driver. But if XMMS is a little too silent, try the OSS driver.

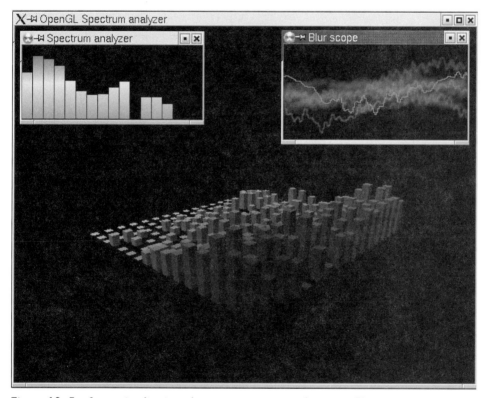

Figure 18–5 *Some visualization plugins accompanying the music. The spectrum analyzer plugin is the small window at the top left, the blur scope is the window at the top right, and the OpenGL Spectrum Analyzer is the larger window behind.*

Tip If you want to use XMMS as your CD player and lightshow combination, you need to activate the CD audio player plugin in digital playback mode. Press <Ctrl+P> to bring up the configuration menu. On the *Audio I/O Plugin* tab, make sure CD Audio Player is enabled (look for the checkbox on the lower right of the plugin list). Click the Configure button to bring up the CD player's configuration options. Look for the radio button labeled *Digital Audio Extraction* and select it. Click OK to close the configuration window, and click OK again to close the XMMS plugin dialog.

I could spend a great deal of time talking about the various options. Instead, I invite you to check out the various options on your own. What I wanted to talk about is the little lightshow effects, the *visualization plugins*. To activate a plugin from Preferences, click on a plugin, and then click the Enable plugin radio button.

We have things here such as Spectrum Analyzer and Blur Scope. Another cool plugin I very much enjoy is the OpenGL Spectrum Analyzer. It provides colorful 3D visuals to accompany your music—you can even launch that one full-screen; sit back, and enjoy the show.

Skinning XMMS

One of my favorite features of XMMS is its *skinability*, if you will. Using skins, I can change XMMS's look from its default black metal face to something more classic, such as cherry wood or a refined brushed aluminum. The <Alt+S> shortcut brings up the Skin Browser, which you can also select through the right-click menu. Mandrake Linux is *particularly nice* this way. This distribution includes a large number of skins for XMMS.

If you don't have any skins in your list, you need to get yourself some skins. For that, head to the XMMS Web site at www.xmms.org and click Skins on the menu. I guarantee you won't be getting bored anytime soon. There are literally tons of skins available.

So how do you install them? All of the skins on the Web site are in either tar.gz or .zip format. Find one that appeals to you, download it, and save it to your $HOME/.xmms/Skins directory. You don't need to extract the file—just save it to the directory. Now right-click on the amplifier, select Options, and click on Skin Browser. Your installed skins should be available for you to select (Figure 18-6). To preview a skin, click on it, and XMMS will change to the new skin. You can even click the Select random skin on play button if you'd like some automatic variety.

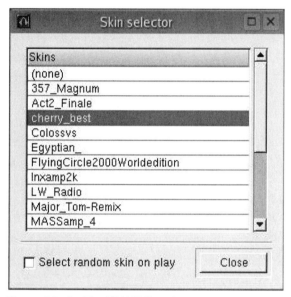

Figure 18–6   The XMMS Skins browser.

I'm going to conclude this discussion of XMMS at this point because the next application also does skins in a great way. I started off with XMMS, but KDE also has an excellent little program called *Multimedia Player* or, more rightly, *Noatun*.

Noatun

Sounds a bit like *know a tune*, doesn't it? You can access the program by looking under the big K, choosing Multimedia, and then clicking on the KDE Media Player, or you can type noatun & at the command line. The problem is that when you fire it up for the first time, it tends to look a little boring, as in Figure 18-7.

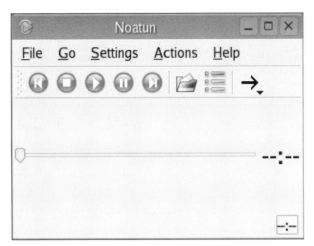

Figure 18–7 Noatun's default look.

Don't let that disappoint you. That is the default skin, named *Excellent*. As with XMMS, you can skin Noatun—in fact, some of Noatun's skins are downright wild. Before we get into that, however, let's talk about playing songs with Noatun.

Click File on Noatun's menu bar and select Open. Navigate your directories until you get to a song you want to play. Select it, and click OK. In all likelihood, nothing will happen at this point. That's because you are loading songs into a playlist. To get to that playlist, click Settings and select Show Playlist. You can also click the Playlist icon just under the menu bar, the second icon from the right. (The final icon lets you select between single play and playlist looping.)

At this point, you can just keep adding songs to the playlist (you can also add directories if you have collections you want to add). Eventually, you'll have your list. Click the diskette icon on the playlist (see Figure 18-8) to save your list. You are all set. Select a starting song in the playlist, and click the Play button on Noatun's main screen (or click the starting song in the playlist).

Noatun's slider is positional within the playing song. You can control volume using your KMix applet in the system tray as well as through Noatun. To see the volume control, click Settings on the menu bar and select Show Volume Control.

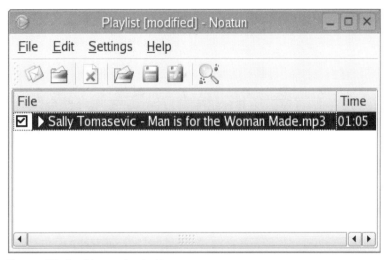

Figure 18–8   Noatun's playlist.

Quick Tip You can also use Noatun to play video clips.

Skinning Noatun

Let's get back to the subject of skinning Noatun. Click on Settings, followed by Configure Noatun. From the pop-up menu that appears, choose Plugins, which will then give you a tabbed menu. Under Interfaces, you'll see four options for player styles. The skinable styles are *K-Jofol* (Figure 18-9) and *Kaiman* (although there is also a Winamp skin loader). In both cases, you can find additional skins on the KDE-Look Web site at `http://www.kde-look.org`.

Start by unselecting the *Excellent* interface and selecting the *K-Jofol* interface. You'll see the menu bar at the left change. It now shows a K-Jofol Skins option. The same would happen with the Kaiman interface but, obviously, with Kaiman skins. If you click on this menu option, you'll see a drop-down list on the right with a preview of the various installed skins.

Quick Tip For the curious readers out there, Noatun skins live under the `$HOME/.kde/share/apps/noatun/skins` directory.

Figure 18–9   Noatun with a K-Jofol skin.

Noatun Lightshows!

When I told you about XMMS, I mentioned the variety of cool plugins you could use for visualization. KDE's media player, Noatun, has these as well. In the Configure Noatun Interfaces menu, select Plugins (from the left-hand sidebar), and then click Visualizations.

Ripping and Burning Songs

Over the years, we have all purchased a lot of music CDs, or, as some of us still call them, *albums*. Many of those albums, unfortunately, have only two or three songs we really liked, so playing the whole album wasn't what we wanted. As a result, we created collections of our favorite songs on tape and played the tapes instead.

These days, with the help of our Linux systems, we can create our own collections from those albums we have purchased and create CD collections of those songs we want to hear. Furthermore, if you have lots of disk space and you spend a lot of time at your computer, nothing beats a collection of songs ready to play without having to change CDs all the time. Pulling songs from a CD and saving them to your system as digital images is what is commonly referred to as *ripping*.

Intermezzo: Digital Audio Formats

Before I get into the mechanics of ripping and burning songs, I'd like to spend a little time discussing music formats. When you purchase a CD, the songs on it are in a format not generally used by your system. In fact, when we copy songs to disk from a CD, we always encode it into another, usually more compact format. The format we transfer to is identified by a three-letter extension on the filename. The most common formats are .wav, .mp3, and (more recently) .ogg.

The *wav* format is one originally created by Microsoft. It is extremely common but not the most efficient in terms of compression. The *mp3* format (from the Motion Pictures Experts Group, aka MPEG), on the other hand, owes its popularity to the high compression ratio it uses—about 12:1. The newcomer on the block is the *ogg* (or Ogg Vorbis) format. Like mp3, it boasts a high compression rate; but unlike mp3, it is completely unencumbered by patents.

To give you an idea of the compression values, I ripped a 3-minute, 46-second song to wav format. It came in at 39,866,444 bytes, while the same song in ogg format required only 3,438,407 bytes. If you do the math, that is a ratio of 11.6:1—a pretty impressive reason for not using wav format files.

KAudioCreator

As you might expect, there are several tools to let you rip songs from your CD collection. One of those tools comes with your KDE desktop. It's called KAudioCreator, and it is a wonderfully easy program to use. Using a library called *cdparanoia* (which I discuss later), KAudioCreator makes it possible to create MP3s or OGGs easily from your favorite CD. You will likely find the program in your multimedia menu. You can also call it by its program name (using the shell or the <Alt+F2> program launcher), kaudiocreator.

When you start the program for the very first time, you may find yourself looking at a message telling you that no encoder has been selected. The message then asks you to select one in the configuration (Figure 18-10). I show you how to do that shortly. For now, click OK.

Start the program without a CD in the drive and you'll be presented with a single window with two tabs (Figure 18-11): *CD Tracks* and *Jobs*. As you might expect, the CD Tracks window will list the contents of your CD, while the Jobs tab will report on the progress of each track as it is ripped and encoded. Along the top is a familiar-looking menu bar with a few command icons below.

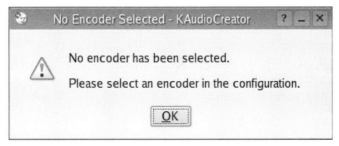

Figure 18–10   When you run KAudioCreator for the first time, no encoder is set.

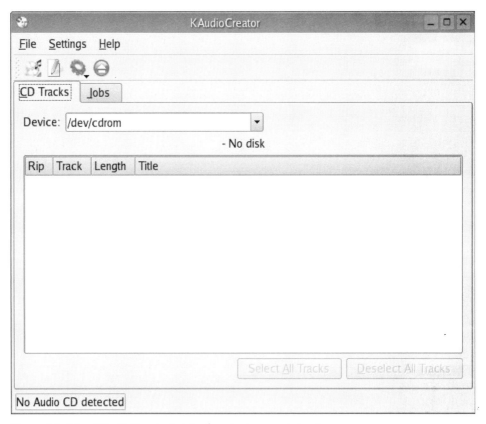

Figure 18–11   KAudioCreator's interface is clean and simple.

Given that we haven't yet selected an encoder, we are getting ahead of ourselves, so click Settings on the menu bar and select Configure KAudio-Creator. The dialog window that comes up (Figure 18-12) is similar to many you have already seen: a menu sidebar with icons leading you to the most common functions, and a larger, left-hand pane where the real work gets done. You'll see a General icon as well as CD, CDDB, Ripper, and Encoder icons. Click on the last icon to configure the encoder.

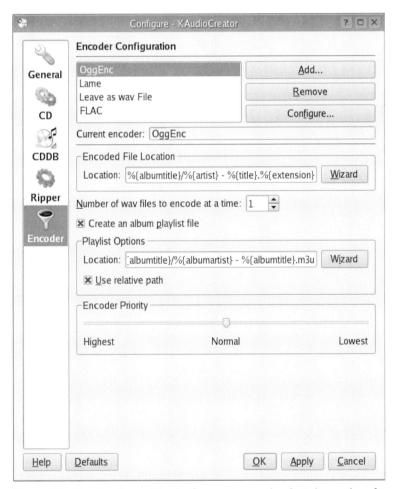

Figure 18–12 Configure KAudioCreator to use the digital encoder of your choice, whether OGG, MP3, or FLAC.

Earlier, I explained the various digital audio formats. If the music is going to stay on your home computer and you like the idea of patent-free compression format, then choose OggEnc or FLAC. If you own a portable MP3 player and you want to take your music with you, then the decision is clear. Choose LAME for MP3 encoding. In this example, that is what I do. There are other options here that are interesting, such as the CDDB lookup (which provides KAudioCreator with a means of downloading song and album information from the Internet), and I invite you to check out those settings. For now, with an encoder selected, you should have everything you need to continue. Click OK.

Now pop a music CD of your choice into your CD-ROM drive. KAudio-Creator will read the information off the disk and display a list of songs in the CD Tracks window (Figure 18-13).

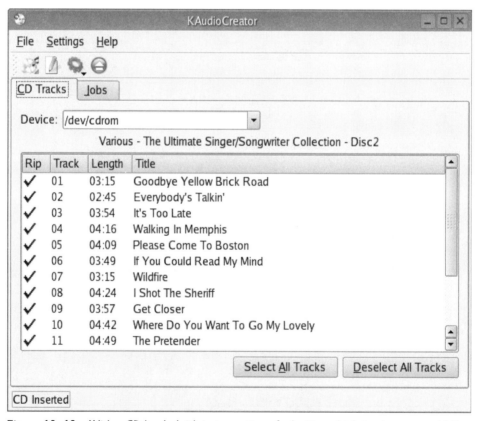

Figure 18–13   With a CD loaded, it's just a matter of selecting which tracks you would like to rip.

Generally speaking, you should see the information you expect to see here: the album name, artist, song titles, and so on. If you don't find what you expected, you may want to click File on the menu bar and select a *CDDB* lookup online (it's also the first icon directly below the File menu). Another way, though not quite as automatic, is to click File and select *Edit Album* (second icon from the left).

When you are satisfied with your choices and settings, click File and select Rip Selection (third icon from the left does the same). Once the process starts, click the Jobs tab to get a progress report. The resulting songs will be saved in your home directory under a folder called *mp3*, using the following format:

```
/home/username/mp3/artist_name/album_name/track_title.mp3
```

Of course, if you chose OGG as your audio compression format, the resulting directory would change accordingly.

KAudioCreator is, of course, strictly a ripping-and-encoding program. If you want to get those songs burned to CDs, you'll need a CD-burning package. Luckily, this won't be a problem.

K3b, for a Friendlier Burn

I still find it interesting to consider the terms that have entered the language when referring to creating CDs. We rip, and then we burn.

Considering the violent-sounding nature of the process, anything that simplifies the process and makes things a little friendlier is certainly welcome. One of the friendliest tools for creating and copying audio and data CDs is called *K3b*. K3b now comes as part of KDE, but you can still keep up with development or pick up the latest version at www.k3b.org. K3b is generally found under the Multimedia menu—the program name (should you wish to run it from the shell or via the <Alt+F2> launcher) is k3b.

When you fire up K3b for the first time, the program will detect the various devices you have for reading and writing. There you will see a pop-up window that asks you to verify those devices (Figure 18-14).

On my test system, I have a CD writer as well as a DVD writer. Unless you know that it is something different, it's usually okay to just accept the burn speed suggested. Click OK, and you'll find yourself at the main K3B window (Figure 18-15).

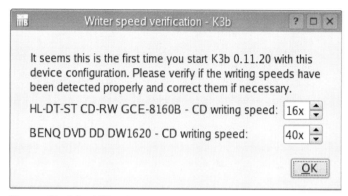

Figure 18–14   K3b asks you to verify the writing speed of your CD and DVD writers.

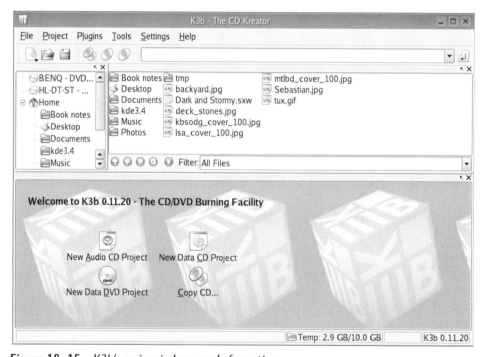

Figure 18–15   K3b's main window, ready for action.

Getting Familiar with K3b

K3b's interface is friendly and very easy to use. It is broken up into three main windows, with two top frames and one larger one at the bottom, all of which can be resized to your tastes. The top left-hand frame is your file navigator, showing your directories in the Konqueror-like tree format you are now familiar with. Just click the plus signs to open a directory or the minus sign to collapse it. The top right-hand frame will display the contents of whatever folder you have selected on the left-hand side.

Creating a CD of any kind in K3b is done with *projects*, and that is where the bottom window comes into play. That window will display details about the CD or DVD you are going to put together. Before you actually do, however, notice the quick-access projects there (Audio CD, New Data DVD, etc.). These just happen to be the most common choices you might make. Click File on the menu bar and select New Project. You'll be presented with several other choices (Figure 18-16).

If you are looking to create an *audio CD*, click File on K3b's menu bar and select New Project; then click on New Audio Project. If you were creating a data CD (which we cover shortly), you would click on New Data Project.

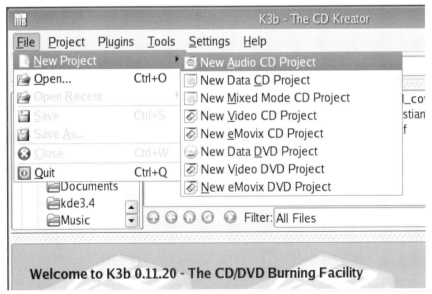

Figure 18–16   This close-up of the File, New Project dialog displays a list of K3b projects.

Backing Up Your Data with K3b

K3b makes a quick and easy tool for backing up your important data. The best approach involves CD-RW, or rewriteable CDs, because you can use them over and over again. Before you reuse your CD-RW, you'll want to blank it first. Pop the disk into your CD rewriter, click Tools on the menu bar, select CD, and then from that submenu choose Erase CD-RW.

A window will appear (Figure 18-17) showing you some options for erasing the CD-RW—just click the drop-down box for other choices. From there, you can select which CD writer you wish to use (if you have more than one), the speed at which you want to perform the operation, and whether you want a fast or a complete erase. When you are happy with your choice, click the button labeled *Start* at the top right-hand corner of the window. Just below all this is an Output window, where the progress of blanking will be displayed. After your successful-completion message, you will still want to click Close to banish the window.

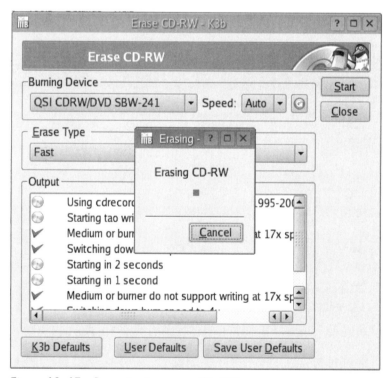

Figure 18–17   Preparing to erase a CD-RW.

Now you are ready to back up your data. Start a New Data Project. A tab with a sequentially generated name will appear (starting with DataCD1) in the bottom Current Projects window. It will be divided into two areas. On the left-hand side, you'll see a small icon representing a CD, with the current project name next to it. On the right will be a blank list with headings for file Name, Type, Size, Local Path, and Link. To fill this project, simply drag directories or files onto the CD icon in the left-hand side of the Current Projects window.

As each directory is added, K3b will calculate the amount of space all of this takes. Consequently, it may take a few seconds for a large directory to appear as these calculations are being made. A colored bar will stretch along the bottom, indicating the amount of space you still have left to create your data CD.

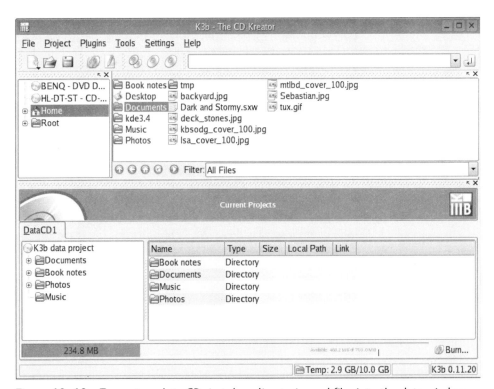

Figure 18–18   To create a data CD, just drag directories and files into the data window.

Quick Tip You have probably already noticed the option for creating a DVD data project. The steps are essentially the same (beyond choosing DVD over CD). The big difference is that you have a much greater capacity on a DVD than on a CD.

After you have added everything you want, click the Burn icon directly below the menu bar. You can also right-click the current project tab and select Burn there. A new Write window will appear, with five tabs, labeled *Writing, Settings, Volume Desc, Filesystem*, and *Advanced*.

I won't cover everything on every tab here, but I will tell you about a few of the more important settings, starting with the Writing tab. If your device is capable of high-speed burning, you may want to change the setting for Speed. The default choice is Auto, which will try to guess the optimal speed for your device. You may, however, feel confident that you can squeeze out a little more performance or accuracy by playing with this setting. Notice also the *Burnfree* checkbox. Most modern devices have Burn-Proof or Burnfree technology built right into the writers. If yours is capable, make sure you check this option on.

Quick Tip A rather odd-sounding option is Simulate, located on the Writing tab. After all, why go through the process and not do anything? The idea is to see whether a disc can be properly written at the current speed. Everything happens as it would, except the laser is turned off. This is also where the Writing on the fly option will come into play. If your system performance is such that you can burn a disc without writing out an image first, make sure you check this option on.

The Volume Desc tab allows you to set some label information for your CD, such as the name, who created it, and what system it was intended for. You don't actually need to enter anything here. It is all optional. Finally, take a look under the Advanced tab, where you'll find a number of miscellaneous options related to how data is written on your CD. For most users, these can be left alone.

Did Someone Say "Backups"?

By now you must be thinking, "Hey, if I can copy data directories to my CD, surely I can use this thing to do backups," and you would be bang on. Other than the limitations of the CD's roughly 700MB of storage, this is a great option. Use CD-RWs, and you can create a rotating set of discs for backup purposes.

Taking all this into consideration, we're onto something here, but there are some things to consider. Look under the Filesystem tab, and you'll find a couple of important settings related to data backups. The first has to do with whether you will ever be looking at this CD using a Windows system. If so, make sure you check on the *Generate Joliet extensions* box. Under Permissions, check on *Preserve file permissions* if this CD is a backup of your data. Should you ever need to recover from this CD, you'll want to have the proper ownership and permissions of files and directories maintained.

When you're done and ready to go, click on the Burn button, located in the top right-hand corner of this dialog box. A progress window will appear, with status information on the current CD creation (Figure 18-19).

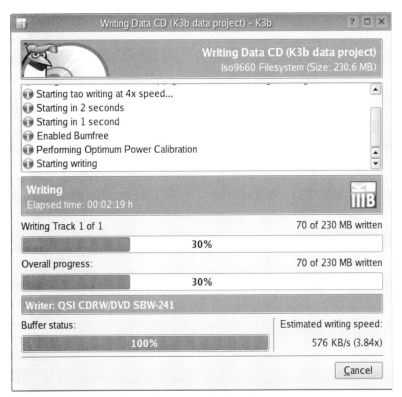

Figure 18–19 Watching the status of a burn in progress.

That's it. With your data safely backed up, you can sleep soundly at night.

Creating a Music CD with K3b

Data is fine, of course, but I started this chapter talking about music. The good news is that if you've already mastered the art of creating a data CD with K3b, you are well on your way to doing the same with music. From the file menu, select New Project; then click on *New Audio CD Project*. Putting your music CD together is just a matter of navigating to the directory in which your music is stored and dragging songs into the Current Projects window at the bottom (Figure 18-20). The window has a tab labeled AudioCD1. You can create multiple projects if you wish, and each will appear with its own tab.

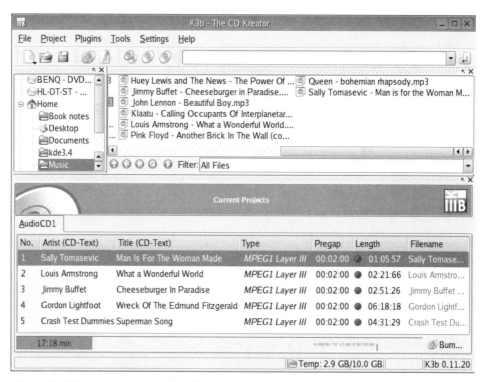

Figure 18–20   Building an audio CD of your favorite songs.

Along the bottom of the audio project window is a green bar indicating how much time the songs you've chosen take up so that you know when to stop. When you have everything you want, click that Burn button in the bottom right-hand corner of the K3b window.

Don't worry about the order in which the songs appear on the list. When you have your selection complete, simply click on the songs in the lower pane, and move them up or down at will. If the song in position 6, for example, would make a better opener, drag it up to position 1. It is that easy.

When you are done, click Burn. As the window appears, you might notice that it looks a little different than the data-burn window. For starters, there are two fewer tabs. We'll start with that one labeled *CD-Text*. Like the Volume Desc tab in the data project, this is for information only. This is where you enter the CD label information, performer name, or other information related to this disc. Should you decide simply to leave this blank, your CD will still work.

The Advanced tab is much simpler than on the *data CD* dialog. The only option is a strange little trick to hide the first track of a song in the first pregap. If you do this, you won't find the song on a straight play. You'll have to seek backward from the first song.

Finally, we'll go back to the Writing tab. There's really nothing new here that you haven't already seen. Select your write speed and click Write.

 Quick Tip If you always use the same settings when burning either a data or a music CD, click the *Save User Defaults* button in the Write CD dialog.

Put Another Nickel In . . .

Ripping songs from your CDs and storing them on your PC so you can listen while you work (or play) is fantastic. Start up Noatun or XMMS, pull a few songs into your playlist, and enjoy the music. Life couldn't be any better. Except . . .

You see, all this collecting of music, ripping of songs, and building of huge libraries of MP3s or OGGs on your computer's hard disk is eventually going to become a nightmare to administer. Sure, all those CDs in jewel cases have disappeared into that virtual space that is your hard disk, but now you have all these songs in a number of large folders with little or no organization. If you want to play something, you have to go searching. What you need is a jukebox.

In a much earlier part of my life, I made extra money babysitting some of my parents' friends' children. One of their friends repaired jukeboxes for a living. Consequently, a real honest-to-goodness jukebox was always in the house, full of 45 RPM singles. From time to time, the model and type of machine would change, but, with the coin mechanism disabled, I had all the music I wanted available. Now, that's entertainment! As luck would have it, your Linux system comes with a very fine jukebox program called Juk, so you won't have to babysit anybody's kids to use it.

Juk

Juk (command name juk) is part of the standard KDE multimedia package, so it is very likely already on your system. This program, being a KDE application, integrates nicely into the KDE desktop, with a tray icon to drop the application out of sight quickly. It includes support for your MP3 and Ogg Vorbis files, collection and playlist management, tag editing, and much more. Look for it in the Multimedia menu, or run the command juk from your <Alt+F2> quick launch.

On startup, Juk asks for folders where music is kept. To tell the program where to find songs, click on the Add folder button. A directory navigator window will appear, from which you can choose the locations of music on your system (Figure 18-21). In my case, I have a separate partition, called /mnt/music, where I keep all my music.

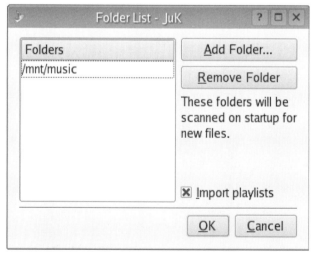

Figure 18–21   Start by adding the names of folders you want Juk to keep track of.

Juk is smart enough to scan all your subdirectories for songs, so there's no need, other than speed, to list each and every directory where you keep music. You don't want to scan the entire system, however, because you won't have permissions for many directories. You can add as many folders or file systems as you want. If you make a mistake, you can select that entry and click the Remove Folder button.

When you press OK, Juk will start scanning those folders and build a base collection. It will read the information tags on each song to try to determine the title, year, etc. of each song. After the process ends, you'll wind up with a collection list similar to the one in Figure 18-22.

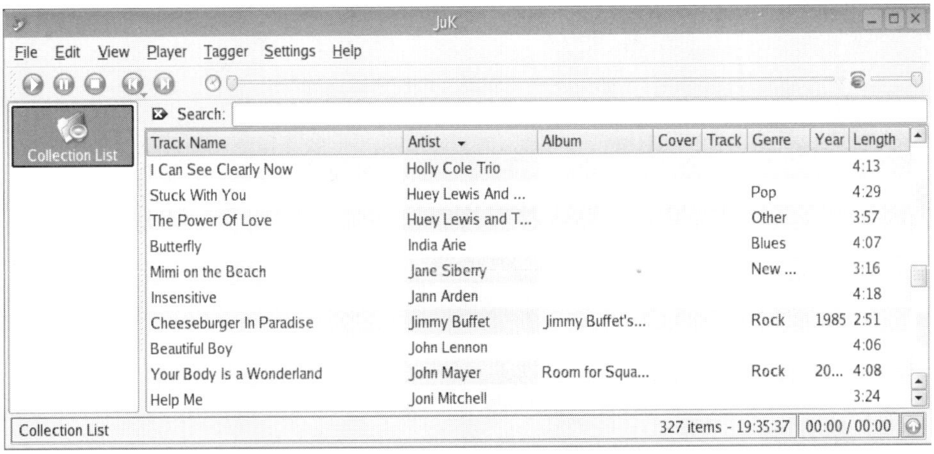

Figure 18–22   Juk creates a default collection list of all the songs in the folders you specified.

Juk uses a fairly simple two-pane interface, with a sidebar on the left and a large work/display window on the right, both of which you can size to suit. The expected menu and quick-access icons are along the top. The sidebar has a single folder icon, labeled Collection List. By default, all your songs appear in the default collection list. Because organization is key, you can create additional playlists by right-clicking in the column under the Collection List icon and then selecting *New* and *Empty Playlist*. Enter a name; then click OK. To populate a new folder, make sure you have your default Collection List selected; then drag and drop song titles into your playlist folder of choice. The titles appear in your new playlist but remain in the master collection as well. Now let's pretend you already have a folder called Love Songs; you could just add that as a predefined playlist. Right-click in the Collections List sidebar again, and select *New* followed by *Playlist From Folder*. No need to add anything else.

From the main track list window, you can click each of the columns to sort by album title, artist, date, or other catalog identifier. At this point, you could just click on a song and press the Play button (directly below the File menu) and your choice would start to play. Double-clicking works as well. When a song starts, the interface changes somewhat to display the current title. As you play more and more songs, a history of the last two titles you have played will appear to the right of the song information (Figure 18-23).

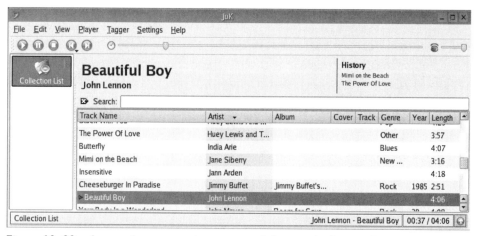

Figure 18–23   As you play more and more songs, Juk starts displaying a history of your past choices.

As anyone with a collection of songs on their computer knows, the information contained in the information tags isn't always perfect. To deal with this problem, we have Juk's tag editor. What I really like about this feature is that you can edit information inline by right-clicking on a song title, artist name, or any of the columns and selecting the appropriate *Edit* option. It gets better, though. Juk can try to intelligently decipher the track information based on the filename or by searching on the Internet. Right-click on the title, select *Guess Tag Information*, and choose *From File Name* or *From Internet* (Figure 18-24).

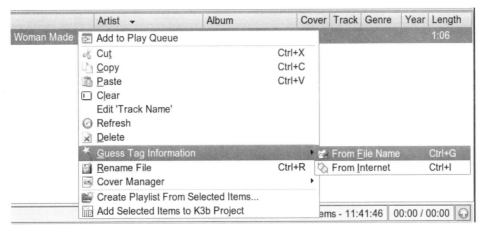

Figure 18–24 Editing tags is easy, but letting Juk figure it out on its own is easier. Choose by filename or from the Internet.

Here's one final treat. When a particular song is playing, it's nice to be able to see the cover of the album it comes from. You could scan each album or CD cover, save the file on your system, and use the Cover Manager to import them. Luckily, there's a much better way. Right-click on a song of your choice, and select Cover Manager from the menu that appears (Figure 18-25). Look to the right of that selection and you'll see two additional options. One lets you import your cover based on a local file (Get Cover From File); the other will connect to the Internet, look for the album cover that fits your song selection, and let you download it automatically.

Figure 18–25 Let Juk search the Internet for album or CD covers and automatically import them.

Now as your song plays, you'll see a nice cover image beside the song title (Figure 18-26). Click on the cover and, depending on the cover you chose to import, a larger version of it will be displayed.

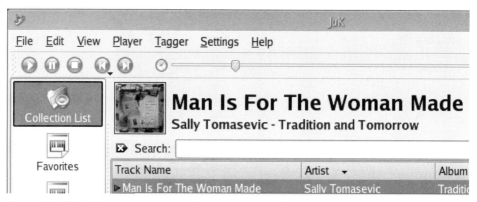

Figure 18–26　After importing an album cover with the cover manager, it is shown to the left of the title while a song from that album plays.

Rockin' On with amaroK

Juk is the standard KDE jukebox program and a fine one at that. Before I move on to other things, I want to tell you about another jukebox program that may not be included in your distribution. Nevertheless, it is impressive enough that I consider it's well worth looking at if you are serious about your music. It's called amaroK, and you can get it from `http://amarok. kde.org/`.

amaroK looks fantastic and comes packed with great features like a powerful cover manager (downloads covers from Amazon), a context browser that keeps track of your favorite and most listened to songs, great visualizations, and more. There's even a lyric download feature so you can sing along with your favorite tunes without worrying about whether you are getting the words right or now.

Lights, Camera, Action: Moving Pictures

Believe it or not, you have already worked with one of the Linux video players in this chapter. It is Noatun, KDE's media player. It is just as adept at playing video clips, such as AVI or MPEG files. Try it!

If you have a DVD player installed on your system, you will likely want to take advantage of it. One very capable and slick-looking video player out there is likely already installed if you are running a system with KDE. It's called KMPlayer, and it plays back video clips, such as AVI, MOV, MPEG, and others. It also handles DVDs as well, allowing you full menu control with the click of a mouse. It can even handle URLs, meaning that you can play remote files on the Internet.

You can start KMPlayer (command name `kmplayer`) from the Multimedia menu. Looking at Figure 18-27, you see KMPlayer at work. At the bottom of the screen are the play controls (play, forward, rewind, etc.). To start watching a DVD, click Source on the menu bar, select DVD, and then DVD Navigator and Start. The DVD will start playing, just as you would expect on your regular player.

While the DVD is playing, you can switch to full-screen mode by pressing the <F> key for the big screen action.

Figure 18–27 Watching a DVD on Linux with KMPlayer. (If you are curious, the DVD image you see if from a comedy show called *Corner Gas*.)

A Note on Encrypted DVDs

You may find as you play DVDs on your Linux system that some DVDs work and others do not. The reason for this is encryption. In an effort to protect against unlawful copying and distribution of movies on DVD, some companies in the motion picture industry have gone to extremes to protect themselves by using a *Content Scrambling System* (CSS). The result of this overreaction curtails the freedom of those law-abiding individuals who are looking to play the DVDs they legally bought and paid for on the DVD player they legally bought and paid for on the computer they legally bought and paid for.

"There's a simple solution," you say. "Why not write or use software that decrypts the DVDs so you can watch them?" Well, it isn't that easy. In some countries, most notably the United States, it is illegal to use software that decrypts any form of encryption put in place by another individual or company, even when it is for private use (do a Google search on *DMCA*). As I write this, legal challenges to this law are currently in the courts, which, in some cases, have already upheld the rights of the individual. This isn't to say that the motion picture industry will give up easily.

For instance, under the DMCA, a small handful of individuals have been charged for distributing a piece of software called *libdecss, libdvdcss* (or simply DeCSS), which lets you play encrypted DVDs on your Linux PC. The California Appeals Court ruled that the posting of source code (in this case, DeCSS) is upheld by the First Amendment.

Meanwhile, in Norway, a young man named Jon Lech Johansen was cleared of wrongdoing for distributing DeCSS software on the Internet. The 19-year-old "DVD Jon" faced two years in prison when the Motion Picture Association of America (MPAA) requested that Jon be arrested (he was only 15 at the time). In fact, the MPAA wanted both Jon *and* his father arrested.

Why am I telling you all this? Because I want you to make yourselves aware of the laws in your area. Playing a DVD on your PC sounds like a perfectly normal and legal thing to do. I agree, but I must repeat myself: You should be careful and make yourselves aware of the laws regarding this as they apply to your state, province, or country. I don't want to hear that any of you are facing jail time just because you decided to watch your legal copy of the latest blockbuster on your Linux system.

It's a Wrap!

It sounds so basic for me to say this, but multimedia *really is* about song and dance, dog-and-pony shows, and gratuitous flash and pizzazz. Judging from everything I've seen out there, our appetite for yet another adventure into sight and sound won't abate anytime soon.

I've shown you a few of the more popular and useful tools to explore Linux sight and sound, but your own appetite for more will likely take you well beyond these pages. On that note, I'm going to give you another handful of Linux tools to excite the ears and eyes.

In the world of audio, check out *KMid* (command name `kmid`) for playing MIDI files. What makes this program particularly fun is that it is a karaoke player as well. Plug the words *karaoke*, *midi*, *files*, and *download* into a Google search form, and you should find plenty of files. Just load them up in KMid, click Play, and you are the next international singing sensation.

 Hint Why not enter the following words into Konqueror's Location field for a quick Google search?

```
gg: karaoke midi files download
```

Feeling creative? Would you like to take a shot at writing your own music? A number of decent music notation programs are available for Linux. They include *NoteEdit* and *RoseGarden*, to name a couple. Links to each follow in the Resources section.

Just as there seems to be no end to the number of songs that humanity can create, so it is with software to manipulate sound. If I haven't mentioned it in this chapter, it certainly isn't because it doesn't exist. Check out the *Sound and MIDI Software for Linux* site at `http://linux-sound.org`.

Resources

Corner Gas

http://www.cornergas.ca

K3b

http://www.k3b.org

Lame Encoder

http://lame.sourceforge.net

MPlayer

http://www.MPlayerHQ.hu

NoteEdit

http://noteedit.berlios.de/

Ogg Vorbis

http://www.vorbis.com

RoseGarden

http://www.rosegardenmusic.com/

Sound and MIDI Software for Linux

http://linux-sound.org/

X-CD-Roast

http://www.xcdroast.org

xine video player

http://xinehq.de/

Chapter

19

Fun and Games (Very Serious Fun)

There's plenty to smile about when it comes to taking a little downtime with your Linux system. A default KDE installation comes with a number of games, as does a standard GNOME installation. If you installed both desktops, you will find plenty to keep you busy and happy for some time.

Expand your mind with one of the many puzzles. Do a little target practice in the arcade. Race down a dizzying mountain slope. Play golf. Sink someone's battleship. Board a space fighter and take on somebody halfway around the world. Play solitaire, backgammon, or poker.

There are tons of games available, and I'm just talking about the ones on your distribution disks. Head off to the Internet and you'll find yourself set for weeks, possibly months. Sit back, relax, and get ready to enjoy a little fun, Linux style.

You'll find most of these games under your K menu, where they'll be ordered according to the type of game each represents. In each case, I also give the command name so that you can either run it from the shell or start it with your program launcher, <Alt+F2>.

Take Me Out to the Arcade

Ah, the video arcade! I'm sure I spent far too much of my youth popping quarters into video game machines. (Yes, kids, it used to cost a mere 25 cents to play a game.) Nevertheless, there was a real flavor associated with the kind of games you found there. In the heyday of the arcade (sorry, kids, it is over), games tended to be fast but easy to learn. You didn't need to spend a small fortune just to get used to what it was the game did. Things came at you—you zapped them or you got out of the way.

With your Linux system, the arcade experience is alive and well. Let's take a look at the sorts of things you have at your disposal.

Cubes and Things That Drop

One of the most enduring games of that period was something called *Tetris*. The concept is simple. Colored geometric patterns fall from above, and as they fall you rotate the pieces so that they fit (like a jigsaw puzzle) into the bottom row. Fill a row, and the pieces disappear. Miss too many of the pieces, and the top crushes the bottom—you lose. As simple as it sounds, this is an amazingly addictive game idea, and your Linux distribution probably came with several games of this type. KSirtet (command name `ksirtet`) is just one such game and an excellent clone of the original. KSirtet (Figure 19-1) can be played with more than one player or against the computer. If you loved Tetris, you will love KSirtet.

Variations included with the kdegames package are KSmileTris (command name `ksmiletris`) and KFoulEggs (command name `kfouleggs`). Both follow a similar concept (dropping pieces that you rotate), but each provides interesting variations on the game.

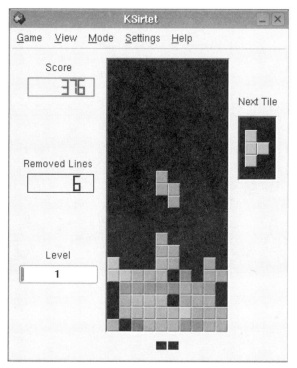

Figure 19–1   KSirtet, a Tetris-like game.

One of my favorite games from the arcade days also had a very simple concept—blast big rocks heading in your direction into smaller and smaller rocks. Did I mention that you are in command of a spaceship and the rocks are asteroids? KAsteroids (command name `kasteroids`) is a wonderful update of the classic arcade game (Figure 19-2). Your spaceship and the oncoming asteroids are nicely rendered in 3D instead of the old vector graphics. Watch your fuel, your shields, and your back.

Perhaps my favorite arcade-style game under Linux also happens to be one of the most addictive I have ever run across. It is called *Frozen-Bubble*. This is a bright, beautiful, and colorful game with dozens of levels featuring a great musical soundtrack, cool sound effects, and at least one penguin. You'll just have to trust me on this one—this game is a must have, and, no, age doesn't enter into it. Still with me? Here's the premise.

Figure 19–2 KAsteroids—break big rocks into smaller rocks.

Frozen, colored bubbles are arranged in various patterns against a wall at the top of your screen. Some kind of hydraulic press behind the wall slowly pushes the bubbles toward you (Figure 19-3). Your job is to guide your cute little penguin gunner (so to speak) to aim the bubble launcher at the oncoming wall of bubbles. If three of more bubbles of the same color are together, fire a similarly colored bubble at that group, and the arrangement collapses. Destroy all the bubble groups, and you win that level. If any of the bubbles at the wall touch you, everything freezes over, and your penguin cries a river of tears. It's silly. It's fun. You are going to love it.

Many Linux distributions do include Frozen-Bubble as part of the install. If you don't find a copy on those CDs, head straight over to the main site at `http://www.frozen-bubble.org/` and pick up a copy. You will be happy you did.

Figure 19–3 The incredibly addictive Frozen–Bubble.

Deal Those Cards, Ace

If you find yourself with five cards in your hands, two of them sevens and the other three queens, and you call that a *full house*, you are my kind of person. We're talking poker, my friends, five-card stud and nothing wild.

The KDE games package comes with a nice poker game called *KPoker* (Figure 19-4; command name `kpoker`) that features sound effects, animated cards, and configurable card fronts and backs (just click Settings on the menu bar and select Configure Carddecks). It's a great way to waste time gambling without losing a fortune. The only downside is that you can't bluff the computer.

Almost anyone who has held a deck of cards knows about solitaire, a one-person card game whose object is to reorder seven piles of cards, drawn at random, into four ordered piles, by suit and in numerical order. You may also know it as patience (as I did, growing up). There are, in fact, many solitaire or patience card games; the most famous and popular is also known as *Klondike*.

Figure 19–4   KPoker is fun. No bluffing.

KPatience (command name `kpatience`) is more than just Klondike solitaire (Figure 19-5). Several games are included (click Settings on the menu bar and select Game Type), such as FreeCell, Grandfather's Clock, and Napoleon's Tomb, among others. As with KPoker, you can change the card styles for both the front and back. You can even change your background graphic.

B-4. Miss. E-7. Hit!

What I find interesting is how many classic, low-tech games (you don't get much lower tech than playing cards) translate well to the computerized world. In the case of multiplayer board games, add a network connection and it all suddenly makes sense. You can play your favorite board games with the person sitting across from you or with someone halfway around the world. The following games can all be played on your local network or with friends in some distant part of the globe.

A number of Linux games take full advantage of this capability, starting with KBattleship (command name `kbattleship`). As you might expect, this is a KDE version of the popular game Battleship. You need two networked computers to play this one. One person runs a server (under the File menu), and the other connects to it.

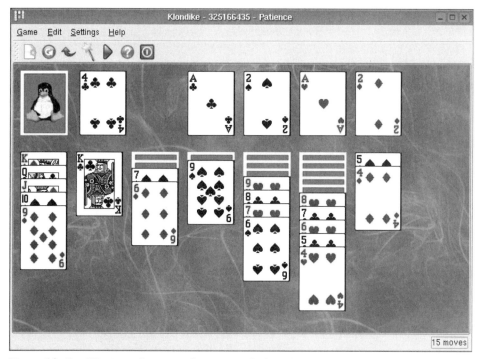

Figure 19–5 KPatience has several games, including the classic solitaire.

The rules are simple. You arrange your ships on a grid. In this version, the grid has no numbers or letters to indicate position. When it is your turn to fire, you simply click on a square, where you have to try to sink the opponent's ships. The game also has sound effects. A miss *splashes* into the water, whereas a hit *explodes* with the sound of the explosion.

One of the things I particularly enjoy about this game is the chat line. The bottom part of the game screen lets you send *instant messages* back and forth between yourself and your opponent (see Figure 19-6). Adding a little witty repartee to the game makes it even better.

Other network-playable games include KBackgammon (command name `kbackgammon`) and Atlantik, a network-playable, real estate, Monopoly-like game. It too features a chat area so that you can play with others around the world. Then there's *Tenes Empanadas Graciela*, or TEG, a network-enabled clone of the Risk world-conquest game. Unfortunately, that one isn't on your disk. But if world conquest appeals to you, visit `http://teg.source-forge.net` and start building your empire.

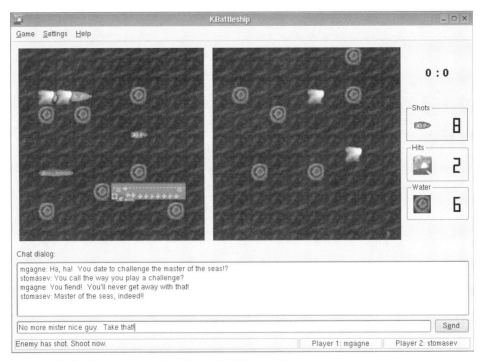

Figure 19–6   Network naval warfare with KBattleship.

Of course, one of the oldest and most popular board games in the world is chess. On your disks and perhaps already installed, you will almost certainly find xboard (and that is the command name). For the Mahjongg (the classic Eastern tile-matching game) fans out there, there is a KDE version (command name `kmahjongg`) and a GNOME version (command name `mahjongg`).

Educational Games

Games can be educational as well. As we all know, having a game that also happens to be educational doesn't automatically eradicate the fun factor. In fact, one of my favorite Linux games just happens to be an educational game. (I tell you what it is shortly.)

KStars

KStars (command name, `kstars`), part of the kdeedu package, is a desktop planetarium program that displays the locations of stars and planets on your desktop. KStars is amazing fun but much more than a toy. With a database of all the planets, 130,000 stars, 13,000 deep-sky objects, and a few thousand near-Earth objects (asteroids, comets, etc.), KStars is an astronomical treasure. With it, you can visually identify the position of stars, galaxies, nebulae, and other glories of the night sky (see Figure 19-7). You can control what is displayed, zoom in on objects, and (I love this part) download images from online resources, such as Hubble and the Space Telescope Science Institute. Just right-click on an object of interest, and the pop-up will offer you both additional information and links to high-resolution images of those objects when appropriate.

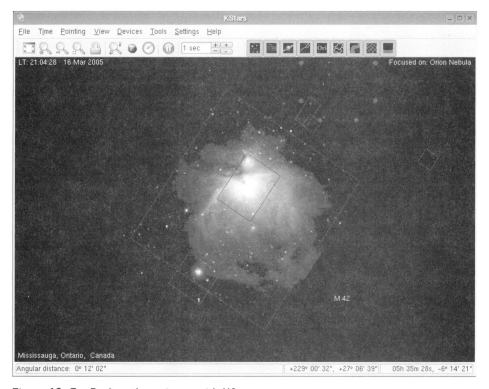

Figure 19–7 Explore the universe with KStars.

When you start KStars, it will open the KStars Setup Wizard. You'll be asked to select your home location by choosing from a fairly extensive list. When you find your location (which you can quickly narrow down by entering your city, state, province, or country), the longitude and latitude will be filled in for you (Figure 19-8).

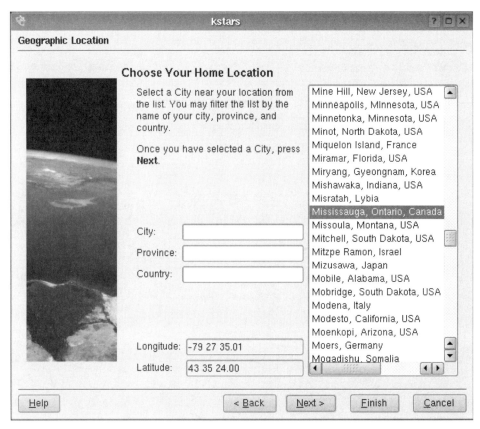

Figure 19–8   Choosing your geographical location for viewing.

When you click Next, KStars gives you the opportunity to download additional data for your catalog. This includes updated Messier object images, more NGC/IC catalog entries, planetary and asteroid data, and the like. This isn't something you have to do immediately. Clicking File on the menu bar and selecting Download data will restart this at a later time.

Explore. Learn. The universe is yours!

Learn to Type

In this day and age, learning to type is a life skill. From what I have seen, a foolproof voice recognition system is still some time off. For years, it has been my dream to be able to speak my thoughts and have them appear in my word processor or text editor, but I have seen nothing that works faster than just typing. What I'm saying is that everyone, including kids, should learn to type.

As part of the kdeedu package, you'll find software called *KTouch* (command name `ktouch`), a great little typing program. Besides being a nice typing tutor, KTouch looks great while doing the job. The display highlights which key to press as you go along, and the color coding tells you which finger to use (Figure 19-9). It supports multiple keyboard layouts, tracks your performance, and automatically changes levels based on that performance.

If the kids are particularly young, KTouch may not seem like a great deal of fun. Another way to get them into the spirit of learning is with a game called

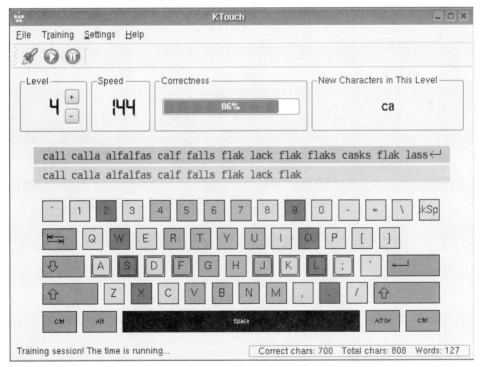

Figure 19–9   Learn to type with KTouch.

TuxTyping (Figure 19-10). This one isn't likely to be on your distribution disk, but head on over to the Web site and pick up a copy at `http://tuxtype.sf.net`.

TuxTyping features a pleasant musical soundtrack, friendly graphics, colorful background images, different game play, and multiple levels of increasing difficulty. Furthermore, when you complete a level, TuxTyping rewards you with applause that can be quite raucous at times. I particularly like waiting until the letters are almost at ground level before I let Tux go for them. It's great fun to see him run for it. Otherwise, he just lazily makes his way over to the fish. If you have kids and you want to teach them to type, get TuxTyping. They will love you for it.

Figure 19–10   Learning to type becomes a game with TuxTyping.

That Potato Guy

I can't honestly say whether this qualifies as educational (although it does force you to use your imagination), but it does qualify as fun. What I am talking about here is Potato Guy (command name `ktuberling`), a computerized version of the potato-head game where you plug various plastic eyes, ears, noses, and hats into a plastic potato to create a funny-looking potato person (Figure 19-11). The *official* Mr. Potato Head is, of course, the famous store-bought version of this game, sold by Hasbro. I'm old enough to remember when the potato wasn't included with the game. You used a *real* potato.

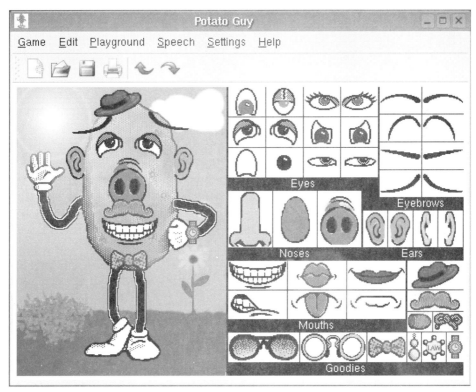

Figure 19–11 KTuberling, aka the "Potato Guy."

As you add the various pieces to the potato guy, a friendly voice speaks out the names of those parts: *"Nose," "Eye," "Spectacles."* Change the playground (click Playground on the menu bar), and you can dress up Tux the penguin or create an aquarium scene in the same way.

Yes, I know it is a kid's game, but I have had a lot of fun with this simple diversion.

The Edutainment Pack

I'm going to wrap up this section on educational games by telling you a bit more about one of the packages that comprises KDE, the one called *kdeedu*. In it, you will find a scrambled word-guessing game called *KMessedWords* (command name `kmessedwords`), as well as *KHangMan* (command name `khangman`), another word-guessing game.

The package also contains some more advanced items, including KPercentage (command name `kpercentage`), a math testing game using (what else?) percentages; KGeo (command name `kgeo`), an interactive geometry program; and KAlzium (command name `kalzium`), an interactive periodic table of the elements with a Web lookup.

There is a quite a lot of work going on in this area. For more details (and to see what else is in the works), visit `http://edu.kde.org`.

3D Accelerated Fun

To truly appreciate the following pastimes, you will require a 3D accelerated video card and OpenGL or Mesa 3D video libraries. Many manufacturers sell these cards, and some are extremely well supported under Linux. Even when the card is supported, the manufacturer of the card may not distribute the accelerated driver for inclusion with the Linux distributions themselves. That doesn't mean they aren't available, but you may have to visit the vendor's site and download them. With some cards, full 3D acceleration is directly supported under X.Org, the graphical environment on which your desktop runs.

A quick way to test for the presence of 3D support is with the following command:

```
glxinfo | grep rendering
```

The system should respond with this:

```
direct rendering: Yes
```

Another nice little test you can perform involves running a program called *gears* (part of the Mesa-demos package). To do this, you need to shell out (open a terminal or Konsole window), type the command name (`gears`), and press <Enter>. A window will appear with three gears spinning on your screen (Figure 19-12).

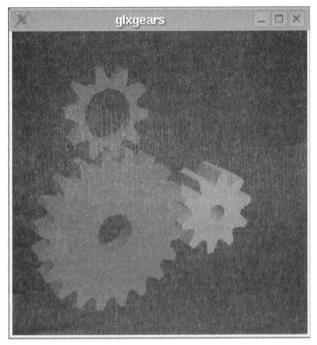

Figure 19–12 gears, a 3D acceleration measuring tool.

Don't get too distracted by the spinning gears. Look back at your terminal window and you will see some statistics regarding the performance of your 3D hardware, for instance,

```
1778 frames in 5.001 seconds = 355.529 FPS
```

That result comes from my test (play) system running with an NVIDIA GeForce2 card, and it is reasonably impressive hardware performance. In contrast, my notebook, which does not have accelerated hardware, yields this result:

```
312 frames in 5.004 seconds = 62.350 FPS
```

Not having acceleration for your card doesn't stop the program from working, it's just that it will run very slowly. On that note, let's have a look at our selection of 3D accelerated games, starting with a personal favorite.

FlightGear

You may not know this (well, you do now), but your humble author is also an airplane pilot. Consequently, I have a warm spot in my heart for FlightGear, an extremely impressive open source flight simulator (Figure 19-13). The developers of this incredible package have produced a beautiful thing. The scenery itself is breathtaking, and the coloration of land and sky is verging on photorealistic. You can also download scenery packs for every bit of land mass in the world, allowing you to fly and explore distant lands from the comfort of your own room. Fancy a lazy flight through the Grand Canyon? With FlightGear, it's not a problem.

FlightGear comes with a number of different aircraft models, from a single-engine Cessna 172 (like the ones I've flown on many occasions; Figure 19-13) to a Boeing 747, an F16 fighter, or even a Sopwith Camel.

Figure 19–13   FlightGear, a truly fantastic flight simulator.

Now that I have sold you on this (hopefully), I should tell you that this is one you will have to get online (http://www.flightgear.org)—many distributions will not include it (partly because it can be a huge program). Multiple packages are also involved in this one (and don't forget the scenery), so make sure you read the information on the Web site carefully. Despite the extra work, the rewards for this one are well worth it.

TuxRacer

Once upon a time, there was the GPL'ed TuxRacer package. Then the author of the program changed his package into a proprietary game. Because of those GPL'ed, open source roots, you can still get your hands on the original TuxRacer from many different download sites. In fact, many distributions include it on the disk, so look there first. There's also the original site at http://tuxracer.sourceforge.net if you can't find it on your disks.

The idea is simple. Tux races down snow- or ice-covered mountains on his belly (Figure 19-14). As the speed increases, you try to dodge obstacles while

Figure 19–14   Fast, frozen fun with TuxRacer.

picking up herring along the way. The action is fast-paced and exciting, with Tux taking flight off the occasional cliff or ramp. All this as you race against the clock.

I should probably mention that another developer has picked up the GPL version of Tux Racer and is continuing the project with some new looks, options, screens, and races. This version, called PlanetPenguin Racer, is available at `http://projects.planetpenguin.de/racer/`, and it's the version of TuxRacer I keep coming back to. It won't likely be on your distribution disks, but it's definitely worth the download.

Need a Belly Rub?

When you think you've mastered all of the courses TuxRacer or PPRacer has to offer, head on over to the TuxRacer Belly Rub Web site at `http://tux-racer.cjb.net/`. There are tons of additional contributed courses you can install on your Linux system. Just create a `contrib` directory in the `.tux-racer` (or `.ppracer`) directory in your `$HOME`. Extract each contributed course into its own directory (most will extract that way), and you are off to yet another race.

The 13-Year-Old's Picks

At the opening of this book, I mentioned my nephew, Paul, now a happy Linux user and, as it turns out, a happy Linux gamer. Since I wanted to know what an expert on video games finds entertaining, I asked him for a list of his favorite games so far. I've already mentioned at least one of the games he likes: PPRacer (or TuxRacer). His list of favorites is pretty varied.

For starters, he thinks FreedroidRPG is awesome. Johannes Prix and Reinhard Prix's FreedroidRPG is a beautiful 3D role-playing game with superb graphics, a cool soundtrack and sound effects, and a well-developed world (Figure 19-15). Here's the back story. Sometime, in the not-too-distant future, a mega-corporation known as *Megasoft* (or MS for short) has effectively taken over the galaxy. They managed to do this by using their vast corporate power to install Trojan horses in every computer-equipped machine on the planet, including those of government and police. As a result, all of humanity was enslaved. Due to some terrible programming error, however, the machines rebelled and took over, thus making things worse than they already were.

The only hope for mankind now is a cyborg version of Tux, a so-called *lunarian*. Equipped with high-tech armor, low-tech magic, and a laser sword, our hero is ready to take on the machines and bring freedom to the galaxy. Along the way, you'll battle numerous villains and monsters, pick up items, money, and weapons, and meet up with all sorts of interesting characters. FreedroidRPG is available at `http://freedroid.sourceforge.net`.

Figure 19–15 FreedroidRPG is a great combination of classic adventure with a post-industrial science fiction theme.

Remember the 1982 Disney movie called *Tron*? Inside the computer, programs engaged in gladiatorial battles, fighting for their *users*. One of the deadly sports in this virtual world was a *lightcycle* race. Contestants rode a kind of motorcycle that left a wall of light in its wake. The cycles themselves can't stop. The only thing you can do is ride, avoiding your opponents' walls while trying to get them to crash into yours. The last program standing wins. A lightcycle called KTron comes with your KDE desktop (program name ktron). The popularity of the lightcycle concept has created a number of variations on the theme, including one of my nephew's favorites. It's called Armagetron (Figure 19-16)—think *Armageddon*. Armagetron is available at `http://armagetron.sourceforge.net`.

Figure 19–16   *Armagetron is an excellent re-creation of the classic lightcycle duel.*

My nephew's list was pretty long, but I'll leave you with a last favorite of Paul's, which also happens to be one of mine. It's called SuperTux (Figure 19-17), a classic jump-and-run platform game in the style of, you guessed it, Super Mario Bros. The story goes like this: Tux and Penny (Tux's love interest) are out for a nice date together when Tux gets knocked out and his lovely Penny gets penguin-napped by the evil Nolok. Held prisoner in Nolok's equally evil fortress, Tux must brave all sorts of perils to save his lovely lady. It is your job to help Tux succeed in his quest. SuperTux is available at `http://super-tux.sourceforge.net`.

Figure 19–17   Help Tux rescue his beloved Penny from the evil Nolok.

More Games! I Need More Games!

Well, it was bound to happen. As you can imagine, tons of games are out there. Some are commercial packages, and others are free for the download (or compile). Still more are in various stages of development and playability.

To satisfy your hunger for Linux games, you might take a little time browsing in the games section on either SourceForge,

```
http://sourceforge.net/softwaremap/trove_list.php?form_cat=80
```

or FreshMeat (`http://freshmeat.net/browse/80/`). You'll find plenty there.

One of my favorite sites for games is the Linux Game Tome at happypen-guin.org. Although not a download site, the Linux Game Tome organizes, reviews, and lets users rate games. It's organized and searchable, and it should be on your list when it comes to adding some new diversions to your system. If you are looking specifically to find games for the younger kids, check out Linux for Kids at `http://linuxforkids.sourceforge.net/`.

Play on!

Resources

FlightGear

http://www.flightgear.org

KDE Edutainment Site

http://edu.kde.org

KDE Games Center

http://games.kde.org

Linux for Kids

http://linuxforkids.sourceforge.net/

Linux Game Tome

http://happypenguin.org

TuxRacer Belly Rub

http://tuxracer.cjb.net/

Appendix

A

The GNU General Public License

This is a copy of the GNU General Public License. Those wishing to see the original can do so by visiting the Free Software Foundation Web site. Here is the direct link to the license:

```
http://www.gnu.org/copyleft/gpl.html
```

On that Web site, you may also want to check out the comparative list of license types (both commercial and noncommercial) and how they compare with the GNU GPL. Most interesting there is the definition of whether a license qualifies as free and whether it is compatible with the GPL. Here is that address:

```
http://www.gnu.org/philosophy/license-list.html
```

Now, without further ado, here is the GNU GPL.

GNU General Public License

Version 2, June 1991
Copyright (C) 1989, 1991 Free Software Foundation, Inc.
59 Temple Place, Suite 330, Boston, MA 02111-1307 USA

Preamble

The licenses for most software are designed to take away your freedom to share and change it. By contrast, the GNU General Public License is intended to guarantee your freedom to share and change free software—to make sure the software is free for all its users. This General Public License applies to most of the Free Software Foundation's software and to any other program whose authors commit to using it. (Some other Free Software Foundation software is covered by the GNU Library General Public License instead.) You can apply it to your programs, too.

When we speak of free software, we are referring to freedom, not price. Our General Public Licenses are designed to make sure that you have the freedom to distribute copies of free software (and charge for this service if you wish), that you receive source code or can get it if you want it, that you can change the software or use pieces of it in new free programs, and that you know you can do these things.

To protect your rights, we need to make restrictions that forbid anyone to deny you these rights or to ask you to surrender the rights. These restrictions translate to certain responsibilities for you if you distribute copies of the software or if you modify it.

For example, if you distribute copies of such a program, whether gratis or for a fee, you must give the recipients all the rights that you have. You must make sure that they, too, receive or can get the source code. And you must show them these terms so they know their rights.

We protect your rights with two steps: (1) copyright the software, and (2) offer you this license, which gives you legal permission to copy, distribute, and/or modify the software.

Also, for each author's protection and ours, we want to make certain that everyone understands that there is no warranty for this free software. If the software is modified by someone else and passed on, we want its recipients to know that what they have is not the original, so that any problems introduced by others will not reflect on the original authors' reputations.

Finally, any free program is threatened constantly by software patents. We wish to avoid the danger that redistributors of a free program will individually obtain patent licenses, in effect making the program proprietary. To prevent this, we have made it clear that any patent must be licensed for everyone's free use or not licensed at all.

The precise terms and conditions for copying, distribution, and modification follow.

GNU General Public License
Terms and Conditions for Copying, Distribution, and Modification

0. This License applies to any program or other work which contains a notice placed by the copyright holder saying it may be distributed under the terms of this General Public License. The "Program," below, refers to any such program or work, and a "work based on the Program" means either the Program or any derivative work under copyright law: that is to say, a work containing the Program or a portion of it, either verbatim or with modifications and/or translated into another language. (Hereinafter, translation is included without limitation in the term "modification.") Each licensee is addressed as "you."

Activities other than copying, distribution, and modification are not covered by this License; they are outside its scope. The act of running the Program is not restricted, and the output from the Program is covered only if its contents constitute a work based on the Program (independent of having been made by running the Program). Whether that is true depends on what the Program does.

1. You may copy and distribute verbatim copies of the Program's source code as you receive it, in any medium, provided that you conspicuously and appropriately publish on each copy an appropriate copyright notice and disclaimer of warranty; keep intact all the notices that refer to this License and to the absence of any warranty; and give any other recipients of the Program a copy of this License along with the Program.

You may charge a fee for the physical act of transferring a copy, and you may at your option offer warranty protection in exchange for a fee.

2. You may modify your copy or copies of the Program or any portion of it, thus forming a work based on the Program, and copy and distribute such modifications or work under the terms of Section 1 above, provided that you also meet all of these conditions:

   a. You must cause the modified files to carry prominent notices stating that you changed the files and the date of any change.

   b. You must cause any work that you distribute or publish, that in whole or in part contains or is derived from the Program or any part thereof, to be licensed as a whole at no charge to all third parties under the terms of this License.

   c. If the modified program normally reads commands interactively when run, you must cause it, when started running for such interactive use in the most ordinary way, to print or display an announcement including an appropriate copyright notice and a notice that there is no warranty (or else saying that you provide a warranty) and that users may redistribute the program under these conditions, and telling the user how to view a copy of this License. (Exception: If the Program itself is interactive but does not normally print such an announcement, your work based on the Program is not required to print an announcement.)

   These requirements apply to the modified work as a whole. If identifiable sections of that work are not derived from the Program, and can be reasonably considered independent and separate works in themselves, then this License, and its terms, do not apply to those sections when you distribute them as separate works. But when you distribute the same sections as part of a whole which is a work based on the Program, the distribution of the whole must be on the terms of this License, whose permissions for other licensees extend to the entire whole, and thus to each and every part regardless of who wrote it.

   Thus, it is not the intent of this section to claim rights or contest your rights to work written entirely by you; rather, the intent is to exercise the right to control the distribution of derivative or collective works based on the Program.

   In addition, mere aggregation of another work not based on the Program with the Program (or with a work based on the Program) on a volume of a storage or distribution medium does not bring the other work under the scope of this License.

3. You may copy and distribute the Program (or a work based on it, under Section 2) in object code or executable form under the terms of Sections 1 and 2 above provided that you also do one of the following:

    a. Accompany it with the complete corresponding machine-readable source code, which must be distributed under the terms of Sections 1 and 2 above on a medium customarily used for software interchange; or,

    b. Accompany it with a written offer, valid for at least three years, to give any third party, for a charge no more than your cost of physically performing source distribution, a complete machine-readable copy of the corresponding source code, to be distributed under the terms of Sections 1 and 2 above on a medium customarily used for software interchange; or,

    c. Accompany it with the information you received as to the offer to distribute corresponding source code. (This alternative is allowed only for noncommercial distribution and only if you received the program in object code or executable form with such an offer, in accord with Subsection b above.)

    The source code for a work means the preferred form of the work for making modifications to it. For an executable work, complete source code means all the source code for all modules it contains, plus any associated interface definition files, plus the scripts used to control compilation and installation of the executable. However, as a special exception, the source code distributed need not include anything that is normally distributed (in either source or binary form) with the major components (compiler, kernel, and so on) of the operating system on which the executable runs, unless that component itself accompanies the executable.

    If distribution of executable or object code is made by offering access to copy from a designated place, then offering equivalent access to copy the source code from the same place counts as distribution of the source code, even though third parties are not compelled to copy the source along with the object code.

4. You may not copy, modify, sublicense, or distribute the Program except as expressly provided under this License. Any attempt otherwise to copy, modify, sublicense, or distribute the Program is void, and will automatically terminate your rights under this License. However, parties who have received copies, or rights, from you under this License will not have their licenses terminated so long as such parties remain in full compliance.

5. You are not required to accept this License, since you have not signed it. However, nothing else grants you permission to modify or distribute the Program or its derivative works. These actions are prohibited by law if you do not accept this License. Therefore, by modifying or distributing the Program (or any work based on the Program), you indicate your acceptance of this License to do so, and all its terms and conditions for copying, distributing, or modifying the Program or works based on it.

6. Each time you redistribute the Program (or any work based on the Program), the recipient automatically receives a license from the original licensor to copy, distribute, or modify the Program subject to these terms and conditions. You may not impose any further restrictions on the recipients' exercise of the rights granted herein. You are not responsible for enforcing compliance by third parties to this License.

7. If, as a consequence of a court judgment or allegation of patent infringement or for any other reason (not limited to patent issues), conditions are imposed on you (whether by court order, agreement, or otherwise) that contradict the conditions of this License, they do not excuse you from the conditions of this License. If you cannot distribute so as to satisfy simultaneously your obligations under this License and any other pertinent obligations, then as a consequence you may not distribute the Program at all. For example, if a patent license would not permit royalty-free redistribution of the Program by all those who receive copies directly or indirectly through you, then the only way you could satisfy both it and this License would be to refrain entirely from distribution of the Program.

   If any portion of this section is held invalid or unenforceable under any particular circumstance, the balance of the section is intended to apply and the section as a whole is intended to apply in other circumstances.

   It is not the purpose of this section to induce you to infringe any patents or other property right claims or to contest validity of any such claims; this section has the sole purpose of protecting the integrity of the free software distribution system, which is implemented by public license practices. Many people have made generous contributions to the wide range of software distributed through that system in reliance on consistent application of that system; it is up to the author/donor to decide if he or she is willing to distribute software through any other system, and a licensee cannot impose that choice.

   This section is intended to make thoroughly clear what is believed to be a consequence of the rest of this License.

8. If the distribution and/or use of the Program is restricted in certain countries either by patents or by copyrighted interfaces, the original copyright holder who places the Program under this License may add an explicit geographical distribution limitation excluding those countries, so that distribution is permitted only in or among countries not thus excluded. In such case, this License incorporates the limitation as if written in the body of this License.

9. The Free Software Foundation may publish revised and/or new versions of the General Public License from time to time. Such new versions will be similar in spirit to the present version, but may differ in detail to address new problems or concerns.

    Each version is given a distinguishing version number. If the Program specifies a version number of this License which applies to it and "any later version," you have the option of following the terms and conditions either of that version or of any later version published by the Free Software Foundation. If the Program does not specify a version number of this License, you may choose any version ever published by the Free Software Foundation.

10. If you wish to incorporate parts of the Program into other free programs whose distribution conditions are different, write to the author to ask for permission. For software which is copyrighted by the Free Software Foundation, write to the Free Software Foundation; we sometimes make exceptions for this. Our decision will be guided by the two goals of preserving the free status of all derivatives of our free software and of promoting the sharing and reuse of software generally.

NO WARRANTY

11. BECAUSE THE PROGRAM IS LICENSED FREE OF CHARGE, THERE IS NO WARRANTY FOR THE PROGRAM, TO THE EXTENT PERMITTED BY APPLICABLE LAW. EXCEPT WHEN OTHERWISE STATED IN WRITING THE COPYRIGHT HOLDERS AND/OR OTHER PARTIES PROVIDE THE PROGRAM "AS IS" WITHOUT WARRANTY OF ANY KIND, EITHER EXPRESSED OR IMPLIED, INCLUDING, BUT NOT LIMITED TO, THE IMPLIED WARRANTIES OF MERCHANTABILITY AND FITNESS FOR A PARTICULAR PURPOSE. THE ENTIRE RISK AS TO THE QUALITY AND PERFORMANCE OF THE PROGRAM IS WITH YOU. SHOULD THE PROGRAM PROVE DEFECTIVE,

YOU ASSUME THE COST OF ALL NECESSARY SERVICING, REPAIR, OR CORRECTION.

12. IN NO EVENT UNLESS REQUIRED BY APPLICABLE LAW OR AGREED TO IN WRITING WILL ANY COPYRIGHT HOLDER, OR ANY OTHER PARTY WHO MAY MODIFY AND/OR REDISTRIBUTE THE PROGRAM AS PERMITTED ABOVE, BE LIABLE TO YOU FOR DAMAGES, INCLUDING ANY GENERAL, SPECIAL, INCIDENTAL, OR CONSEQUENTIAL DAMAGES ARISING OUT OF THE USE OR INABILITY TO USE THE PROGRAM (INCLUDING BUT NOT LIMITED TO LOSS OF DATA OR DATA BEING RENDERED INACCURATE OR LOSSES SUSTAINED BY YOU OR THIRD PARTIES OR A FAILURE OF THE PROGRAM TO OPERATE WITH ANY OTHER PROGRAMS), EVEN IF SUCH HOLDER OR OTHER PARTY HAS BEEN ADVISED OF THE POSSIBILITY OF SUCH DAMAGES.

END OF TERMS AND CONDITIONS

How to Apply These Terms to Your New Programs

If you develop a new program, and you want it to be of the greatest possible use to the public, the best way to achieve this is to make it free software that everyone can redistribute and change under these terms.

To do so, attach the following notices to the program. It is safest to attach them to the start of each source file to most effectively convey the exclusion of warranty; and each file should have at least the "copyright" line and a pointer to where the full notice is found.

<one line to give the program's name and a brief idea of what it does.>
Copyright (C) <year> <name of author>

This program is free software; you can redistribute it and/or modify it under the terms of the GNU General Public License as published by the Free Software Foundation, either version 2 of the License or (at your option) any later version.

This program is distributed in the hope that it will be useful, but WITHOUT ANY WARRANTY; without even the implied warranty of MERCHANTABILITY or FITNESS FOR A PARTICULAR PURPOSE. See the GNU General Public License for more details.

You should have received a copy of the GNU General Public License along with this program; if not, write to the Free Software Foundation, Inc., 59 Temple Place, Suite 330, Boston, MA 02111-1307 USA.

Also add information on how to contact you by electronic and paper mail.

If the program is interactive, make it output a short notice like this when it starts in an interactive mode:

Gnomovision version 69, Copyright (C) year name of author

Gnomovision comes with ABSOLUTELY NO WARRANTY; for details type "show w.". This is free software, and you are welcome to redistribute it under certain conditions; type "show c" for details.

The hypothetical commands "show w" and "show c" should show the appropriate parts of the General Public License. Of course, the commands you use may be called something other than "show w" and "show c"; they could even be mouse-clicks or menu items—whatever suits your program.

You should also get your employer (if you work as a programmer) or your school, if any, to sign a "copyright disclaimer" for the program, if necessary. Here is a sample; alter the names:

Yoyodyne, Inc., hereby disclaims all copyright interest in the program "Gnomovision" (which makes passes at compilers) written by James Hacker.

<signature of Ty Coon>, 1 April 1989
Ty Coon, President of Vice

This General Public License does not permit incorporating your program into proprietary programs. If your program is a subroutine library, you may consider it more useful to permit linking proprietary applications with the library. If this is what you want to do, use the GNU Library General Public License instead of this License.

Resources

Linux Documentation Project

http://www.tldp.org

Linux.org list of LUGs

http://www.linux.org/groups/index.html

B

Installation

A modern Linux installation is easy. I will go so far as to say that it is even easier than installing Windows. For the most part, you boot from your CD-ROM drive, click Next a few times, and you are running Linux. Okay, perhaps there is a bit more to it than that, but not much. Linux will, for the most part, auto-detect nearly all devices on your machine and automatically configure them optimally.

Getting Ready for Your Installation

If your machine has Windows already installed and you have documents, spreadsheets, pictures, or music files you wish to keep, now would be a good time to back those up, either on diskette or burned to a CD-ROM. Even if you plan on preserving your Windows installation for a dual-boot system, it's always prudent to have a good backup if you are going to be doing major work on your hard disk. You might also want to take advantage of all that hard work that was done in preinstalling Windows, and make notes on all the hardware in your machine—the type of network and video cards and anything else you can think of. You do that by clicking the Start button, selecting Settings, selecting Control Panel, and then double-clicking the System icon. Now walk through the hardware profiles and take some notes. Odds are you won't need it at all, but you can never have too much information.

The average Linux installation takes about 30–60 minutes, although I have seen it happen in as little as 5 minutes on a really fast system. That's a fully network-ready, configured, all-set-to-work machine with no rebooting every few minutes to load another driver. It doesn't get much easier than this.

That said, unless you are feeling particularly adventurous, I would highly recommend that you read through this chapter once before actually starting.

Hardware Considerations

Before we move on, let's talk hardware. The sad truth is that not every device will work with Linux. You should not think of this as being strange or as somehow representing a weakness in Linux. After all, Linux is not unique in this. In fact, Linux may be fairly unique when it comes to the sheer number of devices and platforms that it supports. Linux will run on Intel-based systems as well as Alpha, RISC, and Macintosh. IBM's entire line of computers, from small, desktop PCs to large, mainframe systems such as the S/390, run Linux. Then there are MIPS, SPARC, and StrongARM. You can also find Linux embedded in microchips, running on portable MP3 players, PDAs, cell phones, and even digital watches. That's incredible hardware support!

From the perspective of your computer, it is highly unlikely that Linux won't install and run well. If something is going to be unsupported, it will probably involve some Windows-only modems, printers, or scanners. To find out whether or not your computer and its associated devices will work with your Linux installation, the first place to look is your Linux vendor's Web site.

Another great hardware resource is the Hardware HOWTO. You can always find the latest version by surfing on over to the LDP's Linux Hardware Compatibility HOWTO page:

```
http://www.tldp.org/HOWTO/Hardware-HOWTO/
```

As Linux gains in popularity, you'll find that hardware vendors are increasingly interested in tapping into this ever-growing market. I've had the experience of being on site, adding hardware to a customer's system (Ethernet cards come immediately to mind), and finding that the system did not have the drivers. I quickly visited the Ethernet card manufacturer's Web site and found precompiled drivers ready and waiting for me. With the incredible growth of Linux, it won't be long before these issues will be a thing of the past.

Dual Booting Revisited

In Chapter 3, I mentioned dual booting, a means by which you can run both Linux and Windows on one machine. At boot time, a menu lets you start one *or* the other. Let's pretend for a moment that you still want to run Windows from time to time. Perhaps you want the comfort of knowing that you can go back to your old operating system to do certain things. This is where dual-booting comes into play. There are a couple of ways to do this and I will get to those in a moment. Please note, however, that doing this will require a little more up-front work.

One dual-boot scenario involves a completely separate disk that you can dedicate to a Linux installation. Although this is an ideal situation, most people will have a single disk with Windows already loaded. If you have a large disk, chances are good that there are already two partitions. One will be a C: drive and the other a D: drive. What you want to do is erase the D: drive and use it for Linux. If you are going to follow this route, make sure you back up any documents or copy them into folders on your C: drive.

Unfortunately, Windows is just as likely to be taking up the entire partition table. The trick is to *shrink* the existing Windows partition, thereby creating some space on which to install Linux. To do this, you must defragment your disk in Windows before going ahead and resizing your partitions. You do this by clicking the Start button and then selecting Programs | Accessories | System Tools | Disk Defragmenter.

Resizing the partition is your next step. Once again, there are two ways of doing this. Some recent distributions, such as Mandrake and SuSE, will automatically detect a Windows-only disk and offer to shrink the partition for you. Alternatively, you can do this with a little DOS program called *FIPS*, which you can find on your Linux distribution CD. On Debian, check the tools directory. On Red Hat or SuSE, check the dosutils directory.

In most cases, there will probably be a directory called `FIPS` or `FIPS20` with a number of files inside, including the `FIPS.EXE` program itself.

A Sample FIPS Session

Warning When doing anything this drastic with your drives, *always* make a backup. In fact, no matter what you do with your system, always make regular backups.

Let's pretend you've already run your defragmenter and that you have plenty of space on your hard drive. Start by creating a DOS/Windows boot diskette. This is generally done by typing the following command from the DOS/Windows command prompt (after inserting a blank diskette into the diskette drive):

```
FORMAT A: /S
```

The "`/S`" tells DOS/Windows to transfer the system to the boot diskette. You will also want to have a second boot diskette handy, so do this a second time. You'll need it to back up your boot sector. I'll explain why in a moment.

Next, copy the `FIPS.EXE` utility and its associated files from the CD-ROM drive to the first diskette:

```
COPY D:\DOSUTILS\FIPS20\*.* A:
```

Remember that the path to the `FIPS20` directory may vary, depending on your distribution CD.

Now shut down Windows and boot from the FIPS diskette. When the boot completes, you should be at a DOS prompt. This is where the split occurs. Now run the FIPS command:

```
FIPS
```

FIPS will display a partition table showing you how the disk space has been allocated. FIPS will ask which partition you want to split. No doubt, we are taking these steps because there is only one partition, and that makes it easy to answer the query. Enter the partition number and press <Enter>. As a precaution, FIPS will ask whether you want to make a copy of your boot sector on the remote chance that disaster strikes. You probably want to answer Y (yes). This will require a second, preformatted diskette. Put in your second diskette and answer Y to the next question: *"Do you have a bootable floppy disk in drive A: as described in the documentation (y/n)?"* Since you have just inserted the diskette, press *<Enter>*.

Now the fun begins. FIPS will display your partition table. Using the left and right cursor (arrow) keys, change the size of the partition (you'll see the numbers changing each time you press the keys). When you are happy with your changes, press <Enter>. FIPS will ask you to confirm the changes. You can still change your mind at this time. If everything looks good, press <c> to continue; then type y when asked *"Ready to write the new partition scheme to disk?"*

When FIPS completes, you will reboot your system. You might want to reboot into Windows first, just to make sure that things are working properly. If everything looks as you want it to, pop in your Linux installation CD, shut down Windows, and reboot the system.

An Installation Comparison

Modern installations offer a nice, graphical process, and, for the most part, installing Linux today is a point-and-click experience, with help every step of the way. Of course, a graphical installation makes a lot of assumptions that might not necessarily be what you want. Should all else fail, try the text-based installation. Most distributions still provide one, and I don't see that changing anytime soon.

A Very Generic Install

Every installation is similar in many ways, though the order of the steps may vary slightly. After booting, you get a nice welcome screen, usually followed by a request for the language you want to install in. Hot on the heels of this is some kind of basic peripheral selection, namely, for your keyboard and mouse. You'll also be asked for the time zone you live in. Every installation will (somewhere near here) ask you for options on partitioning and formatting your drive. For most users, the defaults should be fine, and your Windows partition (if you opted for a dual-boot system) will be detected and set aside. This is also the point where you are asked to select a boot loader and to confirm the operating systems you want to be able to launch at boot time. Once again, this is particularly important if you are setting up a dual-boot system.

After all these preliminary steps are taken care of, it is time to load your software. Some kind of default collection will be offered (i.e., workstation, server, etc.), at which point your system starts to load. There may be one or more CDs to load, depending on how much you asked for. Once this is over, it is time to configure your network connection, followed by the graphical window setup, also known as the X window system.

You will then get your first introduction to *Linux security*. The installer will ask you for an administrative user (root) password and provide you with the opportunity to create one or more additional users for day-to-day use. Under normal circumstances, the root user should not be used, except to install software or to update and administer your system in some fashion. The separation of administrative from *regular* users is one of the ways Linux protects your system from accidental or malicious damage.

Usually, that is pretty much it. The system will reboot and you'll be running Linux.

Note Installers tend to make fairly intelligent choices as you go. Nevertheless, you should still check to make sure that what is selected is indeed correct.

Another source of information is the distribution itself. Most Linux distribution CDs have extensive installation information on the CD itself, in the box (if you purchased it), or on the distribution's Web site. If you are feeling less than adventurous, print out a copy before you begin your installation.

Remember that until you have actually formatted your drives, you can still change your mind about a great many of the decisions you make along the way. Just click the Back button (or use the <Tab> key to move to it) and reenter the information the way you intended.

Of course, my generic install is just that; generic. In order to give you an idea of just what to expect when you go through the real thing, I have gone through four different installations using some of the more popular Linux distributions and detailed them for you here.

Note As of this writing, Mandrake 10.1 was the current version, Fedora Core 3 was out, and SuSE 9.3 was the new kid on the block. I mention this release information because the screens you see may not be precisely as I describe here—not a big deal, but some things will be a bit different. That's why I want you to look at these install examples *as* examples. They are meant to prepare you for what you will experience during an installation.

Warning Almost any modern PC can boot from a CD-ROM, and this is the easiest way to do this. If your system will not boot from the CD, you can create a boot diskette. If this is a problem for you, put your first Linux CD into the drive and use Windows Explorer (the file manager) to look for a directory called "boot" on the CD. There will be a boot disk image there (the name may vary) and instructions on how to create the diskette.

A Mandrake Linux Install

With this Mandrake install, I used version 10.1. As this book was wrapping up and going to press, Mandrake had just acquired Conectiva Linux and, in the process, changed the company name to Mandriva. So Mandrake is now Mandriva, but the version of Mandriva I used was still called Mandrake.

Reboot your system with the installation CD in the drive. Mandrake boots with a graphical screen with two options. Pressing <F1> will allow you to choose between text and low-resolution install modes, while the default is the standard graphical install. Press <Enter> and you are on your way.

Basic hardware detection takes place at this time, and the installer is loaded into memory. In a few seconds, you'll be at the main install screen. On the left-hand side of the screen is a set of steps, each with a light beside the label to let you know (roughly) where you are in the installation process. The first of these steps involves selecting your preferred language for installation—there are many, organized by continent to help you narrow things down. Select your language of choice, or click OK to accept the *English (American)* default, and continue. On the next screen, read the license agreement (where you learn about the GPL and related licenses). Select the Accept radio button, and then click Next.

The next screen deals with security. Mandrake's default install lets you choose between four different security levels. What each level allows or denies is documented on the page. Take a moment to read it and choose the level that works for you. Most people will choose the default of Standard.

Mandrake's install then automatically detects your hard drive, which means it is time to set up your file systems. The options here involve erasing the entire disk, doing your own custom disk partitioning, or using the free space on the Windows partition. This is quite *interesting* because it makes it possible to automatically resize the Windows partition, making use of the free space in order to install Mandrake. You might remember from my earlier discussion that the only caveat is that the Windows disk must be defragmented first.

Quick Tip With Windows XP, you may need to turn off the swap file before starting your defragment and resize. That's because the swap file is often placed at the end of the disk, making it virtually impossible to resize the partition.

To do this, right-click on the My Computer icon and select Properties. Now click on the advanced tab and look near the top. You'll see a button labeled *Settings* in the *Performance* section. Click Settings and another dialog appears, labeled Performance Options. Again click on the Advanced tab, and look down near the bottom in the *Virtual memory* section. Click Change; then, on the next screen, select the *No paging file* radio button. Click OK on each dialog until you exit system properties. Now you can do your defragment and get access to all your free space. When you are done with the Linux installation, you'll want to turn the swap file back on.

The default option is to *"Use free space,"* and that is probably what you should choose. Click OK to continue. The partitions will be created and formatted and a list of available packages will be pulled from the install disk. Now it is time to decide what kind of a system you want. You will be looking at the *Package Group Selection* screen. A standard Mandrake install is a Workstation install, and that's where the emphasis is placed with the defaults. *Office Workstation* is automatically selected, as is *Internet station* and *Multimedia station*. That means you get your word processors and spreadsheets as well as e-mail clients and Web browsers. If you want to play games, you should click on *Game station*

A few more package groups are preselected, among these, *Development*. Now, once again, I am going to point out that if you want to be able to compile programs (for those bleeding-edge new programs), this one is necessary. *Configuration* and *Console tools* will help with system configuration, while *Network Computer (client)* provides the ssh client. In an office situation, you will most certainly want that. This grouping is rounded off with *Documentation*.

Before you move on, look over on the right. If this computer will be a server, you may wish to add Web, ftp, e-mail, and database servers. Pause your mouse pointer over the choices and a tooltip will give you a short description of what each server offers. Finally, look under *Graphical Environment*. The KDE environment is selected by default; however, you may want to choose GNOME as well here. Furthermore, if you would like to experiment with even more desktop environments at some future time, you might consider checking on *Other Graphical Desktops*. This loads WindowMaker, IceWM, and others. At the bottom of the screen is a checkbox labeled *Individual package selection*. This lets you review your choices and add or remove items as you see fit.

Click Next, and the package installation will begin. You'll be treated to a little slideshow telling you about Open Source software, Mandrake products, joining the Mandrake Club, and information about the various things that come with your Mandrake system (Figure B-1). In short, the show tells you why you are going to love working with Mandrake Linux. Depending on the choices you made, you may need to switch the CD at some point.

When the installation completes, you'll be asked to choose a root password, after which you will have the opportunity to create one or more normal users. You really only need to create one at this time. Notice that the Mandrake install lets you choose a representative icon for your users. Just click on the icon and select one that suits you. *I particularly like the cat, myself.* After entering your information, click *Accept user*, and then click *Next* (unless you are adding multiple users, of course).

Mandrake will then ask you to choose your default Window manager. KDE is displayed as the default, and that will do nicely. You can also choose to have the system automatically log in a single user on boot. While this is fine for a home user who is the only one on the system, I highly recommend that others (particularly in an office environment) make sure this box is unchecked.

Click Next to select a location for the installation of the boot loader. Most people should just accept the default here, which is the master boot record (MBR) of the first disk.

Click Next to continue, and you'll be taken to the a kind of summary screen of various hardware options, such as printer, sound card, and network. Some of these will already be configured; others may need to be set up (the Network/LAN option, for instance). Click the Configure button to make changes. In most cases, a wizard will take you through the various choices available. The installer is very good at auto-detection of printers, network

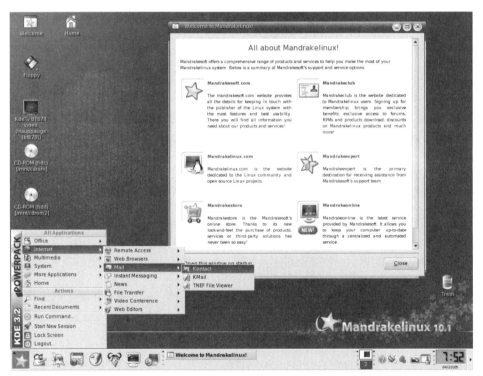

Figure B–1   Your Mandrake 10.1 desktop, ready for use.

connections (LAN, Cable, DSL, etc.), and graphical interfaces, so if you aren't sure, take the defaults. When you are happy with all your choices, click Next.

We're almost done! Ideally, you should have a live Internet connection at this point and high-speed access, because the packages can be *substantial*— downloading the updates can take a long time if your only connection is a dial-up modem. What Mandrake does here is provide you with a chance to load and install any updates and security fixes that may have been released since the OS first came out. Select Yes and then click Next to start the update. But remember what I said about high-speed access.

That's it. Click Reboot to reboot, and make sure you take the CD out of the drive when it is ejected. When you log in for the first time, Mandrake will take you through a Wizard to complete your user setup.

Putting On the Fedora

The version I used for this install was Fedora Core 3, the community-based Linux distribution based on Red Hat Linux. In terms of installation, I could almost as easily have shown you the install for Red Hat Enterprise Linux 4, the famous commercial Linux distribution, whose company financially supports the development of Fedora. Both are essentially identical in terms of the install steps.

Start by putting in the CD-ROM and rebooting your system. The boot menu will appear, giving you the option of choosing either a graphical or text install. For almost every system out there, the graphical install will be just fine. All you need to do is click or press Install and the system will start booting. The system will identify devices and you'll see a number of messages scroll by.

A few seconds later, you'll see an interesting message. Fedora's install has a *media check* option. Here's the idea: You have your installation CDs, but you don't know for sure whether there isn't some kind of surface defect that will make installation impossible. Isn't it better to find out before you start off on all this work? It really is your choice. You can take time to test each CD in your set before you proceed, or you can simply skip the step.

After the media check option, the graphical install screen will appear. This is just a welcome screen, and you can simply click Next and continue on. On the following screen, select the language you would like to use for the installation. I selected English and clicked Next again. What follows is the keyboard

selection screen. Once again, I selected the default of *U.S. English* and clicked
Next, which brings us to the mouse selection screen.

The next screen is for installation type. The default option is *"Personal
Desktop,"* which Fedora suggests is *"Perfect for personal computers or laptops."*
Most people will want to accept the default and click Next.

On the next screen, you have the option of letting the system automatically partition your disk or using Disk Druid to do the job yourself. Unless you
are trying to preserve another operating system, you can accept the default,
which is to allow the install to automatically partition your disk. After clicking
Next, you will be given some choices on *Automatic Partitioning*, which is to
decide how the installer will make use of the available space. The default is to
"Remove all Linux Partitions on this system," and this is probably the right
choice. Another option to consider if you are looking to dual-boot with Windows is the one labeled *Keep all partitions and use existing free space*. If you
want to double-check the decisions made by the installer, make sure that you
check off the option to *"Review (and modify if needed) the partitions created."*

A warning box will appear letting you know that all data will be erased.
Click OK. The *Boot Loader configuration* is next. Fedora Core installs the
GRUB boot loader by default, but it is possible to change it to LILO. Both
work very well, and in the end it is your choice. I have personally grown to like
GRUB quite a bit, but I still use LILO on other systems without a care. At
this point, you also have the option of setting a password on the boot loader.
Home users don't have to worry about this, but some network installations
may want the additional security of having to enter a password when the system is booted. Before you move on, you may want to have a look at the labels
the installer assigns. I mention this because if you are setting up a dual-boot
system, one of those partitions will be Linux and another Windows. Most
people will accept the default. When you are happy with your choices, click
Next.

The following screen is for network configuration. If you do not have a
network card installed, you can skip to the next step. If your Internet connection is through a DSL or cable modem connection, that will likely be the case.
The default is to boot and pull an address via DHCP, and this is what you
would choose. If your PC is on a home or corporate network with fixed
addresses, you will want to click `Edit`, check off the *"Configure using DHCP,"*
and enter your address information. If you are in an office, check with your
systems administrator for this information. Otherwise, enter your IP address
and netmask; then click `OK`. Enter your hostname, gateway, and DNS information; then click Next.

The next section is very important; the *Firewall Configuration* screen. There are many options here, and you should take the time to read what each one offers. Network security is extremely important because the incidence of cyberattacks continues to rise all the time. Linux PCs aren't as susceptible to viruses, particularly if you don't run as the root or administrative user, but that doesn't mean you should let your guard down. If you are a single user on a home PC that is connected to the Internet, choose *Enable Firewall*, and leave the various services checked off.

Tip Before you go ahead and click Next, notice the last item on that screen. It asks, "*Enable SELinux?*" This is a more hardened form of Linux security, which you probably don't need if you are running on a single-user machine or if your system is strictly for home use. It you are interested in learning about and using SELinux, you may want to set this option to *Warn* in the beginning instead of *Enable*. This sets up enhanced security controls on certain programs without enforcing these controls, logging denials rather then denying access. It's a good way to determine whether your system is still usable with these strict security policics in place.

What follows is yet another language selection screen (*Additional Language Support*). That's because the OS can support multiple languages, and you can change that default at a later time. Unless you have another language at your disposal, leave the choice as it is and click Next. On the next screen, you will be asked to enter your time zone (in my case, I chose *America/Toronto*). When you are done, click Next.

When you arrive at the next screen, you will get your first taste of Linux's multiuser nature, with the Account configuration. This is where you set your root password (root is the administrator login). After the installation completes, you have the opportunity to create other, nonroot (regular user) accounts. It's early, but I'll stress it now: You should create at least one nonroot account from which to work on a day-to-day basis.

This brings us to the screen with the goodies, *Package selection*. The packages selected for the *Personal Desktop* are as follows:

```
Desktop shell (GNOME)
Office Suite (OpenOffice)
```

```
Web browser
Email (Evolution)
Instant messaging
Sound and video applications
Games
```

Since, in this book, I concentrate on KDE as the desktop, make sure you click *"Customize the set of packages to be installed"* before you go on. Click Next, and you will be on the *Package Group Selection* screen. Notice that packages are ordered into categories such as Desktops and Applications. Make sure you check off the *KDE Desktop Environment* under Desktops. Then click Details, and make sure that *all* KDE packages have been selected before you click OK.

> *Note* For the most part, you can leave everything else as is, but you may want to consider one other thing here. Despite the fact that most *desktop users* will not want to compile packages, I think that the lure of trying out something that is leading edge or unusual will be more than even home users will be able to resist as they get familiar with their systems. That's why you might want to chose to install the development tools (gcc, perl, python, etc.) as well as X Software Development, GNOME Software Development, and KDE Software Development.

When you are done here, click Next. This is the last step before the installation takes off on its own. You'll be given a final opportunity to change your mind before committing to this installation. Click Next, and a pop-up window will inform you of what other CDs you will need (in my installation, I needed CD #1 and CD #2 and CD #3). Click Continue and you are on your way.

Your partitions will be formatted and a progress bar will keep track of where you are in the installation. As the install progresses, you will be treated to some information about the Fedora project and some of the included products. Incidentally, this is usually a good time to take a break and grab something to drink. From time to time, you'll need to change CDs (you may need all three). When the installation completes, remove the last CD and click *Reboot,* and the system will restart with your Fedora Core installation.

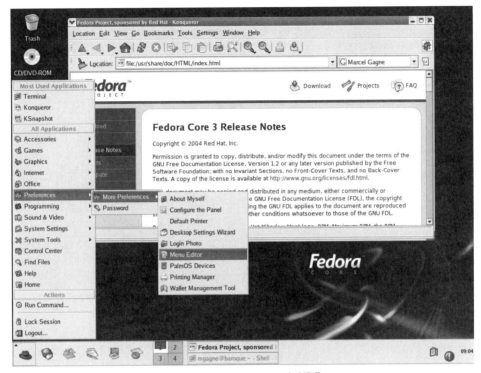

Figure B-2 Your Fedora Core 3 desktop running with KDE.

After the system reboots, you will be presented with a graphical Welcome screen. From here, you will be asked to go through a few final configuration details. Accept the license agreement and click Next. If the date and time are incorrect, you can adjust them here. On the next screen, you'll have an opportunity to fine-tune the display based on your monitor type and the number of colors you want displayed (Figure B-2).

Click Next, and you'll be at one of the more important parts of the process, User Account creation. You must create at least one nonroot user for the system, and this is the time to do so. After clicking Next, the system will let you test your sound card and provide you with a chance to install additional CDs (if you have them), after which you are done. The graphical login manager will start up and you can log in as your nonroot user.

Quick Tip You can choose between the different window managers (desktop environments) at login time by clicking Session on the login screen. Select your environment of choice (KDE, GNOME, etc.) and click OK.

A SuSE Install

For my SuSE install, I used exactly the same machine and started from the same place. Note that I was using SuSE Linux Professional 9.3 for this, which comes with both multiple CDs and a single DVD. The advantage of the DVD, assuming you have a DVD drive, is that you do not have to swap disks.

Reboot your system with the CD (or DVD) in the drive. You now have the option of selecting various install modes. For a fresh installation, select Installation and press <Enter>. The screen at this point is all graphical, with status messages letting you know, among other things, that hardware is being initialized. If you would prefer to see the text boot messages, press the <Esc> key and you'll get more details.

The first screen you'll see after this is a license agreement floating above the YaST installation and configuration screen. Once you have read the license, click *I Agree* to continue. What follows is a nice welcome screen, which also happens to be the language selection screen. The default is *English (US)*, but you can certainly choose something else. Click Accept, and the install process will begin analyzing your system and probing for the various devices and peripherals you have. Once this is done, you'll be provided with some installation choices based on whether your system already has Windows or Linux installed.

At this point, a lot happens in the background as YaST collects all of your installation information. All of these choices are shown to you on a single page; the keyboard, mouse, partitioning, software install, booting, and time zone info are all there on one screen. Notice the *blue underline* on each setting, much like a Web page. Look at the suggested settings to make sure things look right. If you need to change something, click the blue link. For instance, to change your time zone from the default of *USA/Mountain*, click *Time zone*, select from the list, and click Accept.

I would like you to look at *Partitioning and Software* in particular. If you do have a Windows partition, you should see it listed as /windows/C—that will be its mount point unless you would like a different name. The software choices are the *KDE Desktop Environment, Office Applications* (this is Open-Office.org), *Help & Support Documentation*, and *Graphical Base System* (the X window system).

You might recall that I suggested that the lure of playing with some lead-ing-edge software might be overwhelming at some point. You can prepare for that here by clicking on the blue *Software* link. On the screen that follows, click the *Detailed selection* button. On the left-hand side of the next screen, you'll see a number of categories for additional software. If you do want to compile your own programs, you'll want to select the *C/C++ Compiler and Tools*. I'm also pretty sure you'll want the *Games and Multimedia* packages. If I am right, choose those as well.

Finally, there's the GNOME desktop environment. Even though I concen-trate this book on KDE, you might recall that I said it is a good thing to exper-iment with another desktop environment. In the end, you might like GNOME better than KDE. In the Linux world, you have a choice. Further-more, it doesn't hurt anything (other than taking up some disk space) to load it at the same time. When you are done, click Accept to go back to your *Installation Settings* screen. Have a final look and click Accept. You'll be given a final warning regarding installation. If you are ready to start, click *"Install."*

Install Tip Depending on your installation, you may be asked to confirm license agreements for non-GPL packages. For instance, my installation included Macromedia Flash Player 7, which had its own license agreement.

Your drive will be formatted, your Linux system will load, and you'll see a progress bar at the top right. After a little while, the basic installation will complete (you'll get a message to that effect), whereupon you remove the CD and press <Enter>.

During the installation, you'll be treated to a slide show telling you about SuSE Linux, your installation, security features, individual software pack-ages, Novell's involvement, and more. Notice that this is a two-tab window, with one labeled Slide Show and the other Details. If you would rather see which file is being installed at what time, click on the Details tab. How long this process takes depends on what you decided to install and how fast your system is.

If you are using multiple CDs (as opposed to the DVD install), the system will reboot on its own after the first CD has finished installing. This is normal. Just let the system boot without interruption. The process will restart, asking for the remaining CDs in order.

Now we jump to final configuration. The first of these steps is account creation, starting with the setting of the root password. The root account is used for administrative functions, such as installing software. Always remember that you do not want to run as root under normal circumstances, since root is essentially *all powerful*.

After selecting a root password, click Next. The screen that follows is the Network Configuration dialog. Look under Firewall, Network Interfaces, and so on, and make sure you are happy with the settings. By default the firewall is turned on, and, while you may want to make some changes to the policies, you should not turn it off. DSL and cable modem connections are detected automatically. If your system is part of an existing LAN, click on Network Interfaces and enter your settings by clicking the Change button on the selected interface. This process also detects your modem hardware should you have a dial-up network connection. When you are done here, click Next. Your Internet connection will come up and you'll have a chance to download any updates to your system.

When the updates are done, click Next. The YaST installer will take you to the user configuration screen. The first question has to do with your method of authentication, whether local (your password file), LDAP, NIS, or Samba. Home users will want to keep the default of Local. Click Next; then create at least one user login. The SuSE install is interesting here in that it allows you to redirect all of root's mail directly to a user account. Check off the box that says "Receive System Mail" when you are creating your personal user ID. There's also a checkbox for "Auto Login," which logs in this particular user without a password automatically at boot time. This is probably fine if you are running this system at home and are the only user; but in an office environment or with multiple users, you don't want to check this box. You can choose to create additional users at this time (by clicking the *User Management* button), or simply click Next to continue.

After a brief interlude to tell you about some of the changes in SuSE Linux 9.3 (some of these are interesting, so take a moment to read them), you will get to the Hardware Configuration screen. Hardware in this case includes graphics cards, printers, your sound card, TV tuner cards, and other network interfaces, like Bluetooth.

The first item on the hardware lists is your X window graphical configuration. The auto-detect will likely make the right choices, but do take a look at what has been selected. The dialog here will vary, depending on what kind of video hardware you have or whether your card is 3D accelerated. *Just make sure you test out the final settings before moving on.* Even if the information looks right, click the Graphics Cards link on the page where you'll have an opportunity to test your settings. Video settings work perfectly 99.99% of the time. It's just good to be sure beforehand.

When you return to the Hardware Configuration screen, take a moment to test your printer (you can always do this later, if you prefer) and test your sound card, and then click Next. The final hardware settings will be written to disk and the installation will complete.

There is no reboot at this point. SuSE wraps up the final configuration changes and immediately takes you to your desktop (Figure B-3). As the folks at SuSE are known to say, "Have a lot of fun."

Figure B–3   SuSE Linux Professional 9.3 desktop.

Xandros Desktop OS, Version 3.0 Deluxe

I decided to include Xandros 3.0 here for a couple of reasons. One is that it isn't one of the big-name distributions. The second is that its commercial product comes with CrossOver Office preinstalled, making it easy to run a number of Windows applications (e.g., Microsoft Office, Quicken, Adobe Photoshop), should you have a need to do so. While Xandros offers a free distribution version, their commercial product does provide a number of additional products to simplify the switch from Windows to Linux for those who have more of an investment in their legacy operating system.

Let's take a look at the Xandros 3.0 Deluxe install. Start by putting your CD in the drive and rebooting your system. The initial boot screen is kind of nice, with a Xandros logo to the right (Xandros: Making Linux Work for You) and hardware and boot information showing up on the left. Eventually, the logo fades out, very dramatically, to be replaced by the rather classy-looking, graphical Xandros installation screen. There isn't much to do here other than clicking Next.

The screen that follows is the license, which explains that part of the programs included with a Xandros distribution are GPL while others are not (the CodeWeavers CrossOver Office product, for instance), thereby making this a single-user distribution. That said, the license permits you to install Xandros on unlimited home computers (for noncommercial use) and one commercial-use system. Once you accept the agreement, you can click Next.

There are two installs possible . . . an express install and a custom install. I'll give you details on the custom install.

Under Software Selection, you'll find four desktop possibilities. The minimal desktop comes in at 904MB, the standard at 1262, and the complete at 1268; the custom desktop starts at 844MB and goes up from there. Given the small difference between standard and complete, I opted for complete. Below these choices is a software list of the various packages that will be installed. Each has a checkbox to the left so that you can make changes to your selection. Click Next, and the installer moves you to the Disk Configuration screen.

Under Disk Configuration, you have the option of using free space, taking over a disk or partition, or managing the partitions manually. There is also an option for resizing a Windows FAT, FAT32, or NTFS partition. Not having a copy of XP loaded, I did not test this. Finally, there is an option for upgrading an existing Xandros installation.

Since I wanted to give the automatic install as much leeway as possible, I chose "Take over disk or partition" and clicked next. I was presented with a list of existing partitions to choose from. I selected one, clicked Next, and was taken to the summary screen. The partition I chose would be formatted as ReiserFS. As for swap, the installer noticed my existing swap partition and chose to use it. Perfect!

The next screen was for Network configuration, and my card was detected without a hitch. The default is a dynamic setting, which is great for people with a DSL or cable modem connection. Since this machine is to be part of an existing network, I clicked Edit and entered the IP address, default gateway, and DNS info.

Under Administration configuration, I was asked to enter the admin password. Rather than using "root" as the admin username, the system defaults to "Administrator" (presumably to make the Windows users feel at home). I entered the password and gave the computer a name (XANDROS). Before clicking Next here, you might want to look at two additional options for installations. These allow you to *Enforce strong passwords* and *Make user home folders private*.

The next screen had me configure individual nonadmin users (for everyone who will be using the system). Good. I added my own username, chose a password, and moved on.

That was it. An installation summary screen gave me a quick recap of my settings and warned me that it would take over all the data on the chosen partition. Fine with me. I clicked Finish and watched the install take place. A status bar along the bottom showed the progress of the installation.

A few minutes later, the install was complete. Just before exiting, you have the opportunity to create a rescue/boot diskette. This whole process takes a only a couple more minutes. After it was over, I clicked Exit to restart my system.

The boot screen that follows offers three choices: a default boot, a safe mode boot, and an administrator configuration boot. Choose the default option by pressing Enter (or just wait a few seconds), and the system comes up normally.

The login screen is relatively plain, with a graphical box requesting your username and password. If you configured only one user, this will be the default, so enter your password and log in. The first time you log in, you will be presented with the First Run Wizard (Figure B-4). The first screen asks you to customize your mouse preferences for right- or left-hand use. I'm a right-handed guy living in a right-handed world, but I thought this was a rather thoughtful touch.

Clicking Next takes you to the Regional Settings. This is basically your language of choice, keyboard layout, and so on. Click Next again and enter the correct date, time, and time zone. When you are done here, click Next, and the Connection Wizard will help you set up your Internet connection. This wizard will take you through the steps to connect using a DSL line, a local LAN, a SLIP connection, or a modem. Once you are done with this, click Next, and another wizard will let you set up your printer. When you have done so, click Next.

You are almost there. Next, the System Behavior screen offers a number of settings, including window decoration and style, whether you single-click or double-click to launch a program, and so on. For starters, you might want to just accept the default (which is KDE's Plastik theme), but the button labeled "Keep Current Behavior" lists a number of other system defaults, including a Windows-like style. Click Next when you are through here and you will be at the Registration screen, where you can register your copy of Xandros online.

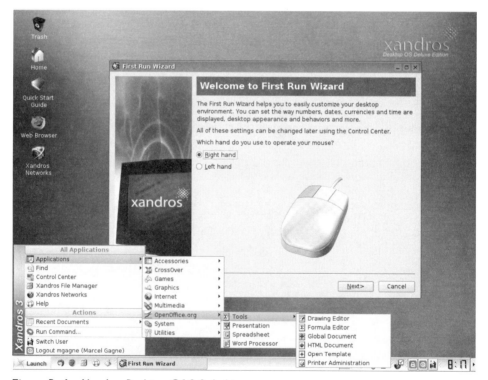

Figure B–4   Xandros Desktop OS 3.0 desktop.

There is only one more screen after this, and it is an important one. Two buttons are available. One is the Xandros/KDE Control Center, from which you can change a number of the settings you have already made. The other button is labeled Xandros Networks. This will allow you to connect to Xandros and download any updates that might apply to your current release.

Software updates are installed by double-clicking on the Xandros Networks icon. Several sections are available through this, including the Xandros online shop, new application installs, and application updates. I checked for updates and found the process very simple. Updates are listed as security updates, driver updates, and so on. Each has a description with an "Install now" link. After clicking on the link, you will be asked for the admin password, after which the process begins.

Not-So-Tough Installs

As you can see, installing Linux isn't difficult, but it does vary from distribution to distribution. The thing to remember is that every distribution has similar steps, such as language, keyboard, and mouse selection. All will ask you about how to deal with disk partitions and offer to do it for you if you would rather keep it simple. For the most part, it's just a matter of accepting the defaults and clicking Next.

Starting and Stopping Linux

This sounds like such a simple thing that you might wonder why I am spending any time on it at all. After all, you turn on the power switch, sit back, and watch Linux come to life. Depending on the installation, you may have more than one boot option. The default will almost certainly be to take you into Linux. If you opted for a dual-boot system, you may have to select Linux from the boot menu.

The lesson here is simply this: Because you do have options, take the time to read what's on the menu and go with that.

 Warning All right. Here is *rule number one* when it comes to shutting down your system: Never, ever simply power off the system. You must do a *proper* shutdown. Oh, and get an uninterruptible power supply (UPS) so that your system doesn't shut down accidentally. I should perhaps make it clear that *you do not need a UPS* to run Linux. However, if you don't want a random power fluctuation or a three-second power outage to take down your system, the added protection of a UPS just makes sense.

Linux is a multiuser, multiprocessing operating system. Even when it appears that nothing is happening, a great deal can be going on. Your system is maintaining disk space, memory, and files. All this time, it is busy making notes on what is happening in terms of security, e-mail, errors, and so on. There may be open files or jobs running. A sudden stop as a result of pulling the plug can damage your file systems. A proper shutdown is essential. Even in the world of your old OS, you still had to do a proper shutdown—it is no different here.

There are a few ways of shutting down your system. You start by logging off from your system. Make sure you've closed all your applications and saved anything you might have been working on. Now right-click on the desktop and select Logout from the pop-up menu. You should get something that looks similar to the screen shown in Figure B-5.

Figure B–5
Here are the available options when preparing to end a login session.

This particular logoff screen is from a SuSE system, but the types of options will be similar regardless of what system you are on. At this point, select *"Turn off computer."* There's rarely any need for a *"Restart computer"* in the Linux world—when you shut down, it's usually because you intend to power off the system.

 Shell Out You can also log out from the command line, but it must be done from the root login. From a terminal window, switch to root with "su - root" (you'll be prompted for the password), and type the following:

```
shutdown -h now
```

When shutdown is called with the -h option, it is another way of saying, "Shut the system down and keep it down." On some systems (and with proper hardware), this option will power off the system after it is down: Another option is to type the following:

```
shutdown -r now
```

The -r option tells Linux to reboot immediately after a shutdown. A reboot option is usually used after a kernel rebuild.

Resources

FIPS Home Page

http://www.igd.fhg.de/~aschaefe/fips/fips.html

Mandriva Linux (Mandrake)

http://www.mandriva.com

Fedora Linux

http://fedora.redhat.com

SuSE Linux

http://www.novell.com/linux/suse/index.html

Appendix

C

Taking Command of Linux

Think of this appendix as an extended Shell Out section. That means it is time to transform you into a master or mistress of the shell. In deciding to join me here, you have identified yourself as one of the bold and curious explorers who really want to know their Linux systems. Sure, it is possible to work day in and day out with your Linux system and rarely use the command line, but the command line is power. Your reward for continuing to this next level will be a deeper understanding of your system and the power to make it do whatever you want.

The things I want to talk about here are basic commands that will serve you well throughout your time with Linux. One of the things I hope to show you is how flexible some of these commands are. With most, you can modify the basic function with command-line switches, flags, or options and thereby have them yield far more information than a simple execution of the command itself. A little thirst for exploration will open you up to the real potential of everyday commands.

Linux Commands: An Easy Start

When you talk about commands, it invariably means working at the shell level: the command prompt. That's the dollar sign prompt ($), and it is common to many command shells. When logged in as the root user, you will usually have a different prompt. That symbol (#) goes by many names. In North America, we call it the "pound sign" or the "hash mark." My English lit friends tell me it's an "octothorpe." Others call it the tic-tac-toe board. I'm going to call it the **root prompt**.

Anyway, you want to be at just such a command prompt to begin your experimentation. If you are running from a graphical environment, click the terminal window icon to start a terminal (or shell) session. KDE users will be starting a Konsole (command name `konsole`). Konsole (Figure C-1) supports tabbed shells, so you can run multiple shell sessions from one Konsole window. Just click Session on the menu bar and select New Session. You can then click back and forth from one shell to the other. You can even cut and paste between sessions. This is very handy if you are working on multiple systems.

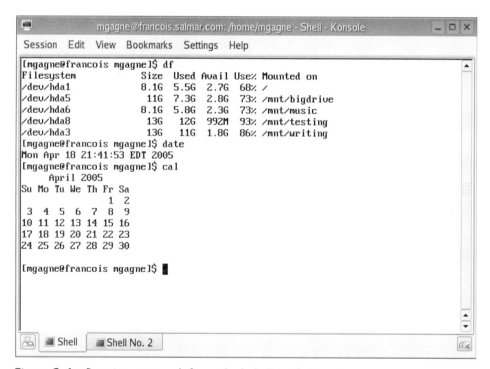

Figure C-1   Running commands from a bash shell inside Konsole.

GNOME users, meanwhile, will likely start up a gnome terminal. Like Konsole, it features tabs to give you easy access to multiple sessions. To say that there are a great number of terminal emulators might be understating things. You also have the venerable xterm, rxvt, and Eterm, to name just a few.

As you work your way through this chapter, you'll notice that I toss in little lists, like the one that follows. If these commands are not already in your arsenal, then spend a few minutes playing with them and finding out what they do.

Commands to Know and Love, Part 1

`date`	Date and time.
`df`	Show me how much free space my disks have.
`who`	Who is logged on to the system?
`w`	Similar to `who` but with different information.
`cal`	Show me a calendar
`tty`	Identify your workstation.
`echo`	Hello, ello, llo, lo, o, o, o . . . .
	Try typing `echo "Hello world."`
`last`	Who last logged in, and are they still logged in?

Working with Files

Let me tell you the secret of computers, of operating systems, and of the whole industry that surrounds these things: Everything is data. Information is the be-all and end-all of everything we do with computers. Files are the storehouses for that information, and learning how to manipulate them, use and abuse them, and otherwise play with them will still be the point of computers 20 years from now.

The next thing I want to do is talk about the three most overlooked files on your system: standard in, standard out, and standard error. A facility in manipulating these "files" will provide you with amazing flexibility when it comes to doing your work.

Commands to Know and Love, Part 2

`ls`	LiSt files.
`cat`	conCATenate files.
	Try "`cat /etc/profile`".

sort	SORT the contents of a file (or any output for that matter). Try "`sort /etc/passwd`".
uniq	Return only the UNIQue lines—you do this after sorting.
wc	Word Count (returns a count of words, characters, and lines). Try "`wc /etc/passwd`".
cp	CoPy files.
mv	MoVe, or rename, a file.
rm	ReMove, or delete, a file.
more	Allows easy paging of large text files.
less	Like the more command, but with serious attitude.

File-Naming Conventions

Valid filenames may contain **almost** any character. You do have to pay some attention to the names you come up with. Your Linux system will allow filenames up to 255 characters in length. How you define filenames can save you a lot of hassle, as I soon demonstrate.

Some valid filename examples include the following:

```
fish
duck
program_2.01
a.out
letter.to.mom.who.I.dont.write.often.enough.as.it.is
.bash_profile
```

Notice the last name in particular. It starts with a period. Normally, this type of file is invisible with a default listing. Starting a filename with a period is a way to make a file somewhat invisible. This is good to know if you don't want to burden file listings with a lot of noise. It is also the way that a system cracker might hide his or her tracks when breaking into your system—by creating a directory that starts with a period. To see the so-called dot-files, use the ls command with a -a flag (ls -a).

Listing Files with Emotion!

The ls command seems so simple, and yet it has a number of options that can give you tons of information. Change to something like the /etc directory and try these options if you never have:

```
cd /etc
ls --color
ls -b
ls -lS
ls -lt
```

The first listing will show different types of files and directories in color. The second (-b) will show octal representations for files that might have been created with control characters. Depending on the terminal you are using, the default is to show question marks or simply blanks. If you need to access (or delete) the file, it helps to know what it is really called. The third and fourth options control sorting. The -lS option gives you a long listing (lots of information) sorted by file size. The last option (-lt) sorts by time, with the newest files at the top of the list and the oldest at the bottom.

A Peek at Metacharacters

Metacharacters are special characters that have particular meaning to your shell—that dollar sign or hash mark prompt where you do your work. The two I want to look at are the asterisk and the question mark. The following is what they mean to the shell:

*	Match any number of characters.
?	Match a single character.

Extending our talk of listing files, you could list all files containing "ackle" by using this command:

```
$ ls *ackle*
hackle hackles tackles
```

Similarly, you could find all the words that start with an "h" like this:

```
$ ls h*
hackle hackles
```

Now, if you want to see all the seven-letter words in your directory, use this command:

```
$ ls ???????
hackles tackles
```

Each question mark represents a single letter position.

File Permissions in the Shell

Back in Chapter 5, I showed you how to look at file permissions with Konqueror. When you use the `ls -l` command, you are doing the same thing—looking at basic Linux security at the file (or directory) level. Here is an example of a long `ls` listing:

```
$ ls -l
total 3
drwxr-x---  5 root     system   512  Dec 25 12:01   presents
-r-xr--r--  1 zonthar  users    123  Dec 24 09:30   wishlist
-rw-rw----  1 zonthar  users    637  Nov 15 09:30   griflong
```

The first entry under the total column shows a directory (I talk about the next nine characters in a moment). The first character is a d, which indicates a directory. At the end of each line, you'll find the directory or filename—in my example, they are `presents`, `wishlist`, and `griflong`. Because the first character in the permissions field is d, "presents" is a directory.

On to those other nine characters (characters 2 through 10). These indicate permissions for the user or owner of the file (first three), the group (second group of three), and others or everyone else (last three). In the first line, user root has read (r), write (w), and execute (x) permissions, while the system group has only read and execute. The three dashes at the end imply that no one else has any permissions. The next two files are owned by the user called zonthar.

Quick Tip Remember user, group, and other (ugo). You will find them useful later when I cover changing file and directory permissions.

Not-So-Hidden Files

When you take your first look at valid filenames, remember that I mentioned that files starting with a period are hidden. As a result, creating directories or files in this way is a favorite trick of system crackers. Get used to the idea of listing your directories and files with a -a option so that you see everything that's there. Look for anything unusual.

Keep in mind, however, that a number of applications create dotted directory names in your home directory so that you are generally not burdened with seeing all these configuration areas. That's great, except you should know what you've got on your disk. Always balance your need for convenience with a healthy curiosity. A quick ls –a in your home directory will show you some files (and directories) you will become very familiar with as time goes on. Here is an example of what you will see:

```
Xclients  .bash_history  .bash_profile  .gnupg  .kde
```

Strange Filenames That Just Won't Go Away

Every once in a while, you will do a listing of your directory and some strange file will appear that you just know isn't supposed to be there. Don't panic. It's not necessarily a cracker at work. You may have mistyped something and just need to get rid of it. The problem is that you can't. Case in point: I *accidentally* created a couple of files with hard-to-deal-with names. I don't want them there, but trying to delete them does not work. Here are the files:

```
-another_file
 onemorefile
```

Here's what happens when I try to delete them:

```
[mgagne@scigate tmp]$ rm -another_file
rm: invalid option -- a
Try 'rm --help' for more information.
```

What about that other file?

```
[mgagne@scigate tmp]$ rm onemorefile
rm: cannot remove 'onemorefile': No such file or directory
```

The problem with the first file is that the hyphen makes it look like I am passing an option to the `rm` command. To get around this problem, I'll use the double-dash option on the `rm` command. Using two dashes tells the command that what follows is not an option to that command. Here I go again:

```
[mgagne@scigate tmp]$ rm -- -another_file
[mgagne@scigate tmp]$
```

Bravo! By the way, this double-dash syntax applies to many other commands that need to recognize potentially weird filenames. Now, what about the second file? It looked fine, didn't it? If you look very closely, you'll see a space in front of the leading o, so simply telling `rm` to remove the file doesn't work either, because "onemorefile" is not the filename. It is actually " onemorefile". So I need to pass that space as well, and to do that I give the full name (space included) by enclosing the filename in double quotes:

```
[mgagne@scigate tmp]$ rm " otherfile"
[mgagne@scigate tmp]$
```

More on `rm` (or "Oops! I Didn't Really Mean That.")

When you delete a file with Linux, it is gone. If you didn't really mean to delete (or `rm`) a file, it is time to find out if you have been keeping good backups. The other option is to check with the rm command before you delete a file. Instead of simply typing `rm` followed by the filename, try this:

```
rm -i file_name1 file_name2 file_name3
```

The `-i` option tells `rm` to work in interactive mode. For each of the three files in the example, `rm` will pause and ask if you really mean it:

```
rm : remove 'file_name1'?
```

If you like to be a bit wordier than that, you can also try

```
rm --interactive file_name
```

but that goes against the system administrator's first principle.

Of course, in following that principle, you could remove all the files starting with the word `file` by using the asterisk:

```
rm -i file*
```

Making Your Life Easier with `alias`

You might find that you want to use the `-i` option every time you delete anything, just in case. It's a lot easier to type Y in confirmation than it is to go looking through your backups. The problem is that you are adding keystrokes, and everyone knows that system administrators are notoriously lazy people. Then there's that whole issue of the first principle. That's why we shortened "list" to simply `ls`, after all. Don't despair, though—Linux has a way. It is the `alias` command:

```
alias rm='rm -i'
```

Now every time you execute the `rm` command, it will check with you beforehand. This behavior will only be in effect until you log out. If you want this to be the default behavior for `rm`, you should add the `alias` command to your local `.bashrc` file. If you want this to be the behavior for every user on your system, you should add your `alias` definitions to the systemwide version of this file, `/etc/bashrc`, and save yourself even more time. Depending on your distribution, `alias` definitions may already be set up for you. The first way to find out is to type the `alias` command on a blank line:

```
[root@website /root]# alias
alias cp='cp -i'
alias ls='ls --color'
alias mv='mv -i'
alias rm='rm -i'
```

Using the `cat` command, you can look in your local `.bashrc` file and discover the same information:

```
[root@website /root]# cat .bashrc
# .bashrc
# User specific aliases and functions
alias rm='rm -i'
alias cp='cp -i'
```

```
alias mv='mv -i'
# Source global definitions
if [ -f /etc/bashrc ]; then
        . /etc/bashrc
fi
```

Well, isn't this interesting? Notice the two other commands here, the cp (copy files) and mv (rename files) commands, and both have the -i flag as well. They too can be set to work interactively, verifying with you before you overwrite something important. Let's say I want to make a backup copy of a file called important_info using the cp command:

```
cp important_info important_info.backup
```

Perhaps what I am actually trying to do is rename the file (rather than copy it). For this, I would use the mv command:

```
mv important_info not_so_important_info
```

The only time you would be bothered by an "Are you sure?" type of message is if the file already existed. In that case, you would get a message like the following:

```
mv: overwrite 'not_so_important_info'?
```

Forcing the Issue

The answer to the inevitable next question of "What do you do if you are copying, moving, or removing multiple files and you don't want to be bothered with being asked each time when you've aliased everything to be interactive?" is this: Use the -f flag, which, as you might have surmised, stands for "force." Once again, this is a flag that is quite common with many Linux commands—either a -f or a --force.

Imagine a hypothetical scenario in which you move a group of log files daily so that you always have the previous day's files as backup (but just for one day). If your mv command is aliased interactively, you can get around it like this:

```
mv -f *.logs /path_to/backup_directory/
```

Musing Yes, I know that mv looks more like *move* than *rename*. In fact, you do move directories and files using the mv command. Think of the file as a vessel for your data. When you rename a file with mv, you are moving the data into a new container for the same data, so it isn't strictly a rename—you really are moving files. Looked at that way, it doesn't seem so strange. Sort of.

The reverse of the alias command is unalias. If you want your mv command to return to its original functionality, use this command:

```
unalias mv
```

Standard Input and Standard Output

It may sound complicated, but it isn't. *Standard in* (STDIN) is where the system expects to find its input. This is usually the keyboard, although it can be a program or shell script. When you change that default, we call it *redirecting* from STDIN.

Standard out (STDOUT) is where the system expects to direct its output, usually the terminal screen. Again, redirection of STDOUT is at the discretion of whatever command or script is executing at the time. The chain of events from STDIN to STDOUT looks something like this:

```
standard in   -> Linux command   ->   standard out
```

STDIN is often referred to as *fd0*, or file descriptor 0, while STDOUT is usually thought of as *fd1*. There is also *standard error* (STDERR), where the system reports any errors in program execution. By default, this is also the terminal. To redirect STDOUT, use the greater-than sign (>). As you might have guessed, to redirect from STDIN, you use the less-than sign (<). But what exactly does that mean? Let's try an experiment. Randomly search your brain and pick a handful of names. Got them? Good. Now type the cat command and redirect its STDOUT to a file called random_names:

```
cat > random_names
```

Your cursor will just sit there and wait for you to do something, so type those names, pressing Enter after each one. What's happening here is that `cat` is taking its input from `STDIN` and writing it to your new file.

You can also write the command like this:

```
cat - 1> random_names
```

The hyphen literally means `standard in` to the command. The `1` stands for file descriptor 1. This is good information, and you will use it later. Finished with your random names list? When you are done, press <Ctrl-D> to finish. <Ctrl-D>, by the way, stands for *EOF*, or *end of file*.

```
Marie Curie
Albert Einstein
Mark Twain
Wolfgang Amadeus Mozart
Stephen Hawking
Hedy Lamarr
^D
```

If you `cat` this file, the names will be written to `STDOUT`—in this case, your terminal window. You can also give `cat` several files at the same time. For instance, you could do something like this:

```
cat file1 file2 file3
```

Each file would be listed one right after the other. That output could then be redirected into another file. You could also have it print out the same file over and over (`cat random_names random_names random_names`). `cat` isn't fussy about these things and will deal with binary files (programs) just as quickly. Beware of using `cat` to print out the contents of a program to your terminal screen. At worst, your terminal session will lock up or reward you with a lot of beeping and weird characters.

Quick Tip If you get caught in such a situation and all the characters on your screen appear as junk, try typing `echo` and then pressing <Ctrl+V> and <Ctrl+O>. If you can still type, you can also try typing `stty sane` and then pressing <Ctrl+J>. Some systems also provide a command called `reset` that will return your terminal session to some kind of sane look.

Redirecting STDIN works pretty much the same way, except you use the less-than sign instead. Using the sort command, let's take that file of random names and work with it. Many commands that work with files can take their input directly from that file. Unless told otherwise, cat and sort will think that the word following the command is a filename. That's why you did the STDIN redirection thing. Yes, that's right: STDIN is just another file. Sort of.

```
sort random_names
```

The result, of course, is that you get all your names printed out in alphabetical order. You could have also specified that sort take its input from a redirected STDIN. It looks a bit strange, but this is perfectly valid:

```
[mgagne@scigate tmp]$ sort < random_names
Albert Einstein
Hedy Lamarr
Marie Curie
Mark Twain
Stephen Hawking
Wolfgang Amadeus Mozart
```

One more variation involves defining your STDIN (as you did previously) and specifying a different STDOUT all on the same line. In the following example, I am redirecting **from** my file and redirecting that output **to** a new file:

```
sort < random_names > sorted_names
```

Pipes and Piping

Sometimes the thing that makes the most sense is to feed the output from one command directly into another command without having to resort to files in between at every step of the way. This is called *piping*. The symbolism is not that subtle: Imagine pieces of pipe connecting one command with another. Not until you run out of pipe does the command's output emerge. The pipe symbol is the broken vertical bar on your keyboard, usually located just below or (depending on the keyboard) just above the Enter key and sharing space with the backslash key. Here's how it works:

```
cat random_names | sort | wc -w > num_names
```

In this example, the output from the `cat` command is piped into `sort`, whose output is then piped into the `wc` command (that's "word count"). The -w flag tells `wc` to count the number of words in `random_names`. So far, so good.

That `cat` at the beginning is actually redundant, but I wanted to stack up a few commands for you to give you an idea of the power of piping. Ordinarily, I would write that command as follows:

```
sort random_names | wc -w > num_names
```

The `cat` is extraneous because `sort` incorporates its function. Using pipes is a great timesaver because you don't always need to have output every step of the way.

tee: A Very Special Pipe

Suppose you want to send the output of a command to another command, but you also want to see the results at some point. Using the previous word count example, if you want a sorted list of names but also want the word count, you might have to use two different commands: one to generate the sorted list and another to count the number of words. Wouldn't it be nice if you could direct part of the output one way and have the rest continue in another direction? For this, use the `tee` command:

```
sort random_names | tee sorted_list | wc -w > num_names
```

The output from `sort` is now sitting in a file called `sorted_list`, while the rest of the output continues on to `wc` for a word count.

STDERR

What about `STDERR`? Some commands (many, in fact) treat the error output differently than the `STDOUT`. If you are running the command at your terminal and that's all you want, there is no problem. Sometimes, though, the output is quite wordy and you need to capture it and look at it later. Unfortunately, using the `STDOUT` redirect (the greater-than sign) is only going to be so useful. Error messages that might be generated (such as warning messages from a compilation) will go to the terminal, as before. One way to deal with this is to start by redirecting `STDERR` to `STDOUT` and then to redirect that to a file. Here's the line I use for this:

```
command_name 2>&1 > logfile.out
```

Remember that file descriptor 2 is STDERR and that file descriptor 1 is STDOUT. That's what that 2>&1 construct is all about. You are redirecting fd2 to fd1 and then redirecting that output to the file of your choice. Using that program compilation example, you might wind up with something like this:

```
make -f Makefile.linux 2>&1 > compilation.output
```

Quick Tip The final greater-than sign in the preceding example could be eliminated completely. When using the 2>&1 construct, it is assumed that what follows is a filename.

The Road to Nowhere

If the command happens to be verbose by nature and doesn't have a quiet switch, you can redirect that STDOUT and STDERR noise to what longtime Linux users like to call the *bit bucket*, a special file called /dev/null—literally, a road to nowhere. Anything fed to the bit bucket takes up no space and is never seen or heard from again. When I was in school, we would tell people to shut up by saying, "Dev null it, will you?" As you can see, we were easily amused.

To redirect output to the bit bucket, use the STDOUT redirection:

```
command -option > /dev/null
```

If, for some strange reason, you want to sort the output of the random_names files and you do not want to see the output, you can redirect the whole thing to /dev/null in this way:

```
sort random_names > /dev/null
```

Using the program compilation example where you had separate STDOUT and STDERR streams, you can combine the output to the bit bucket:

```
make -F makefile.linux 2>&1 /dev/null
```

That's actually a crazy example because you do want to see what goes on, but redirecting both STDOUT and STDERR to /dev/null is quite common when dealing with automated processes running in the background.

Linux Commands: Working with Directories

There is another batch of commands suited to working with directory files (directories being just another type of file):

```
pwd       Print Working Directory.
cd        Change to a new Directory.
mkdir     MaKe or create a new DIRectory.
mv        MoVe directories, or, like files, rename them.
rmdir     ReMove or delete DIRectories.
```

One way to create a complicated directory structure is to use the mkdir command to create each and every directory:

```
mkdir /dir1
mkdir /dir1/sub_dir
mkdir /dir1/sub_dir/yetanotherdir
```

What you could do instead is save yourself a few keystrokes and use the -p flag. This tells mkdir to create any parent directories that might not already exist. If you happen to like a lot of verbiage from your system, you could also add the --verbose flag for good measure:

```
mkdir -p /dir/sub_dir/yetanotherdir
```

To rename or move a directory, the format is the same as you used with a file or group of files. Use the mv command:

```
mv path_to_dir new_path_to_dir
```

Removing a directory can be just a bit more challenging. The command rmdir seems simple enough. In fact, removing this directory was no problem:

```
$ rmdir trivia_dir
```

Removing this one, however, gave me this error:

```
$ rmdir junk_dir
rmdir: junk_dir: Directory not empty
```

You can only use `rmdir` to remove an empty directory. There is a `-p` option (as in *parents*) that enables you to remove a directory structure. For instance, you could remove a couple of levels like this:

```
rmdir -p junk_dir/level1/level2/level3
```

> *Warning* Beware the `rm -rf *` command. Better yet, *never use it*. If you must delete an entire directory structure, change directory to the one above it and explicitly remove the directory. This is also the first and best reason to do as much of your work as possible as a normal user and not as root. Because root is all powerful, it is quite capable of completely destroying your system. Imagine that you are in the top-level directory (`/`) instead of `/home/myname/junkdir` when you initiate that recursive delete. It is far too easy to make this kind of mistake. *Beware.*

All the directories from `junk_dir` on down will be removed, but **only** if they are empty of files. A better approach is to use the `rm` command with the `-r`, or *recursive*, option. Unless you are deleting only a couple of files or directories, you will want to use the `-f` option as well:

```
$ rm -rf junk_dir
```

There's No Place Like $HOME

Yeah, I know. It's a pretty cheesy pun, but I like it.

Because you've just had a chance to play with a few directory commands, I'd like to take a moment and talk about a very special directory. Every user on your system has a home directory. That directory can be referenced with the $HOME environment variable. To get back to your home directory at any time, simply type `cd $HOME`; then no matter where you were, there you are. Actually, you only need type `cd`, press <Enter>, and you are home. The $HOME is implied.

The $HOME shortcut is great for shell scripts or anytime you want to save yourself some keystrokes. For instance, say you want to copy the file remote.file to your home directory and you are sitting in /usr/some_remote/dir. You could use either of the next two commands:

```
cp remote.file /home/my_username
cp remote.file $HOME
```

The second command saves you keystrokes, and the more time you spend doing system administration, the more you will love shortcuts like this. To save the maximum keystrokes, you can also use the tilde (~), a special character synonym for $HOME:

```
cp remote.file ~
```

More on File Permissions

What you can and can't do with a file, as defined by your username or group name, is pretty much wrapped up in four little letters. Look at the following listing (using ls -l) for an example. The permissions are at the beginning of each line.

```
-rw-r--r--  1 mgagne mgagne       937 May 17 13:22 conf_details
-rwxr-xr-x  1 root   root   45916220 Apr  4 12:25 gimp
-rw-r--r--  1 root   root        826 Feb 12 09:43 mail_test
-rw-r--r--  1 mgagne mgagne     44595 May 17 13:22 sk_open.jpg
```

Each of these letters in turn can be referenced by a number. They are r, w, x, and s. Their numerical representations are 4, 2, 1, and "it depends." To understand all that, you need to do a little binary math.

Reading from right to left, think of the x as being in position 0. The w, then, is in position 1 and the r is in position 2. Here's the way it works:

2 to the power of 0 equals 1   (x is 1)
2 to the power of 1 equals 2   (w is 2)
2 to the power of 2 equals 4   (r is 4)

In order to specify multiple permissions, you can just add the numbers together. If you want to specify both read and execute permissions, simply add 4 and 1 and you get 5. For all permissions (rwx), use 7.

File permissions are referenced in groups of three rwx sections. The r stands for "read," the w means "write," and the x denotes that the file is executable.

While these permissions are arranged in three groups of three rwx combinations, their meaning is the same in all cases. The difference has to do with who they represent rather than the permissions themselves. The first of these three represents the user, the second trio stands for the group permissions, and the third represents everybody that doesn't fit into either of the first two categories.

The commands you will use for changing these basic permissions are chmod, chown, and chgrp.

chmod	CHange the MODe of a file (aka its permissions).
chown	CHange the OWNer of the file or directory.
chgrp	CHange the GRouP of the file or directory.

User and Group Ownership

Let's pretend you have a file called `mail_test` and you want to change its ownership from the root user to natika. You first have to log in as root, because only root can change root's ownership of a file. This is very simple:

```
chown natika mail_test
```

You can also use the -R option to change ownership recursively. Let's use a directory called `test_directory` as an example. Once again, it belongs to root and you want to make every file in that directory (and below) owned by natika:

```
chown -R natika test_directory
```

The format for changing group ownership is just as easy. Let's change the group ownership of `test_directory` (previously owned by root) so that it and all its files and subdirectories belong to group accounts:

```
chgrp -R accounts test_directory
```

You can even combine the two formats. In the following example, the ownership of the entire `finance_data` directory changes to natika as the owner and accounts as the group. To do so, you use this form of the chown command:

```
chown -R natika.accounts finance_data
```

 Quick Tip You can use the -R flag to recursively change everything in a subdirectory with chgrp and chmod as well.

So now files (and directories) are owned by some user and some group. This brings us to the next question.

Who Can Do What?

From time to time, you will need to modify file permissions. One reason has to do with security. The most common reason, however, is to make a shell script file executable. This is done with the chmod command:

```
chmod mode filename
```

For instance, if you have a script file called list_users, you make it executable with the following command:

```
chmod +x list_users
```

That command will execute permissions for all users.

If you want to make the file executable for the owner and group only, you specify it on the command line like this:

```
chmod u+x,g+x list_users
```

The u means user (the owner of the file, really), and g stands for group. The reason you use u for the owner instead of o is that the o is being used for "other," meaning everyone else. The chmod +x list_users command can then be expressed as chmod u+x,g+x,o+x list_users.

Unfortunately, this starts to get a bit cumbersome. Now let's look at a much more complicated set of permissions. Imagine you want your list_users script to have read, write, and execute permissions for the owner, read and execute for the group, and read-only for anybody else. The long way is to do this is as follows:

```
chmod u=rwx,g=rx,o=r list_users
```

Notice the equal sign (=) construct rather than the plus sign (+). That's because the plus sign adds permissions, and in this case you want them to be absolute. If the original permissions of the file allowed write access for "other," the plus sign construct would not have removed the execute permission. Using the minus sign (–) removes permissions. If you want to take away execute permission entirely from a file, you can do something like this:

```
chmod -x list_users
```

One way to simplify the chmod command is to remember that r is 4, w is 2, and x is 1 and to add up the numbers in each of the three positions. rwx is then 4 + 2 + 1, or 7. r-x translates to 4 + 1, and x is simply 1. That monster from the second-to-last example can then be rewritten like this:

```
chmod 751 list_users
```

Who Was That Masked User?

Every time you create a file, you are submitted to a default set of permissions. Go ahead. Create a blank file using the touch command. I am going to call my blank file "fish."

```
[mgagne@testsys tmp]$ touch fish
```

Now have a look at its permissions by doing an ls -l:

```
[mgagne@testsys tmp]$ ls -l
total 0
-rw-rw-r--    1 mgagne   mgagne          0 Nov  5 11:57 fish
```

Without doing anything whatsoever, your file has read and write permissions for both the user and the group, and read permission for everybody else. This happens because you have a default file-creation mask of 002. You can discover this using the umask command:

```
[mgagne@testsys tmp]$ umask
002
```

The 2 is subtracted from the possible set of permissions, rwx (or 7). 7 − 0 remains 7, while 7 − 2 is 5. But wait—5 stands for r-x, or read and execute. How is it that the file only shows a read bit set? That's because newly created files are not set executable. At best, they provide read and write permissions for everyone. Another way to display this information is by using the -S flag. Instead of the numeric output, you'll get a symbolic mask displayed.

```
[mgagne@testsys tmp]$ umask -S
u=rwx,g=rwx,o=rx
```

If you have an application that requires you to provide a default set of permissions for all the files you create, change umask to reflect that inside your scripts. As an example, let's pretend that your program or script created text files that you wanted everyone to be able to read (444). Because the execute bit won't be a factor anyway, if you mask out the write bit using a 2 all around, then everybody will have read permission. Set your umask to 222, create another file (called "duck" this time), and then do an ls -l to check things out:

```
[mgagne@testsys tmp]$ umask 222
[mgagne@testsys tmp]$ touch duck
[mgagne@testsys tmp]$ ls -l
total 0
-r--r--r--    1 mgagne    mgagne            0 Nov  5 12:58 duck
```

The **setuid** Bit

Aside from those three permission bits (read, write, and execute), there is one other very important one: the s bit, sometimes referred to as the setuid or setgid bit, depending on its position.

The reasoning behind this particular bit is as follows. Sometimes you want a program to act as though you are logged in as a different user. For example, you may want a certain program to run as the root user. This would be a program that you want a nonadministrative user to run, but (for whatever reason) this program needs to read or write files that are exclusively root's. The sendmail program is a perfect example of that. The program needs to access privileged functions in order to do its work, but you want regular (nonroot) users to be able to send mail as well.

The setuid bit is a variation on the "execute" bit. In order to make the hypothetical program, `ftl_travel`, executable by anyone, but with root's privileges, you change its permissions as follows:

```
chmod u+s ftl_travel
```

The next step, as you might guess, is to combine full permissions and the `setuid` bit. Start by thinking of the `setuid` and `setgid` bits as another triplet of permissions. Just as you could reference `r`, `w`, and `x` as 4, 2, and 1, so can you reference `setuid` as 4, `setgid` as 2, and other (which you don't worry about).

So, using a nice, complicated example, let's make that command so that it has read, write, and execute permissions for the owner, read and execute permissions for the group, and no permissions for anyone else. To those with execute permission, though, you want to have it `setuid`. You could also represent that command either symbolically or in a numerical way:

```
chmod u=rwxs,g=rx,o= ftl_travel
chmod 4750 ftl_travel
```

The 4 in the front position represents the `setuid` bit. If you want to make the program `setgid` instead, you can change that to 2. And, yes, if you want the executable to maintain both the owner's permissions and that of the group, you can simply add 4 and 2 to get 6. The resulting set of permissions is as follows:

```
chmod 6750 ftl_travel
```

Changing the `setuid` bit (or `setgid`) is not strictly a case of providing administrative access to nonroot users. This can be anything. You might have a database package that operates under only one user ID, or you may want all users to access a program as though they were part of a specific group. You will have to decide.

Finding Anything

One of the most useful commands in your arsenal is the `find` command. This powerhouse doesn't get anywhere near the credit it deserves. Generally speaking, `find` is used to list files and redirect (or pipe) that output to do some simple reporting or backups. There it ends. If anything, this should only be the beginning. As versatile as `find` is, you should take some time to get to know it. Let me give you a whirlwind tour of this awesome command. Let's start with the basics:

```
find starting_dir [options]
```

One of those options is `-print`, which only makes sense if you want to see any kind of output from this command. You could easily get a listing of every file on the system by starting at the top and recursively listing the disk:

```
find / -print
```

While that might be interesting and you might want to redirect that to a file for future reference, it is only so useful. It makes more sense to search for something. For instance, look for all the JPEG-type image files sitting on your disk. Because you know that these images end in a .jpg extension, you can use that to search:

```
find / -name "*.jpg" -print
```

Depending on the power of your system, this can take a while and you are likely to get a lot of "Permission denied" messages (particularly as you traverse a directory called /proc). If you are running this as a user other than root, you will likely get a substantial number of "Permission denied" messages. At this point, the usefulness of find should start to become apparent, because a lot of images stashed away in various parts of the disk can certainly add up as far as disk space is concerned. Try it with an .avi or .mpg extension to look for video clips (which can be very large).

If what you are trying to do is locate old files or particularly large files, then try the following example. Look for anything that has not been modified (this is the `-mtime` parameter) or accessed (the `-atime` parameter) in the last 12 months. The `-o` flag is the "or" in this equation:

```
# find /data1/Marcel -size +1024 \
\( -mtime +365 -o -atime +365 \) -ls
```

A few techniques introduced here are worth noting. The backslashes in front of the round brackets are escape characters, there to make sure the shell does not interpret them in ways you do not want it to—in this case, the open and close parentheses on the second line. The first line also has a backslash at the end. This is to indicate a line break, because the whole command will not fit neatly on one line of this page. Were you to type it exactly as shown, without any backslashes, it would not work; however, the backslashes in the second line are essential. The preceding command also searches for files that are greater than 500 KB in size. That is what the -size +1024 means, because 1024 refers to 512-byte blocks. The -ls at the end of the command tells the system to do a long listing of any files it finds that fit my search criteria.

Earlier in this chapter, you learned about setuid and setgid files. Keeping an eye on where these files are and determining if they belong there are important aspects of maintaining security on your system. Here's a command that will examine the permissions on your files (the -perm option) and report back on what it finds:

```
find / -type f \( -perm -4000 -o -perm -2000 \) -ls
```

You may want to redirect this output to a file that you can later peruse and decide on what course of action to take.

Now let's look at another find example to help you uncover what types of files you are looking at. Your Linux system has another command, called file, that can deliver useful information on files and what they are, whether they are executables, text files, or movie clips. Here's a sample of some of the files in my home directory as reported by file:

```
$ file $HOME/*
code.layout:    ASCII text
cron.txt:       data
dainbox:        International language text
dainbox.gz:     gzip compressed data, deflated, original
filename, last modified: Sat Oct 7 13:21:14 2000, os: Unix
definition.htm: HTML document text
gatekeeper.1:   troff or preprocessor input text
gatekeeper.man: English text
gatekeeper.pl:  perl commands text
hilarious.mpg:  MPEG video stream data
```

The next step is to modify the find command by adding a -exec clause so that I can get the file command's output on what find locates:

```
# find /data1/Marcel -size +1024  \
\( -mtime +365 -o -atime +365 \) -ls -exec file {} \;
```

The open and close braces that follow -exec file mean that the list of files generated should be passed to whatever command follows the -exec option (in other words, the command you will be **exec**uting). The backslash followed by a semicolon at the end is required for the command to be valid.

As you can see, find is extremely powerful. Learning to harness that power can make your administrative life much easier. You'll encounter find again as you work more and more with the shell.

Using grep

grep: Global regular expression parser.

That definition of the acronym is one of many. I've been told that the "p" also stands for print. Don't be surprised if you hear it called the "gobble research exercise program" instead of either of those two. Basically, grep's purpose in life is to make it easy for you to find strings in text files. This is its basic format:

```
grep pattern file(s)
```

As an example, let's say you want to find out if you have a user named "natika" in your /etc/passwd file. The trouble is that you have 500 lines in the file:

```
[root@testsys /root]# grep natika /etc/passwd
natika:x:504:504:Natika the Cat:/home/natika:/bin/bash
```

Sometimes you just want to know if a particular chunk of text exists in a file, but you don't know which file specifically. Using the -l option with grep enables you to list filenames only, rather than lines (grep's default behavior). In the next example, I look for Natika's name in my e-mail folders. Because I don't know whether Natika is capitalized in the mail folders, I'll introduce another useful flag to grep: the -i flag. It tells the command to ignore case.

```
[root@testsys Mail]# grep -i -l natika *
Baroque music
Linux Stuff
```

```
Personal stuff
Silliness
sent-mail
```

As you can see, the lines with the word (or name) "Natika" are not displayed—only the files.

Here's another great use for grep. Every once in a while, you will want to scan for a process. The reason might be to locate a misbehaving terminal or to find out what a specific login is doing. Because grep can filter out patterns in your files or your output, it is a useful tool. Rather than trying to scan through 400 lines on your screen for one command, let grep narrow down the search for you. When grep finds the target text, it displays that line on your screen:

```
[root@testsys /root]# ps ax | grep httpd
 1029 ?        S       0:00 httpd
 1037 ?        S       0:00 httpd
 1038 ?        S       0:00 httpd
 1039 ?        S       0:00 httpd
 1040 ?        S       0:00 httpd
 1041 ?        S       0:00 httpd
 1042 ?        S       0:00 httpd
 1043 ?        S       0:00 httpd
 1044 ?        S       0:00 httpd
30978 ?        S       0:00 httpd
 1385 pts/2    S       0:00 grep httpd
```

Here, the ps ax command lists the processes, and then the "|" pipes the output to the grep command. Notice the last line, which shows the grep command itself in the process list. You'll use that line as the launch point to one last example with grep.

If you want to scan for strings other than the one specified, use the -v option. With this option, it's a breeze to list all processes currently running on the system but ignore any that have a reference to root:

```
ps ax | grep -v root
```

And speaking of processes . . .

Processes

You are going to hear a lot about processes, process status, monitoring processes, or killing processes. Reducing the whole discussion to its simplest form, all you have to remember is that any command you run is a process. Processes are also sometimes referred to as **jobs**.

Question: So what constitutes a process?

Answer: Everything.

The session program that executes your typed commands (the shell) is a process. The tools I am using to write this chapter are creating several processes. Every terminal session you have open, every link to the Internet, every game you have running—all these programs generate one or more processes on your system. In fact, there can be hundreds, even thousands, of processes running on your system at any given time. To see your own processes, try the following command:

```
[root@testsys /root]# ps
  PID TTY          TIME CMD
12293 pts/5     00:00:00 login
12316 pts/5     00:00:00 su
12317 pts/5     00:00:00 bash
12340 pts/5     00:00:00 ps
```

For a bit more detail, try using the u option. This will show all processes owned by you that currently have a controlling terminal. Even if you are running as root, you will not see system processes in this view. If you add the a option to that, you'll see all the processes running on that terminal—in this case, revealing the subshell that did the su to root:

```
[root@testsys /root]# ps au
USER       PID %CPU %MEM    VSZ  RSS TTY       STAT START   TIME COMMAND
root     12293  0.0  0.4   2312 1196 pts/5     S    21:23   0:00 login --
mgagne
mgagne   12294  0.0  0.3   1732  976 pts/5     S    21:23   0:00 -bash
root     12316  0.0  0.3   2156  952 pts/5     S    21:23   0:00 su - root
root     12317  0.0  0.3   1736  980 pts/5     S    21:23   0:00 -bash
root     12342  0.0  0.2   2400  768 pts/5     R    21:24   0:00 ps au
```

The most common thing someone will do is add an x option as well. This will show you all processes, controlled by your terminal or not, as well as those of other users. The administrator will also want to know about the l option, which stands for "long." It is particularly useful because it shows the parent process of every process, because every process has another process that launched (or spawned) it. This is the parent process of the process ID. In sysadmin short form, this is the PPID of the PID. When your system starts up, the first process is called init. It is the master process and the superparent of every process that will come until such time as the system is rebooted. Try this incarnation of the ps command for an interesting view of your system:

```
[root@testsys /root]# ps alxww | more
  F   UID   PID  PPID PRI  NI   VSZ  RSS   WCHAN STAT TTY         TIME COMMAND
100     0     1     0   0    0  1120  120 134005 S      ?        0:07 init [3]
040     0     2     1   0    0     0    0  12d42b SW     ?        0:00 [kflushd]
040     0     3     1   0    0     0    0  12d4a0 SW     ?        0:03 [kupdate]
040     0     4     1   0    0     0    0  123282 SW     ?        0:00 [kpiod]
040     0     5     1   0    0     0    0  126896 SW     ?        0:03 [kswapd]
140     1   336     1   0    0  1212    0  134005 SW     ?        0:00 [portmap]
040     0   350     1   0    0     0    0  1ad198 SW     ?        0:00 [lockd]
040     0   351   350   0    0     0    0  1aa906 SW     ?        0:00 [rpciod]
```

Again, this is a partial listing. You noticed, of course, that I threw a couple of new flags in there. The double w, or ww, displays each process's command-line options. A single w truncates the options at a half a line.

The columns you see there tell you a little bit more about each process. The F field indicates the process flag. A 040 in that position indicates a process that forked but didn't exec, whereas a 140 means the same, but that superuser privileges were used to start the process. The UID field represents the user ID, while PID and PPID are, respectively, the process ID and parent process ID that I covered earlier. PRI and NI (priority and nice number, respectively) will feature later when I discuss performance issues. In fact, there are quite a number of information flags for the ps command. Every system administrator should take some time to read the main page. More important, play with the command and the various flags. You will be enlightened.

Forests and Trees

With all the information displayed through ps, you can be forgiven if your head is starting to hurt a bit. It is a little like trying to see the forest but being overwhelmed by the sheer number of trees. And yet, all these processes are linked in some way. Luckily, your stock Linux distribution contains tools to make this easier. One of them is called pstree. Here's a sample of what you get by simply typing the command and pressing Enter:

```
init-+-aio/0
     |-atd
     |-bonobo-activati
     |-crond
     |-cupsd
     |-devfsd
     |-events/0
     |-gconfd-2
     |-httpd2-+-advxsplitlogfil
     |         `-5*[httpd2]
     |-ifplugd
     |-kalarmd
     |-kblockd/0
     |-kdeinit-+-artsd
     |         |-karm
     |         |-12*[kdeinit]
     |         |-kdeinit---bash
     |         |-kdeinit-+-aspell
     |         |          `-2*[gs]
     |         |-kdeinit---bash---pstree
     |         `-soffice.bin
     |-12*[kdeinit]
     |-kdeinit---perl
     |-kdesud
     |-kicker
     |-klogd
     |-knotes
     |-kontact
     |-kopete
     |-lockd
     |-login---bash---startx---xinit-+-X
```

This is only a partial listing, but notice that everything on the system stems from one super, ancestral process called `init`. Somewhere under there, I have a login that spawns a shell. From that shell, I start an X window session, which spawns a WindowMaker application. Even so, GNOME and KDE applications are in there as well.

If you want a similar output but in somewhat more detail, you can go back to your old friend, the ps command. Try the f flag, which in this case stands for "forest," as in forest view. The following output is the result of my running "ps axf". Once again, this is a partial listing, but unlike the pstree listing, you also get process IDs, running states, and so on.

```
$ ps axf
1894 tty6      S      0:00 /sbin/mingetty tty6
 2513 ?        S      0:00 /sbin/ifplugd -w -b -i eth1
 3099 ?        S      0:00 login -- mgagne
 3169 tty1     S      0:00  \_ -bash
 3228 tty1     S      0:00      \_ /bin/sh /usr/X11R6/bin/startx
 3241 tty1     S      0:00          \_ xinit /home/mgagne/.xinitrc --
                                                            -deferglyp
 3242 ?        S     65:16                  \_ /etc/X11/X :0 -deferglyphs 16
 3247 tty1     S      0:00                  \_ /bin/sh /usr/bin/startkde
 3256 tty1     S      0:13                      \_ magicdev
 3304 tty1     S      0:00                      \_ kwrapper ksmserver
 3270 tty1     S      0:00 /usr/lib/gconfd-2 13
 3273 ?        S      0:01 kdeinit: Running...
 3278 ?        S      0:01  \_ kdeinit: klauncher
 3300 ?
```

In the Linux world, you can find a number of programs devoted to deciphering those numbers, thereby making it possible to find out what processes are doing and how much time and resources they are using to do it, making it possible to manage the resultant information.

Killing Processes

You can usually interrupt a foreground process by pressing <Ctrl+C>, but that does not work with background processes. The command used to terminate a process is called `kill`, which as it turns out is an unfortunate name for a command that does more than just terminate processes. By design, `kill` sends a signal to a job (or jobs). That signal is sent as an option (after a hyphen) to a process ID:

```
kill -signal_no PID
```

For instance, you can send the SIGHUP signal to process 7612 like this:

```
kill -1 7612
```

Signals are messages. They are usually referenced numerically, as with the ever-popular `kill -9` signal, but there are a number of others. The ones you are most likely to use are 1, 9, and 15. These signals can also be referenced symbolically with these names.

Signal 1 is SIGHUP. This is normally used with system processes such as xinetd and other daemons. With these types of processes, a SIGHUP tells the process to hang up, reread its configuration files, and restart. Most applications will just ignore this signal.

Signal 9 is SIGKILL, an unconditional termination of the process. Some admins I know call this "killing with extreme prejudice." The process is not asked to stop, close its files, and terminate gracefully. It is simply killed. This should be your last-resort approach to killing a process, and it works 99% of the time. Only a small handful of conditions will ever ignore the –9 signal.

Signal 15, the default, is SIGTERM, a call for normal program termination. The system is asking the program to wrap it up and stop doing whatever it was doing.

Remember when you suspended a process earlier? That was another signal. Try this to get a feel for how this works. If you are running in an X display, start a digital xclock with a seconds display updated every second:

```
xclock -digital -update 1 &
```

You should see the second digits counting away. Now find its process ID with `ps ax | grep xclock`. Pretend the process ID is 12136. Let's kill that process with a `SIGSTOP`:

```
kill -SIGSTOP 12136
```

The digits have stopped incrementing, right? Restart the clock:

```
kill -SIGCONT 12136
```

As you can see, `kill` is probably a bad name for a command that can suspend a process and then bring it back to life. For a complete list of signals and what they do, look in the man pages with this command:

```
man 7 signal
```

If you want to kill a process by specifying the symbolic signal, you use the signal name minus the `SIG` prefix. For instance, to send the –1 signal to `xinetd`, you could do this instead:

```
kill -HUP `cat /var/run/xinetd.pid`
```

Note that those are backward single quotes around the previous command string.

Forging On . . .

I'm going to end this extended Shell Out section here. Given the sheer number of Linux commands and the incredible flexibility of the shell language, I could write an entire book on the subject. Who knows?

I hope you enjoyed this foray into the nongraphical world of Linux. Furthermore, I hope it has whetted your appetite for more. Once you get comfortable with the shell, nothing is impossible.

Meanwhile, if you want to learn more about the shell and what can be done with it, I refer you to a couple of excellent bash shell references at the Linux Documentation Project Web site: the *Bash Prompt HOWTO* and the *BASH Programming—Introduction HOWTO*. Look for the links in the References section, which follows.

Resources

BASH Programming—Introduction HOWTO

http://www.tldp.org/HOWTO/Bash-Prog-Intro-HOWTO.html

BASH Prompt HOWTO

http://www.tldp.org/HOWTO/Bash-Prompt-HOWTO/index.html

Appendix

D

The Barnes and Noble Special Edition CD: Game On!

Welcome to the Barnes and Noble special edition appendix. Your copy of *MOVING TO LINUX* came with one extra CD filled with some fantastic Linux games. In that regard, you can consider this as Chapter 19, part 2, since I take you on a tour of your special edition CD and the great entertainment it contains.

In terms of setting up and configuring your WFTL Knoppix Game CD, the information covered in Chapter 2 still applies. Some of the games are networked games that you can play with others on the Internet or on your local network. I mentioned one of these, KBattleship, in Chapter 19; I show you some others in this appendix.

I've arranged this appendix into major game styles or type: puzzles, board games, arcade action, and so on. To cover every game on this CD, I would need the space of a whole other book, space I don't have at the moment. What I do, then, is highlight one game from each category and then offer a list of other games I think you'll enjoy from that category (again, this doesn't cover all of the games on the CD). Furthermore, whenever I mention a game, I also provide the command name in parentheses (command_name) so that you can launch it from your <Alt+F2> quick program launcher if you would rather skip the menus.

Ready to play? Game on!

Adventure and Strategy

Adventure games represent some of the earliest form of computer games. Originally text-based dungeon crawlers, adventures have come a long way. Great graphics and special effects accompany the games of today, and exploring your fantasy world is more than just discovering buried treasure. Strategy, cunning, and hard-earned battle skills are all necessary.

Battle for Wesnoth

Wesnoth has fallen to the evil hordes and you, as the rightful heir to the throne of Wesnoth, assemble an army to regain what is rightfully yours. You recruit fighters, train them, build up your resources, and lead campaigns against your enemies. The land is populated with elves, orcs, wizards, and humans alike. Friends or foes? Choose wisely and lead well, and in time you may be able to return to Wesnoth.

This fantasy-based adventure game is fully graphical (Figure D-1) with a rich story line. You can play it alone or against others on the Internet. Make sure you try the training mode before you jump right in. Remember, Wesnoth isn't just one story. You can edit and create your own levels, and you can download many different scenarios from the Internet.

Many other games can quench your thirst for adventure and test your strategic skills. Why not try some of the following?

- Freeciv (civclient)—Recreate civilization, build, conquer, and expand. Similar to the popular game Civilization.
- Falcon's Eye (falconseye)—A graphical version of the classic Nethack.

- Pingus (`pingus`)—An excellent Lemmings clone.
- Lincity (`lincity`)—Build and maintain a city. Similar to SimCity.

Figure D–1   Set a quest for adventure in the Battle for Wesnoth.

Long Live the Video Arcade!

Arcade games . . . ah, if I could find a way to collect all the quarters I've poured into those machines over the years. Arcade means action, and action raises your heart rate, gets your blood pumping, and starts your fingers dancing over the controls with deadly fury. Your game CD contains tons of arcade games, more than enough to get you excited and keep you excited.

Neverball

Suspended in 3D virtual space, Neverball (neverball) seems as though it should be extremely simple. You navigate a rolling ball across a variety of playing fields, collecting coins as you make your way to the goal on the other side (Figure D-2). Except it's much harder than that. Advancing to the next level requires a minimum number of coins. To make this coin gathering just a tad harder, the platform rocks back and forth as you try to stabilize it with your mouse. Your point of view shifts dynamically with each tip of the playing surface, and the movements can get downright dizzying. And be careful that you don't go over the edge.

Neverball is a challenging game that requires nerves of steel. Just when you think you've got this thing licked, you remember that this is just Neverball's beginner levels. The difficulty of the higher levels borders on the impossible.

Figure D–2   Neverball's constantly shifting landscape requires nerves of steel to conquer.

Did you beat all the levels? All right, then. Why not try a few other arcade challenges.

- Armagetron (`armagetron`)—Great recreation of the famous lightcycle battles from the movie Tron. You can even play others on the Internet.
- Blob Wars (`blobwars`)—You are a blob soldier out to rescue some blob MIAs. Any questions? Fun, fast-paced platform game.
- TuxKart (`tuxkart`)—Race with Tux the penguin and friends on some interesting go-kart tracks. Oliver's Math Class is particularly interesting. Great for the kids.
- KGoldrunner (`kgoldrunner`)—Run, dig, and collect gold while avoiding the enemy. A Loderunner clone. Check out X Scavenger as well (`scavenger`).
- GL-117 (`gl-117`)—Aerial jet fighter combat simulation. Choose your plane, your weapons, and your mission. My advice is to start with the training missions.
- X-Bill (`xbill`)—Stop the evil hacker known only as "Bill."
- Chromium (`chromium`)—Fast-paced space shoot-'em-up. Great soundtrack. Those alien ships seem never to stop coming.
- LBreakout2 (`lbreakout2`)—The classic breakout game updated with slick graphics, great sound effects, and clever game play. Play it against others over the Internet.
- Tux, A Quest for Herring (`tux_aqfh`)—Help Tux, the penguin, find the missing herring, and help feed the wild penguins of the world.

Dice, Cards, and Boards

Even as we talk about faster video processors, cutting-edge graphics, and pixelated action, the classic games live on in our computers. In fact, I might argue that card games are the most popular type of game on personal computers. I deduce this from the many solitaire games I've seen played on PCs in numerous homes and offices.

Speaking of solitaire . . .

PySol

You might wonder why I'm mentioning yet another solitaire game when I already talked about one in Chapter 19. My explanation is that this standout version of solitaire is for the truly serious card player. I'm talking about PySol (Figure D-3).

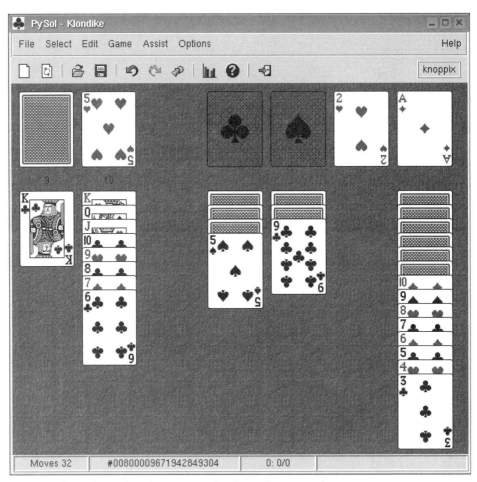

Figure D–3   PySol is the solitaire game for the truly serious player.

So what makes PySol (pysol) so special? For starters, it includes some 200 different games and game styles. Add to that different card styles and backs, configurable animation, statistics gathering, a demo mode, bookmarks (so you can return to a game in progress), a playable preview, and a great music soundtrack, and you've got yourself a whole new kind of solitaire game.

Have you played all the solitaire you can handle? Why not try these games when you think you are ready?

- Blackjack (blackjack)—Place your bets! 21 is the magic number.
- GNOME Tali (gtali)—Poker dice, anyone? Think Yahtzee.

- Mahjongg (`mahjongg`)—The classic Eastern tile game.
- Shisen-Sho (`kshisen`)—Another great match-the-tiles game. Very addictive.
- KBackgammon (`kbackgammon`)—Play against others locally or on the Internet.

Codebreakers and Other Puzzlers

Sometimes what makes a game interesting is that it leaves you scratching your head. Anyone who has spent hours working a Rubik's cube knows what I am talking about. Puzzles are games, but they are also the most entertaining way to stretch those mental muscles.

gTans

I've always been fascinated by the classic Tangram puzzle. I suppose that's the reason I chose to highlight it as a representative of this category. Here's how it works. A wooden square is cut into seven pieces. There are five triangles (three different sizes), a square, and a parallelogram. The obvious idea is to recreate the square from the seven pieces, but the puzzle lends itself to many more interesting possibilities. You can create hundreds of different figures and symbolic shapes—birds, animals, flowers, or other objects. Philippe Banwarth's gTans is a great re-creation of the Chinese Tangram (Figure D-4).

To move a piece, click and drag it into the central area, where you assemble the Tangram. Right-click on a piece to quickly rotate it 180°. Left click around the outside to rotate it more accurately around its axis (a 180° rotation isn't always what you need). When you've solved the puzzle, click the up arrow on the figure number and move on.

When you are done with gTans, try a few of the following.

- Code Breaker (`codebreaker`)—Similar to MasterMind.
- Four-in-a-row (`gnect`)—Think "Connect Four."
- Gnome Robots (`gnobots2`)—Avoid capture by evil robots.
- Gnome-Stones (`gnome-stones`)—This also has an adventure game feel to it.
- Mirror Magic II (`mirrormagic`)—Aim lasers using mirrors and then zap things.

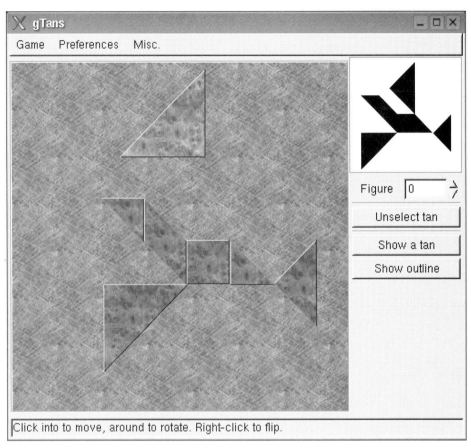

Figure D–4   gTans is a very nice implementation of the classic Chinese Tangram puzzle.

Indoor and Outdoor Sports

Every once in a while, somebody tries to convince me that I should learn to play golf. Given my skills on the miniature golf course, I'm a little reluctant to do so. Besides, I've yet to master the game on a computer. Then there's pool. You would think knocking balls into the pockets of that small table would be simple.

Thank goodness for computer simulations!

BillardGL and FooBillard

Florian Berger's BillardGL (command name `billard-gl`) is an extremely realistic billard game with a 3D table floating in virtual space. Yes, that's *billard* and not *billiards*. Florian based the name on the German spelling for billiards. Spelling aside, this is a great game that looks fantastic (Figure D-5). The table has a green felt top with polished wood trim. The tabletop is textured, and the balls cast appropriate shadows. The sound effects are great as well.

Figure D–5 FooBillard provides a great-looking and realistic game of billiards.

The physics of this particular game make for a simulation that feels very real in terms of what happens, compared to what you expect to happen. You can control the orientation of the table as well as shoot by using both the mouse and the keyboard. The function keys enable rapid changes between various views of the table. The Page Up and Page Down keys let you zoom in and out between close-up and wide-angle views of the table. To locate a particular ball, click on its icon at the bottom of the screen.

To get you used to the feel of the game, there's a training mode. When you feel ready, find yourself a worthy opponent. BillardGL is a two-player game. If you don't have a 3D accelerated video card, try running the non-GL version, called FooBillard, instead (command name `foobillard`). While not quite as slick looking as BillardGL, it's still a great game.

Now that you've shown your skill on table green, why not try a different surface, one where the green gets interrupted by a variety of obstacles. Break out your virtual putter and check out these miniature golf games.

- Neverputt (`neverputt`)—Neverball's version of miniature golf.
- Kolf (`kolf`)—A two-dimensional miniature golf game with multiple courses.

Play On . . .

Here is where I end this tour of your WFTL Edition Knoppix Game CD. This introduction is by no means all you'll find on the disk. Look through the Games menu (under the K program launcher) and have fun. When you are ready for more, remember to check out the resources I told you about in Chapter 19.

Would you like to play a game?

Index

Also from Marcel Gagné

Moving to the Linux Business Desktop

ISBN: 0-13-142192-1

The Complete Technical Resource for Migrating Your Business Desktop to Linux

Respected *Linux Journal* columnist Marcel Gagné walks you step-by-step through planning and managing the transition, getting users up and running, administering the desktop efficiently, and using it to drive cost savings throughout your organization. Gagné covers hardware, productivity applications, messaging, coexistence with Windows environments, support, and much more. *Moving to the Linux Business Desktop* is also the first book with in-depth coverage of using Linux Terminal Server Project (LTSP) thin clients to dramatically reduce the cost and complexity of computing.

Linux System Administration: A User's Guide

ISBN: 0-201-71934-7

A Comprehensive, Hands-On Guide to Linux System Administration

Linux System Administration: A User's Guide provides you with the deeper understanding of Linux and pragmatic techniques you need to become an outstanding Linux system administrator—whether you are a career administrator in a corporate environment or simply administering your home system. Written for both those who are new to Linux and those who are already proficient and wish to hone their skills, *Linux System Administration* starts with the basics and builds up to more sophisticated material.

Visit us online for more books and more information, and to read sample chapters: http://www.awprofessional.com

Register
Your Book

at www.awprofessional.com/register

You may be eligible to receive:

- Advance notice of forthcoming editions of the book
- Related book recommendations
- Chapter excerpts and supplements of forthcoming titles
- Information about special contests and promotions throughout the year
- Notices and reminders about author appearances, tradeshows, and online chats with special guests

Contact us

If you are interested in writing a book or reviewing manuscripts prior to publication, please write to us at:

Editorial Department
Addison-Wesley Professional
75 Arlington Street, Suite 300
Boston, MA 02116 USA
Email: AWPro@aw.com

Addison-Wesley

Visit us on the Web: http://www.awprofessional.com

CD-ROM Warranty

Addison-Wesley warrants the enclosed CD-ROM to be free of defects in materials and faulty workmanship under normal use for a period of ninety days after purchase (when purchased new). If a defect is discovered in the CD-ROM during this warranty period, a replacement CD-ROM can be obtained at no charge by sending the defective CD-ROM, postage prepaid, with proof of purchase to:

Disc Exchange
Addison-Wesley Professional
Pearson Technology Group
75 Arlington Street, Suite 300
Boston, MA 02116
Email: AWPro@aw.com

More information and updates are available at:
http://www.awprofessional.com/